# Empire on the Adriatic

## Mussolini's Conquest of Yugoslavia

## 1941–1943

Also published by Enigma Books

*Hitler's Table Talk 1941–1944*
Hugh Trevor-Roper, Ed.

*In Stalin's Secret Service*
W. G. Krivitsky

*Hitler and Mussolini: The Secret Meetings*
Santi Corvaja

*The Jews in Fascist Italy: A History*
Renzo De Felice

*The Man Behind the Rosenbergs*
Alexander Feklisov and
Sergei Kostin

*Roosevelt and Hopkins:
An Intimate History*
Robert E. Sherwood

*Diary 1937–1943*
Galeazzo Ciano

*The Battle of the Casbah:
Terrorism and Counter-Terrorism in
Algeria 1955–1957*
General Paul Aussaresses

*Secret Affairs:
FDR, Cordell Hull, and Sumner
Welles*
Irwin F. Gellman

*Hitler and His Generals:
Military Conferences 1942–1945*
Helmut Heiber & David M.
Glantz, Eds.

*Stalin and the Jews: The Red Book*
Arno Lustiger

*The Secret Front:
Nazi Political Espionage 1938–1945*
Wilhelm Höttl

*Fighting the Nazis:
French Military Intelligence and
Counterintelligence 1935–1945*
Colonel Paul Paillole

*A Death in Washington:
Walter G. Krivitsky and the Stalin
Terror*
Gary Kern

*Hitler's Second Book
The Unpublished Sequel to* Mein
Kampf
Gerhard L. Weinberg, ed.

*At Napoleon's Side in Russia
The Classic Eyewitness Account*
Armand de Caulaincourt

*The Atlantic Wall
Hitler's Defenses for D-Day*
Alan F. Wilt

*Double Lives*
Stephen Koch

*France and the Nazi Threat*
Jean-Baptiste Duroselle

*Top Nazi*
Jochen von Lang

H. James Burgwyn

# Empire on the Adriatic

## Mussolini's Conquest of Yugoslavia

## 1941–1943

Enigma Books

Enigma Books
580 Eighth Avenue, New York, NY 10018
www.enigmabooks.com

Copyright © 2005 by H. James Burgwyn

ISBN 1-929631-35-9

Printed in the United States of America

Library of Congress Cataloging-in-Publication Data


Burgwyn, H. James, 1936-
  Empire on the Adriatic : Mussolini's conquest of Yugoslavia 1941-1943
/ H. James Burgwyn.

    p. : ill. ; cm.
  Includes bibliographical references and index.
  ISBN: 1-929631-35-9

1. Mussolini, Benito, 1883-1945. 2. Yugoslavia—History—Axis occupation, 1941-1945. 3. Balkan Peninsula—History—World War, 1939-1945.
4. Italy—History, Military—1914-1945. I. Title.

DR1298 .B87 2005
949.702/2

# Empire on the Adriatic

## Mussolini's Conquest of Yugoslavia

## 1941–1943

To Diana

# Table of Contents

## Chapter IV
## The "Pax Romana"

## Chapter V
## Friends and Enemies

## Chapter VI
## Četniks, Jews, and Partisans

## Chapter VII
## Operation *Weiss*

## Chapter VIII
## End of the *Spazio Vitale*

## Chapter IX
## Italy's Götterdämmerung in Yugoslavia

# Preface

The earth-shattering events that shook the Balkans in the 1990s made headlines for over a decade. Television audiences viewed shards of buildings scarring the landscape and bands of roving refugees scavenging for food—victims of the raging strife that had torn the country of Yugoslavia apart. The later discovery of mass graves and the roundup and trial of war criminals at The Hague continues to fuel the hatred of peoples still wracked by martyrdom complexes and the desire for revenge.

The roots of Balkan conflict, as pointed out by historians and newspaper reporters, lie buried in the deep past. But little attention has been given to one short period of Balkan history that likewise resulted in destruction, slaughter, and ethnic cleansing, and laid the groundwork for the current ghastly events. This was during World War II, when, in 1941, the Axis Powers, Italy and Germany, invaded Yugoslavia, triggering a cycle of violence that equaled that of the 1990s. The focus of this book is the Italian occupation of Yugoslavia between 1941 and 1943 and the role that Fascist Italy played in this tragic time.

The Italian constitutional monarchy that came into existence in 1861 carried imperialism in its baggage of traditional European liberal principles. No sooner was unification achieved than eyes began to turn toward the Mediterranean and Africa. But a more immediately urgent battle cry was heard, *Italia irredenta*, which demanded that all lands belonging to the Habsburg Empire containing a majority of Italian-speaking peoples be joined to the motherland. This dream was largely realized after World War I.

Italy's nationalists, however, were not content with nationhood defined solely by fulfillment of irredentist claims; they sought to expand beyond "natural frontiers" by turning the Adriatic into an Italian lake as a first step to domination of the Balkans. Such gains, joined with an overseas empire in the Middle East and Africa, would define Italy's status as a European Great Power. But Italy's Balkan expansion was hampered at the Paris Peace Conference of 1919 when the victors brought to birth a new union of South Slavs— Yugoslavia—minus the Bulgarians, whose misfortune it had been to have joined the "wrong" side in the war. The Italian foreign minister, Sidney Sonnino, vowed to crush the fledgling polyglot state because it stood as a barrier to expansion, but was restrained from doing so by Italy's erstwhile wartime allies. Later, the Duce of Italian Fascism, Benito Mussolini, would try to accomplish the same feat. He too was thwarted for most of his rule by a seemingly invincible French alliance system that provided Yugoslavia a defense against Italian aggression. Only after he had gained an ally in Nazi Germany did expansionist prospects in the Balkans open up. But it was not until Hitler had unleashed World War II and vanquished Yugoslavia in April 1941 that Mussolini could send his legions across the Adriatic to claim Italy's vital living space (*spazio vitale*).

Problems arose at once. After all the rhetoric of conquest and imperialism, Mussolini was caught without any real plan for empire-building. Since Italian troops were heavily engaged elsewhere—in Northern Africa and Greece—military resources were at a premium. The Germans seized the initiative and practically dictated the allocation of occupied territories and the delineation of frontiers. The Italians were allowed to take possession of major portions of Dalmatia, the southern half of Slovenia, and Montenegro. By the grace of Hitler, Mussolini set up a puppet Ustaša regime in Zagreb to preside over an elephantine Croatia that was supposed to evolve as an Italian protectorate alongside the newly constituted satrapy of Montenegro. But when the Italian 2nd Army arrived to occupy Croatia, it was immediately confronted by chaos. The Yugoslav state had vanished and Fascist Italy's Ustaša henchman, Ante Pavelić, had initiated the vicious ethnic cleansing of Orthodox Serbs, Jews, and gypsies. The 2nd Army intervened to quell the violence. To the dismay of Rome, Zagreb, and Berlin, the Army gave refuge to the persecuted peoples and tolerated—and eventually befriended—Četnik bands that the harried Orthodox had spontaneously organized to defend their communities from Ustaša outrages. All this before the Communist Partisans moved from propaganda to open revolt against the occupying Axis forces.

In the annexed territories of Dalmatia and Slovenia, the story turned out differently. When the Croats and Slovenes of these provinces failed to welcome the Italian conqueror, the Fascist civilian rulers immediately launched Italianization programs as their method of assimilating a "culturally inferior" people into the "civilized" Roman imperium. Rather than comply, the native population rose up. The Italian 2nd Army retaliated with a vicious policy of repression that eventually backfired, fanning ever-greater hatred of Italy on the part of the persecuted Slav peoples.

The government in Zagreb vehemently protested in Rome against the 2nd Army's preference for Orthodox Serbs over Croatian Roman Catholics. The Germans also proved to be an uneasy ally. In spite of many protestations that they regarded Croatia as lying in Italy's sphere, they swept into the country with infinitely greater strength and resources to nail down already acquired economic privileges and advance political influence. Finally they were able to dominate Italian policy by prevailing on the Duce to abandon the Četnik ally and to hand full military leadership over to the Wehrmacht in suppressing insurgency. But nothing the Axis Powers did could stem the Partisan tide. It was merely a question of time. As the dream of Balkan empire faded from view, the 2nd Army commanders, who had been so snarled in controversy with Rome over the Croatian Ustaša regime and who bristled over German arrogance and subterfuge, finally cast aside their differences by lining up behind Mussolini. All in Rome would stand by Pavelić to the end and tie the fate of the country indissolubly with the Third Reich.

The Italian army was handicapped during World War II by antiquated equipment and inefficiency, its morale undermined by corruption, rigidity, and a top-heavy officer class riddled with backbiting and careerism. As the military correspondence shows, the Italian commanders in the Balkan theater were quite aware of shortcomings in strategy and training. Many a general despaired over the difficulties encountered in taking troops prepared for conventional warfare and retraining them in wholly new tactics to defeat a highly mobile guerrilla force in a generally hostile environment.

Beyond fighting the Partisans, the high army commanders played hardball politics. This was not in accordance with historical tradition but imposed by the conditions of military occupation. An amazing lack of concord is seen in the military correspondence. The 2nd Army was entangled in negotiations with the Croatian regime, the German Balkan command, and with various and sundry Četnik leaders. As for the Italian Foreign Ministry, its files reveal dogged loyalty to Mussolini's alliances and empire building. Caught in the middle of the dispute between the 2nd Army Command and Mussolini, the Foreign Ministry frequently strove to play the role of honest broker—or buffer—between them.

Thanks to the grim reality of omnipresent ethnic violence, the crazy-quilt pattern of Italian presence, Mussolini's sporadic attention to Balkan affairs, and the 2nd Army's freelance scheming, Italian policy in the lands of Yugoslavia was neither linear nor coherent. While civil war, triggered by the Axis invasion, tore the country apart, the Axis powers and their proxies faced each other with drawn daggers. Since the Italians did not have nearly the strength and power to put an end to the death and destruction, their empire-building proceeded more in an ad hoc fashion than through a fixed plan. Encountering tough Partisan resistance and determined German rivalry, the engine of Italian imperialism frequently sputtered and eventually burned out, leaving behind many enemies and few heroes to honor at home. But the picture is not entirely bleak. The Italian 2nd Army salvaged some degree of honor by providing refuge for thousands of Orthodox Serbs and Jews, thus saving them from the German and Croatian death camps.

* * * *

This study, I believe, represents the first attempt in any language to describe the interplay of forces at work during Italy's invasion and occupation of Yugoslavia: the institutional conflicts, diplomatic rivalries, and the military's relations with the occupied peoples. Moving beyond the Italian empire-builders and the military, I discuss in some detail the puppet governments, ethnic cleansing, and insurgency movements that resulted from the Axis invasion of Yugoslavia. An analysis of the Ustaša, the Partisans, and the Četniks will provide the reader with an in-depth picture of the Italian occupation. Information on the terrible massacres and destruction that occurred in Yugoslavia during the war years—whether caused or contained by Italian troops—will, I hope, lead to a deeper comprehension of the history behind the horrors that have recently been visited on the brave and hardy Balkan peoples.

In narrating the search for empire in the Balkans, I have let the Italians involved in this tragedy tell much of their own story. The book rests primarily on research done in the Italian military, diplomatic, and state archives and gleaned from captured Italian military files currently available to researchers on microfilm. Trips to Belgrade and Ljubljana enabled me to consult Italian military files captured by the Partisans. Of particular value were the Pietromarchi diaries in the Fondazione Einaudi. The United Nations War Crimes Commission provided me with arresting testimony on what the Titoist government regarded as Italian war crimes. Without the comprehensive three-volume work by Oddone Talpo, which contains many printed documents from the Italian military archives, my study would not have been possible. Providing me a broad picture of politics and ethnic turmoil in wartime Yugoslavia were the books of Srdja Trifkovic, Jozo Tomasevich, Stefan Pavlovich, and Matteo Milazzo.

Amplifying my knowledge of events and compelling me to re-think various episodes were two recently published books. Davide Rodogno has written a comprehensive and detailed study of Mussolini's empire-building during World War II, *Il nuovo odine mediterraneo*. His study is arranged topically and focuses almost exclusively on the particulars of Italian policy, whereas mine is narrative and seeks to place the Italian occupation in a broader perspective. Klaus Schmider has produced an equally detailed work from the German angle entitled *Partisanenkrieg in Jugoslawien 1941–1944*. His exhaustive research in German archival materials yielded important new information that I have utilized to enrich my discussion of the Axis partnership. The scholar from whom I have learned the most is Enzo Collotti, who, in his numerous articles and books, has written wisely on the various aspects of Italy's occupation of Yugoslavia.

I owe thanks to many and varied people. The archivists at the Italian Foreign Ministry and the Central State Archives directed me to obscure and hard-to-find documents and inventories. With the help of Elisabeth Giansiracusa, I was able to consult files in the Italian military archives. Dottoresse Dorigo and Giordana, the chief archivists at the Fondazione Einaudi, gave me permission to consult the Pietromarchi papers and diary; their kindness made a Turin visit memorable. Captain Dragan Nenezić, chief of the military archives in Belgrade, not only helped me locate important documents but provided me invaluable advice and insights regarding the tangles of Yugoslav politics during the war. Special thanks are owed an old friend and one of Yugoslavia's finest historians, Dragoljub Živojinović, for his great hospitality, his encouragement, and his wise counsel during my visit to Belgrade. In Ljubljana, Professor Tone Ferenc kindly granted me a couple of interviews during which I learned much about the Italian occupation of Slovenia. Yelena Stjepanović helped me by translating into English important materials in the Serbian language. Lutz Klinkhammer kindly read and critiqued an earlier draft of the manuscript. Philip Cannistraro gave it a thorough reading and made countless valuable suggestions. Richard Bosworth helpfully indicated areas where interpretation and analysis could be strengthened. Diana Burgwyn succeeded in turning my sometimes rough prose into something faintly resembling her inimitably graceful style. It was distinct pleasure to work with Robert L. Miller, publisher and editor of Enigma Books, and his associate, Jay Wynshaw. I need not emphasize that whatever errors in fact and judgment one might find in this book are mine alone.

# Abbreviations

| | |
|---|---|
| ACS | Archivio Centrale dello Stato, Rome |
| ADAP | *Akten zur Deutschen Auswärtigen Politik 1918–1945* (Baden-Baden, Frankfurt a.M., 1950-) (cited as series, volume, document number) |
| AP | Affari Politici |
| ARS | Archives of the Slovene Republic, Ljubljana |
| ASMAE | Archivio Storico-Diplomatico del Ministero degli Affari Esteri (Foreign Ministry diplomatic archives) |
| AVII | Institute of Military History, Belgrade, Serbia |
| b. | busta (envelope) |
| bk. | book |
| CC.NN. | Blackshirts |
| CC.RR | Royal Carabinieri |
| CS | Comando Supremo |
| D. | Document |
| DDI | *I documenti diplomatici italiani* (Rome: 1952-) (cited as series, volume, document number) |
| DGFP | Documents on German Foreign Policy (cited as series, volume, document (number) |
| DS | Diario storico |
| f. | fascicolo |
| fr | frames |
| GABAP | Gabinetto armistizio-pace, Ministero degli Affari Esteri |
| MAE | Ministero degli Affari Esteri |
| MI | Ministero dell'Interno (ACS) (Ministry of the Interior) |
| MVAC | Anti-Communist voluntary militia |
| n. | note |
| NAW | National Archives Washington (cited as microcopy, followed by reel number, and frame(s) only, sender and receiver, and date) |
| NDH | Nezavisne Države Hrvatske (Independent State of Croatia) |

| | |
|---|---|
| OF | Slovene Liberation Front (Communist) |
| OKW | Oberkommando der Wehrmacht (Supreme Command of the German Army) |
| OO | Benito Mussolini, *Opera Omnia*, Edoardo and Dulio Susmel, eds. (Florence, 1951–78) (cited as volume number) |
| p. | posizione |
| PC | Presidenza del Consiglio (ACS) (Prime Minister's secretariat) cited by year and file number) |
| PCM | Presidenza del Consiglio dei Ministri—1940–1943 |
| PP | Pietromarchi Papers: Diary and manuscripts |
| PS | Public Security Forces |
| r. | reel |
| s. | series |
| sf. | sottofascicolo |
| SIM | Servizio Informazioni Militari (Italian Army Intelligence) |
| SME | Stato Maggiore dell'Esercito |
| SMRE | Stato Maggiore del Regio Esercito |
| SPD | Segretaria Particolare del Duce (Mussolini's papers, confidential correspondence) |
| SME | Stato Maggiore del Esercito |
| USSME | Ufficio Storico dello Stato Maggiore dell'Esercito |
| US | Ufficio Storico |
| Zbornik | *Zbornik dokumenata i podataka o Narodnooslobodilačkom ratu naroda Jugoslavije* (Belgrade: Vojnoistorijski Institut, 1949–86) |

# A Note on Sources

Far and away the most valuable military archive source consists of the 505 reels of microfilm containing captured Italian military archives that fell into the hands of the Allies at the end of the war. After the US government returned the original materials to the Italian government, they were placed in the Italian military archives located on Via Lepanto in Rome and can be found in Series M-3. Many duplicates are housed in Ljubljana and Belgrade.

Soon after the end of the Second World War, the Yugoslav government commissioned the publication in some 80 volumes of materials that had been recovered by the victorious Yugoslavs—Partisan, Četnik, Croatian government, and captured Italian and German documents. As for Italy, the most important information is to be found in series XIII, which consists of three volumes, translated into Serbo-Croatian. In this excellently arranged series, the origin of each document is cited. In my view, most of the significant documents in the Zbornik collection were not drawn from the 2nd Army files captured by the Partisans, but reproduced from the NAW-821 collection, as indicated by the editors. It is therefore quite easy to determine their veracity. Much of this material consists of battlefield deployments not relevant to my study. All the original captured Italian documents published in the Zbornik series can be found in the Military Archives in Belgrade. The biggest prize consists of copies of General Roatta's 3C pamphlet of 1 March 1942 and its expanded re-edition of 1 December 1942.

A vast treasure trove is found in the Italian XI Army Corps documents captured by the Slovene Partisans. The major correspondence from it has been translated and published in many volumes into Italian by Professor Ferenc, happily for this researcher who reads no Slavic language. They are listed in the bibliography. After taking a few days in Ljubljana to verify the existence of the originals, I emerged completely confident that the Slovene archivists, like their Serb counterparts, have observed rigorous professional standards in reproducing the captured Italian documents.

# Chapter I

# Italy's Ambitions in Yugoslavia
## 1918–1940

The Paris Peace Conference
Mussolini Confronts Yugoslavia
War: Yugoslavia or Greece?

*The Paris Peace Conference*

When World War I broke out on 1 August 1914, Italy aban
doned its Triple Alliance partners, Germany and Austria-
Hungary, by declaring neutrality. In early 1915, fearing it would be
left out of the division of spoils, the Italian government engaged
in negotiations with both sides. The Allies—Great Britain, France,
and Russia—held bargaining advantage over the Central Powers. At
no territorial sacrifice of their own, they could entice Italy with valuable lands of the Habsburg enemy. After arduous negotiations the
Pact of London was signed on 26 April 1915. Italy would enter the

war a month later in exchange for the Friuli-Julian area eastward to
the watershed of the Julian Alps, Trieste, the Istrian peninsula, and
several islands lying off the Dalmatian coastline—lands containing
approximately 700,000 Slavs. Italian security in the Adriatic was
further strengthened by clauses that called for the neutralization of
most of the Dalmatian coast left to Serbia. Italy stood to benefit
immensely from other provisions of the pact as well: gain of the
Trentino and South Tyrol to the Brenner Pass and the port city of
Valona, control over Albania, a sphere of influence stretching across
the southern coast of Anatolian Turkey, and a share in any future
division of German colonies in Africa.

Although a latecomer to the fray, Italy fought a long and hard
war and suffered considerable casualties. After many offenses failed
to crack the Habsburg lines in the desolate regions of the northeast, the country sustained a great military reverse at Caporetto in
October 1917. But the Italian line held at the Piave River. After a
year of recuperation, the Italian armies went on the offensive, knifed
through the Habsburg lines, and achieved victory at the Vittorio
Veneto. The battered Habsburg enemy begged for an armistice,
which was signed at the Villa Giusti. As the Empire proceeded to
fall apart, the Italian people looked to reap large rewards for their
losses—at least 600,000 dead and a ravaged economy.

Most Italians rejoiced over the defeat of an ancient foe that had
long thwarted fulfillment of Risorgimento ideals. The foreign minister, Sidney Sonnino, certainly shared in this triumph but was shaken
by the huge political vacuum created by the Dual Empire's demise—
a vacuum that he had neither anticipated nor welcomed. The would-
be Yugoslavia, in his view, yearned to be the Habsburg heir by absorbing not only Dalmatia, certain islands off the coastline, and
Fiume, but also Istria, Gorizia, and Trieste. Sonnino thus devoted
himself to strangling Yugoslavia at birth.

While Sonnino prepared to cash in the Pact of London at the
upcoming peace conference, Prime Minister Vittorio Emanuele
Orlando stoked up *la passione Adriatica* by claiming Fiume, which had
belonged to the Hungarian half of the Habsburg Empire. Untroubled that the tiny Adriatic port formed no part of any Allied

treaty commitment owed Italy, Orlando, without consulting the Allies, ordered the city occupied on 17 November. Simultaneously, the army swiftly moved into areas delineated by the Villa Giusti armistice that approximated the Pact of London line.

Emerging from the war triumphant with its honor reaffirmed, the army turned antagonistic when the troops found that local Slavs had wantonly destroyed property, blown up railroads, and carried out methodical looting. Since the Slovenes and Croats had been among the most tenacious and fiercely anti-Italian warriors in the Habsburg armies, they could hardly expect courteous treatment from their conquerors. The stage was set for a harsh Italian occupation of Dalmatia and the Friuli-Julian Alps region. In contrast to a certain openness toward the Yugoslavs and the Adriatic problem during the war, the Italian Supreme Command, after the armistice, forbade the display of anything suggesting Yugoslav authority or South Slav ethnic rights. Since no objection was raised in Rome as the *regio esercito* spread panic in the occupied territories, the Italian commanders saw no reason why they should obey Orlando's injunctions to refrain from treating territory falling under the armistice terms as Italian.

By striking out on its own in the Adriatic, Italy challenged the peacemakers in Paris. Unable to prevent the establishment of the Yugoslav union, Sonnino applied an economic blockade. In this spirit General Pietro Badoglio, chief of the general staff, suggested on 3 December that the new Adriatic neighbor be broken up by promotion of internal conflicts. Sonnino replied:

I have the honor to inform you that, following discussion between the president of the council [Orlando], the Chief of the General Staff [Diaz] and myself, your project for *action to be undertaken among the Yugoslavs has been accepted.* You may begin the action elaborated in the project immediately, turning for any elucidation that you may need directly to H. E. General Diaz.[1]

At the Paris Peace Conference, the Italians encountered opposition to fulfillment of the London Pact primarily from the American president Woodrow Wilson. As regarded the Adriatic, Wilson threw his weight behind the polyglot Yugoslav state, which he imagined would be both democratic and ethnically cohesive, against a grasping and imperialist Italy. But the South Slav union of Croats, Slovenes, Serbs, ethnic Albanians, and Magyars, like the newly formed Czechoslovakia and Poland, resembled more a miniature Habsburg empire than a state resting firmly on the nationality principle dear to his heart. Making Italy a test case, the American president insisted that boundaries in the Adriatic be drawn along ethnic lines. This would deprive Italy of many territories in the Julian Alps and in Dalmatia claimed under the London Pact.

Many liberals in Italy, anticipating friendly relations with their Adriatic neighbor, viewed the "Wilson line" as an equitable one. The more imperialistic Italian delegation was doggedly opposed to Wilsonian "idealism," but, in plotting a course of aggressive diplomacy, fell into disagreement. Orlando was prepared to trade Dalmatia for Fiume while Sonnino stood firm on the London Pact. Unable to compromise, the two Italian statesmen ended up claiming both. While this outlandish position made banner headlines in the Italian nationalist press, it deepened Italy's isolation in Paris. An irate Wilson quickly moved to exploit the Italian *faux pas* by lining up the Allies, who had been searching for an opening to chasten their Italian ally, to assist him in opposing "the London Pact plus Fiume." Encountering such stiff resistance, the Italians left for Rome in a huff. But the Western Powers and the United States remained unmoved, and the Allied press had a field day portraying Italian greed. Although hailed as saviors of Italian honor at home, Orlando and Sonnino crept back to Paris discredited and diplomatically bankrupt. The cabinet resigned on 22 June, leaving the Adriatic controversy simmering.

In the view of many Italians, erstwhile allies had sullied the honor of their nation by depicting it as a prima donna addicted to egoistic and petty intrigue. Forgotten in the humiliation were substantial gains: the hereditary Habsburg enemy had been destroyed, *Italia irredenta* was fulfilled, and predominance, if not outright hegemony, had advanced in the Adriatic. Other than the Socialists, a handful of liberals, and influential conservative Catholics, Italians on the whole resented the Allied refusal to recognize Italy as a heroic war victor and a Great Power of equal rank. This lack of Allied respect exacerbated the disparity in Italian minds between what had been promised and what was gained. Denied gratitude and rewards for its considerable economic sacrifices and the heavy loss of life sustained in a long and bloody war, many Italians surrendered to the legend of the "mutilated victory."[2] Such a sentiment informed the collective memory of Italian military commanders operating in the Balkan theater during World War II.

A new government formed under Francesco Nitti, a member of the old leadership of liberal notables, attempted to tie up the loose Adriatic strings in Paris left by Orlando's cabinet. But Nitti's efforts to achieve a settlement were hampered by the Italian poet Gabriele D'Annunzio, who, leading an expedition of ex-Arditi, seized Fiume in September 1919 and proclaimed himself dictator. Since the army would not act against D'Annunzio, Nitti hoped that in time the problem would go away. In this he was correct. Elections in November foretold that a march on Fiume would not be followed by a march on Rome. Thus the ground was cut from under D'Annunzio, who skulked away from Fiume on 18 January 1920, castigating the Italian people for their failure to throw out the "renouncers" in Rome.

Giovanni Giolitti, Nitti's old rival, formed a new cabinet in June 1920. Carlo Sforza was named to the foreign ministry, which suggested that a liberal program would become the basis of Italian foreign policy. Sforza pursued friendship with Yugoslavia by means of a bargain. Yugoslavia would make concessions on Istria, and Italy would sacrifice Dalmatia. On 12 November 1920 the Treaty of Rapallo was signed. Italy obtained a strategic frontier at the Monte Nevoso line, territorial contiguity with a small free state of Fiume, four islands, and sovereignty over Zara. Yet hostility still smouldered between the two Adriatic neighbors. The "mutilated victory" theme persisted, enabling Mussolini to pick up where Sonnino had left off.

## Mussolini Confronts Yugoslavia

When Mussolini came to power in 1922, he wanted to conduct foreign policy on a grand scale. War and the threat of war would be employed to build an empire in Africa and in the Balkans. But during the 1920s all this saber-rattling took place against a background of more rational behavior in the world of diplomacy. Still, in Eastern Europe, Italy, under Mussolini's tutelage, aimed at a revision of the Paris peace settlement that would enable him to extend Italian influence in the Balkans and along the Danube. To be sure, Mussolini's "revisionism" would be selective. There would be no changes in Italy's northern frontier, fixed at the Brenner in the Versailles settlement. Elsewhere, Mussolini reserved the right to take unilateral action, notably in Yugoslavia, the major obstacle standing in the way of an Italian hegemony in the Balkans. After a period of dithering, he seized Fiume in September 1923 with hardly a whimper from the Yugoslavs, who enjoyed no support from Wilson's successor or the indifferent Western Powers.

The stick was followed by the carrot. On 27 January 1924 Mussolini concluded the Pact of Rome with Yugoslavia. Long in gestation but short in life, this pact included neutrality and friendship clauses: the two signatories would collaborate on the maintenance of the peace treaties, remain neutral in case of a non-provoked aggression against either, and give diplomatic support if their interests or security were threatened by a third power. On 20 July 1925 Italy and Yugoslavia signed the Nettuno Conventions, which regulated the rights of Italians living in Dalmatia. The Yugoslavs were pleased that Italy had apparently closed the books on the Adriatic statutes of the 1915 Pact of London. Salvatore Contarini, secretary-general of the foreign ministry, hoped that the Rome treaty would lead to stability in the Adriatic, promoted by an understanding with Belgrade over Albania. The Duce, however, had other ideas born from a different set of assumptions. Catering to the rabid anti-Slavism among many Fascists, he pondered revisionist strategies to push Italian expansion beyond the limits of irredentism. That objective involved the breakup of Yugoslavia—a natural concomitant of the ruthless Fascist Italianization of Slavs inhabiting the acquired provinces in the Julian Alps.

Behind Mussolini's ceaseless meddling in the domestic politics of Yugoslavia was an abiding insecurity over the future of Albania, which had begun an uneasy existence in 1913. Mussolini thus moved to establish a patronage over Albanian King Zog. When the Yugoslavs expressed their concern over Italy's inroads in that desolate little country, Mussolini perceived an ulterior motive to supplant Italian influence in Tirana with their own. And when Belgrade professed a desire for a return to the spirit of the Rome treaty of 1924, Mussolini sensed weakness.

A not entirely misplaced suspicion gripped Mussolini that the Serb army was preparing for assaults against Albania—further proof that the Yugoslav regime was inimical to Italy. In his mind the French were the abettors who manipulated Belgrade. Suddenly, on 2 October 1926, the Duce ordered General Badoglio to mobilize twenty divisions; in July 1927 he told his military chiefs: "The attack [against Yugoslavia] must be aggressive, unexpected."[3] At the same time he resorted to diplomacy by establishing a virtual protectorate over Albania through two treaties of Tirana, signed in 1926 and 1927. The Yugoslavs answered by obtaining a commitment from France to defend them from Italian aggression. As was his habit, the Duce wrote of a "masonic-democratic" conspiracy to strangle Fascism and thwart Italian aspirations in the Balkans.[4] The battle lines were being drawn; Sforza's Adriatic reconciliation hung by a thread.

Mussolini's misjudgment of Belgrade's bellicosity abetted by France was exacerbated by subjective reports on Yugoslavia from Italy's representatives in the field. Fascist language and anti-Slav prejudices crept into the writings not only of Mussolini's personal emissaries but also the old-guard diplomats. They peppered their reports were such phrases as the "atavistic impulses" of Serbs, the "social-democratic, masonic, Jewish internationalist plot" underlying the Franco-Yugoslav pact, and the occult influence of "Grand Orient masonry and its funds."

In June 1927 Mussolini authored a memorandum that called for Italian support of rightist revolutionary movements in the Balkan and Danube regions, whose major aim was the destruction of Yugoslavia. Fascist Italy did not set any nefarious example in trying to subvert the governments of foreign countries deemed to be hostile, for this was a practice common to the Great Powers of Europe. But Mussolini, feeling estranged from erstwhile wartime allies, did demonstrate a novel independence by befriending the defeated powers of the Great War. Furthermore, since Italy lacked economic wherewithal and diplomatic leverage, he did not shrink from doing business with nasty subversive movements as long as they shared his desire to reconfigure the peace settlements in Eastern Europe. In this effort Mussolini expended more money and energy on the Internal Macedonian Revolutionary Organization (IMRO) than he did on the Croatian separatists. This preference derived from an Italian inclination to contrast Croatian timidity unfavorably with Macedonian audacity and expertise in the use of terrorist weapons. During World War II the Duce may have seen matters in a different light when the Croats carried out far more ferocious deeds than were ever wrought by the IMRO.

Mussolini's half-hearted support of Croatian separatism revealed many shortcomings: a confusing overlap between secret agents and official channels and insuperable diplomatic obstacles. Even the matter of coordinating the small number of Croatian separatists willing to listen was taxing, for they were at odds with one another and widely scattered in and around Croatia. Dr. Ivo Frank, who had been living in exile in Hungary since 1922, maintained contacts with the Magyars, allies of Italy; the Fascist sympathizer Ante Pavelić, whom Mussolini would name ruler of Croatia in 1941, presided over covert operations in Zagreb; and General Sarkotić, another rightist with pronounced monarchist leanings, preached independence from his domicile in Vienna. The most successful among the disaffected Croats was Pavelić, who, with the help of Italian agents, was able to forge links with the IMRO and receive the bulk of Italian money. To consolidate these anti-Serb terrorists, the Italians brought them together with agents of the Albanian Committee of Kosovo.

On the whole Mussolini urged both his agents and diplomats to be discreet while culling information on Croatian affairs and personalities. But even this restricted task was made difficult by changing and contradictory commands. In 1925 the agent Vittorio Mazzotti was assigned to coordinate all contacts with the expatriate Croats; later he was supplanted by the newspaperman Italo Zingarelli. Yet Colonel Vecchiarelli, the military attaché in Vienna, and Eugeneo Morreale, a correspondent of *Il Popolo d'Italia,* continued to receive various Croatian representatives with no apparent disapproval from the Palazzo Chigi. The Croatian Peasant party leader, Vladko Maček, who played a leading role in the drama, simultaneously beseeched the Duce to receive one of his men. Mussolini placed Maček under the supervision of Ubaldo Rochira, the Italian consul in Zagreb.

Within Croatia Mussolini moved to bring order by giving Rochira sole responsibility for conferring with Croatian dissidents. Zingarelli would have been a wiser choice, but he was shunted off to Austria on another assignment. The less levelheaded Rochira took to harping on the imminence of civil war in Yugoslavia, the reliability of Pavelić, and the potential for insurgency among Croatian soldiers should Italy intervene militarily. Rochira's monopoly on Croatian affairs was contested by the Italian minister in Belgrade, Carlo Galli, who felt that he should be the one to coordinate the flow of information. Rochira was not Galli's only headache; he found himself surrounded by independent-minded Fascist agents who cut into his influence.

The droves of Italian press, undercover agents, military attachés, and diplomats who fanned out in Eastern Europe searching for Croatian separatists amounted to wasted effort. There were only a handful of separatist terrorists around, and Italy lacked the funds to bankroll a broader-based movement. The commanding objective, the promotion of Yugoslavia's disintegration, suffered, moreover, from a widening discrepancy between the activity of Mussolini's agents and the Fascist press, which persisted in lumping Yugoslav ethnic groups together as Italy's implacable foes. Moreover, Mussolini was unable to resist adorning his news columns with strident irredentist claims on Dalmatia. The Roman Catholic Croats, who far exceeded the Italian-speaking population in numbers, were deeply offended.

Here, perhaps, was opportunity missed. Having cultivated a strong sense of identity, the Croats considered themselves more civilized and advanced than the "primitive" Greek Orthodox Serbs dominating the Belgrade regime. Disgruntled, they longed to free themselves from the Serb yoke by means of autonomy or independence, but thanks to "*Dalmazia irredenta*," hardly any Croats took up the Italian call for insurgency against the Yugoslav state. Following King Alexander's imposition of military dictatorship in 1929, further Croatian dissidence was squelched in both Dalmatia and Zagreb, which ended all contacts between Mussolini's emissaries and disaffected Croats in Yugoslavia. But clandestine Italian support on Italian soil continued. Mussolini provided camps for training for a sparse Ustaša cohort led by Pavelić, who was given run of a villa located near Pesaro. His henchmen, Gustav Perčec and August Košutić, received money for recruitment and weapons.[5]

Beyond acting as a bad neighbor to Yugoslavia, Mussolini had not seriously pursued a coherent policy aimed at destroying his major Balkan rival. And he certainly had not with any zeal or consistency devoted military resources for an invasion. Confronted with Italian pinpricks and bombast, the French alliance system in Eastern Europe had no problem in holding together, and Yugoslavia declined to break up under Italian pressure.

A few months before taking up his duties as minister of foreign affairs, Dino Grandi, a renowned radical Fascist of the first hour, rose before the Fascist Grand Council on 5 February 1929 to address the "burning Adriatic question" that still aroused Italian nationalists:

The Adriatic no longer suffices to defend our independence as a Mediterranean race from the Slav races. There must be, beyond the Adriatic and its banks, a chain of states running from the Otranto Canal to the Nevoso that virtually serves as a trench dividing the Orient from the Occident—bridgeheads commanded by Italy. We have made Albania; now we must make

Croatia. It is the ancient policy of Caesar, a policy pursued by
Napoleon, and it is the current policy of Mussolini. Destiny
decrees that the boundaries between the Occident and Orient
lie on the Save, which Diocletian marked as the frontier between
the empire of the Occident and the empire of the Orient. The
Save is also the frontier that the Congress of Nicaea delineated,
which today is still valid for dividing the Catholicism of Rome
from the Eastern Church.[6]

Grandi, however, perhaps sobered by the responsibilities of
office, was worried that Mussolini's aggressive Balkan policy would
involve Italy in a two-front war against Yugoslavia and France. To
"cloroformizzare" (anesthetize) what he perceived to be over-
wrought Yugoslav nerves, Grandi posed as an exponent of détente.[7]
Orders were given out to the Fascist press to cease attacks against
Serbia; the mastermind of Croatian insurrection, Eugenio Coselschi,
was told to wind down the Dalmatian irredentist campaign; and the
military attachés running riot in the Belgrade legation were packed
up and sent home.[8] In a word, Grandi wanted to spare his unprepared country a premature war. As he wrote Mussolini, there would
be a day of reckoning with Yugoslavia.[9]

Rather than allow Grandi to reach a settlement with Belgrade
in good faith or bad, Mussolini proceeded to negotiate behind his
back through an interior decorator, one Malagola Cappi, who conducted a shuttle diplomacy with King Alexander. In February 1932
the king proposed an alliance with Italy and a break in the ties binding Yugoslavia to France. But no accord ensued. Bypassed and eventually cashiered in mid 1932, Grandi in the privacy of his diary wrote
that Mussolini's "ferocious" press polemics had made Italy the dupe
by turning Yugoslavia into a martyr.[10]

Eyeing the problem from a different perspective, Mussolini
zeroed in on a Yugoslav state he thought to be fast disintegrating.
A Croatian office in the Foreign Ministry was set up under Paolo
Cortese to orchestrate terrorism and contrive a policy to keep Yugoslavia weak, divided, and inactive while Italy pursued hegemony
in the Balkans. The door swung open again for Ante Pavelić. The

Dalmatian coast, spotted with Italian-speaking communities, seemed an ideal place to begin. In September 1932 Ustaša men, jumping off from camps in Zara, attempted to trigger an uprising in Croatia by rampaging through the region of Lika. But nary a Croat stirred. Yugoslav activists answered the Ustaša provocation with the senseless decapitation of the famous Lions of Trau, statues that commemorated Venetian rule in Dalmatia.

Simultaneously, Mussolini unleashed a press war that was hobbled by the same self-defeating message that marked his previous propaganda. How could irredentist claims on Dalmatia persuade Croats to look to an anti-Slav Fascist Italy for salvation against Serb domination? They would rather suffer the Belgrade regime. Nor did the Duce seem to be aware that an independent Croatia, instead of shoring up the defense of Austria in cooperation with Italy, would, as a barely viable entity, be an inviting target for German expansion. (This is exactly what happened after Italy's supposed takeover of the country between 1941 and 1943.) Mussolini's policy toward Yugoslavia in 1932 and January 1933 degenerated into aimless provocation in the misguided hope that somehow the Yugoslav state would dissolve from ethnic tensions exacerbated by Italian subsidies and terrorism. He entertained war with Yugoslavia and on one occasion thought that the "Latin Sister" would let matters take their course. "If there is only trouble between us and the SHS [Yugoslavia], France won't move."[11] But few around him were so deluded. Succumbing to the restraint advised by the crown, military, and the Palazzo Chigi, Mussolini shelved an attack on Yugoslavia and placed the Ustaša on hold. By February the crisis had eased. The rise to power of the Nazis in Germany, might, paradoxically, have had something to do with this.

Hitler's accession to the chancellorship of Germany on 30 January 1933 initially delighted the Duce. The surge to power of a kindred movement validated the Fascist idea. But the Führer's unabashed intention of annexing Austria, whose independence stood as the linchpin of Italy's security in Europe, threatened to put a quick end to the Nazi-Fascist honeymoon. Mussolini moved to befriend rightist elements in Vienna and to prop up Austria's independence against Nazi pressure by creation of a Roman Protocols bloc consisting of Austria, Hungary, and Italy. The looming specter of Anschluss made Mussolini more amenable to rapprochement with France and reconciliation with Yugoslavia.

During the last weeks of September the French foreign minister, Louis Barthou, was ready to resume Franco-Italian talks on the whole range of colonial questions that had divided the two countries ever since the Paris Peace Conference. The Italians prepared for serious negotiations by presenting a set of proposals, and, as an earnest gesture of good will, Mussolini promised to downgrade support of Croatian separatism and discuss the tangled Albanian question directly with Belgrade.

Impressed by a less intransigent Italy, Barthou invited King Alexander to France, where he intended to stress the importance of Austria's independence to Yugoslav security and the necessity of cooperation with Italy in fending off Nazi-inspired Anschluss pressure.[12] But this diplomacy was aborted when members of the Croatian Ustaša, some of whom were known to have resided in Italian training camps, assassinated Alexander and Barthou in Marseille on 9 October.

Many fingers pointed at Mussolini for ordering the king's murder. There was a good deal of circumstantial evidence to support this view. Known Croatian terrorists moved freely between camps in Italy and Hungary, and the Ustaša Eugen "Dido" Kvaternik, an associate of Pavelić, who had found refuge in Italy, was a chief plotter behind the assassination.[13] But no evidence emerged implicating the Duce directly in the crime. It seems logical to believe that it was indeed a Croatian, not an Italian, deed, for why should Mussolini want suddenly to provoke Yugoslavia when his diplomacy aimed to include Belgrade in an anti-Anschluss front? The French seemed to understand this point, since they subjected the Croats to a half-hearted European manhunt directed mainly at Hungary rather than Italy and sponsored by the impotent League of Nations. On 18 October the Italian police arrested Pavelić and Kvaternik in Turin and sent them off to prison.[14] In protest against their hasty lockup, the two Ustaša leaders conducted a short-lived hunger strike.[15]

The willingness in Rome to resolve old differences with a former bitter enemy was chiefly induced by the change in the constellation of power in Eastern Europe wrought by Hitler's threat to Austria's independence. Mussolini's efforts to shore up the government in Vienna, however, faltered badly when his authoritarian protégé, Chancellor Engelbert Dollfuss, was felled by Nazi bullets in July 1934. Unable to forge the same unity of purpose with his successor, Mussolini, in January 1936, braced for the inevitable Anschluss. He hoped to rekindle Belgrade's interest in a Rome-led alignment that would serve as a replacement for the Roman Protocols to halt the German *Drang nach Südosten* short of Trieste and the Adriatic. In contemplating this new approach, he did not abandon the longstanding goal of splitting Yugoslavia from the Little Entente and France. Rome was fortunate that Milan Stojadinović, the new Yugoslav premier, was partial to authoritarian government and an admirer of the Duce.

Stojadinović and Ciano signed an agreement on 25 July 1937. Italy promised to respect the territorial integrity of Yugoslavia and, in a secret provision, agreed to intern Pavelić and Kvaternik and demobilize the rest of their following. On the Albanian question the Yugoslavs tacitly recognized Italy's "acquired position" as delineated in the Ambassadors' Conference of 1921. It was clear to everyone that the Yugoslav premier had downgraded France and the Little Entente in favor of alignment with Rome. Ciano paid him the ultimate complement: "Stojadinović is a Fascist."[16]

When Stojadinović fell from power in February 1939, Ciano noted that Yugoslavia had lost "90 percent of its value."[17] Hostility quickly replaced rapprochement, normality restored. The army staff proceeded to prepare *Progetto C* to occupy key towns in Croatia hand-in-hand with a Croatian uprising. But Germany, rather than Italy, seemed to be the Axis power most determined to exploit secessionist agitation in Croatia. Desperate to outbid the Third Reich, Ciano hurried to resume contacts with Croatian separatists—Pavelić the terrorist and Maček the Peasant party leader. It was typical that the Italians would engage themselves in contradictory intrigues. At the same time Ciano tried to interest the Yugoslavs in a non-aggression pact, but was turned down. Belgrade did not want to compromise its claim to neutrality, which was contrived as a defense against ever-growing German pressure on Yugoslavia to leave the League of Nations and adhere to the anti-Comintern pact.[18]

On the eve of the German attack on Poland, Hitler surprised Rome by suddenly encouraging Italy to dismember Yugoslavia. Was this a ploy to bring Italy into the war? But Mussolini, restrained by Ciano and Badoglio, did not bite. The pace of events quickened. In a *Sporazum* (agreement) signed on 23 August, Maček agreed to join a new cabinet in Belgrade in return for limited autonomy for Croatia, which showed the Italians that all along he had feigned collaboration with them only to bolster his bargaining power in Belgrade.[19] On 1 September Hitler invaded Poland, which triggered the outbreak of World War II. Woefully unprepared, Italy declared non-belligerence.

While Mussolini pondered whether or when he should enter the war on Hitler's side, Pavelić became the Croatian man of the hour in Rome. In a chatty exchange on 23 January 1940, he and Ciano partitioned Yugoslavia. The Ustaša would instigate insurrection in the Croatian areas of Yugoslavia, seize Zagreb, and proclaim independence. To block a Yugoslav counterattack, Pavelić would invite Italian troops to occupy Croatia. Italian hegemony would be established at a later stage by a Croatian monarchy under the House of Savoy, bound to Italy by a personal union with the Savoyard ruling family. A customs union between the two countries would turn Croatia into an Italian "Manchukuo." The Germans would be paid off with Slovenian Maribor, but, as Pavelić emphasized, their Adriatic plans would be thwarted by an Italo-Croatian "Catholic front." Montenegro would receive independence, and Italy's protectorate, Albania, would be enlarged by the annexation of Kosovo, a province located in southern Yugoslavia that contained a majority of Muslims.

In spite of these titillating possibilities, Ciano cautioned Pavelić that the time was not yet ripe for action.[20] The big issues—how much of the Croatian coastline Italy would take and how much control it would exercise over the Croatian state—were left untouched. Ciano confided to his diary that Mussolini's hands fairly "itched" for action, and, after another meeting with Pavelić on 10 May, he mused: "The Croatian situation is getting ripe and if we delay too long the Croats will sign up with Germany." The Duce agreed: "We must act quickly."[21] That same day Hitler invaded France, which made Mussolini ever more desirous of French imperial booty. A month later the Ustaša sent Ciano a memorandum appealing for Italian military aid in detaching Croatia from Yugoslavia and proclaiming an independent Croatian state under Italian auspices.[22] As Mussolini scrambled to place his country on a war footing, he pondered the Adriatic question burdened by illusions: that the Germans could be made to forget Trieste and Fiume, and that Berlin would leave him a free man to act against Yugoslavia.

*War: Yugoslavia or Greece?*

Convinced that the Wehrmacht had delivered France a knockout blow, Mussolini on 10 June took a fairly united country into the war on Germany's side. Many of Italy's ruling elite, in the specific circumstances of late May and early June, fell into line despite their qualms. The timing seemed right, even for a country as deplorably prepared for war as Italy. For who could question the Duce's calculation that England would not be able to stand alone against the full fury of the Führer's wrath? After a short but sharp and victorious fight, Italy would control the gates of the Mediterranean and pick up imperialist treasures at the expense of the hapless Western Powers.

While declaring war Mussolini grudgingly announced that he would refrain from attacking Yugoslavia and Greece. A reluctant Supreme Command and the long arm of Germany were what kept the Duce under a pained restraint. Indeed, the Germans had quite a different agenda than he toward Yugoslavia, one that transgressed Italy's "parallel war." (This was the formula spelling out Mussolini's plan to assert Italy's political autonomy in a war that would complement Germany's campaigns in Europe while he independently pursued Italy's imperialist aims in North Africa and in the Balkans under cover of the Axis.) Hitler's definition of Europe's New Order required that Germany exercise hegemony over Yugoslavia, defined by bilateral economic agreements that would provide the Third Reich with much-needed raw materials at a favorable rate of exchange. Whereas Mussolini eagerly anticipated aggression against either Yugoslavia or Greece—or both at once—Hitler strove to keep the Balkans quiet. Italy's ambition to win glory on the battlefield, he thought, should be confined to North Africa. The tacit assumption between Germany and Yugoslavia, gratefully appreciated in Belgrade, was that Berlin would caution Italy from undertaking any "mad-dog act."[23] If Mussolini did not fully comprehend German efforts to pluck Yugoslavia from his orbit, his peaceful demeanor of June hardly constituted a permanent disavowal of a Balkan adventure in the future.

The Yugoslavs had long learned to take Mussolini's conciliatory words with a grain of salt. They were hardly appeased by Ciano's soothing assurances that Italy harbored no aggressive intentions.[24] But such reassurances were in keeping with Mussolini's endless assertions to Berlin that Italy contemplated no action against Yugoslavia or Greece.[25] Oddly, it was Hitler who on 1 July informed a delighted Mussolini that the Wehrmacht had discovered a treasure-trove of French and Allied documents that had been abandoned in a railway wagon at La Charité-sur-Saône. These captured materials contained evidence that the Yugoslav and Greek governments, while mouthing words of friendship to Italy and Germany, had solicited Allied support in language with anti-Fascist overtones. Offhandedly Hitler suggested that Italy settle accounts with its Adriatic archenemy.[26] Buoyed by the Führer's support, the Duce looked forward to a strike across the Adriatic to avenge himself against a state he saw no place for in a Fascist-remodeled Europe.

During Ciano's visit to Berlin on 7 July, it occurred to Hitler that, by playing on Mussolini's eagerness to wage war in the Balkans, he was jeopardizing his own plans. Germany's timetable for aggression against the Soviet Union took precedence over Italy's "parallel war." In reply to Ciano's comment that the Duce was prepared to "liquidate" Yugoslavia, the Führer delivered the message that, short of a general Balkan conflagration, the risks of such an attack were too great. Of course the Duce could intervene in Yugoslavia but not until the appropriate hour had struck.[27]

To prepare for that hour, Mussolini instructed his military to ready itself for the invasion of Yugoslavia. General Mario Roatta, deputy chief of the army staff, produced a plan in early July that called for an Italian troop movement to outflank the main Yugoslav defenses with an attack through Austria, synchronized with a thrust across the Julian Alps. But it would not be easy. A massive deployment of troops was in order and the Po Valley contingents suffered from severe shortages of tanks, trucks, and anti-tank guns. To dodge the logistical problems of attacking Yugoslavia by an arduous climb through the Julian Alps, Roatta wanted Berlin's permission to scout out the Yugoslav fortifications along its frontier with Germany. His hope was to carry out an Italian attack through Austria with an army numbering eight to ten divisions borne on 9,000 German trucks. Would Hitler allow Italy free passage through German territory? Presented this fantasy, Badoglio procrastinated. Action against Yugoslavia would be feasible only after Italy had wound up the North African campaign. In the meantime German cooperation should be secured and the Hungarians drawn in—a tall order indeed.

During August the Germans headed the Italians off a collision course with Yugoslavia. General Franz Halder, chief of the German army staff, was dismissive: "Italians propose to invade Yugoslavia, and want German help: German transport for the build-up, German supply organization . . . What incredible nerve!"[28] Alarmed by his trigger-happy ally, Hitler killed the Italian plan by reflecting that he was "totally uninterested in any attack on Yugoslavia." The British "should not be given an opportunity to create bases in Yugoslavia, and German-Italian staff talks on the subject were not necessary."[29]

On receiving this discouraging news, Mussolini told Badoglio "to slacken the tempo" on war preparations against Yugoslavia. Relieved, Badoglio put all such plans "in a drawer to be taken out only after England had been finished off."[30] Roatta easily fell into line.[31] This placed Mussolini back on square one. He would only invade Yugoslavia following a violent internal upheaval.

In honoring the German veto over any military action against Yugoslavia, Mussolini failed to challenge a number of unstated assumptions in German policy: Hitler's determination to dominate the Yugoslav economy, Nazi machinations with the Croatian Ustaša, and Germany's refusal to recognize that Yugoslavia lay in Italy's orbit. Furthermore, Mussolini did not shed his own unstated assumption: that Greece, touching the Mediterranean, "Italy's sea," was fair game for Italian aggression.

As if fighting a difficult campaign with slender resources in North Africa was not enough, the Supreme Command, at Mussolini's request, weighed the pros and cons of an attack on Greece. On 16 July Contingency "G," a limited offensive, was drawn up. The plan drew its inspiration from Ciano, who yearned to enlarge his Albanian "grand duchy." As General Roatta explained, "the undertaking was not conceived as a 'war' against Greece, but as a simple precautionary measure, which could be carried out without combat."[32] Since the General Staff had its hands full fighting the British in North Africa, it did not warm up to any Balkan adventure. The generals counted on the Germans to stay Mussolini's hand on Greece as they had on Yugoslavia.

On 12 October German troops moved into Romania without any prior consultation with Italy or invitation for joint action. Angry over being upstaged by Berlin for the nth time, Mussolini summoned his army commanders three days later and unfolded a plan to occupy the whole of Greece, an intention that he carefully concealed from Hitler. Mussolini took for granted that an impoverished Greece could be terrified into an immediate surrender. Following the advice of dilettantes, who convinced him that a few bribes would buy off Greek resistance, Mussolini ignored both unresolved logistical problems and the dour prospect of launching an invasion at the onset of the rainy season in craggy mountain terrain. Although opposed, his generals drifted along lest any criticism impugn the Duce's expertise in military matters.

Barely weeks after a 28 October attack on Greece, a country one-fifth the size of Italy, Mussolini's legions suffered the humiliation of being driven back across the Albanian frontier. Panicked by the prospect of an Italian Dunkerque, Mussolini asked the Germans to rescue his bottled-up troops. The Führer promised Operation *Marita*. An Italian invasion of Yugoslavia disappeared into the Greek night, replaced by fear that the vengeful South Slav state would fall on Italy's vulnerable flank in Northern Albania. Italy's "parallel war" seemed to have disappeared in the smoke of battle against Greece. As the year 1941 turned, an unforeseen German invasion of Yugoslavia would revive the dream of Italy's *spazio vitale* in the Balkans and renew the military's determination to fight a "parallel war" unhindered by German interference. All the contradictions and illusions in Mussolini's Croatian policy over the past years would be carried over without any serious reappraisal. History, therefore, would repeat itself. In his search for empire in ex-Yugoslavia, Mussolini would lurch forward as a junior partner in an Axis alliance destined for an eventual Götterdämmerung.

# Chapter II

# The Dismembering of Yugoslavia

Italy and the End of Yugoslavia
Mussolini and the Ustaša
Boundary Controversies
Mangled Montenegro
The Partition of Slovenia
Italy's *Spazio Vitale*

*Italy and the End of Yugoslavia*

Mussolini had long held the Yugoslav peoples in contempt for being nothing more than an agglomeration of primitive tribes unworthy of nationhood; he also profoundly resented the fledgling state's annexation of "Italian" Dalmatia in 1919. Belgrade answered in the same coin by belittling Fascism as a masquerade of spoiled Italian children pretending to be a nation of virile warriors. Thanks to this mutual disdain, war loomed as a premeditated act, preemptive strike, or as a result of miscalculation. Two accidental Italian air raids in early November on the Macedonian border town of Bitolj nearly persuaded the Yugoslavs to fall on the exposed northern flank of Italian armies fighting the Greeks in Albania, but, unsure of French support, they instead engaged in a simulated effort of rapprochement. An undercover agent of Prince Paul, the lawyer Vladislav Stakić, met Ciano secretly on 11 November 1940 in Rome with the purported goal of clearing up past misunderstandings and exploring a transformation of the 1937 pact into an alliance that would include a demilitarization of the Adriatic. Mussolini was "encouraged" by this move, and Ciano looked forward to utilizing Yugoslavia as a buffer against both the Soviet Union and Germany.[33] Hitler, anxious to prevent further Italian aggression in the Balkans, urged Mussolini to bargain: an Italian guarantee of Yugoslavia's frontiers and the prize of Salonika,[34] in exchange for a Yugoslav recognition that Italy ruled the Adriatic sea. Thanks to the Italian setbacks in Albania—as well as Hitler's warnings not to stir up trouble in the Balkans—Mussolini was amenable, but only after Italy had inflicted a decisive blow on Greece.[35] To inspire confidence in Belgrade, Ciano, with the full concurrence of the Duce, "demobilized" Pavelić.[36]

The Yugoslavs were caught in a fearful bind. They wanted to be left alone, but could neither avoid the frightening mien of the Third Reich nor ignore rapidly unfolding events. Leading from weakness, they tried to play Rome off against Berlin to buy time for rearmament of the country. Behind every calculation lay the hope of a British landing in the Adriatic. This chancy assumption was kept alive by attempts to hold off the Axis Powers with non-binding and meaningless agreements: a non-aggression pact with Germany and renewal of the Italian-Yugoslav neutrality treaty of March 1937. The "dynamic" Third Reich, however, scorned non-aggression treaties as part of a bygone world of emasculated pacifists. Only by acceding to the Tripartite Pact could Yugoslavia keep in step with the Nazi New Order.[37] Hungary had signed up on 20 November 1940, Romania on the 23rd, followed by Slovakia the next day. On 1 March Bulgaria was brought in. Now it was the turn of the Yugoslavs.

During January and February 1941, Stakić and Mussolini took stock of each other. At the outset Mussolini believed that the

Yugoslav go-between wanted to take advantage of the stalemate on the Greek front to extort concessions from him. But in their common desire to check German expansion in the Balkans, they sketched out a rough plan. Before agreeing to the Tripartite Pact, Yugoslavia would sign a strengthened version of the 1937 pact with Italy. Belgrade thus would be provided an escape from German dictation and Rome would enjoy a better equilibrium with the Third Reich within the Axis. Cooperate with Italy and Mussolini would drop the Ustaša. On the war front, the Duce believed that alignment with Yugoslavia would "hasten the collapse of Greece."[38] Operation *Marita*, the German plan to invade Greece, would be rendered superfluous and German occupation of Salonika unnecessary. In his typically abrupt manner, Mussolini suggested a vast population exchange to take place as soon as Italy had annexed territory still under Greek sovereignty: a transfer of the majority Albanian population of Kosovo to Italian-dominated Albania and a move of the Slavs living in the Julian Alps into Yugoslavia. For these advantages Belgrade would have only to demilitarize the Dalmatian coast.[39]

Although Mussolini confided in Hitler that the "vague and bombastic" Serbs were "inwardly hostile to us,"[40] he had sought, through backdoor channels with Stakić, to make Italy, rather than Germany, predominant in Belgrade. The Germans, however, put to rest whatever notions Rome harbored of a direct arrangement with Belgrade by informing Mussolini that Yugoslavia must adhere to the Tripartite Pact. Belgrade had nowhere to turn.[41] Neither did Mussolini. Aware that military weakness left him little leverage in Berlin, and stung by Prince Paul's aloofness, Mussolini left Hitler *carte blanche* in Belgrade.[42] The Germans were grateful to learn that the Duce was on board, but they, as always, would decide Yugoslav affairs according to their own interests.

The Yugoslavs signed the Tripartite Pact on 25 March 1941. This should not be dismissed as abject capitulation, for, by escaping the onerous military obligation to provide free passage for Hitler's legions heading towards Greece, the Yugoslavs obtained a privileged position in the Tripartite bloc denied to the other captive members. Yugoslav sovereignty and territorial integrity were guaranteed, and

*23*

Salonika, the "symbol of salvation" for Serbia in World War I, lay within reach. The government in Belgrade had made a momentous decision in abandoning its historical ties with Britain and France in favor of alignment with the Axis Powers. Faced by dire necessity, the Yugoslav leadership saw no other way of saving the country's independence. Many critics have severely chastised the government for violating the soul of the country by joining the Axis.[43] This is a touch overdrawn. Britain and America urged them to "save their souls" by defying Hitler, but offered no military support.[44] And no Allied landing of Salonika—the city that stood as a symbol of Yugoslavia's link with the West—was in sight. Still, Realpolitik aside, in joining the Tripartite Pact the Yugoslav regime appeared to be an Axis collaborator and accomplice to Nazi aggression, determined to save its skin at whatever the moral cost. For his part, Hitler was glad to have ended Yugoslav foot-dragging; the German generals, however, grumbled over the long detour around Yugoslavia for their troops heading south.

Two days later, out of the blue, Belgrade was shaken by a coup d'état engineered by military officers and politicians unhappy with the drift of Yugoslavia toward the Axis Powers. Serbs, relieved over the demise of their pro-Axis government, surged through the streets of Belgrade shouting "Better grave than slave" and "Better war than pact,"[45] without much reflection on how Berlin and Rome would react. The new Yugoslav government was headed by an air force general, Dušan Simović, who believed that the decision to join the Tripartite Pact had compromised the integrity of the nation. Prince Regent Paul was dismissed in favor of Prince Peter. The unseasoned rulers in Belgrade thought they could avoid antagonizing Berlin by maintaining the delicate diplomatic balances contrived by their predecessors. Britain was informed that Yugoslavia would neither denounce nor ratify the Tripartite Pact. In the absence of concrete military support from England, the Yugoslavs refused to receive British Foreign Secretary Anthony Eden.[46] But nobody was fooled by this neutrality posturing; Belgrade was headed on a collision course with the Third Reich. The Serbs, in Churchill's quip, may "have found their souls"—helped by British gold. Most certainly they were embarked on a martyr's odyssey, based upon the mythical tradition of Prince Lazar's "Kingdom of Heaven" in the 1389 epochal Battle of Kosovo.[47]

The changing of the guard in Belgrade caught the two dictators by surprise. In Berlin an enraged Hitler promised to exact revenge against a country that he felt had double-crossed him. A punishing invasion would also satisfy important strategic imperatives by rendering safe the movement of a German army across Bulgaria to the Greek frontier and by quieting down the Balkans on the eve of Operation *Barbarossa*, Hitler's planned invasion of the Soviet Union.

In Rome pandemonium ensued. Michele Lanza, the second secretary at the Italian embassy in Berlin, reported: "What are they saying in Berlin? What should we do? What if the Yugoslavs attack us? We're not ready."[48] Mussolini was ambivalent. He welcomed the turn of events that would enable the Axis to sweep away this last artificial state created at Versailles under American President Wilson's sponsorship. Avenging the "vittoria mutilata" had always been an urgent Fascist priority. At the same time Mussolini wondered how Dalmatia and Croatia could be saved from Germany's clutches. And he was oppressed by fear of a catastrophe for his troops in Albania if the Yugoslavs joined the Greeks. As usual, he kept his Axis chin up when addressing the Germans: "I have already personally ordered General Cavallero to call off the offensive which was about to be launched [against Greece]," he assured Hitler. Troops would be moved to the Yugoslav frontier in the north and Pavelić summoned to Rome "in a war that would be popular in Italy."[49] Mussolini could not allow a German attack to proceed without Italian participation for fear of being left out of the division of spoils.

The Germans, meanwhile, smoothly and quickly altered their war plans to knock out Yugoslavia before attacking Greece. Simultaneously, the Italians were expected to knife across the Julian Alps and destroy the Yugoslav navy in the Adriatic.[50] Hitler kept up a relentless pressure on Mussolini to meet the challenge of a new war front.

Not one to show weakness, the Duce ordered his generals to resist a feared Yugoslav offensive *à outrance* in Fiume and in northern Albania.[51] On 29 March, he wrote Cavallero: "At the beginning of hostilities in Yugoslavia, instruct those [soldiers] who are assembled on the Julian frontier that whoever, officer or soldier, retreats without orders from positions that must be defended at all costs, will be immediately shot."[52] Embarrassed by the memory of Greeks fighting Italians to a standstill on the Albanian front, Mussolini was perhaps not amiss in doubting the resilience of his troops. But since no Yugoslav offensive materialized, his orders did not have to be carried out.

In contrast to the confidence at the command of the German armed forces (OKW), the Italian Supreme Command was enveloped in gloom during these dark days of the Greek campaign. Cavallero bleakly observed that Italy could not at the same time fight Greeks, hold Albania against a Yugoslav force of "no less than 200,000 men," and hasten troops and artillery to the Julian Alps to meet an attack there.[53] Roatta cringed at opening a new front before the Germans had crushed Yugoslav resistance.[54] Only a swift German advance, the generals held, could save Italy from military disaster.[55] But if there had to be an attack, General Roatta, for one, was ready for unorthodox warfare: "Let it be understood that 'Četniks,' or civilians, coming from beyond the frontier who commit acts of hostility, sabotage, or rebellion will be immediately shot."[56]

Faced by his military's pessimism, Mussolini, on the sly, moved to delay an outbreak of war by instructing his special envoy in Belgrade, Francesco Giorgio Mameli, to act as a mediator. Simović, in turn, wanting to mobilize, rebuild internal unity, and extract firm guarantees from the Allies, sounded out Mussolini for Italian support in staving off a German attack on Salonika. But hardly in discreet diplomatic form. If the Germans should move on the coveted Aegean port, he warned Mussolini, the Yugoslavs would fall on the exposed Italian troops in northern Albania.[57] Offended by this pressure, but worried by unfavorable developments in the war against Greece, Mussolini temporized, hoping that the crisis would pass. But the joint desire of Rome and Belgrade to avoid war was only a transient coincidence. Prince Paul, for one, was unapproachable. He neither trusted the Italians nor was interested in population exchanges.[58] His use of middlemen to explore the Duce's intentions was a ruse to spin out negotiations as long as possible in the hope that a miracle would save his country from the Axis. And Mussolini was not one to stand against Hitler's determination to crush the hapless Yugoslavs.[59] The Führer wrote: "Above all, Duce, I consider *one* thing important: *Your front must in no case give way in Albania.*"[60] His words sufficed: Mussolini, emboldened, rushed to arms.

Without warning, on 6 April, the day that the Yugoslavs signed a non-aggression treaty with the Soviet Union, German Stukas rained bombs down on a defenseless Belgrade, followed by a swift and deadly invasion. Simultaneously, Italian bombers struck towns in Dalmatia. Before an advancing enemy composed of Germans, Italians, Hungarians, and Bulgarians, the poorly trained and equipped Yugoslav army, strung out over a vast area, did not stand a chance. The ranks were drained by the defection of soldiers from minority nationalities. Many Croats thronged into their favorite drinking places to toast the demise of Serb hegemony. On the 17th, routed and outflanked, the demoralized Yugoslav army bent to the inevitable and signed an unconditional surrender. By the end of April, German forces had rectified Italy's reverses at the hands of the Greeks by crushing them. Southeastern Europe lay at Hitler's feet.

The Italians were active on three fronts. In Albania, since the war against Greece was still raging, the troops hardly stirred. The thinly manned lines, however, held their ground against a few spirited Yugoslav assaults, which were less intense than the Supreme Command had originally feared. After a short period, the Italians went on the offensive and overran the Yugoslavs, who bravely defended their positions or surrendered long after the general cessation of hostilities. On 11 April the Italians met the German motorized columns striking out from Bulgaria at Lake Ochrid and Debar in Albania. By the 17th the Italians moved into Kotor and Cetinje. Military intelligence (SIM), under the able leadership of General Cesare Amè, was able to ease the Italian task on the Albanian front by cracking the Yugoslav code describing the disposition of enemy troops.[61] The Yugoslav command was completely disoriented when Italian intelligence infused disinformation into Yugoslav radio communications. In Zara Italians forged ahead; after a couple of setbacks they reached the important railhead at Knin and successfully cut off a Yugoslav retreat to Bosnia, where, if they had been able to reach this mountainous terrain, they would have been in a position to fight a grueling and prolonged guerrilla war. That day was merely postponed. In the north, encountering no resistance, a detachment of motorcyclists, determined to beat the Germans to Ljubljana, sped in on 11 April and quickly took control of the city.[62]

The Hungarians and Bulgarians, doing little of the fighting, scurried in to partake of the plunder. The Magyars claimed the Banat, while the Bulgars gathered in most of Macedonia. The Germans quickly withdrew their crack units for more important business pending on the Eastern Front and left mopping-up operations to their Tripartite allies. In the resulting void many Yugoslav units were able to steal away with their arms to fight another day in guerrilla warfare. Only a skeleton German occupation force was left behind for garrison duty in a rump Serbia.

In spite of much talk of war against Belgrade over the years, Mussolini had not fine-tuned the Italian military machine for a lightning military strike. Bellicose posturing hid the lack of careful preparations. As usual, Mussolini expected Yugoslavia to dissolve from within. The dizzying speed of the Axis victory caught the Duce without a plan either for the ultimate disposition of Yugoslav territory or for the establishment of a new Croatian regime. Who would serve as the Italian puppet in Zagreb? The moderate Croatian separatists, whose chief spokesman was Vladko Maček, would not do, for the peasant leader had irked Mussolini in 1939 by joining the Yugoslav cabinet instead of intriguing with him for a Croatian uprising. Only the minuscule radical fringe—the Croatian Ustaša—found credibility in Rome. Thus did Mussolini's eye fall on Ante Pavelić, whose major skill lay in the employment of knives and bombs.

## Mussolini and the Ustaša

When Hitler informed Mussolini of his intention to attack Yugoslavia on 27 March, he made no mention of Pavelić and the Ustaša.[63] (Small wonder, for on that same day Hitler had assured the Hungarian regent, Miklos Horthy, that Croatia was his; Horthy, two days later, wisely declined the offer.[64]) The Duce hastened to fill in the lacunae by talking up Pavelić's separatism.[65] There was no time to lose. Determined to have his minions in place in Zagreb before Hitler arrived with his Quislings, the Duce summoned Pavelić to Villa Torlonia on 29 March, the first time they had met face to face since the Croatian refugee had arrived on Italian soil twelve years before. After a disjointed conversation, Mussolini promised to set him up as maestro in Zagreb in exchange for Italian annexation of the Dalmatian coast. Pavelić agreed, but flinched from having to face compatriots already distressed by Italian irredentism.[66] Nothing, however, was submitted to writing. Mussolini allowed the Ustaša, who had been interned on the Lipari Islands, to be transferred to Pistoia, where they were supplied with uniforms and equipment. Pavelić was given a radio station in Florence for late evening broadcasts to Croatia.

The Duce's fears were not misplaced, for after the outbreak of hostilities against Yugoslavia, the Germans poured into Croatia determined to dominate the economy and control the government. Germany had already secured important concessions and by 1941 held first place in Yugoslav exports and imports.[67] A strong 5th column of 150,000 *Volksdeutsche* eagerly lent a helping hand. The Italophobe Edmund Glaise von Horstenau, German general plenipotentiary in Zagreb, supported the Croatian argument that economic viability would be crippled if Dalmatia were lost to Italy. He informed Hitler that Zagreb was strongly pro-German in contrast with the uniform hostility toward Italy prevalent throughout the country.[68]

The Germans first singled out the popular Maček to be leader of Croatia. A government in Zagreb supported by a majority of Croats would allow them to pare down their occupying forces—a more practical answer than turning to an unknown expatriate who, if more ideologically in tune with the Nazi regime, might need a heavy Wehrmacht presence to keep him in power. As the acknowledged head of the Peasant party, which had deep roots in the Croatian countryside, Maček had once exclaimed: "We are Yugoslavia's Sudeten Germans!" But when he showed a disinclination to sign on with the

Third Reich, the Germans transferred their attentions to Colonel Slavko Kvaternik, who was certifiably Ustaša and avowedly anti-Italian. Pavelić, an Italian stooge with no popular following in Croatia, could easily be shoved aside. As a former Habsburg officer, Kvaternik was susceptible to German blandishments. The notorious Nazi Siegfried Kasche, German envoy in Zagreb, worked assiduously to marry the local Croatian Ustaša to Germany. He was prepared to ignore Italy and the group of exile Ustaša surrounding Pavelić. The table was set for a German coup. Nazis descended on the farmland retreat of Maček and browbeat him to accept a Kvaternik-led regime. Maček obliged by calling on the Croatian people to swear allegiance to the new government. The last barrier to Ustaša rule had been removed. Thus was born the so-called Nezavisna Drzava Hrvatska, the Independent State of Croatia (NDH), which was officially proclaimed on 10 April.[69] History has rendered Maček a harsh judgment. He fled Belgrade while still a member of the Yugoslav cabinet and, failing to provide leadership to his fellow Croats, abandoned them to the Ustaša.[70] But he refused to serve as a German stooge and did not hide his disgust over the Ustaša's efforts to open Croatia to German and Italian forces.

That Croatia seemed to be falling under Germany's spell produced panic in Rome. Mussolini met hastily with Pavelić on 11 April, reconfirmed their oral bargain of 29 March, and bundled him off to Croatia to claim political power before it was too late.

Shortly after stepping on his homeland's soil for the first time in a decade, Pavelić on 13 April met with German representatives and Kvaternik at Karlovac some 40 miles southwest of Zagreb. Mussolini rushed Ciano's right-hand man, Filippo Anfuso, there to make sure that Pavelić would toe the Italian line rather than the German. But aware of Germany's preference for Kvaternik and his own narrow support in Zagreb, Pavelić knew that he was in no position to defy Mussolini. Accordingly, he sent the Duce a telegram promising to honor Italy's special interests in Dalmatia. Rome reciprocated by recognizing him as Poglavnik, or leader, of a newly proclaimed government in Zagreb.

How would Pavelić with a bedraggled band of some hundreds of followers still outfitted in uniforms from the Italian Ethiopian campaign—and trailed by a breathless Anfuso—gain the upper hand over the German-supported Kvaternik?[71] It seemed like a hopelessly uphill climb. Zagreb was teeming with haughty, goose-stepping Wehrmacht troops and Nazi agents, surrounded by a cohort of fanatic ethnic Germans, who brandished swastikas and cheered wildly as the tanks rumbled over the cobbled streets of the capital. Thanks to the large turnout of ethnic Germans, Zagreb was the only occupied city outside Austria that welcomed the German legions with open arms. But, according to Glaise, "this revolution knows how to fire up only very few of the people."[72] A Teutonic takeover of a country whose Croatian population was stunned by the sudden collapse of political order seemed imminent. To the chagrin—and puzzlement—of all around him, Hitler, however, checked a German coup by granting Mussolini the honor of elevating Pavelić to power. The Croatia that emerged was a mongrel entity with a grafted-on government recognized only by the Axis Powers and their satellites. Some of the most fanatic Nazis and signature Italian-haters never ceased to be baffled when trying to plumb Hitler's devious mind.

*Boundary Controversies*

In spring 1941 a new department was established in the Palazzo Chigi called the "Cabinet of Armistice and Peace," whose purpose was to deal with the economic and political affairs of European countries brought under Italian domination. Count Luca Pietromarchi, a long-standing Fascist, remembered for having shouted down the Ethiopian representative at the League of Nations in the early 1920s, was appointed head of this department, directly responsible to Ciano. After the outbreak of the war, when relations were broken off with the rest of the world save the Axis bloc, the Palazzo Chigi had little else to do. Ciano, frequently distracted by the enticements of the *haute monde,* left the day-to-day work regarding Yugoslavia to Pietromarchi.

Shaken by the rapidity of the German conquest, the Italians hurriedly worked up suggestions for the disposition of the Yugoslav state. Dalmatia had highest priority. The Palazzo Chigi wrestled with the question of whether Dalmatia should be annexed outright or given an autonomy under Italian hegemony that would allow the majority of Croats a certain participation in local government. This latter solution had the double advantage of offsetting Croatian ethnic resistance to Italian authority and, by dodging boundary disputes with Zagreb, rendering Dalmatia immune to territorial amputations.[73]

Before discussing the matter with Mussolini, and in the absence of any directive from above, Pietromarchi spelled out his own views: "I support the maximum thesis;" that is, a "totalitarian" solution: annexation of Dalmatia from head to foot and from the Adriatic litoral to the Dinaric Alps and beyond.[74] "It is not possible to ask less than what the Italian government of 1915 demanded."[75] There could be no half-measures when it came to ports, he insisted; Italy must have them all. For if one single port should go to the Croats, they would be able to starve Fiume and other territories ceded to Italy by diverting all traffic emanating from the hinterland to Zagreb's exclusive advantage.[76] In the back of Pietromarchi's mind, as he planned the future of Dalmatia, was Germany. If the Third Reich should extend its occupation as far as Salonika, Italian control over the Adriatic would not be secure unless its control over Dalmatia extended to the crest of the Dinaric Mountains.

Blessed with mineral sources powered by cheap hydroelectric energy, Dalmatia, in Pietromarchi's view, stood to enjoy a splendid future of industrial development. But an Italian Dalmatia, he acknowledged, would not be self-sufficient unless joined to the Bosnian interior. Containing what Dalmatia lacked—farm animals, cereals, and forestry lands—Bosnia, linked "in indissoluble unity" with Dalmatia, would assure a prosperous and self-sufficient unity under Italian imperial rule. No matter that Bosnia was filled with Serbs and Muslims incapable of holding steady jobs; skilled workers from Italy could be imported to exploit resources and build up industry as in Roman days when the long arm of empire stretched far beyond the Dinaric Alps. "For about two millenniums, save for brief parentheses, Dalmatia has lived in the orbit of Italian history and civilization. Italy could not ever have done without it, because Italian power without the Dalmatian shore is inconceivable."[77] Pietromarchi jotted down these thoughts in the learned journal *Storia e politica internazionale* in March 1942.

Echoing Pietromarchi were vociferous nationalist partisans of an Italian Dalmatia in the Senate, who demanded restoration of a Venetian-style Lordship. Senator Alessandro Dudàn thought that the Croats and Slovenes would seek Italian help to free them from the Yugoslav yoke; Italy had better move in before the Germans. Senator Francesco Salata assumed that the Dalmatian Croats, anxious to distance themselves from Zagreb, would be grateful for Italian protection over a "historical Dalmatia." The Italian senators were in no compromising mood. A 1915 Pact of London-style solution was deemed untidy and unacceptable because it would chop up the Dalmatian coastline.[78] The national advisor of the Fascist party, Giovanni Maracchi, wrote Mussolini that Dalmatia, Herzegovina, and the Adriatic territory from Zara to Albania and from the Adriatic to the watershed of the Danubian basin should be part of the metropolitan territory.[79]

Surprisingly, the so-called "Duke of Albania" and instigator of the war against Greece, Foreign Minister Galeazzo Ciano, had no patience for the "blathering" senators, who were conducting an "absurd" campaign to deny even a "centimeter of coast" for Croatia. The king was even less supportive.[80] The armed forces were divided. To assure mastery of the Adriatic, the Navy lobbied for an "Italian Adriatic," whereas the Supreme Command was more leery. Should the eastern boundary line be drawn far from the coast, the problem of peacekeeping in vast hostile territory would be daunting.[81] As opposed to the heated atmosphere of the postwar era, the country was too shell-shocked by the Greek imbroglio to care much about Dalmatian irredentism. Giovanni Ansaldo, the director of the newspaper *Telegrafo* and close confidant of Ciano, noted that for the Italians the occupation of Dalmatia was spectacular choreography that did not touch the heart.[82]

On 17 April Mussolini roughed out his own ideas: enlargement of Fiume and annexation of an indivisible Dalmatia, its eastern boundary defined by the crest of the Dinaric Alps, which would give Italy undisputed mastery over the Adriatic. "We will give Dalmatia an autonomous regime," Mussolini told Pietromarchi; "we could call it the regency of Dalmatia or an Illyrian kingdom reminiscent of the Napoleonic era . . . but under an Italian flag." Croatia would be provided an outlet to the sea at Fiume-Sušak, and Serbia given use of Dubrovnik.[83] Mussolini was opposed to "the formation of tiny states having an operatic character." Benefiting from a friendly tutorial administered by high-minded Italians, the Croatian majority would learn ethnic brotherhood and love of Italian civilization. The Duce's essay in map-making contained no allocation of Bosnia and Herzegovina to Croatia.

The thinking in Berlin proceeded along somewhat different lines. To be sure, the official German position, as explained in Rome, held that Yugoslavia lay in Italy's sphere of influence. The Italians expected that the military collapse of the country would not result in any change in German policy. But the Wehrmacht wanted to secure lines of communications through the Balkans to their far-flung outposts in Greece,[84] and the war machine needed Yugoslavia's rich mineral deposits. Ciano was given a harbinger of things to come by Ribbentrop. Italy, he said, would acquire southern Slovenia and areas in the Adriatic, thus forming a long common boundary with Germany from Monte Bianco to Ljubljana. The rest of Yugoslavia would be settled in conformity with "our mutual interests"[85]—a comment that hardly squared with the Italian notion of *spazio vitale*.

Ribbentrop, meeting with Ciano in Vienna 21–22 April, unveiled yet another ploy to win Zagreb's allegiance: the creation of an elephantine Croatian state that would include Bosnia-Herzegovina and large tracts of the Dalmatian coast. When Ciano claimed Dalmatia and announced Italy's intention to install an Italian king on the Croatian throne, Ribbentrop "did not conceal his personal, although disguised opposition." But since Hitler had cautioned his foreign minister to respect Mussolini's sensibilities, Ribbentrop declared that the Führer would have no objection either to an Italian Dalmatia or to a personal union between Italy and Croatia.[86] The Wilhelm-strasse was momentarily compelled to yield some of its heart's desires to Italy.[87]

On 23 April Ribbentrop announced that Berlin had decided to maintain an occupation force in "a strip of Croatia running from northwest to southeast in order to safeguard the railroad communications with Serbia." Hence the origin of the demarcation line, "purely for contingent military purposes," as Ribbentrop put it, that would separate the Italian and German occupying forces in Croatia for the duration of the war. The Germans made sure that communication lines of strategic importance, as well as major urban areas such as Sarajevo, Banja Luka, and the capital Zagreb, would rest on their side of the demarcation line. "The boundaries traced [by the Germans]," Pietromarchi noted, "are uniquely based on economic considerations."[88] In addition, the Germans staked out economic privileges, particularly bauxite mines, in the proposed Italian-occupied zone.[89] Italy emerged from the German *Diktat* with one advantage: the *Drang nach Südosten* had not yet reached the Adriatic. Instead of an Italian *spazio vitale* in Croatia, the country had been divided into two Axis spheres of interest, but with German economic domination assured in the area assigned to Italy, which made Croatia a German semi-protectorate just as Italian troops took up their positions in the lands across the Adriatic.

In the aftermath of their talks, Ciano and Pietromarchi had this exchange: "We have returned to the concept of the Versailles peace," Pietromarchi observed; "we thought we were working on the plan of the 'spazio vitale,' which is the negation of the nationality criterion." Ciano replied: "It is evident that they [the Germans] want to impose the nationality principle on us while insisting on *Lebensraum* for themselves."[90] Ciano likened Italy's situation to Piedmont facing the mighty France of Louis XIV—and worse, without allies to counterbalance the overwhelming power of the Third Reich. Feeling the disproportionate strength between the two Axis Powers, the Italians could only fume impotently among themselves while the Germans made mincemeat of Hitler's oral promises to regard Croatia as lying within the Italian sphere of interest.

Pavelić's word to the Italians was equally faithless. In a bid for German support, the Poglavnik informed Berlin that he would not give away any part of Dalmatia "either now or tomorrow" and eventually would throw the Italian troops out of his country. But the Germans would not be sucked into Croatian-Italian disputes by Pavelić's confidences or by Ciano's "dialectical tricks" to have Berlin coax the Poglavnik into acceptance of Italian aspirations.[91] Official German policy was clear: Pavelić was an Italian problem to be settled by Italians with no support from Berlin.[92] This was hardly an expression of Axis solidarity. Hitler decidedly was not ready to relinquish Croatia to Mussolini. As the Führer coyly told Glaise, allowing Dalmatia to become Italian could be useful by creating "a permanent basis for conflict between Italians and Croats, whereby Germany could always reserve the role of an arbiter."[93]

Hitler was quite happy to see Italy make enemies of the Croats and the Croats make enemies of the Serbs even if the country dissolved into turmoil. The Wehrmacht had the quite different purpose of creating stability and would support any government in Zagreb that would assure this. Hitler's confidence to Glaise went directly counter to Weizsäcker's instructions that Kasche avoid Italo-Croatian controversies.[94] While the Wilhelmstrasse would use strong-armed diplomacy to advance German interests at the risk of alienating Mussolini, the Führer employed guile to keep him in line. A German-dominated Croatia could wait. If Pavelić should be swept from office by a population outraged over the loss of Dalmatia, the Germans could feign surprise, deny responsibility, and take control of the country.

Emerging from the Vienna talks with many imperialist dreams already shattered, the Italians, armed with Mussolini's maximum program, were faced with a hard sell to Pavelić and his following when they arrived in Croatia to negotiate boundaries. Ciano gives a vivid description:

> In Ljubljana. A hell of a day. It is raining and there is a freezing wind. The people have a distraught air but are not hostile. I see Pavelić surrounded by his band of cutthroats. He declares that

the solutions proposed by us would have him thrown out of a job . . . His followers are more radical than he. They invoke statistics to prove that in Dalmatia only the stones are Italian.[95]

Pavelić insisted that Italy restrict itself to the zones assigned by the Pact of London. Croatia would take possession of Spalato, Ragusa, and the islands facing them. The atmosphere suddenly became "red hot," but both sides backed off and deferred further discussion for later.[96]

By 26 April Mussolini had altered his thinking. "Except for Spalato," Ciano records, "Mussolini is in agreement with Pavelić and justly maintains that it is better to attract Croatia into our political orbit than to gain a little more territory populated by hostile Croats."[97] Afraid that Pavelić would slip from their grasp, they prepared to trim Italian demands.

On 6 May Mussolini and Ciano departed by train for Monfalcone to sign an accord with Pavelić. The Italian delegation was met by the Poglavnik, escorted by a squadron of cars full of Ustaša toughs armed with machine guns, like "gangsters in American movies."[98] To prop up a wobbly Pavelić, Mussolini suddenly decided not to insist on a customs union or to claim the entire Dalmatian coast. The ultimate status of Spalato would be left for future negotiations. Pavelić, in turn, showed a disposition to meet Italy's demands regarding Spalato.[99] Raffaele Casertano, the Italian minister plenipotentiary in Zagreb, and Ciano were dismayed by Mussolini's unexpected abandonment of a customs union, key to an Italian protectorate, which held out the only hope of safeguarding the country from German economic inroads. The only light moment came when Pavelić claimed territory up to the gates of Budapest. "Pest," he told the bemused Italians, "is a Croatian word and signifies port. Croats were once the masters there."[100] Back in Zagreb, Pavelić boasted to Glaise von Horstenau that he had achieved a diplomatic victory. Italy's control over Spalato was only nominal, and if an Italian king were enthroned, he would be a figurehead unable to threaten his "Führerstaat."[101]

The understandings reached at Monfalcone were codified in the Treaty of Rome signed on 18 May. Italy guaranteed Croatia independence and promised to develop and train its armed forces. The settlement provided Italy with territory not much greater than that granted by the Pact of London. The cities of Zara, Sebenico, and Cattaro became provinces of the motherland with groups of islands tacked on; the territory around Fiume was enlarged. Spalato's ultimate status remained undecided. The remainder of Dalmatia, with a broad strip of its hinterland, was divided into three occupation zones in which the Italians exercised a control that diminished by degrees from the coast to the interior. Required to relinquish areas occupied in anticipation of annexation, below Split, and to the Croat Littoral from the Bay of Bakar to Senj, Italy was left holding slips of territory not much wider than a few kilometers in some places, while the main rail and road links passed over long stretches beyond their control. Italian Dalmatia would function as an economically backward territory filled with nearly a half-million alienated Croats whose numbers dwarfed the ethnic Italians.

The Navy was happy to have acquired domination of the Adriatic by the annexation of all suitable harbors and by the provision in the treaty that denied Croatia war ships. The Croats were compelled to demilitarize their portions of the Adriatic coast and inland up to 80 kilometers; only civilian administrators were allowed there to exercise power. The Italians reserved the right to garrison these demilitarized areas at any time. No map was published showing in detail the Croatian national boundaries. Only on 15 July was the frontier between Croatia and the Italian-annexed part of Slovenia fixed; the frontier between Croatia and Italian-occupied Montenegro was not worked out until 27 October.

Pietromarchi expressed no dissatisfaction with the mutilated Dalmatia that Italian diplomacy had produced. The Croats would ultimately not care, in his view, since Zagreb would be grateful that the country had been given life by Fascist largesse. Collaboration was guaranteed by "the ties of solidarity between the two revolutions, the friendship between the two governments, and the military alliance against Communist enemies."[102] It was obvious to all that Italy could not hope to predominate in Croatia without a friendly NDH, and it was equally obvious that, by insisting on a de-militarized zone and on a prohibition of a Croatian navy, the Ital-ians, in spite of Pietromarchi's optimism, had little confidence in the loyalty of their newly acquired satellite.

The shortcomings of the Rome Accords were patent: ambigu-ity over the legal status of Spalato, a disfigured Italian Dalmatia, a broken railroad line from Fiume to Spalato, and deprivation of important hydroelectric plants left to Croatia, essential to the life and economy of the Italian towns on the coast. Proclamation of the accords spread such consternation among Dalmatian Italians that when Giuseppe Gorla, the minister of public works, landed in Spalato, he thought he had arrived at a funeral. Hugely important was the Italian failure to prevail on the Croats to sign a customs union, the key to a protectorate and a far better imperial device, in the opinion of many Italian experts, than possession of barren is-lands and rocky Dalmatian territory.[103] Equally telling, the Italians acquired no domination over the Croatian armed forces. Soon af-ter the treaty was signed, Pavelić formally asked King Victor Emmanuel III to designate a member of the House of Savoy as king of Croatia. The king immediately named his nephew Aimone, Duke of Spoleto. But the king-designate, having little stomach for a coun-try torn by ethnic strife, preferred not to accept the crown as Tomislav II after the first medieval Croatian king crowned in 925. This came as no disappointment to Pavelić, who spun out matters to avoid acceptance of a kingdom of Croatia under the Savoy dy-nasty, which, if realized, would have defined Croatia, based on the example of Albania, as an Italian protectorate. The matter was left indefinitely suspended.[104]

Pavelić was certainly not happy when his aroused people called him a "renouncer" for the Dalmatian sell-out—land thought by many Croats to be the political and cultural cradle of their nation.[105] The huge territorial acquisitions of Bosnia and Herzegovina that included well over 2,000,000 Serbs destined to live in the "reborn"

Croatia[106] (a gift from the Third Reich, not from Mussolini) did not make up for "unredeemed" Dalmatia. No matter how much Pavelić expatiated on "independence," it appeared to the mainstream Croat that Italy intended to call the shots in Zagreb. If ever Pavelić were to taste power, however, he had no choice but to sign on with Mussolini, a choice made painfully clear to him by Hitler's postured "disinterest." But the Poglavnik was determined not to be Italy's minion. To keep an even keel between the Axis Powers, he ceded to Berlin, in a confidential protocol of 16 May 1941, a package of economic privileges that guaranteed German domination over the natural resources of the country.[107] By the end of the month Germany had successfully claimed chromium mines in Macedonia and the lead deposits in Mitrovica located in rump Serbia. The "anti-German" Count Ciano offered no objection.[108]

Mussolini was not pleased with his own Dalmatian patchwork. He confided to Athos Bartolucci, the newly appointed civil commissioner for Dalmatia: "A body has been cut in two that should have remained united; it can only survive united. This population, emerging with many memories of a Venetian and Roman past— excluding the usual nationalists originating from other places in Yugoslavia—is now oriented toward a slow appreciation of a strong, generous, and well organized Italy, as exemplified by our magnificent troops." When Bartolucci pointed out that Dalmatian Slavs of every stripe were inveterate enemies of Italy, the Duce replied: "All those problems will be taken care of at the peace table."[109] Meanwhile, Pavelić would be his man in Zagreb.

Since Germany's military setbacks in the Soviet Union were still to come, and America slumbered in neutrality, Mussolini crafted an Italian policy on the expectation of an Axis victory. For him the Rome Accords with Croatia comprised a makeshift arrangement until Italy was in a position to dictate new terms. To leave himself wide latitude for maneuver in an ultimate Balkan settlement, Mussolini chose not to present the Rome Accords to the Senate for final validation.

*Mangled Montenegro*

T he Italians approached Montenegro with the same frivolity and lack of preparation they displayed elsewhere in the Balkans. Mussolini on 17 April envisaged a union of Montenegro with Albania to promote Italian hegemony over the entire Adriatic coast.[110] Later, in Vienna, Ciano acquainted Ribbentrop with the idea of an Italian protectorate over Montenegro sealed by a personal union under the Italian royal dynasty. The Albanian fiefdom would be aggrandized by territory sheared from Montenegro and Macedonia. Ribbentrop, however, had to answer to the greedy demands of Germany's client, the Bulgarian King Boris: Macedonia, the shrine of Ohrid, and Salonika. Ciano conceded the shrine,[111] but avoided commitment on precise frontiers in the hope that his Albanian state would eventually fall heir to the parts of Kosovo and Macedonia populated by ethnic Albanians. When Ribbentrop ceded Kosovar lead deposits in Mitrovica to German-occupied rump Serbia and claimed the rich chrome deposits west of Skopje in Macedonia plus bauxite mines located in Dalmatia,[112] Ciano raised no objection, for Albania was still the main beneficiary of Yugoslavia's break-up, having gained slices of Montenegro and most of the former Yugoslav province of Kosovo. After fully satisfying Germany's economic interests, Ribbentrop accepted the idea of an independent Montenegrin state united to Italy.

In Italy a "greater Montenegro" had only one stout supporter, King Victor Emmanuel III, but only for reasons of family prestige. As opposed to the Duce, who wanted an Albanian-Montenegrin union, the Italian king favored Montenegrin "independence" under Prince Michael of the Petrovic dynasty, who had married into the Italian royal house. From Ciano's standpoint this choice would merely complicate matters. His favorite was the king's wife, Queen Elena of Italy, as she was the daughter of King Nicholas, Montenegro's last independent ruler. Italian control over the country would thereby be assured. The Italian king pestered Ciano to restore Montenegro's 1914 boundaries. "I do not think this is possible," noted the Italian minister, for "Albania would start an uprising,"[113] adding: "Frankly, I never dreamed we should waste so much brain power on a country like Montenegro."[114] Various other schemes were bandied about until the Montenegrin uprisings of mid July, which spiked further talk of kingdoms, princes, and regents.

Montenegro had many Italians *in loco* opposed to both Croatian predators and Albanian annexationists in Rome. Captain Ugo Villani, serving on a mixed Italian-German boundary commission, reported that the Croats had occupied Prijepolje, which lay in the heart of old Serbia, and mistreated Muslims and Serbs. To spare the local population further abuse in a region where no Croats lived, Villani urged that Prijepolje be given to Montenegro.[115] The Italian high commissioner in Montenegro, Serafino Mazzolini, mused on the injustice of compelling the Montenegrins to yield land to Albania that they had heroically fought for at great cost in blood.

Pavelić created yet more problems for Italy by laying claim to the Sandžak, which had never been a part of historic Croatia, had not been mentioned in previous negotiations with Italy, and contained nary a Croat, even if "you looked for one with a flashlight."[116] Mazzolini predicted that if the Montenegrins were deprived of the Sandžak, they would revolt.[117] Diplomacy was overshadowed by violence in the second half of June when armed clashes occurred between Croats and Montenegrins in the disputed territory; during these incidents some soldiers of the Italian "Marche" division were killed and wounded by Ustaša elements.[118]

This unruly Croatian behavior stimulated controversy in the Palazzo Chigi. Ever the stalwart supporter of a "resurgent" Croatia, Casertano thought to give the disputed territory to Pavelić in return for his acceptance of a customs union with Italy. Pietromarchi would have none of this "blackmail,"[119] certain that the Croats would demand Spalato next. Resorting to "hard language," he warned Stijepo Perić, the Croatian minister in Rome, that his salami tactics were leading the two countries straight to war. [120]

The stalwarts in the Palazzo Chigi devised a solution by establishing the boundary between Croatia and Montenegro at the river Drina, which would leave the Sandžak in the latter. Mussolini readily accepted their proposal: "We must do as the Germans. When we went to Vienna [in April], they told us 'this is the boundary.' We will do the same."[121]

Still, Montenegro stood to lose substantial territory. In the ex-Yugoslav province of Kosovo that was handed over to Albania, the majority Muslim population, which had been persecuted by Serbs ever since the collapse of the Ottoman Empire, now had their chance to strike back. Five thousand terrorized Montenegrins fled to their homeland where they were joined by compatriots fleeing the Ustaša from the borderland areas with Croatia in the Sandžak.[122] The atmosphere crackled with ethnic rage. The 9th Army command in Albania, responsible for the garrisoning of Montenegro, assumed the functions of civilian commissariats. As the troops set about the task of provisioning the towns and countryside, however, they found themselves the object of hatred for trampling on the independence and territorial aspirations of the country. The Montenegrin pot was about to boil over.

## The Partition of Slovenia

The Italians were almost defeated before they got started in Slovenia. While Hitler gave lip-service to Italian primacy in Croatia, he dictated "irrevocable" boundaries for the hapless Slovenia, grabbing the rich mineral deposits and industrial sectors in the north—the strategic Ljubljana-Zagreb line, the coal mines of Trbovlje, and the steel mill at Jesenice, leaving Italy the rest: pastoral lands and an overpopulated capital.[123] This nettled Ciano, who was surprised to learn that the German-dictated frontiers ran considerably further south than he expected by passing a mere three kilometers north of Ljubljana. There was nothing to do but bend to the Führer's will.

The ensuing partition of Slovenia, the heartland of which was split for the first time in history, defied economic logic. The German north contained the best forestry lands plus productive industrial and agricultural regions, all now deprived of their markets in the south. The impoverished and barren Italian south was weighed down by a bureaucratic apparatus rendered useless and costly by cession of the northern areas to Germany. Chemical firms in the south were cut off from primary materials in the north. Ljubljana suffered the same fate as Vienna following the amputation of Habsburg territory after World War I: a city cut off from its food supply. Electrical power in the provincial capital was rendered uncertain and made more expensive by the loss of free access to power generators located in the German sphere. This economic anomaly exacerbated the nationalistic spirit of the population and provided an incentive for rebellion.

Although only 458 Italians lived in Slovenia, the territory was annexed to the mother country. Slovenia would not be a puppet state, like Croatia, but an Italian province. There was a peculiarly Fascist logic to this. The Fascists had long experienced great difficulty in suppressing the local Slovene minority in the Venezia Giulia, whose rebellious spirit was kept alive by propaganda and weaponry emanating from the safe haven in Slovenian Yugoslavia. By annexing the "Province of Ljubljana," the Fascist authorities thought they could quite easily stamp out Communist and nationalist cells there that would leave the anti-Fascist resistance in the Venezia Giulia to wither and die. No longer would there be a "Slovenian question," because Slovenia had simply ceased to exist. Ciano boasted that the Province of Ljubljana would rest on "liberal principles,"[124] which for him meant Italianization and the granting of a miserly autonomy. An old revisionist ambition was reawakened: expansion of Italian interests in the Balkans and Danube, a central feature of Mussolini's policy during the twenties. No matter that the major obstacle was no longer posed by a debilitated France but by an aggressive Third Reich. Slovenia would become an appendage of Italy in the heart of Mitteleuropa and buffer the *italianità* of the acquired irredentist lands against the expansionism of both Germany and Croatia. Mussolini could show Hitler that Italy, too, knew how to encroach on territory held dear by an Axis partner. To overcome the Italian fiasco in Greece, he hoped to revive Rome's "*spirito conquistatore.*" But the province of Ljubljana ended up a poor choice—a poverty-stricken region on the periphery, simmering in discontent. Slovenia was not Dalmatia, which evoked old irredentist passion, or even

Montenegro, which was tied to the Savoyard dynasty. It was a foreign entity that for reason of state had been grafted on to the "healthy body" of the mainland.

Giovanni Ansaldo summarized Italian peacemaking in the Balkans:

> The settlement of the Yugoslav carcass is comical. I listen to all of this kaleidoscope of annexations, partitions, divisions, and restorations with a secret desire to laugh. All this is constructed in sand, fleeting as an unsettling dream, and destined to founder in European chaos. We lack everything to made this system endure: military force, administrative capability, the right, and perhaps the interest. Ciano actually realizes this. The discussions in Vienna about the partition divert him like a sport.[125]

## Italy's *Spazio Vitale*

In *Mein Kampf*, Hitler set aside the Ukraine as Germany's *Lebensraum*; the existing populations would be pushed off to distant regions or simply exterminated to make place for German settlement. Mussolini, in contrast, had only inchoate ideas on how to proceed in Italy's Balkan *spazio vitale* after the Germans had wiped Yugoslavia off the map. An Italian "living space" in the Balkans and Mediterranean had been twin fixtures in Mussolini's imperialist panorama ever since the inception of his regime. At first he speculated on Italian expansion in only short, staccato outbursts. Many Fascist writers took up the cue by musing on the grandeur of imperialism. Italy was destined to conquer and dominate lands over which Mussolini would rule as emperor, applying Fascist law and civilization. Colonial war would forge a hard Fascist warrior and turn Italy into a modern-day Sparta, prepared to do battle with the "effete" western democracies who blocked Fascism's will to found an empire. Throughout the thirties Africa held center-stage. After the conquest of Ethiopia and the outbreak of World War II, Mussolini combined a Balkan *spazio vitale* with an African imperium under what a recent writer has dubbed "The New Mediterranean Order."[126]

After the Axis conquest of Yugoslavia, aficionados of empire-building could draw upon Italy's African experience for a model to apply in the Balkans. In Libya and Ethiopia the conquerors not only had fought a savage war against the native peoples but subjected them to inhumane and destructive treatment. There was no thought of a Fascist "civilizing mission" here, only a biologically defined apartheid.

Then there was Albania, already in place as a first piece of the yet-to-be-realized Italian imperium in the Balkans. Albania had been conquered in 1939 and turned into a protectorate. King Victor Emmanuel of Italy ruled as sovereign over the impoverished country, which was fractured by warring clansmen. The Fascist party, although given its head in the cultural sphere, was answerable to a luogotenente, or deputy of the king, who held the real power. The Italian Foreign Ministry played a preeminent role by imparting political directives to the luogotenente. This confusing setup reflected a compromise worked out by competing pressure groups and lobbies in Rome. Foisted on a hapless country, the Fascist government in Albania hardly pretended to answer the needs of the restive and discontented native peoples. Rather, a system was created that featured corruption and official banditry, which deferred a true Fascist *civiltà* to a remote future.

Although conquest of Yugoslavia as a "living space" had been much talked about in Italy between the wars, it was not until after the 2nd Army had landed that a plethora of differing plans for the *spazio vitale* appeared, typically vague and impractical. Mussolini himself rarely joined this debate. Rather than tie his hands by allegiance to any set doctrine or course of action, he would improvise, mediate, and decide as he went along, for this was the Fascist way. Empires emanated from an *élan vital*, an act of will, and were always a work-in-progress. But if there was little agreed-upon theoretical guidance, the conquerors were at one in rejecting the traditional kind of plutocratic, or financial, imperialism found in British-style indirect rule. Mussolini was determined to crowd his conquered territories with a host of administrators and colonists from the motherland.

The *spazio vitale* assumed concrete definition in parts of Yugoslavia by virtue of Italy's annexation of major portions of Dalmatia, the expansion of Fiume, attainment of the province of Ljubljana, and a protectorate over Montenegro, but remained inchoate in Italian-occupied Croatia. As opposed to Italy's prostrate African holdings and a ground-down Albania, the conquerors found themselves in an enlarged Croatia as only one among many independent forces contending for power: Croats, Orthodox Serbs, and, eventually, Communist Partisans. Furthermore, they were hampered by little preplanning, a critical shortage of trained personnel, and an omnipresent Nazi Germany.

Regarding Croatia, there were throughout the Italian occupation decided differences of opinion in the Fascist establishment over how the *spazio vitale* should be realized. The Realpolitikers argued that a tightly knit alliance between Rome and Zagreb would provide Italian Dalmatia with a strong strategic defense. Better yet would be a protectorate over Croatia, which would enable Italy to safeguard its settlements and exercise full and unimpeded exploitation of the country's economic resources. For many Italian expansionists, however, such utilitarian logic was thinking too small. They imagined a manifest destiny that enjoined Fascist Italy to hew out commodious spaces in the Balkans to receive the mainland's overpopulation. Fascists and Ustaša would provide ideological definition and spiritual unity by collaborating in cultural programs designed to turn all faces toward Rome. However, Germany's "zone of preeminent economic interests," which Ribbentrop had spelled out in April before cowed Italians, deflated these high-flying *ballons d'essai*. In the sure knowledge that the determined German ethnic minority would easily forge a political sway over the country, Hitler fed these Italian imperialist fantasies with oral promises to respect Italy's living spaces.

While Fascist visionaries were contriving wild theories of the future Italian imperium, Mussolini was unable to ensure the military's compliance with the regime's ideological precepts. Unlike Hitler and Stalin, he had no Italian counterpart to the Nazi SS policeman and Soviet political commissar who could look over the shoulders of the 2nd Army commanders in the field and intimidate them into acceptance of any particular party line on empire-building. The Italian military was, therefore, free to absorb and impart to the troops what they wanted of regime-defined imperialism, or they could simply emphasize traditional military values and objectives, many of which had been absorbed into the Fascist credo. Disdainful of theoretical speculation, the 2nd Army commanders viewed empire-building in Yugoslavia as a practical challenge that required on-the-spot decisions and constant adjustment to changing battlefield conditions.

Italy, so held the military commanders, should turn the Balkans into a "vital space" all right, where there would be no resistance—an area that would provide the motherland with a safe haven for economic exploitation and the extraction of natural resources. No less important, Italian-occupied territory should be defended against an ongoing German *Drang nach Südosten*. In contrast with the 2nd Army commanders, who had no interest in Fascist social engineering, the "idealistic" Fascist overlords whom Mussolini would appoint to rule in the annexed territories intended to inculcate "barbaric" Slavs with Roman *civiltà* by assimilating them. But when this essay in empire-building encountered sullen hostility, the Fascist rulers were prepared to reduce unreceptive members of the native population to an underclass. When Communist insurgency engulfed their fiefdoms, they joined the military in outright subjugation.

# Chapter III

# Ethnic Cleansing in Croatia

Italy's Infamous Ustaša Ally
Italian Military Assumes Command
The Serbs Fight Back
Reactions in the Field
Into the Croatian Whirlwind

*Italy's Infamous Ustaša Ally*

A nte Pavelić was on the hot seat from the moment he arrived in Zagreb. To secure a modicum of independence and himself in office, Pavelić tried to maintain a balance between the two Axis Powers. But his deep resentment over Italy's seizure of Dalmatia found expression in a confidence conveyed to the Germans that he could hardly wait for the "later disintegration" of the Italian army that would allow Croatia to fulfill its rights on the Adriatic.[127] Meanwhile, Italians were at one in attributing a basic pro-Germanism to everyone in Zagreb save Pavelić, whom they regarded, in face of strong evidence to the contrary, as their Trojan horse in a hostile camp. It is surprising that Mussolini and his hard-bitten advisers would place such trust in Pavelić 's professions of loyalty despite his many acts of defiance. This speaks of desperation. Without Pavelić Italy's *spazio vitale* would be swamped by a German *Drang nach Südosten*. Yet, in looking to the branch of the renegade Croatian Ustaša for support, Mussolini was clutching a weak reed. The émigré group surrounding Pavelić was no more than an outlaw minority that had arrived in Zagreb in the baggage of the enemy Italians. There was also a homegrown Ustaša of about 4,000,[128] whose influence would have been negligible had it not received support from the invading Germans. The majority of Croats favored independence, but not a Ustaša regime. In a population of 6,700,000, of which Croats numbered some 3,300,000, the movement at most had about 40,000 followers or barely six percent of the population.[129] The rest consisted of approximately 2,200,000 Orthodox Serbs, 750,000 Muslims, some 45,000 Jews, and 30,000 gypsies.[130]

When Croatia annexed Bosnia and Herzegovina with their large Serb population, it was almost certain that Zagreb would have to govern by strong-arm methods, but the Ustaša immediately went far beyond that, employing unrestrained terror in the endeavor to found a "pure" Croatian state. The political consciousness of the Ustaša was based on mistrust and hatred of Serbs, an irrational response growing out of folk memory. It is a terrible tragedy that in regions with mixed Croatian and Serbian populations, which had lived side-by-side in relative, if uneasy, peace in Habsburg times and in interwar Yugoslavia (where ethnic intermarriages were not rare), the Ustaša was able to ignite long-dormant religious conflicts and tribal hatreds.[131] The new government was staffed with inefficient and corrupt personnel—or none at all—but the Ustaša squads were surprisingly unified and prompt in launching their extermination programs.

Taking their cue from the Germans, the Ustaša built concentration camps—the most infamous being at Jasenovac—where hundreds of thousands of Orthodox Serbs, Jews, and Croatian dissidents perished by unspeakably sadistic methods that offended the more fastidious German killers. The Ustaša regime introduced the genocidal terror and extermination later perfected by the SS *Einsatzgruppen.*[132] Croatian Minister of Education Mile Budak echoed the Ustaša belief that the Serbs, "the refuse of the Balkans," were brought to Croatia by the Turks to plunder the people. On 22 June in Gospić, the center of the Ustaša killing fields, he outlined a diabolic program under the motto "Either submit or get out."[133] "For... Serbs, Jews, and Gypsies, we have three million bullets. We shall kill one-third of all Serbs. We shall deport another third, and the rest of them will be forced to become Roman Catholic."[134] Before May was out, thousands of Serbs had been driven from their homes or simply massacred. In the crazed atmosphere of bloodletting, even those beleaguered Serbs who thought they had found safety in Catholic baptism were still rounded up for torture and death. Between 1941 and 1945, some 30,000 Jews, roughly 27,000 gypsies, and an estimated 487,000 to 530,000 Orthodox Serbs perished under the Croatian regime.[135] In its effort to set up a pan-Croatian state from the ruins of Yugoslavia, Pavelić's movement was responsible for starting a horrendous fratricidal war. The NDH's efforts to purify the state by terror would be answered, atrocity by atrocity, in a vicious struggle of mutual extirpation into which was drawn an ill-prepared and unsuspecting Italian army of occupation.

As opposed to its big sister totalitarian parties in Germany and Italy, which enjoyed sizeable support, the Ustaša rested on a small popular base. No spellbinding mass rallies or midnight torchlight parades, the trademarks of Fascism and Nazism, were staged. The Poglavnik remained far from view and a mystery to his country. But his Ustaša movement was able to fill a massive void created by military defeat and the breakup of Yugoslavia.

A largely rural population formed the backbone of Vladko Maček's Peasant party. When the "master of the villages" disappeared into exile, thence to the infamous Croatian concentration camp of Jasenovac, and ultimately to house arrest, the countryside was left without leadership and sank into indifference. Many political allies of Maček fled abroad or withdrew into passivity; the right wing of the Peasant party was drawn to the Ustaša. Conservative and clerical elements, including Croatian officers of the former Yugoslav army, drifted into the Ustaša movement, and splinter groups of the Croatian Catholic movement, supported by the Church, joined forces too. The urban upper classes—the financiers and industrialists who had lived comfortably in the old Yugoslavia—viewed the future fearfully, while the working class remained enamored of Marxism. The Ustaša picked up limited support in the lower-middle class of artisans and small-time merchants in the larger towns. A small fringe of "frustrated intellectuals," passing time on university campuses and in sophisticated salons, embraced xenophobic and anti-Serb nationalism. The economic depression of the 1930s contributed to the general unrest through the loss of jobs. Lower-level Croatian functionaries smouldered in resentment against Serbs who filled many high posts in the administration. Social advancement, political participation, and job security could be found in a Croatian New Order.

Although the urban areas supplied the Ustaša with fanatical supporters and intellectual leadership, in the main the movement found its spiritual home in the poorest villages and parched mountain areas of Croatia and Herzegovina, whose peasantry was inspired by Ustaša terrorist nationalism. Indoctrinated in armed struggle, the Ustaša developed the cult of the knife, the revolver, and the bomb. Glaise von Horstenau observed that the Croatian revolution "is largely the revolution of old men and, last but not least, of former imperial Austrian officers."[136] This quasi-feudal elite joined the lumpen proletariat, the economically squeezed, and restless village toughs to make up the Ustaša's hard-core band of frenzied killers.

The *raison d'etre* of Ustaša ideology lay in a fusion of Catholic religion and Croatian romantic nationalism that developed into a religious crusade as ferocious as the Catholic inquisition inflicted on the heretical Albigensians in the twelfth century. The NDH enjoyed the strong support of the Franciscan monastic order and the ecclesiastical Croatian Catholic church. Alojzije Stepinac, the Catholic archbishop of Zagreb and a vocal nationalist Croat, conferred respectability on the Ustaša regime by his immediate approval of the new government, whose puritanical program included stiff jail sentences for indecent advertisements and thievery, and the death penalty for abortions. But in this community, he had doubts about the methods, if not the honesty, of its "elders." A devout and austere man, who was distressed by the deportations and mass killing around him, Stepinac was no admirer of the Nazi and Fascist creeds beyond their authoritarian ideas and anti-Communism. But throughout most of the Italian occupation, he refrained from open criticism of Pavelić's blood-soaked rule and kept silent over the Ustaša murders of the Orthodox. Only late in the day, in 1943, did he speak out, informing Pavelić by letter that the Jasenovac camp represented a gaping wound in the Croatian soul.[137] In his own cathedral in May of that year, he openly criticized the regime by stating that it should not deny life, a gift of God, to Jews and Orthodox Christians.[138] Stepinac is today a strong candidate for beatification in the Catholic Church.

The Catholic Franciscan order in Croatia encouraged the NDH's forced conversion of the Orthodox to the Catholic faith and looked on unmoved when the Ustaša subjected the unrepentant to brutal torture.[139] An alarming number of countryside Catholic priests eagerly participated in Ustaša rallies. As bigoted authoritarians and anti-modernists they shared a hatred of the Yugoslav idea, Jews, democracy, the Serbs, Orthodoxy, and Communism.[140] The Croatian Catholic press stood firmly behind Pavelić and the Ustaša regime throughout the war.[141] In Croatia religious faith was equated with nation and race, obscuring the universalist Catholic message. The Ustaša cult, which romanticized Croatian peasant life, paid only lip service to Christ's transcendent message of peace and love. Through its elemental appeal, it tapped atavistic impulses to carry out "natural justice." Those anxious to find relief from suppressed guilt were legitimized as Christians by the Ustaša regime and the fanatical branch of the Catholic church.[142] Without the urging of prelates and priests, many Croats, who otherwise would have turned their backs on Ustaša atrocities, allowed themselves to be co-opted by Pavelić's regime.

When the Ustaša launched its massacres, the Holy See took no overt measures to bring them to a halt. Consistent with his proclivity for silence, Pope Pius XII avoided taking a public position. The Holy See did not recognize the NDH, however, and continued to maintain diplomatic relations with the Yugoslav government-in-exile. But in May 1941, the pope received Pavelić informally, sent a legate to Croatia, and carried on confidential relations with the Ustaša regime. For the pontiff Croatia represented a bastion of Catholicism against the "schismatic" Greek Orthodox Church in the Balkans. The Vatican never protested publicly to Croatian authorities against Ustaša persecution of the Serbs and the Orthodox Church, let alone the Jews and Gypsies.[143]

The one religious group that escaped the Ustaša's vengeance were the Muslims, whom the regime considered as ethnically pure Croatians. Zagreb granted them religious freedom and even appointed a small number of Muslim dignitaries to cabinet posts,[144] but this amounted to mere tokenism—a far cry from the teachings of Croatia's spiritual father, Ante Starčević, who once described the Muslims as the "flower" of the Croatian nation.[145]

If Rome's reliance on Pavelić was de rigueur, confidence in his popularity should have been reassessed on the strength of a report submitted to Mussolini by Manlio Morgagni, a pressman of impeccable Fascist credentials who visited Zagreb on a fact-finding mission in May 1941. A high-ranking member of the official Stefani press agency, Morgagni reflected on the "absolute indifference, coldness, and anomie" with which the Croatian people welcomed Pavelić to power. The Ustaša, he reflected, was accepted with "ostentatious resignation." Their violent persecution of the Jews and Serbs, who, admittedly, were not liked, sickened local Croats and played directly into the hands of the Communists.[146]

How quickly Pavelić and the Ustaša were to squander political opportunity. Not unhappy over the breakup of Yugoslavia, the Croatian people as a whole welcomed independence. At the same time they were stunned by the Axis invasion and dismayed by the immobility and disappearance of their old leaders and parties. Feeling utterly powerless, they submitted to Pavelić's government, hoping for the best. At least he was a Croat, not an Italian, German, or Serb. But the Poglavnik was destined to conjure up their worst nightmares.

## The Italian Military Assumes Command

U nder the command of General Vittorio Ambrosio, the Italian 2nd Army moved through the annexed areas to bivouac on Croatian territory in the demilitarized zone near the Adriatic coast. Facing no competition from Italian civilian functionaries in supervising the public order, the 2nd Army initially had a free hand.[147] The military leaders were not bashful in propagating the view that Italy was a proud military conqueror. Dalmatia was merely the first step. In late April, speaking for the Duce from his new headquarters in Sušak, Ambrosio laid down the indispensable preconditions for the Italian New Order: a roundup of weapons, the taking of hostages, disarmament of the native population, the arrest of all undesirable elements, the suspension of nationalist organizations, mandatory flying of the Italian flag, prominent public display of images of the king and Duce, the posting of popular Fascist dictums, and the death penalty for threats on the lives of Italian military and civilian personnel.[148]

By these measures the Duce placed the 2nd Army and the Fascist commissars on the same page. Both strove to create a tyrannical Italian imperium over the Slav population in Italian-annexed territories in Yugoslavia. But not all was harmonious between Sušak and Rome. General Ambrosio in his initial reports made the following points: The "Italianità" of Dalmatia was a distant memory preserved only in monuments. The Croats living there, believing that Italian rule was a transitory and unfortunate necessity, were ostentatiously hostile. The NDH spread anti-Italian propaganda and appointed vocal irredentists to important administrative posts, while the Ustaša, without an Italian warrant, seized the arms stockpiled by the defeated Yugoslav armies. Pavelić was politically "immature," every Croat believed that Dalmatia belonged to him, and the Italian troops were greeted like aliens from space.[149] From the moment he assumed command Ambrosio felt offended by the Pavelić regime that Mussolini had set up. Eventually, differences of opinion between the 2nd Army and the warlords in Rome about the Pavelić regime would evolve into distinctly conflicting policies in Italian-occupied Yugoslavia.

In Croatia's demilitarized zones, Italian military authority was undermined by the Rome Accords of 18 May. As a concession to Pavelić, the Italian commissioners, who had exercised power in a number of towns assigned to Croatia, were instructed to relinquish their authority to Zagreb's representatives. This was followed up by a directive from Mussolini on the 20th that the troops were to behave like guests of a friendly and sovereign country.[150] Accordingly, the Carabinieri and the customs guards [guardia di finanza] withdrew, and the 2nd Army dismantled its checkpoints, but left garrisons in their fortified positions. The Italian soldiers were instructed to take no part in local politics.[151] But local politics would not leave them alone. Outraged ethnic Croats who refused to accept the Pact of Rome fled Italian Dalmatia for refuge in the NDH. Those who remained were sullen and alienated, or flocked to the Ustaša. Orthodox Serbs and Jews hounded by Ustaša persecution scrambled out of the Croatian towns handed by Italy to Zagreb's authority and tried to cross over into the Italian-annexed areas. Some were able to slip through the porous borders, while others were caught and deported.

Stripped of authority by the Duce's order, the Italian soldiers, engulfed in murderous ethnic strife, were helpless bystanders as Croatia turned into a slaughterhouse. Italian troops stationed behind the Dinaric Alps (with the exception of Knin) were withdrawn to Dalmatia, which opened the way for the Ustaša to fall on undefended Serbs. Instead of disengaging Italy from the maelstrom of Croatian politics, the Duce's "declaration of neutrality" did precisely the opposite. The Croats, angered by the loss of Dalmatia, instigated fights with Italians. Under this barrage the 2nd Army thirsted to avenge itself against the Duce's ally, the Pavelić regime, but could not openly defy Mussolini's non-intervention orders.

Remarkably, the Fascist-controlled Italian press, led by the Turin *Gazetto del Popolo* and the Bologna *Il Resto del Carlino*, echoed the 2nd

Army's criticisms by inveighing against Ustaša criminality. Corrado Zoli of the Italian Geographical Society described the massacre of Orthodox Serbs by Croatian bands and Catholic priests, which "signifies a return to medieval times."[152]

## The Serbs Fight Back

The Ustaša initially struck Orthodox Serbs in urban areas; panic quickly spread to the massifs, basins, and canyons of the rugged countryside. Many Muslims, whose landlord ancestors had exploited Serb sharecroppers until 1919, joined the Ustaša expeditions. At first the Serbs reacted incredulously; they were accustomed to living in relative peace with their Croatian neighbors and believed that reports detailing the terror were exaggerated.[153] But by the end of May the Serb village heads were no longer able to ignore the horror around them. In desperation they approached the Italian garrisons to request food and protection.[154] Throughout the summer Serbs offered their services for road repair or as guides and informants. In the Lika area and in Herzegovina, unable to leave or resist, the menaced Orthodox begged the Italian army to extend its military occupation to cover the entire Croatian state.

Moved by sympathy for the suffering of the Serbs and Jews, the Italian field commanders filed reports that were replete with the phrase *"la scena pietosa."* But Mussolini's nonintervention orders tied their hands. The patience of the troops had neared exhaustion, wrote General Furio Monticelli of the "Sassari" division that was deployed between Dalmatia and Croatia; they could not forever be passive witnesses of the outrages occurring around them.[155] Ambrosio, besieged by violated women and abused children begging for Italian protection, warned Raffaele Casertano, the Italian minister plenipotentiary in Zagreb, that his troops might fire on the marauding Ustaša gangs if such violence did not cease.[156] General Renzo Dalmazzo, commander of the VI Army Corps, wrote Bastianini in the same vein: "I would like to inform you, Excellency, about my impressions as a man and soldier. Notwithstanding a profound sentiment of discipline that animates me, my officers, and my soldiers—

let alone our will to obey orders loyally—I cannot guarantee that when confronted by such acts of violence there will not be an energetic response."[157] Not a few ordinary soldiers were outraged by barbarities perpetrated against women and children and took the initiative in carrying out acts of kindness to the beleaguered Serbs.[158]

No wonder, therefore, that areas under Italian occupation should become sanctuaries for the thousands seeking to avoid execution, internment, deportation, and forced conversion to Catholicism. But since the Italians were in no position to offer blanket protection, and since the NDH was unable to extend its writ over many mountainous areas in Bosnia and Herzegovina, Serb self-defense units sprang up spontaneously among isolated villagers and mountain folk.[159]

At the same time a group of disbanded Yugoslav officers under the leadership of the Serb military officer Dragoljub-Draža Mihailović, who had refused to recognize the capitulation and had eluded capture, set up a clandestine military organization in the Ravna Gora area deep in the mountains of western Serbia. Mihailović liked to call his following "the Yugoslav Home Army," but they were pinned with the sobriquet "Četnik," a generic name for irregulars fighting for freedom against the Turks and guerrillas operating behind enemy lines during the First World War. Unfortunately the term had been employed in the interwar period by the right-wing Association of War Veterans, whom the monarchy had used as auxiliary police, particularly in the Croat regions where the Serbs were in the minority. As if to emphasize their connection with an earlier heroic era, Mihailović and his followers wore beards and long hair and adopted not only old Serbian symbols but flags adorned with skull and crossbones and bearing the slogan "Freedom or Death."[160]

As a representative of the king and government-in-exile, Mihailović, by founding a resistance movement in Serbia, hoped to overcome the mood of defeatism that had swept the country following the crushing Axis victory. In his rare excursions into the political realm, Mihailović talked of friendship with the other non-Serb communities in a federally reconstructed Yugoslavia.[161] A small group of civilian personalities who joined him in his mountain retreat had the narrower aim of Serb supremacy within a resurgent Yugoslavia. Revenge against those whom they deemed responsible for Yugoslavia's collapse and against Croats and Muslims who had visited atrocities on Orthodox Serbs was a driving force.

In the lands of war-torn Yugoslavia, Mihailović, harassed by relentless German pressure, was faced with the daunting task of establishing his authority over officers who had evaded capture. Some were openly collaborationist and ready to cooperate with the German-occupied Serb state, while others disagreed with him on fundamental strategy. Several acted as virtual warlords within their regions or headed homeless bands.

The Četnik movement that eventually sprang up in the Italian-occupied areas to resist Ustaša violence defies easy description. The term embraced the officers and their following as well as a number of small homegrown Serb formations under the guidance of free-lance civilian and military leaders. The Četniks were local, frag-mented, and diverse, comprising enlightened and liberal Serbian nationalists, terrified peasant masses who longed for the restoration of simple ancestral village life, and protagonists of a Great Serbia imbued with religious myths, martyrdom, and folklore.

Lacking centralized leadership, the disparate groups of Serbs in Croatia had to shift for themselves. Mihailović in faraway Serbia had only a handful of immediate followers and was isolated and alone, barely eluding capture by the Germans. His contact men did not reach Herzegovina until January 1942. Lacking effective communi-cations, Mihailović was dependent on personal couriers to contact followers among the *prečani* Serbs—those living in communities outside "Old Serbia"—who were spread thinly in mountain hide-aways of a lawless countryside. Frequently Mihailović's confeder-ates lost track of his whereabouts as he shifted ground to escape his pursuers. Still, Mihailović gradually became a mythic figure. If not able to command obedience from the far-flung *prečani* Serb bands, he was at least recognized as a ceremonial leader.

As guardians of the pre-1941 Yugoslavia, which was composed of bourgeois politicians, businessmen, and a hardy independent peasantry, the Officers (followers of Mihailović who held commissions in the former Yugoslav army) hoped to restore the old social order with a strong dose of military authority. As ardent nationalists they tended to be avowedly Pan-Serb. Mihailović, on the other hand, attempted to squeeze "Greater Serbia" into a restored Yugoslavia. His outlook often changed to reflect a constantly shifting coalition of supporters. He also had to keep an eye out for the balances among the ethnic groups in the London-based Yugoslav government-in-exile, which were frequently upset by polarized ethnic politics and the frequent resignation and dismissal of cabinet members. But since Mihailović and his Četnik following felt themselves bound to the Karageorgević dynasty, the rest was detail, and that placed them in an irreconcilable position vis-à-vis a Yugoslav Communist movement that looked to Moscow for its cues. Either alone, or through temporary cooperation with the Italian military, and, eventually, with the help of an Allied landing in the Adriatic, the Officers and Mihailović were destined to move in lockstep to crush a rival Communist-inspired insurgent movement led by Josip Broz Tito.

While Mihailović's cause was spawned in the rubble of military defeat, the Communist party of Yugoslavia, whose roots lay in the period of Lenin, had already acquired a tough discipline under Tito's leadership. Tested by persecution and incarceration during the inter-war period, the party was able through extensive underground organization to form a cadre fit for clandestine activity. But while the Nazi-Soviet pact of August 1939 was in force, the Comintern ordered the Yugoslav Communists to cultivate an alliance of workers and bourgeoisie, observe neutrality in the war, and keep their heads down. But Tito was impatient. In May 1941 he proposed to his comrades that they bypass the "democratic" stage of revolution on the road to the collapse of capitalism in favor of an immediate seizure of power during the course of the war. The party, as the vanguard, must be in a position to seize control when the Axis and their minions were defeated. A "dictatorship of the proletariat," imposed on a classless society, was the ultimate objective.[162] In Tito's mind, resistance and revolution were bound together in an indissoluble whole. His drastic shortening of the classical Marxist historical cycle was prompted by the expectation that the Red Army would make short shrift of the Germans, whose defeat would spark a chain reaction of proletarian revolutions throughout Europe.

In the chaos produced by Yugoslavia's invasion, Tito was able to forge a guerrilla force, the Partisans, to combat the occupying powers. His following did not come into existence as a grass-roots movement like the Četniks but was part of the Comintern's global warfare against "capitalist-imperialism" orchestrated by Moscow. Although required by the Comintern in July to modify his radical line in favor of a "United Front of National Liberation," Tito was at first unwilling to do so. Among the various wartime Communist movements, his party stood out as radically intransigent, but that did not stop him from meeting with the Četniks and engaging in truces with the Germans. As time passed and the Partisans suffered extraordinary vicissitudes in a struggle against an incomparably better-equipped and ruthless enemy, Tito resorted to tactical ruses. To expand the membership, he urged all patriotic and "progressive" forces in the country to join him in a "Popular Front" against the invader. But not as a Serb nationalist. He meant to reconstruct Yugoslavia on an entirely new basis. Unquestioning loyalty to the party—"democratic centralism"—would provide a rigidly centralized and unified state in place of the old Yugoslavia torn by separatist strains and ethnic strife.

Given this unhappy period in Yugoslav history, Tito's message was a powerful one. The notions of a classless society and ethnic reconciliation drew many idealists, who had been alienated both by the dictatorial and class-ridden Karageorgević regime favoring Serbs and a Četnik movement that eventually became tainted by collaboration. As the acid test for a Communist revolutionary, Tito demanded total obedience and commitment to an unflinching struggle against the Axis Powers. This was in keeping with his perceived Communist mission of aiding the Soviet Union by diverting German resources from the Eastern Front. In accomplishing this task, Tito aimed to involve the entire population in sabotage and guerrilla warfare. But he would tolerate no competition for the hearts and minds of the Yugoslav peoples; he turned on the Četniks with the same ferocity as he did the Axis Powers, and sometimes he singled out Mihailović and his following as the first enemy to be destroyed.

During the war Tito led well-trained and disciplined warriors from one end of Yugoslavia to the other in seemingly constant flight from encirclement and pincers movements devised by powerful Axis forces and their allies. While Tito faithfully enacted Moscow's directives in July 1941 to commence "Partisan warfare," small groups of clandestine Partisan bands spontaneously sprang up from Ljubljana to the mountains of Montenegro, their composition, numbers, and leadership frequently depending more on local circumstances than on orders and directives emanating directly from Tito's headquarters. He was thus faced with a major logistical problem in keeping the various branches of his movement under control and forced to exercise restraint in advocating social revolution—an unpromising prospect for a small conspiratorial following. Party organization was therefore based on Croatian, Slovene, or Montenegrin components, which had evolved pretty much on their own after the fall of Yugoslavia, but all were defined by Communism and the Yugoslav idea. In each ethnic region the party appealed broadly for national and social liberation. Die-hard Communists formed the core, flanked by progressive liberals and mainly apolitical people who hated the imperialist occupier and whose rude but sturdy sense of justice had been violated by the senseless and inhumane outrages occurring around them.

Since Tito was constantly on the run, he frequently lost touch with these nascent "national" Partisan movements spreading throughout Yugoslavia. But a vague Marxism, heavily infused by a visceral patriotism and the simple desire of wanting "to do something," held the disparate Partisan bands together in loyalty to Tito as unquestioned leader. The hammer and sickle proved to be a symbol of messianic faith that rallied doubters to the community of the persecuted and the brave. The will to revolt was spawned by collective outrage against the occupier; sacrifice was prompted by a mythology that promised a just world of brotherhood among the Balkan peoples. The war would be short, Tito promised; following the Red Army's rapid defeat of Germany in Russia, it would rush to the rescue of the Partisans.

In the early stages of the Communist rebellion in summer 1941, Tito gained immediate popularity in Serbia, his first home base of operations, but he exercised little influence over the *prečani* Serbs living on the front lines of Ustaša butchery in Croatia. Rough-hewn patriots and followers of the Orthodox Church, they viewed Communists as urban detritus bearing an atheistic message that aimed to break up their clans and small land holdings by an imported "social revolution." Faced by deadly threats everywhere they turned, the *prečani* Serbs looked mainly to the Italians for protection.

*Reactions in the Field*

When the 2nd Army first deployed in Croatian territory, it did not immediately face armed insurgency, only an angry ally housed in Zagreb. In its rage against Italy for annexing major portions of Dalmatia, the NDH erected a high customs barrier around the contested city of Spalato to obstruct the flow of agricultural products into the port and urged civilians everywhere to boycott Italian goods.[163] Pavelić made no move to stop agitators from flooding into Dalmatia to stir up irredentist passion among the Croatian population, and he mocked Italian pride by permitting the Germans to recruit freely among Croatia's *Volksdeutsche* for the SS Prinz Eugen division. Experiencing hostility from both Germans and Ustaša, the 2nd Army was anxious to silence opposition by occupying the whole country. Mussolini on 10 June vented his frustration to Ciano: "It is of no importance . . . that the Germans recognize our rights in Croatia on paper, when in practice they take everything and leave us only a heap of bones. They are dirty dogs, and I tell you that this cannot go on for long . . . Personally I've had my fill of Hitler and the way he acts."[164]

Mussolini issued an order that same day to halt any further withdrawal of Italian troops from the demilitarized zone. Pavelić must sign the customs union agreement and concede Italy favorable autonomy for Spalato. Absent, however, was any effort to defend the

Serbs against Ustaša atrocities. On receiving petitions begging protection, the Duce "lowered his eyes and said in a hushed voice: 'The Serbs now have the terror of having to pay some accounts opened during their domination.'"[165] Absent too was any modification of the nonsensical order for the Italian troops to stay at their posts but desist from involvement in local affairs.

Fascist representatives were sent to Croatia on fact-finding missions. The party's voice in Zagreb, Eugenio Coselschi, did not conceal Ustaša excesses or the "wild support" provided by the Roman Catholic Croatian parish priests to Pavelić in their "holy crusade against the infidel Orthodox." This admittedly "barbaric behavior," however, did not, in Coselschi's view, go beyond "legitimate" responses, for Croatia was undergoing a Fascist-style revolution. Indeed, for Coselschi, Ustaša excesses paled before the German menace. The SS and Gestapo, 2,000 strong, obstructed Pavelić and disseminated the insidious view that Italian Dalmatia rightly belonged to Croatia. The 2nd Army was an object of criticism too, for sabotaging the Italian alliance with Croatia and for Pavelić's "fundamental loyalty" to Italy.[166] Because of a spat with Casertano, Coselschi was withdrawn in December 1941. Fascist influence quickly sank under the leadership of his successor, Balestra di Mottola. Regarded by both Croats and Germans as a *"quantité negligeable,"* who partied in fashionable nightclubs, Mottola made no impact on the rude Ustaša.[167]

A report filed by an agent of the ministry of interior reinforced the Fascist perspective: one should not worry about Croatian persecution against the Orthodox faith, for Serbs, permeated by Jewish influence, spread anti-Fascist doctrines. Italy must be vigilant against an essentially expansionist Serb movement, which, in its implacable hatred of Italy, aims to reach the shores of the Adriatic.[168]

No less than Coselschi, the Palazzo Chigi was prone to acknowledge Croatian charges that the Italian military was collaborating with the enemy Serbs. Casertano moved to prop up the rickety government in Zagreb against the Orthodox, Communists, and Germans. He found Ambrosio's missives criticizing the NDH for failure to discipline the Ustaša to be inadmissible and only reluctantly handed them on to Pavelić. The crux of the problem for Casertano was the

2nd Army's "pietism" toward Serbs and Jews.[169] The Croatian government could only build authority in the country by taking stern action against them, he opined. The military ignored the revolutionary nature of Fascism's adopted son, the Ustaša; moreover, its hobnobbing with the Četniks threw the NDH into the welcoming hands of the power-hungry Germans. Pavelić, insisted Casertano, felt bound to Italy and stood firmly against the pro-German intrigues of the Kvaternik clique. The Poglavnik deserved Italy's unquestioned support and the 2nd Army should carry out Rome's political directives.[170]

The informants of Aimone d'Aosta, Duke of Spoleto, provided a different view:

> To look at the photographic evidence of the atrocities committed by the Ustashas on Serbian women, old people and children, on Orthodox and Jews, is enough to understand that generations will not suffice to assuage the feeling of revolt and the spirit of revenge animating the survivors.[171]

The Italian consul in Sarajevo put the matter succinctly: "It is known that the Pavelić regime is maintaining itself exclusively on German bayonets."[172]

Italian economic experts gloomily concluded that Italy could not compete with the Germans in dominating the Croatian economy. Amedeo Giannini, a diplomat expert in economic matters, complained that the Germans had willfully undermined Italy's *spazio vitale* in Croatia by stealthily acquiring monopolies in bilateral agreements with Zagreb.[173] Giovanni Host Venturi, the minister of communications, wrote Mussolini that the Germans, who arrived in Croatia first, had already robbed Italy of vital economic resources by "carrying away everything."[174]

No one in official Rome advised contacting the many educated Croats and followers of Maček as a counter to the German onrush and Ustaša terror, for such a move would have implied a partiality to the enemy Western Powers and a repudiation of empire-building (Maček, however, was hardly a democrat). Italian dislike of Maček was certainly not mitigated by rumors that the Germans "every evening consumed pasta" with the peasant party leader and maintained a cordial rapport with him as a backup to Pavelić .[175]

General Ambrosio, speaking for the majority of his commanders, filed a report on 8 August that differed markedly in tone from the views of the policymakers in Rome and their agents in Zagreb. Government officials, the army, and the Ustaša, he wrote, bore an angry grievance against Italy owing to the mutilation of Dalmatia and suspected that Italy would next annex Bosnia and Herzegovina (a not unjustifiable fear). There was, Ambrosio pointed out, "a profound democratic tradition in the country that resists totalitarian ideas . . . The masses are profoundly convinced that the regime, carried on the bayonets of the Axis, will be overthrown by the followers of Maček." The opposition coalesces around the peasant party's leader, who is "loved and venerated by the country. . . Thanks to the vigorous irredentism unleashed by Italian annexation, we have alienated the sympathy of the Croatian intellectuals as well as the middle bourgeoisie."[176] The Italian general further concedes that the "democrat" Maček, supported by the majority of the population, "resists totalitarian ideas" and is far more popular in Croatia than Pavelić , the leader of the kin Ustaša ally. By seizing Dalmatia, Italy, Ambrosio concludes, is at fault for arousing such an outcry in Croatia against his country. In all, this was a remarkably straightforward document for an Italian general to compose in Fascist Italy.

But on one important point Ambrosio was in agreement with Rome: that Pavelić was an innocent witness of "medieval barbarity" perpetrated by men "blinded by passion and the desire for vendetta" who surrounded him.[177] As a lonely ally besieged by bloodthirsty comrades and domineering Germans, Pavelić, in Ambrosio's view, needed Italy for defense against a *coup de main* engineered by Berlin through the Croatian National Socialist party, the *Volksdeutsche*, which was closely aligned with the pro-German Croats who dominated the military and government. Doubtless there was truth in this observation, but Ambrosio and his superiors in Rome were fooling themselves: Pavelić was no true ally. But what would Italy and the Poglavnik do without each other? Italy's position in Zagreb would crumble and Pavelić would fall. Pavelić knew that Mussolini had for long stood as his only reliable protector against local Ustaša rivals who hated Italy and were pro-German. Overlooked by Ambrosio and many other Italian observers, however, was the unarguable fact that Pavelić prospered as Croatia's leading hangman of Orthodox Serbs and Jews. By purging Croatia of "alien peoples," Pavelić justified his position as Poglavnik. One has only to read Glaise von Horstenau's memoirs and reports for confirmation of this.

*Into the Croatian Whirlwind*

In June and July a revolt broke out in the zone of Gospić-Gračac-Knin, where the Serbs interrupted railroad service and cut telegraph wires, killing and capturing Ustaša and Croatian gendarmes. When the Italians retreated from the demilitarized areas in Croatia, the Serbs armed themselves to meet the Ustaša danger in a defense of the classic Četnik tradition. In this early stage the Communists played only a small part.

In early June Pavelić asked Ambrosio to reduce substantially the number of Italian troops occupying his country.[178] But the 2nd Army, displaying more sympathy for the persecuted Serbs than loyalty to their Croatian ally, not infrequently shooed away the Ustaša raiders and in some instances shot them. By observing Casertano's "pietism" toward the Orthodox and Jews, the Italian troops earned their gratitude, thereby incurring the wrath of Zagreb, which sent Rome heated protests against Italian favoritism toward Serbs at the expense of a loyal Croat ally.[179] Yet, because the Italian troops were frequently caught off guard, had no orders, or were stationed far from the scenes of pillage and death, Serbs continued to be massacred. Before word of this reached the distant and remote Serb communities, and before the Italians could do much to stop them, the Ustaša reaped a terrible harvest of vengeance. The lid had blown off.

General Dalmazzo, the commander of the VI Army Corps, stands out as an Italian commander ready for bold initiatives to curb violence in the Croatian countryside. Like Ambrosio, he believed that the real peace-breakers were not the Serbs but the Ustaša. Croatian racial laws banning the Orthodox from employment in certain firms resulted in the hiring of untrained Roman Catholics, which depressed the economy. By allowing the Serbs to take over the town of Knin after Italian troops had disarmed and expelled the local Ustaša, Dalmazzo broke new ground. In gratitude the Serbs throughout the Lika area promised not to attack railroad lines and to respect Italian authority as long as these were not used to transport Croats and Ustaša troops.[180] The Serb assertion that they were no friends of the Partisans, and that their rebellion was aimed only at the Ustaša, resonated credibly throughout the 2nd Army.[181] Since, in the view of the soldiers, Partisan insurgency throve on Ustaša terror, the 2nd Army would, as a prelude to snuffing out Communist insurgency in Croatia, work hand-in-hand with the Serbs to immobilize Pavelić's desperadoes.

The 2nd Army commanders proceeded to pacify the Lika region at little loss to Italian lives or treasury. It did not matter to them if, in the suppression of the Ustaša, Zagreb's feelings were bruised. But this approach did not catch on in Rome and hence could not become official 2nd Army policy. Shackled by Mussolini's restraining order, other officers in the nether reaches of Croatia looked on helplessly—or insensitively—as the Ustaša proceeded in its ghoulish massacres. Many Croatian followers of Maček took such Italian passivity for approval and as part of a diabolical plan to create an unbridgeable chasm between Serbs and Croats. More than a few Orthodox Serbs, for their part, developed a strong suspicion of Italian motive that would be difficult in the future to overcome.[182] This suspicion was corroborated by the behavior of the unfeeling power brokers in Rome who stood firmly behind the Poglavnik's regime. Yet some Italian officers and troops in the field defied the official restraining order by affording Serbs and Jews comfort and protection. There was no military logic in this morality play, only acts of spontaneous compassion.

By midsummer the Partisans had established a foothold in the Dalmatian towns and Ljubljana. But the rugged Lika area was a tough nut to crack, for the Partisans could not compete with the 2nd Army in providing sustenance and arms to the beleaguered Orthodox and their parish priests, and the peasant farmers there were a poor recruiting ground. Those who hardly had heard the name of Mihailović knew even less about Marxism. But gradually the Partisans were able to penetrate the many weakly organized Serb bands in Italian-occupied Croatia and take them over. Instead of challenging the well-armed Germans, the Partisans attacked local Croatian administration posts and slashed communications systems. Village heads associated with collaboration were murdered to persuade the local inhabitants to keep their distance from the occupying powers. A particularly cold-blooded Partisan strategy involved provocation to stimulate Axis reprisals that would further radicalize the civilians and create more recruits from the enraged population.

Soon the Italians began to experience difficulty in stamping out the small pockets of Partisan insurgency in Slovenia and the Italian Adriatic ports. In Drvar, the heart of western Bosnia, the Partisans were able to establish a base for 2,500 warriors. An Italian detachment set out in September to break up the camp. In response, the Partisans torched a complex of sawmills and cellulose factories. The Italians called in fire engines from Knin and Sebenico to douse the blaze that cost hundreds of Serbs their jobs. Overpowered by the Italian rescue squad, the Partisans fled the scene, which brought an end to the "Republic of Drvar."[183]

By Fall 1941 the Italians in Yugoslavia faced serious problems: Partisan insurgency, Ustaša atrocities, Croatian charges of Italian connivance with the Orthodox Serbs, unresolved frontiers, Croatian foot-dragging on the customs union question, and the unsettled status of Spalato. There was a serious refugee problem too. Ustaša terror caused a growing number of desperate and embittered people to take flight for Serbia. The Germans at first did nothing, but eventually closed the gates and created large new numbers of refugees through mopping-up exercises conducted in their areas. There being no other exit, refugees swarmed into Dalmatia, but were not welcome there either. Governor Bastianini frantically asked Rome for a solution. Ciano agreed to house refugees on the Italian mainland, but this ran into a snag at the Interior Department, which admitted that it had only recently launched a crash program of camp construction. The 2nd Army was caught in the middle. Bastianini reproached Ambrosio for allowing the Serb refugees into the new provinces and for a sloppy job in providing defense against "10,000 rebels" supposedly bearing down on Dalmatia.[184] The governor, the Croats, and Serbs demanded strong Italian military support. All were disappointed over what they got.

Mussolini for an instant questioned himself: "It's true. I'm starting to ask myself if I have not played the wrong card . . . I want to ask the Germans what game we are playing given the fact that they are helping themselves to everything. We talk a lot about comradeship between the armed forces but when it comes to deeds they leave us with our hands empty. For example, we have not obtained a single mine in Croatia."[185]

Much to Bastianini's satisfaction, Mussolini took action on 13 August against Zagreb by ordering the 2nd Army to occupy the entire demilitarized zone; the Croatian government was required to hand over authority to the Italian military.[186] Order in the Dinaric region would be restored and railroad lines and communications through Dalmatia secured from insurgent attacks. Mussolini intended to restore Italy's prestige and, by asserting himself, be in a position to roll back German influence in Croatia, which tallied exactly with the thinking of his generals. In advancing Italy's occupation, both Rome and Sušak were swayed by Realpolitik rather than humanitarian impulse to save Serb lives.

Soon after Mussolini's order, the Ustaša were told to shed their arms and leave the demilitarized zone.[187] The Orthodox Serbs breathed a sigh of relief. But if the Duce had given way to the 2nd Army's plea for more power, he was not about to repudiate the alliance with Pavelić. Pietromarchi regarded Mussolini's order as an effective compromise that both placated the military and left life in the NDH.[188] While Mussolini shifted his position, Casertano in Zagreb defended the NDH against the 2nd Army's preference for Orthodox Serbs over the Ustaša, which, in his view, undermined popular support for Pavelić , whom he regarded as Italy's strongest Croatian barrier to further German penetration. In a dig at Bastianini, Casertano questioned whether Italian policy was made in Zara or Rome.[189] A confirmed Fascist (he would continue to serve

Mussolini in the Republic of Salò), Casertano was not one to challenge Rome's support of the Pavelić regime.

Angered by Mussolini's about-face on the question of military and political power in the demilitarized zone,[190] Pavelić and his circle charged Italy with switching sides and reducing the country to civil war. Pavelić was irritated by the crossed religious lines: Catholic Italy defending Orthodox Serbs against Catholic Croatia. Typically, he complained to the German minister in Zagreb, Siegfried Kasche, who, because he was pro-Ustaša,[191] took matters immediately to Berlin.[192] Glaise too was up in arms because he was anti-Italian and distressed over Italy's determination to establish control in old Habsburg lands. Hitler concluded that the Italians had gone mad,[193] but did nothing to support Pavelić for fear of antagonizing the Duce. Thereupon Ribbentrop reminded Kasche that "the alpha and omega of our foreign policy in the Mediterranean area is the preservation of our cordial alliance with Italy."[194] This was often repeated to the Italians too and believed by a gullible Mussolini.

General Ambrosio was pleased to implement the Duce's new policy by taking over political and military power in the 2nd zone.[195] For long he had resented Pavelić's complaints and was indignant over Ustaša assassinations and pillaging. Serb and Croatian victims sought Italian protection, he proudly affirmed, *"because we are just and humanitarian."*[196]

On 7 September Ambrosio issued a proclamation announcing that the 2nd Army would assume ultimate responsibility for the civil authority in the 2nd and 3rd zones. Zagreb would be allowed to nominate a General Administrative Commissioner, who would supervise the civilian Croatian authorities but be answerable to the commander of the Italian 2nd Army. By this measure, the Italians had unilaterally abolished Croatia's discriminatory tariffs directed against them. Insurgents of all stripes were invited to return home and hand in their weapons upon pain of severe penalty for noncompliance by specially appointed local tribunals. The Serbs, where they were a majority, would manage their own affairs; their property confiscated by the NDH would be returned and Orthodox churches reopened. To restore ethnic peace, Ambrosio planned to separate the Croatian and Serb communities and encourage each to be self-reliant. He did not intend to employ Serbs to fight as auxiliaries of the 2nd Army, only to guarantee them a safe life in their homelands. The NDH would be still sovereign, but its actions subject to Italian review.[197] By acting as an impartial mediator, Ambrosio hoped to prevail on both Croats and Serbs to collaborate with Italy in the struggle against the common Partisan enemy. Doubtless Ambrosio believed that he was acting as a humanitarian who would bring ethnic peace to the Croatian countryside, but one must recognize that his underlying motive was more calculating. By placating the Orthodox Serbs, he hoped to dissuade them from joining the Partisans.[198]

Ambrosio's measures instigated no end of Croatian complaints and retaliation. In dissolving the Ustaša, the Italians, by Zagreb's reckoning, had left the Croatian people at the mercy of vengeful Serbs "armed to the teeth."[199] Croatian General Zupano wrote: "For him [Ambrosio], there are no differences between Jews, Orthodox, and Catholic Croats."[200] If the Croats could do nothing to reverse this latest Italian annulment of their sovereignty in the 2nd zone,[201] they did their best to sabotage Ambrosio's proclamation by dressing up dissolved elements of the Ustaša as gendarmes, disrupting commercial traffic to Serb communities, and unleashing a new wave of terror against Serbs in the 3rd zone.[202]

No matter how high-minded, much of Ambrosio's 7 September manifesto was largely unenforceable. The Italian soldiers were unable to establish a credible presence beyond the roads and towns. In an atmosphere of ethnic animosity, few Serbs returned to claim their burnt-out homes and resume life in a fractured civil society. Those who did were unable to recover their possessions and were locked out of their shops and factories by the Croats who had seized them.[203] The 2nd Army commander pointed out that the Croats were incapable of administering impartially and he rebuked them for failing to remove functionaries with a proven record of cruelty treating Orthodox Serbs.[204] Local Italian commanders were having great difficulty in identifying Communist infiltrators in Serb neighborhoods.[205] Since Italo-Croatian cooperation had completely broken down, Ambrosio was unable to restore public order, which gave the NDH the opportunity to bring home the point that Croatian auxiliaries were needed to control the turbulence.[206] The Partisans and Četniks, too, paid no heed to Ambrosio's urging that they resume a pastoral life. The Partisans easily moved into the cracks of the Italian military occupation, while the Četniks sniped at will against the hated Ustaša enemy. Ambrosio's essay in peacekeeping lay in tatters.

General Ambrosio was one of the more authentic and straightforward of Italy's generals, devoted to his country and respectful of the political hierarchy. But his judgment was clouded. He held that arms given to the Četniks would not be turned on Croats, that Italian support for the fine people in the NDH was undercut by local Ustaša, and that "our soldiers" were spilling blood to consolidate the new state. Under his watch, however, the Serbs were using Italian arms to avenge themselves against the Croats and Muslims, and rarely did Pavelić or anyone in his entourage do much to bring the Ustaša under control. Perhaps, most tragically, "our soldiers," were indeed bleeding and dying, not in nation-building, however, but in pursuing the chimera of an Italian protectorate over Croatia.

Before the summer was over, relentless Ustaša terror had triggered Serb uprisings throughout the ethnically mixed areas in Croatia. Entire Serb villages became guerrilla bands who swore eternal vengeance on their Croatian tormentors. There were old scores to settle, too, with those ethnic Serbs who during Ottoman rule had converted to the Muslim faith and landed favored positions within the Turkish Empire. Worse still, many Muslims joined up with the Ustaša and eventually would make their way into German SS formations. The Serb onslaught against these "apostates" was pursued in a deadly spirit of religious holy war that would later recur throughout the Sandžak, Montenegro, and eastern Bosnia-Herzegovina. Bewildered, the Italians had no idea how to stop the strife. To secure their survival, the Muslims frequently sought Italian protection but, in their siege mentality, constantly shifted sides depending on which was the strongest. Surrounded by malicious enemies, the Muslims seemed always to be uprooted and on the run.

*73*

On 25 September Mussolini, taking note that the Germans had initiated a large-scale action to repress the Communist rebellion in Serbia, directed Ambrosio to make contact with the Wehrmacht troops in the demarcation area by means of a coordinated pincers movement.[207] This was an astonishing and bold move that aroused enthusiasm everywhere. The Palazzo Chigi's appetite for a protectorate over all Croatia was whetted, for the troops would be in a position to cross the demarcation line into the German side up to the river Drina.

To soothe Zagreb, Cavallero, speaking for Rome, prompted the 2nd Army to desist from the exercise of civilian power in the 3rd zone as the troops marched in. As once prevailed in the 2nd, they would be "guests" of the Croatian government.[208] Ciano told Ambrosio that he must acknowledge the Croatian commissioner of general administration at Karlovac as the individual responsible for upholding law and order. Ambrosio replied that implementation of this measure would render the Orthodox defenseless before an unsupervised Ustaša. "The Office" agreed, but would not further slight Pavelić.[209]

When the Ustaša predictably declined to disarm, withdraw, or refrain from violence,[210] the Palazzo Chigi floundered in confusion. Lacking reliable information from those turbulent and faraway places, Pietromarchi asked his friend Bastianini about the "rebels"— how many, their leaders, aims, and finances. The demarcation zone was "as an area of dark shadow if not absolute obscurity," the territory beyond the demarcation line (the German occupation zone in eastern Bosnia) "*terra incognita*."[211] But topographical ignorance did not obscure the image of empire. Pietromarchi wrote Host Venturi:

> Our true empire is Croatia, the only country which benign fate has placed into our arms. But it seems that we do everything possible to reject this precious gift. We waste blood for a country like Montenegro, which contains only stones and misery, and we avoid making the slightest effort to take possession of Croatia, one of the most pleasant, fertile, and rich countries of

Europe, which could assure us, during the war, the most important reserves of farm animals, cereals, wood, and minerals in proximity to our frontiers.[212]

In pursuit of this reverie, the Palazzo Chigi advocated a large contingent of fresh troops,[213] but Ambrosio asked for only limited reinforcements.[214]

After the German invasion of the Soviet Union, the Partisans gradually built up their strength and established clandestine cells throughout Yugoslavia. But they posed their most immediate threat to the Germans in the heart of old Serbia. Berlin moved to set up a puppet ruler. The Serb General in Belgrade, Milan Nedić, emerged waving an anti-Communist banner on 29 August to take office as head of what became known as the Government of National Salvation. A Pétain-style ruler, Nedić did what he could to prevent Belgrade from falling into complete Nazi darkness, despite the efforts of the far more pronounced pro-Nazi Dimitrije Ljotić.

When the Partisan resistance in Serbia flared in early fall 1941, the Germans resorted to massive reprisals. The Gestapo imprisoned much of the Serbian intelligentsia in Belgrade and spread terror throughout the city. In line with an order by Hitler, the chief of the OKW, Field Marshal Wilhelm Keitel, issued the notorious edict of 16 September that called for the death of a hundred native hostages for every German killed; fifty would be executed for every German wounded. In reprisal for some twenty German deaths in October, 1,200 hostages were killed in Belgrade,[215] and approximately 2,300 civilians, including schoolboys, according to German estimates, were executed in the village of Kragujevac.[216] This was only the most ferocious of many reprisals. The German armies conducted punitive expeditions that laid waste to a large area of northwest Serbia, accompanied by the usual hangings and shootings, and inflicted substantial losses on both Partisans and Četniks. In their determination to pacify the countryside, the Germans distinguished themselves by taking counter-terror to new heights.

Wilting from Germany's relentless military pressure, Tito and Mihailović, who were both camped out in Old Serbia, were persuaded to meet during the fall 1941 to consider merging their forces. Neither arrived in a spirit of compromise nor was prepared to subordinate himself to the other. Each bore nonnegotiating demands and tried to establish a personal ascendancy. Mihailović would not permit Communist commissars to set up political institutions, and Tito derided the suggestion that Mihailović serve as supreme commander. Tito was prepared to wage relentless war on the principle, "the worse the better."[217] He was convinced that German reprisals, rather than destroying the spirit of the Serbs, would galvanize them to exact revenge by joining the Partisans. Mihailović was astonished that Tito could favor a general insurrection at a time when the prospects of an Allied landing were remote and when nothing, not even a united resistance force, could stand in the way of Germany's brutal reprisals. Contrary to Tito, Mihailović was determined to avoid a repetition of the terrible slaughter visited upon his country by the marauding forces of the Habsburg Empire during the Great War. Premonitions of biological extinction at the hands of the Nazis were heightened by the reality of Ustaša mass murder. Convinced that the Axis would ultimately be defeated and determined to avoid foolhardy and extravagant actions, Mihailović chose to husband his resources and Serbian lives until the Allies had established a new Salonika front.

Given the wide disparity in outlook, it is not surprising that the two sides could agree only to a sharing of weapons and participation in joint operations, but even these arrangements were halting and partial and soon fell apart. Mutual suspicion between the ideological hardliners on both sides gave rise to unpleasant incidents and skirmishes. The broken dialogue could never be renewed so long as Tito intended to destroy everything that Mihailović was fighting to preserve. Mihailović was unable to gain a foot in the Partisan camp and, as a result of his half-hearted commitment to the resistance, exposed himself to the charge, rightly or wrongly, that he was a collaborator no better than Germany's new Quisling ruler in Belgrade, Milan Nedić.[218] Tito was already beginning to win the propaganda war as a more resolute and self-sacrificing warrior.

Alarmed at the rapid growth of Communist strength, the Officers decided to attack Užice in Serbia, the seat of Tito's headquarters, in late October. A spirited contest between the rival insurgent groups ensued before both were swept away by the Germans, who captured the town on 29 November. Reinforced by two divisions in latter 1941, the Wehrmacht chased the Partisans out of Serbia by the end of the year. Both Tito and Mihailović were forced to flee German-occupied Serbia for refuge in the more chaotic and less well-policed Italian areas of control in Croatia and Montenegro. Like it or not, one is tempted to conclude that, as opposed to the less vigilant and sloppy Italian counterinsurgency, the draconian reprisals employed by the Germans had worked. Oddly, however, the Germans in Serbia did not proceed to the mass slaughter that distinguished their occupation in Poland and the Ukraine, perhaps because they had to thin out their forces by sending troops to the Eastern Front. In any event, the spiral of violence against the Serb population began to slow down.[219]

Tito and his decimated forces fled Serbia across the mountains to eastern Bosnia and set up new headquarters at Foča. The ideological line became more militant. In the village of Drenova, the Politburo declared that the "worker-peasant core within the Liberation Front" should be strengthened; Tito's anti-Fascist war was yielding to class war.[220]

Mihailović reacted somewhat differently by dispersing his troops and infiltrating Nedić's gendarmerie. Running out of ammunition and desperate, he decided to engage in discussions with the Germans. In the hope of deepening the split between the Četniks and Partisans, German intelligence service agents met with Mihailović on 11 November to devise a modus vivendi between the occupation authorities and the Četniks. For his part, Mihailović wanted to secure weapons and security from German attack that would allow him to proceed unhindered against the Partisans, whom he now completely distrusted. But General Franz Böhme, who commanded the German troops in Serbia, demanded that the Četniks turn over their arms and place themselves under German custody. The Wehrmacht warlords would only be satisfied by a fully pacified countryside of cowed shepherds. Since Mihailović shrank from taking such a drastic step, the state of belligerency between the two sides continued.[221]

Hemmed in on all sides, the Officers, sometimes on their own initiative and sometimes prodded by the Italians, engaged in dialogue with the Ustaša, but such talks were halting and inconclusive. The Officers had much more luck with the Italians. Not infrequently certain leaders expressed interest in an Italian patrimony over a Serb-dominated Bosnia-Herzegovina.[222] The Italian military commanders did not fall for this ruse, but, in their determination to spare Italian blood in the war against the Partisans, played along with the Serb line to gain their military assistance. It was devilishly complicated work. Since throughout 1941 Mihailović had been unable to impose discipline or a coherent line of action on the wide assortment of Serb bands operating in Croatia, the Italians frequently lost the thread.

The Partisan drive in Croatia, which had been slow to get started, moved into high gear during the last few months in 1941. Communist propaganda portraying Pavelić as the Axis devil began to attract attention. Rendered leaderless by Maček's disappearance, progressive-thinking Croatians, sickened by ethnic violence, saw in Tito's folk-style Pan-Slavism the lone voice openly espousing true equality and reconciliation among the peoples of Yugoslavia.

The Partisans broke the calm in eastern Bosnia with a series of hit-and-run operations after the Germans had swept them out of Serbia. In early October the Italians undertook a major *rastrellamento* (mopping-up expedition) against them dubbed Nota Z to deal with uprisings that the Germans had been unable to suppress.[223] But as the 2nd Army deployed in the 3rd zone, it overreached itself. This additional chunk of Croatian territory included some of the wildest mountain landscape in the Balkans. The more the Italians pushed their occupation sphere inland from the Adriatic, the more they were compelled to confine their troops to the populated centers, neglecting the surrounding hills and countryside. In the mountainous territory, the troops were too widely dispersed to police such vast spaces. The field commanders also faced insuperable operational difficulties in carrying out orders to flush the guerrillas from their rocky caverns. Air support was negligible. Apart from indiscriminate burning of villages, the planes failed dismally in providing tactical support for the troops. In an era preceding helicopters, the conventional army units fought frustrating battles against guerrilla forces who simply vanished into the hills or merged with local populations. The Italian soldiers were constantly surprised by ambushes of their military convoys. Given a large numerical advantage and heavy artillery, they were able to inflict substantial casualties on the Partisans in any pitched battle. On the whole, however, the slow-moving Italian infantry had no answer to the tactics employed by the far more nimble guerrilla forces. Harsh winter weather also impeded their operations.

As nothing before, the events at Pljevlja in Montenegro opened the military's eyes to Partisan ingenuity. Titoist forces launched a strong attack on the Italian garrison stationed there in early December and were able to break into the city. The Italians counterattacked and trapped the Partisans, who put up a desperate resistance. During the course of this epic struggle, the wounded of both sides were massacred.[224]

When the Italians advanced from the upper Drina valley to relieve a besieged Croatian garrison in Višegrad, they promised friendship with the local Četniks and relief from Ustaša atrocities. Faced with a resurgence of the uprisings in Montenegro, the Italians decided to evacuate a large number of the more exposed garrisons. The abandoned outposts were taken over by Četniks, Muslims, and Croats. In the upper Drina, the Četniks fell on the hapless Muslims in their first large-scale massacre of the hated religious enemy.[225]

Life for the Italians in Zagreb was no less complicated. By November the evidence of Croatian misdeeds had become apparent even to the most die-hard Italian supporters and apologists of Pavelić. Casertano finally woke up to the NDH's disloyalty and sabotage of trade with Italian Dalmatia.[226] Inspector General of Public Security Ciro Verdiani wrote that Pavelić presided over a Croatia festering in disorder. There was nothing "wholesome" and "sane" to report, only arrests and summary executions of innocent people. Having cleared out the Jews, he declared, the regime turns on intellectuals and students. Pavelić does nothing to prevent the government from collapsing into German arms. Collaboration with Croatia has broken down, and Italian troops exhausted by Ustaša perfidy are victims of "puerile" charges of complicity with the Serbs.[227] Only two major players, Mussolini and Cavallero, unabashedly defended Pavelić, untroubled that he was running a slaughterhouse in Croatia.

To brace Pavelić, the Duce informed Ambrosio on 2 November 1941 that the military objective in the 3rd zone of normalizing the life of the population must be undertaken in a spirit of friendly collaboration with the Croats at every level of government. At all costs military personnel must avoid creating the impression that they favored the Orthodox population. Mussolini maintained that "the cessation of atrocities perpetrated by uncontrolled and irresponsible elements is in principle achieved." In defiance of the detailed reports from the field, he closed his eyes to the ongoing Ustaša horrors. Brushing aside humanitarian concerns, the Duce aimed to align with the Germans by breaking off contacts with the Serb bands. The order to restore civilian authority to the NDH was in fact a stiff reprimand to General Ambrosio. Almost as an afterthought, Mussolini forbade contact, apart from official business, between the Jews and the Italian military.[228]

General Dalmazzo was convinced that application of Mussolini's 2 November directive would worsen matters, since the Serbs would feel betrayed by Italy and more prone to follow the Communists, who were ready to exploit their fears and discontent. But this approach, while listened to at Sušak, found no hearing at the Supreme Command in Rome. In lockstep with the Duce, Cavallero pointed out that the Croats and the Ustaša—but not the Četniks— were allies of Italy.[229] The Palazzo Chigi fell into line. Fresh from a meeting in Zagreb with Pavelić, in which the NDH was required to renounce the Sandžak for a slightly less ambitious frontier at the river Drin,[230] Pietromarchi spoke of a productive collaboration between local Croatian authority and the Italian command in the war against Partisan insurgency, despite all evidence to the contrary.[231]

The Croats arrived at Abbazia on 15 November for a meeting with Italian officialdom. They bore with them a long list of com-

plaints. The Italians had put Pavelić in power only to cripple his
regime at birth by swarming deep into the Croatian interior. By
usurping authority in the 2nd and 3rd zones, the Italians had unilaterally annulled the Treaty of Rome of 18 March 1941, which
granted the NDH sovereignty over these areas. The 2nd Army supported their enemies and Rome held them in an economic bind. By
terms of a lopsided agreement signed a month before, on 27 October 1941, the Italians had obliged the NDH to terminate its boycott of goods to Dalmatia and adhere to a customs union. More
onerous still, Zagreb was saddled with the responsibility of provisioning the Italian 2nd Army in the occupied zones with lumber,
potatoes, vegetables, meat, wheat and fodder. In addition the NDH
was required to supply the civilian population in Italian Dalmatia
and Fiume with food. If the Croatian government did not honor
its responsibilities by providing the provisions demanded, the governor of Dalmatia would be free to requisition what he thought
was needed.[232]

In a comradely spirit the Italian delegation, overlooking the 2nd
Army's objections, endorsed the Croatian exercise of political authority in Italy's occupied zones and agreed that the Fascist party,
not the Italian military, was to impose discipline on the fraternal
Croatian Ustaša. As for the restoration of law and order, the Croats
promised to turn over a new leaf. Just give us the power and amnesty will be declared, schools for the Orthodox reopened, and
irredentists who claim Italian Dalmatia silenced.[233] By accepting a
Croatian commitment to reform, the Italians overlooked the psy-
chopathological nature of the Ustaša regime and persisted in pursuing a harmony with the NDH that simply did not exist. Moreover, Italian magnanimity was severely compromised by an unwillingness to address directly Croatia's economic woes or to reduce the
huge financial burden on the national treasury imposed by the occupying 2nd Army.

Under the shadow of Mussolini's pro-Croatian order of 2 November, Pietromarchi and Ambrosio met on the 12th and passed
on to Rome a summary of their findings.[234] Since Italy's military
resources could no longer support garrison duty in the far-flung

spaces of the 3rd zone, the troops would have to be pulled back, concentrated, and trained for mobile warfare against the unorthodox and grueling tactics employed by the Partisans. In cooperation with the Wehrmacht, the newly refurbished Italian contingents would sweep across eastern Bosnia to the Drina River. But could the Italian military be remolded overnight? How would the Croatian Domobrani [Home Guards] be factored in?

If the decision had been left to Ambrosio, he would have had nothing to do with the Croats. Only from a sense of duty would he obey Rome's wish to train and equip a disintegrating and morally bankrupt Domobrani to hold the line against the advancing Partisans in areas vacated by the Italian military. Plainly there were too many contradictory aims to sort out. Ambrosio wanted to check the overweening ambitions of the Ustaša and the Germans,[235] but was under Mussolini's order that placed civil power in the hands of the Croatian government in the 3rd zone.[236] The vast Croatian hinterland, which was filled with wood and minerals, should round out an Italian Dalmatia, insisted Ambrosio,[237] but in the next breath he admitted that nothing could be done without the help of the Wehrmacht.

Ciano naively wrote that "the Croatians are very sympathetic toward us. Pavelić also likes us."[238] In truth, the Croats generally hated Italians, a fact frequently pointed out by Ambrosio. Pavelić was unfailingly friendly, but at the same time made sure that everything was in order with the Wehrmacht. On Germany Ciano was fatalistic. Italy, like the NDH, could not "offer resistance to any pressure from Berlin."

> It all depends on the Germans. If they keep their obligations under which Croatia has become a zone of Italian influence, a great deal can be accomplished by us yet. If, on the contrary, they should again try to force our hand and press their penetration, there is nothing for us to do but to haul down our flag and return home.[239]

Unexpectedly, the OKW on 16 December directed Field Marshal Wilhelm von List, commander of the Army Southeast, to release forces in the Balkans for the Eastern Front against the Soviet Union. Italy and Bulgaria would be called on to fill the void in eastern Bosnia left by the departing Wehrmacht units. For the local German command, which believed that Italian politicking with the Četniks had fanned rather than suppressed the revolt, this news spelt disaster. Should the Italians by some miracle reach Sarajevo on their side of the demarcation line, they would tread on mineral sources needed by the German war economy.

The reports from Germany titillated Rome. Pietromarchi welcomed Berlin's announcement of an imminent withdrawal; the Italian troops would move right into the abandoned German-occupied areas.[240] At a top-level meeting Mussolini declared his readiness to order the 2nd Army across the demarcation line, while Ambrosio anticipated a German-free Croatia. With five additional divisions and armed Serbs at the ready, the Italian commander would make Croatia free of both Partisans and Ustaša.[241] The twin objectives of defeating the Partisans and rounding out the *spazio vitale* that had seemed so remote finally appeared a real possibility. When Ambrosio insisted that Germany undertake a total withdrawal from Croatia—troops, air force, overt and occult agents, and military advisors, Mussolini simply kept "very silent."[242] It was Roatta who spoiled the party by skeptically remarking that the Germans would never relinquish their economic stranglehold on Croatia;[243] moreover, Italy did not have the wherewithal to move into German-abandoned areas in eastern Bosnia. As Ciano noted: "he [Roatta] does not want to start something he cannot finish."[244]

On 24 December Hitler suddenly reversed himself by rejecting any plans for the entry of the 2nd Army into German-occupied eastern Bosnia. The Wehrmacht would itself undertake mopping-up operations to the demarcation line and insist on Italian cooperation from the other direction. Hitler had resumed his usual lip service to Italian predominance in Croatia while quietly abetting the NDH's dependence on the Third Reich. Possibly this reversal was less a German initiative than a reaction to Italy's wavering spirits.[245]

Rather than being upset, the Italians were actually relieved. Ciano remarked that perhaps it was not such a bad thing for the Germans to change their minds, "because in the spring Bosnia, Serbia, and Montenegro will give us plenty of headaches."[246] Concerned over a Četnik move to within 20 kilometers of Zagreb, which "agitated" the city, Pietromarchi resignedly observed: "The time has passed [for Italy] to mount guard on the demarcation line"; Italy could no longer waste blood, money, energy and prestige in any more forays into the 3rd zone.[247] Cavallero wished to avoid new undertakings in Croatia because he had no troops to spare, and Pietromarchi told Rintelen flatly that Italy was not in a position to proceed with a comprehensive military occupation of Bosnia. Mussolini quickly yielded to Hitler's about-face by ordering Ambrosio to meet the Germans at the demarcation line instead of crossing it.[248]

Mussolini took out his frustration on the Croats by telling them that he intended to advance the boundary of Italian Dalmatia further into the interior. If certain garrisons would have to be withdrawn from the 3rd zone, Italian troops would stay put in the 2nd—a reminder to Zagreb that they were there to stay. The Duce would allow no strengthening of Croatian forts or any place for the Ustaša in Italian-occupied territory. These ruminations, if they signified a trimming of Italy's imperial designs on Croatia, revealed Mussolini's intention of providing Italian Dalmatia with a strong defense belt.[249]

On 19 January 1942 Ambrosio and Roatta switched offices. Ambrosio was appointed head of the Army general staff, and Roatta took over the command of the 2nd Army. The Germans were glad to see the "enemy of Croatian independence" go. In a farewell speech before an assembly of Croatian notables, Ambrosio sharply criticized the clique surrounding Pavelić for questioning Italy's special position in the country, which left an "unpleasant aftertaste" in the mouth of German Oberst Rohrback, who was in attendance.[250] Settling in his new quarters, Ambrosio on the 23rd handed Cavallero a testy bill of particulars against the Croatian regime whose contents would not have surprised the Axis ally. Power in Zagreb, it claimed, had shifted from the pro-Italian Pavelić to the Italian-hater Kvaternik. To discredit Italy, the Croats had committed crimes dressed in Italian uniforms and ascribed Partisan victories to the 2nd Army's connivance with the Četniks. By failing to treat the Serbs equitably, the NDH had created chaos. The Ustaša were savages who melted before the Partisans, failed to carry out their agreements with Italy, and showed bravery only in butchering defenseless people. Ambrosio concluded that his country should never have made Croatia an independent state. Nor did he spare the Germans. Glaise von Horstenau had besmirched Italian prestige, trampled on Italy's prior rights in the Balkans, and encouraged the Croats to absorb Italian Dalmatia.[251] Ambrosio's reproof of Mussolini for supporting the Pavelić regime was now carved in stone.

In the same defiant mood, Ambrosio pointed out to Mussolini the virtues of the Četniks, whose friendship enabled him to focus on the Partisans and stifle Croatian irredentist claims on Dalmatia. His orderly mind taxed by the claims of disputatious Croats and Germans, Ambrosio advocated a union between Croatia and Bosnia-Herzegovina under the Crown of Savoy, which would give Italy the power, assisted by "the Bosnians" [*prečani Serbs*], to govern the area unchallenged.[252]

In 1941 the 2nd Army in Italian-occupied Croatia devoted much time to protecting the Orthodox Serbs against the Ustaša and in disputes with the regime of Ante Pavelić. The Partisans, with the exception of the uprising in Montenegro, were mainly held in check. But when Partisan insurgency broke out in 1942 and spread simultaneously to many parts of Italian-occupied territory, the 2nd Army, urged on by Mussolini, retaliated with a stepped-up program of counterinsurgency designed to establish a Roman peace. Since the Italian empire-builders were still relentlessly pursuing their will-o'-the-wisp in Yugoslavia, they would continue their deadly anti-Partisan warfare against a background of ongoing Ustaša massacres.

# Chapter IV

# The "Pax Romana"

The Fascists Move In
Uprising in Montenegro
The "Italian Province of Ljubljana"
Hurly-Burly Life in Dalmatia

*The Fascists Move In*

I f the Italian troops and their civilian collaborators encountered
hazardous byways as they wended their way through Croatia,
even more perilous journeys awaited them in the annexed territories of Slovenia and Dalmatia and in the Montenegrin protectorate. To exercise authority over these unfamiliar lands, Mussolini appointed Fascists of high standing as civilian commissioners who
stood at the apex of a centralized system of local power. Anxious
to prove their mettle as imperial lords, these newly arrived rulers
unleashed a torrent of ordinances and laws aimed at inculcating the
Fascist spirit of mainland Italy in the annexed provinces. Through

domination of the cultural domain—education, literature, the arts and social sciences—they were determined to establish a Fascist presence in the daily life of the conquered Slav peoples. Mandatory use of the Italian language in the schools and mass media was considered to be the key in shaping the minds of future generations for existence.

Bent on denationalization, the Fascist commissars moved to break the spiritual and national consciousness of the Slavs by suppressing local newspapers, native cultural organizations, and sports clubs. They requisitioned arms, petroleum, and radios. Fascist squads swaggered about singing Mussolini's praises and Italy's military exploits, somehow imagining that the local residents would believe all the hyperbole. But if persuasion would not shepherd the native population into the Italian "New Order," the Fascist commissars would turn to coercion. The occupied Slavs did not oblige. Instead of showing deference, they derided the conquerors and their Italianization programs. Later they would resort to insurgency.

## Uprising in Montenegro

On 17 April 1941, the Italian lieutenant general of Albania, Francesco Jacomoni, authorized General Giuseppe Pafundi, commander of the XVIII Army Corps, to set up a new government in the old Montenegrin capital of Cetinje. The Italian occupation of the country had begun. The "Committee for the Liberation of Montenegro" had been organized in Tirana to attract pro-Italian Montenegrins to its standard and to avoid administrative chaos. Behind this façade, the Italian army proceeded to occupy the country and reactivate the old Yugoslav civil service. Italian flags flew everywhere, photos of king and Duce were posted in public places, the Roman salute was made obligatory, and censorship of the press was promulgated.

Rome named Serafino Mazzolini civil commissioner of Montenegro on 28 April 1941; he possessed judiciary power but remained subordinate to the head of the Italian Albanian Command. The "Committee for the Liberation of Montenegro" was dissolved on 22 May. On receiving the title high commissioner on 19 June, Mazzolini decided to leave in place former Yugoslav functionaries including under-prefects, financial personnel, and gendarmes—provided they paid an oath to Italy.[253] As a squadrista and vice secretary of the Fascist party (who ultimately became foreign minister of the Republic of Salò), Mazzolini undertook to Italianize Montenegro and set up Fascist organizations such as after-work recreation programs, youth groups, and sporting clubs. (Licio Gelli of future P-2 fame received a thorough grounding in Blackshirt violence during these years.) Mussolini approved monies for public works that would give employment to destitute people,[254] and funds were released to assist the 25,000 Montenegrins returning home from the rest of Yugoslavia and to pay the wages of the local public employees retained by the new Italian government.[255] As in the case of Slovenia, however, and to a lesser extent Dalmatia, the Italianization programs were bold in print but small in effect. A modest Italian presence and inadequate funds added up to a comparatively mild rule that barely touched the country districts. Milovan Djilas commented on the relaxed atmosphere:

> It was striking to see how well the Italian troops behaved, on entering the Montenegrin towns. In contrast to the simple Italian soldiers who played marbles with the children in Podgorica streets, the Blackshirts stood out threateningly. Yet there was no plundering, no arrests, and no use of force. Communists openly walked the streets and sat quietly in cafés. The only innovation was the compulsory greeting, a raised arm, on entering government buildings. This situation in Montenegro lasted, without basic change, until the German attack on the Soviet Union.[256]

Montenegro was a burden to the Italian treasury from the start. Although rich in forestlands and minerals, the country's resources had hardly been tapped due to a lack of investment capital. Of rocky terrain, the impoverished land needed substantial food imports to stay above the poverty line.

Mazzolini turned to a handful of separatists ("Greens"), mainly nostalgic older politicians, to appoint village committees throughout the country that would send delegates to a National Assembly in the capital. The majority of the country, which supported union with Serbia and defeat of the Axis ("Whites"), was left out of the selection process. On 12 July the Assembly proclaimed the independence and sovereignty of Montenegro as a constitutional monarchy. But everyone, regardless of political orientation, knew that Mazzolini, instead of granting Montenegrins political power, had made of that country an Italian protectorate, its life and destiny linked with the occupier.

Mazzolini had the less rewarding task of informing his Montenegrin audience that they stood to lose prized lands to hated enemies–the port of Cattaro to Italy, portions of Herzegovina (and possibly the Sandžak) to Croatia, and prime grazing lands and salt works to Albania. When the Montenegrins reacted angrily to this news, Mazzolini protested to Rome that such mutilations were undermining his popularity. Administering the country with an insolvent treasury and a lack of trained personnel exacerbated his inauspicious debut. Most embarrassing was Montenegrin derision of his Italianization programs. On the eve of the rebellion, Mazzolini wrote Pietromarchi that "disorder runs rampant everywhere."[257] Mazzolini was ready to wash his hands of Montenegro and depart for home.

The next day a rebellion, instigated by ex-officers, Pan-Serbs, and Communists, broke out. The insurgents were moved not so much by a spirit of revenge against Italian occupation, but rather by anger that distant overlords in Rome should contemplate the dismemberment of their country. In the early stages the uprising was spontaneous and chaotic—an exercise in grass-roots protest that lacked centralized leadership and direction. But because the territory was so thinly garrisoned by Italian troops, the insurgency spread rapidly. Only a small minority of Montenegrins, consisting of separatists under the leadership of the elderly General Krsto Popović, were initially willing to collaborate with Italy.

Drawing on the large cache of arms and munitions secreted away by soldiers of the ex-Yugoslav army, the insurgents caught the unsuspecting occupier napping. Within a matter of days they cut off the Italian troops at Cetinje from the rest of the country and pounced on their weakly defended outposts outside the capital, capturing quantities of equipment and taking 3,000 prisoners.[258] General Alessandro Pirzio Biroli, commander of the 9th Army, reacted immediately by ordering a repression of "extreme rigor and of exemplary solemnity, but without the character of reprisal and without useless crudity."[259] Staggered by these unfolding events, General Cavallero, the supreme commander, ordered Pirzio Biroli on the 16th to break the rebellion "at whatever cost."[260] He must have wondered whether the Greek fiasco was being reenacted in Montenegro. Ciano was also beset by fears that "our military men" would not be able to restore order without the help of the Germans.[261]

Political errors in Rome stemming from illogical border manipulations and laxity on the part of the occupation forces undoubtedly contributed to the initial success of the uprising. In response, Mazzolini overreacted by arresting not only sympathizers of the insurgents but many innocent people and adversaries of Communism as well.[262] The Italian commanders lashed back blindly too. General Pedrazzoli, commander of the "Taro" division, ordered that after each mopping-up expedition all captured "rebels" be shot, hostages taken, and the population living in the vicinity deprived of victuals.[263]

In the face of the uprising the Italians abandoned the farce of Montenegrin "independence." On 24 July Mussolini dissolved the High Commission and recalled Mazzolini; the next day he gave Pirzio Biroli full military and civil power. Pirzio Biroli, in turn, placed General Luigi Mentasti in command of the military in Montenegro and then proceeded to assemble 70,000 Italian troops to put down the uprising. Like other Italian generals serving in the Balkans, Pirzio Biroli smarted from Slav criticism: "Diffused among the masses is a feeling of superiority over Italians. That conviction must be overcome by means of strong action in grand style that will once and for all eradicate these ideas."[264]

The uprising now met serious reverses, and the Italians, through their crushing superiority in weapons and numbers, were able to scatter the enemy. Muslim irregulars from Kosovo and the Sandžak took the opportunity to pay off old scores by massacring Montenegrins, while, under the cover of Italian masters in Tirana, the collaborationist Albanian government forced thousands of Serbs to emigrate from the newly acquired province of Kosovo. Mass migrations and ethnic strife further weakened Montenegrin insurgency. General Mentasti issued harsh orders to execute all captured "rebels" even if they surrendered their arms and sent family members of "fugitive" partisans and their sympathizers to internment camps in Italy.[265]

In these unsettled conditions Pirzio Biroli, admitting that his forces had committed "useless violence" and indiscriminate reprisals, attenuated his repressive measures by issuing orders on 8 August that houses earmarked for destruction should be merely confiscated, thus sparing Italy the expense of rebuilding them. Leaving people homeless, he added, would only exacerbate Montenegrin hatred.[266] By the 12th order had finally been restored in the populated areas, while the rugged countryside settled into an uneasy standoff. By tacit arrangement the Montenegrins stopped resisting, the Albanians were withdrawn, the Italians marched back into the towns—and no one in Montenegro was disarmed.[267]

The Italians also benefited from Partisan zealotry, which split the ranks of the insurgents. The Partisans were determined to transform Montenegro into a miniature Red Republic, convinced that the wheel of revolution would crush all who stood in the way. Milovan Djilas, the Partisan leader in Montenegro, propagated Tito's version of Lenin's Marxist message that the party should prepare itself for the immediate seizure of power. Surprised by the rapidity and scale of the insurrection, Djilas quickly mobilized his troops to take it over. No revolution would erupt under his watch without Communist leadership. As for Tito, he did not regard the Montenegrin venture as anything more than a feint to draw Axis troops from the Russian front and simultaneously harden the Communist will to fight. In the aftermath of failure, Tito admitted that there had been a singular lack of grass-roots political preparation.[268] It was clear, too, that the Communist maxims "dictatorship of the proletariat" and "expropriation of private property" did not attract broad sections of the independent peasantry, who strongly valued their small plots of land.[269]

Still, many of the Montenegrin mountain folk, carried away by millennial expectations, waited impatiently for Soviet parachutists to escort them into the Communist utopia. Undismayed by their reverses, the hard-core Communists, many of them veterans of the Spanish civil war, stubbornly conducted a reign of terror against waverers, doubters, and "kulaks." To revive the fractured revolutionary movement, Tito replaced Djilas with Ivan Milutinović who, however, was unable to expand membership or seize the initiative.

The Partisans were frequently their own worst enemy, effecting ill-considered attacks on the Italians that provoked brutal reprisals and imposed unbearable pain on the Montenegrin population. Instead of concentrating on the occupier, moreover, the Partisans seemed more intent on carrying out summary execution of opposition groups and imagined "fifth columnists" before they had the chance to coalesce into a rival movement. They burned and pillaged villages that did not sympathize with them and suppressed tightly knit clans who resisted proletarian unity or showed partiality toward the Četniks. Partisan reprisals against compatriots unwilling to take up arms cost the movement dearly by driving them into the ranks of the Četniks, who eventually would regroup under the Italian umbrella.[270] The people's uprising was degenerating into civil war.

Pirzio Biroli had no doubt that Communists were at the bottom of the revolt; they had succeeded in shaking "a primitive, warlike and excitable people" from their "torpor." The new governor rounded up hostages from among the notables as a means of intimidation and established a tribunal to try those suspected of rebellion. His was to be "an exemplary, implacable punishment of rebels."

> Peoples of the Balkan peninsula respect only the strong. They take good will as weakness, they require tough but just treatment as all rude and primitive peoples. It is a grave error to use only caresses and blandishments. One must resort to force, which naturally requires men, time, and money.[271]

Although Pirzio Biroli denied it,[272] the Blackshirts, who made up a separate unit under his command, committed deeds so violent that this became their trademark in the lands of Yugoslavia. While reviling the insurgents for executing captured Fascists, Pirzio Biroli admitted that the enemy freed captured foot soldiers of the regular army.[273] Inexperienced on the battlefield and unfamiliar with guerrilla warfare, his troops struck back blindly at civilians and resorted to reprisals and summary executions.[274] People were indiscriminately jammed into jails and internment centers.[275] General Giovanni Esposito, commander of the "Pusteria" division, deported about a thousand people to concentration camps, burned villages, and shot not a few of their inhabitants, while General Pedrazzoli, largely inspired by the comportment of the German ally, carried out a fearful scorched-earth policy that earned him an indictment as a war criminal by Tito's postwar Communist government.[276]

In the July uprising some 5,000 Montenegrins died, 7,000 were wounded, and 10,000 deported to concentration camps.[277] The Italians suffered a total of 1,079 dead and wounded.[278]

Pirzio Biroli was aware that the Italian military had mishandled repression. Hereafter it would be organized and disciplined according to the laws of Italy. The Carabinieri would be responsible for arrests, a job not suited for undisciplined army units and irresponsible Fascist squads. Justice would be administered by appropriate judicial tribunals and not randomly by kangaroo military courts. In short, "Roman justice" would replace suppression by terror—even if the Montenegrans failed to appreciate the difference.

In spite of the insurrection, Pirzio Biroli claimed that he liked Montenegrins. As opposed to the "unctuous, false, and hypocritical Croats," he found the Serbs and Montenegrins to have a dashing, warlike spirit. He wanted to make the country work. If Montenegrins were relieved of starvation and provided with decent jobs, he believed that they would eschew Communism and accommodate to a "just," if "stern," Italian rule.[279] But would Rome provide him the funds for large-scale public works and food? Another worry was the general Montenegrin disenchantment over the boundaries. "The conviction is diffused among cultivated circles as well as the masses that the state cannot exist. Either Montenegro should be enlarged or annexed to Italy."[280] In stating that Serbs had the "spiritual quality, intellectual capacity and temperament that distinctly set them apart" from the other Balkan peoples,[281] Pirzio Biroli paid no mind to the German work-in-progress of reducing Serbia to a supply depot for raw materials.

On 3 October 1941 Mussolini created the governorship of Montenegro. Pirzio Biroli, appointed as governor, presided over the armed forces but had to answer to the Palazzo Chigi for political and administrative matters. His military superior was the Supreme Command, not the 2nd Army.

Notwithstanding these changes, the country did not quiet down following the harsh repression of the July 1941 uprising and the population's disillusionment with the Partisans. There were several reasons for this. Pirzio Biroli was hobbled by a lack of good maps, accurate topographical information, and knowledge of local languages. He had no help from informants who constantly led the troops down blind alleys and who, rather than providing information on hidden nests of Partisans, set up hostile clans for Italian reprisal by falsely incriminating them. The Italian troops let him down too. Having a faulty grasp of mountain warfare, they were, in his opinion, more fit for performing garrison duty than for chasing down the "seasoned and ardent" enemy.[282]

Against this background Pirzio Biroli hoped to win over Montenegrins by setting up a collaborationist regime consisting of a constituent assembly and a national gendarmerie. To promote "spiritual progress and prosperity," he proclaimed a general amnesty to the "rebels" as well as a release of those interned for security purposes and those taken in indiscriminate roundups.[283] Partisans at large would have thirty days to hand in their weapons and return home.[284] The hope was that these seasoned veterans in guerrilla warfare would abandon insurgency and join Italy in the anti-Communist crusade. Pirzio Biroli still pursued the practice of taking hostages to assure the good behavior of the population. At solemn ceremonies he supervised the rotation of hostages every week or ten days. By affording them decent food and lodging, and by promising to punish any Italian soldier guilty of maltreating his captives, he hoped to make the point that his military was merciful and solicitous.[285] Envisioning a Partisan-free Montenegro, Pirzio Biroli went so far as to ban Fascist party organizations in the country.[286] As opposed to the brutish repression that he formerly had carried out in Africa, Pirzio Biroli wanted to pass himself off in Montenegro as a humane and just ruler worthy of the old Roman imperium. His would be a government of laws, not of arbitrary power administered by renegade forces of public order.[287] As a gesture of reconciliation, the governor ordered the release of about 3,000 internees.[288]

Pirzio Biroli's "dovish" policies provoked a barrage of criticism. Following a long tour of the country, Guglielmo Rulli, the head of the civil affairs department in the Governor's office on loan from the Foreign Ministry, complained to Ciano that Italian authorities "were lavish with acts of clemency." Instead, they should be conducting reprisals, shooting hostages, and dispatching all men of fighting age to concentration camps. Montenegrins hate Italy, he insisted; they are Pan-Serbs determined to dominate the Adriatic shore.[289] The Italian prefect of Cattaro, Francesco Scassellati, criticized the "differing criteria applied by authority," which had turned Montenegro into a "hospital" for the Partisans fleeing from other parts of Yugoslavia.[290] Gasparino Langhella, a Carabinieri officer, was more scathing still: "Things would have been different had there been fewer proclamations and more shootings . . . Let's be done with these incorrigible brigands once and for all."[291] Cattaro's Carabinieri chief, Major Carlo Caggiati, wrote on 6 December: "Informers from Montenegro say that this new act of clemency is interpreted as a sign of weakness and of an inability to apply the repressive measures that have been threatened."[292] Bastianini sarcastically asked why Pirzio Biroli should expect the "generous and chivalrous Montenegrin people" to live peacefully when "rebels" were disemboweling Blackshirts![293]

Pirzio Biroli quickly reversed himself. On 1 December, the day that the Partisans surprised his legions with a fierce attack on Pljevlja, he noted that conciliation, instead of producing pacification, had yielded "sterile" results. Henceforth villages harboring suspected

"rebels" would be razed to the ground and their farm animals confiscated.[294] Pirzio Biroli's turnabout was timely, for the next day he
learned that Mussolini would tolerate no indigenous Montenegrin
movement for fear it would evolve into an independent force. The
military governor was under orders to eschew employment of collaborationist organizations as auxiliaries in repression.[295] Not surprisingly, Cavallero supported the Duce. Observing that the uprising was led by former Yugoslav officers, he rejected Italian cooperation with native bands no matter how anti-Partisan.[296]

Although the Italians had dealt the Partisans a shattering defeat,
there was no letup in counterinsurgency. Like Roatta, Robotti, and
Armellini, Pirzio Biroli would not tolerate any dissent. He had come
around to the view of his critics that concessions to the population
designed to appease constituted weakness. Perhaps the "tireless"
prefect of Cattaro, Scassellati, was right after all in proposing that
not only adults "captured with arms in hand," but also women,
children, and Orthodox priests should be shot.[297] His days as a
"dove" long behind him, Pirzio Biroli proclaimed to his soldiers in
April 1942:

> The fable of the *buono italiano* must cease! The Italian sol-
> dier is above all a warrior. He who does not wish to understand
> the generosity of a friendly hand will now feel the force of our
> fist...Let there be no pity for whose who cowardly kill our broth-
> ers and show no quarter for those who shoot our comrades and
> make war prisoners in contempt of international conventions.
> Show these barbarians that if Italy is the master and mother of
> civilization, it also knows how to punish with the inexorable laws
> of justice . . . Do not let the misery of the people whose land
> you occupy today move you to pity. The Montenegrin peoples
> have wished this misery upon themselves . . . He who hates
> Fascism hates Italy.[298]

At the same time Pirzio Biroli announced that for every Italian officer killed or wounded, fifty Montenegrins would die.[299] "The whole
country is in revolt," he told Pietromarchi. "Men of fighting age

should be sent to concentration camps." Pietromarchi agreed: "We should have done this sooner."[300] The "Lion of Gondar" had indeed roared.[301]

## The *"Italian Province of Ljubljana"*

On 3 May 1941, when Italian-occupied Slovenia was officially annexed and became a province of Italy, Emilio Grazioli, formerly federal secretary of the Fascist party of Trieste, received the title of High Commissioner. The newly acquired province was granted administrative, cultural, and financial autonomy but was politically dependent on Rome. On 21 May the High Commissioner obtained the civil authority that had previously been exercised by the command of the XI Army Corps stationed in his province. Grazioli presided over a land containing close to 340,000 Slovenes, 17,000 refugees fleeing from German-occupied Slovenia, and 458 Italians. He arrived with a group of party members who had made a name for themselves in the Venezia Giulia. Grazioli interpreted the autonomy that Mussolini had conceded to the new province not as self-government for Slovenes but as his right to Italianize, or Fascistize, society and apply an Italian paternalism similar to that exercised in Albania. He fully expected collaborators representing the middle and upper classes to participate wholeheartedly in his Italianization programs and pondered ways to bind commercial interests to Italy.

Slovenes were relieved of obligatory military service and allowed use of their language in the primary schools, while Italian was rendered optional in the secondary and higher levels of education. Bilingualism prevailed in official business. Since there were not enough Italians to man the administrative posts, Grazioli had to rely on Slovene functionaries of the former Yugoslav province. But not in the security forces where only police from Italy were welcome. Grazioli searched for a formula that would confirm Italy's imperial presence as an ineluctable fact while respecting the culture and traditions of the native population. A benign Fascist administration that looked after the interests of the people and governed with authority, order, and justice was what Grazioli had in mind. Ironically, his intention of granting the Slovenes a certain, if ill-defined, autonomy in schools, administration, and the cultural sphere in the province of Ljubljana contrasted sharply with the outright Fascist repression of the Slovene population in the Venezia Giulia. Grazioli's policies, however, can in no way be described as "liberal." By denying civil liberties and political opposition, he aimed to forge a spiritual identity and totalitarian "unity" similar to that which the Fascists believed they had achieved in the motherland. Since it was clear to Grazioli that Italy, in *la provincia Lubiana*, represented a civilized progression over centuries of "feudal" Habsburg domination and years under the "barbarian" Serb yoke, he expected the Slovenes to recognize this themselves.

As a bona fide Fascist, Grazioli intended to run society through a network of Fascist organizations covering all walks of life, and he replaced Slovene unions with Fascist-style syndicates. But when given a choice, the Slovenes snubbed Grazioli's programs. Only a tenth of the youth enrolled in Fascist organizations, and in the university student body of 2,474, a mere 98 signed up. The Fascist squads of Ljubljana recruited from the Slovene population reached the trifling figure of 144 members. After-work recreation programs made small headway, and the first session of the corporativist provincial council was delayed till 23 February 1943.[302] General Roatta, in his self-exculpatory memoirs, discovered too late the folly of Fascist imperialism in Slovenia.[303]

The Italian occupiers were initially treated to demonstrations of loyalty on the part of politicians and notables of Ljubljana, who were stunned by the rapidity of defeat. City mayors sent an address of welcome to the Duce, while the upper clergy, ultra-conservative and outspokenly anti-Communist, greeted the Italians as stalwart defenders of the Catholic faith.[304] To impart a feeling of local participation, Grazioli created a Consulta, an advisory body of fourteen Slovenes chosen from the "productive categories"—politics, business, and culture. But this turned out to be just window-dressing. The Consulta met and debated in a void, its collaborative purpose undermined by complaints: necessities were short and food prices exorbitant, innocent people were being arrested, and unemployment was rampant.[305] Disabused of Fascist paternalism, the Consulta soon withered away. In June 1942 the Italians appointed a former Yugoslav general, Leo Rupnik, a conservative and determined enemy of Communism, as mayor of Ljubljana, but gave him scant authority. It was obvious from the start that Grazioli had made little headway in summoning local Slovenes to share power. The negative press on the harsh Fascist rule over Slovenes living in the Venezia Giulia during the inter-war period only deepened his general unpopularity throughout the province.

As opposed to the brutal denationalization and forced deportations characterizing German-occupied Slovenia, Italian rule was relatively mild in the first months of occupation. The Catholic church, led by Monsignor Gregorij Rožman, archbishop of Ljubljana and a self-proclaimed collaborator, emphasized ties with Catholic Italy. His flock, though sullen, tolerated the Italian regime and was sufficiently obedient as to render outright repression less necessary. Only a handful of Slovenes appreciated the conquering Italians and wished to emulate the Fascist New Order. Most anti-Communist and patriotic Slovenes retreated into "absenteeism," hoping to be liberated by the Allies rather than by Stalin. When insurgency in Slovenia first flared in July 1941, its home of operations was Ljubljana, where Italian surveillance had been lax, unlike the efficiently policed German areas where every peep of dissent was answered by ruthless retaliation.[306] Over time, however, under the impress of Partisan activity, Italian oppression in Slovenia became no less severe than the German.

When Germany invaded the Soviet Union on 22 June 1941, hopes rose among the Slovenes that the thousand-year Reich was doomed to a premature end; perhaps the makeshift Fascist regime would fall even sooner. Moved by a hatred of the Italian occupier and a determination to recover their political will and cultural identity, many Slovenes headed into the resistance formed and led by dedicated Communists. But many newly recruited Partisans typically gave scant thought to the intricacies of Marxist doctrine. More important to them was Slavic brotherhood, a visceral solidarity with their Russian brothers. Simple patriotic duty to free the country from the Fascist invader provided no less incentive for underground work. There were many degrees of resistance. Peasants and urban dwellers provided refuge to fugitive Partisan warriors; individuals participated in local hit-and-run operations; and the intrepid risked family, home, jobs, and comfort by signing on for full-time guerrilla duty. However, a large number of Slovenes, many of whom were devoutly Catholic, sat on the fence either from fear of Italian reprisals or hatred of Communism. Many Catholic organizations had a large following and might have been willing to collaborate with Italy in the crusade against Communism if granted civil rights, political involvement, and respect for their cultural institutions. But since Grazioli ruled surrounded by Fascist trappings and defined his regime by Italianization programs, he was unable to tap this potential reservoir.

The most influential party in Slovenia before the fall of Yugoslavia was the Popular party led by Anton Korosec. Composed mostly of the urban upper classes and independent peasantry, it looked to a misty Habsburg past rather than to the Fascist-inspired totalitarian social order. Rural and populist—a clerical movement of the Right—the party honored traditional hierarchical values, esteemed the paternalism of the state, and yearned to restore Catholic family ties in a community free of democratic chaos, free-wheeling capitalism, and the atheistic socialism of a rootless urban proletariat. The party proudly touted itself as a redoubtable foe of Communism and was not bashful in displaying an anti-Semitism that, however, stopped short of the nightmarish biological variety found in German Nazism.

Many of Korosec's followers formed the backbone of the White Guards, who, during the unsettling days following World War I, sprang into existence to combat the threat of Bolshevism. Led by large landowners and industrialists, the White Guards absorbed the spirit of the parish priests. Terrorized by Béla Kun's seizure of power in next-door Hungary, the clergy called the rural population to arms. The factory owners needed no persuasion to lock out strikers prowling the streets of Ljubljana in search of revolutionary opportunity.

Undoubtedly there were similarities between the White Guards and
the Ustaša, but the Slovene organization rested on tradition and the
Catholic church, while the Ustaša utilized the concept of faith primarily as an instrument to wage ethnic cleansing against Orthodox
Serbs and Jews.[307]

Situated to the right of the Popular party were the "Storm
Guards." Led by Lambert Ehrlich, priest and Jesuit professor at the
University of Ljubljana, the Guardia made its mark in scuffling with
leftist students. Modeled on the Spanish Falange, the Guardists admired Fascist principles and favored collaboration with Italy. As well
there were smaller radical right cults of diverse Fascist hues whose
underlying common denominator was hatred of democracy, Jews,
ethnic tolerance, and Communism.[308]

By September Grazioli apparently realized that forced Italianization was alienating Slovene conservatives inclined to view Italy as
a bulwark against Communism. He pondered what to do. Since the
German program of fierce repression and denationalization was winning no friends among them, it should not, he observed, serve as a
role model for the Italian province of Ljubljana.[309] But Grazioli did
not shy from severe punishment for anti-Italian transgressions.

On 11 September 1941, in a measure designed to maintain public
order, Grazioli instituted an Extraordinary Tribunal with sweeping
powers.[310] Slovenes found in possession of literature, emblems, and
other materials deemed subversive would receive summary justice.
Those judged to be politically dangerous were subject to internment.
The death penalty was reserved for anyone harming the Italian
armed forces and police. Italian justice was strengthened by a military tribunal set up on 7 November in Ljubljana. Since Grazioli
presided over the forces of public order, it was in his power, through
the Questura, to call on the military to assist the police in quelling
the spreading insurgent uprising. Police units under his jurisdiction
were many and varied: 1,500 Carabinieri assisted by 500 former
Yugoslav gendarmes, as well as financial guards and urban police.[311]
Having been appointed federal secretary of the Fascist party in
Ljubljana in October, Grazioli had control over the Militia and Fascist squads, which he used liberally in *rastrellamenti* to round up all

Jews and citizens of enemy states for expulsion or internment.[312] But Grazioli did not have enough men to protect his public security forces, thinly spread out in the countryside, from attack by the insurgents who were disrupting railroad lines and communication systems.

General Ambrosio shared Grazioli's frustration over the effort to put down rebellion. For him the major fault lay with Rome. "Our proclamations to break this vast agitation with grave sanctions against the criminals aimed to slow down the uprising have failed." The Extraordinary Tribunal, he believed, had rightly handed out death sentences that sought to control terrorism by intimidation, but Rome intervened by inexplicably downgrading these "just sentences" to long prison terms. As compared to the "exemplary punishments in German Slovenia," Italy has shown "hesitations . . . and perplexities," which resulted in "burning setbacks" and loss of prestige.[313]

The only means of persuading a Slovene population terrified of the Communist menace to cooperate with Italian authority would have been a grant of Italian citizenship. Grazioli was on to this and petitioned Rome for permission, but to no avail.[314] Still, by his high-handedness and haughty deportment, Grazioli managed to induce what few collaborators there were to abandon political life. The president of the Consulta, Marco Natlačen, resigned in December 1941, trailed by other notables and conservative party representatives. In their minds liberation from the Serb yoke had been replaced by the worse fate of forced Italianization and underclass status. When the Partisan movement picked up momentum during the autumn, it faced a Slovene collaboration fragmented by Grazioli's unwillingness to empower conservative anti-Communists with even a modicum of political authority.

Grazioli was also harried by a lack of finances to run the government, which involved him in a protracted tug-of-war with the Interior Ministry. The "superprefect" of Ljubljana was likewise frustrated by Rome's failure to grant a statute of autonomy and an extension of Italian laws to his province.[315] Grazioli therefore floundered in a world of hazy laws and undefined power. Having arrived in Slovenia on short notice, he had neither the resources, nor carefully prepared plans, nor an efficient bureaucracy to carry out

Italianization. This contrasted vividly with the careful preparations the Nazis made for their part of Slovenia through a well-oiled administration that instantly carried out deportation of "undesirable" Slovenes and introduced programs designed to Germanize those who remained.[316]

Paradoxically, a threat to Grazioli's authority—no less serious than that caused by Partisan insurgency—came from General Mario Robotti, commander of the X1 Army Corps stationed in Ljubljana. Awash in Partisan activity, Robotti bitterly complained that Grazioli's police were negligent in clamping down on subversion. More than the Fascist High Commissioner, Robotti demeaned Slovenes. The great benefits of German civilization that had laboriously brought this "fistful" of Slavs into Europe, he reflected, have unfortunately been undone by twenty years of primitive Serb rule. The Slovenes have relapsed into barbarity, and their brutish youth understand only force. Grazioli should have understood, Robotti held, that good will and civilizing missionary work were unfailingly taken as weakness. He dismissed the High Commissioner's notion that "enlightened" Italianization would lead ultimately to assimilation of the Slovene population in the larger Italian community.[317] As unreconstructed haters of Italy and Fascism, the Slovenes, he contended, deserved savage repression.[318] Casting his eye over a territory that was nearly one hundred percent Slovene, Robotti saw enemies far and wide.[319] But initially he could not move freely since responsibility for the maintenance of public order resided in the office of the High Commissioner.[320]

By early January General Ambrosio, worried about the security problem in Slovenia, pointed out that, thanks to Grazioli's "weak and indecisive" police, "rebel bands" were reassembling for new "terrorist acts" against Italian authority.[321] Mussolini, after a long silence, decided on 19 January 1942 to deprive the High Commissioner of the power to deploy army troops in civilian-led expeditions against the Partisans.[322] A distinction was contrived: the military would be responsible for "the defense of the public order" and the police entrusted with "the protection of the public order." This meant that the task of suppressing insurgency was now in the hands of Robotti, while Grazioli was left with strictly police duties.

Robotti had finally acquired all the tools of repression.[323] In an opportune follow-up, General Roatta broadened his latitude by inviting him to "shoot a certain number of detained Communist rebels for every soldier treacherously despoiled, when—let it be understood—the guilty ones cannot be identified."[324] With no hesitation Robotti proposed to Grazioli that hostages be taken for collective reprisals from among known Partisans and suspected fellow travelers engaged in subversive activities; such reprisals could include death before a firing squad. This became law and was publicly posted on 24 April and 6 May.[325]

After encircling Ljubljana in barbed wire reinforced by machine gun nests and artillery, Robotti conducted a major roundup between 23 February and 15 March of weapons and people suspected of Partisan ties, 878 of whom, he noted, were arrested.[326] Grazioli reported that 20,037 Slovenes were stopped for questioning, of whom 936 were arrested, and one shot.[327] Roatta endorsed Robotti's operations by stating that Mussolini had ordered the adoption of "energetic and exemplary" measures. Roatta added his own word: Robotti should dispatch all captured officers and non-commissioned officers of the former Yugoslav army (they had been re-arrested as "interned civilians") to the Gonors concentration camp. He further urged Robotti to sequester all radios and prohibit the use of bikes passing from one region to another. The roundup in Ljubljana was to be followed by a dragnet covering the entire province of Slovenia.[328]

While Robotti soldiered on against the Partisans, Mussolini in April came within a hair's-breath of cashiering Grazioli over his inept handling of the public security forces and his wooly views on Italianization. To recover standing as a redoubtable Fascist, the High Commissioner told Robotti: "If the military doesn't shoot 'em, I will."[329] Against a background of ongoing rancor between Grazioli and Robotti, and Partisan success in infiltrating Italian defenses, Ciano recorded:

In Slovenia things are not going so well. The High Commissioner asks us to send twenty-four thousand men. It appears that the streets of Lubiana are now unsafe for our troops; every doorway and every window hide potential danger.[330]

During June 1942 Robotti, on Roatta's orders, orchestrated another methodical roundup of "Communists"—students, professionals, and insurgents. His objective was to break the links between the Partisans hiding out in Ljubljana and those fighting in the countryside. Robotti hated the capital and its people: "our enemy is the intelligentsia of Ljubljana."[331] By applying an "iron fist," he would break the city's "criminal underworld."[332] Robotti complained that Grazioli had made his an uphill battle by retaining Slovene functionaries who assisted Communist agents in establishing a spy network in the city. To quell such clandestine activity, the XI Army Corps commander strengthened the barbed wire surrounding Ljubljana, dug a vast network of bunkers, and conducted periodic roundups. He had a particularly zealous accomplice in General Taddeo Orlando, commander of the "Granatieri di Sardegna" division, who assiduously carried out Robotti's orders by evacuating all manner of university students from Ljubljana.

To counter the relentless Partisan attacks on railroads and forays across the frontier, Robotti ordered the expulsion of people living within 1–2 kilometers of the tracks and 2–4 kilometers from the frontiers of Fiume and Croatia.[333] Commissioner Rosin, one of Grazioli's subordinates, noted that such territory, emptied of its inhabitants, would serve as a "rebel" nesting place and result in the loss of the entire harvest season; 10,000 angry refugees would be created without resolving the problem of the "bands."[334]

Robotti's ongoing and indiscriminate raids inflicted heavy losses on the Partisans and resulted in massive deportations. In the mopping-up operation in Ljubljana from 27 June to 1 July 1942, 17,076 Slovenes were arrested, of whom 2,663 were sent to internment camps in Italy.[335] Thirty-one hostages were shot in reprisal for Partisan-inflicted deaths of Italian soldiers.[336] Of Ljubljana's 80,000 residents, General Orlando reported that 2,858 had recently been arrested. Added to the previous number of 3,000 rounded up, he had taken into custody one-fourth of all men of fighting age.[337] Fascists played a prominent role in all phases of the operation.[338]

The heavy crackdown, however, though it disrupted Partisan communications between Ljubljana and the countryside, did not break the resistance.[339] And the job was botched. Grazioli stated that the "totalitarian" roundup of intellectuals in Ljubljana included friends of Italy, some of whom were members of the Ljubljana branch of the Italian youth organization![340] His "captains," who served as local commissioners throughout the province, reported chaos, irregularities, and unfairness in the military roundups and interrogations.[341] Carabinieri officers were no less critical, reserving their sharpest volleys for the "Granatieri di Sardegna" division. The guiltless were interned while many of the culprits remained at large. Military interrogators responsible for sorting out the innocent from the "criminals" were hoodwinked by clever Slovene informants, who, to make themselves indispensable and assure good payment, gave compromising testimony or incriminated personal enemies to carry out private vendettas.[342] Commissioner Rosin overheard a nasty whisper: "The Italians have become worse than the Germans."[343] Although they had an axe to grind against the military, it is fair to assume that Grazioli's men submitted reasonably accurate reports. The reports of the Carabinieri, who hardly had a reputation for gentle treatment of occupied peoples, constituted a heavy indictment of General Taddeo Orlando and his troops for their brutality in rounding up people en masse in Ljubljana.

To justify his harsh reprisals, Robotti typically pointed to the savagery in the Partisan tactic of killing off collaborating Slovenes.[344] This the Partisans did—an average of sixty people "liquidated" each month.[345] Motivated by ideological fanaticism, they instituted a service of security and information (OF) that became an efficient command post for the elimination of "traitors of the people" by means of witch-hunts and "revolutionary justice."[346] According to Robotti, the OF's major moral and material support came from the "plutocratic bourgeoisie" and its "running dogs"—Catholics, students, intellectuals, and fellow travelers.[347] There is no doubt that the OF, by summarily executing collaborators and their accomplices, intended to send a message to the Slovene people: don't dare sell out to the enemy or you'll suffer the same fate. Such calculation had the further purpose of provoking the Italians to lash back against the innocent. Robotti was clay in the Partisans' hands. By predictably overreacting, he enabled the OF to tell the fence-sitters: your turn will be next if you don't join the insurgency. The Slovene Liberation Front knew no middle ground. So it was for Robotti. Either you were a collaborator who faithfully informed on the Partisans, or you were an enemy to be shot. And there was no sympathy for those caught in contested territory between Partisans and the occupying forces. The population in surrounding areas, assured Robotti, must know when "rebels" are about to attack military outposts or barracks. "If the people have a fear of dying at the hands of the Partisans if they talk, let them have as much fear of dying at our hands if they don't talk."[348]

The Partisans did not restrict terrorism to bourgeois class enemies; they committed atrocities against the Italian troops too, but in this they were selective. Captured officers and proven Fascists were commonly shot; the lower ranks, however, were frequently set free. The Italian commanders sent former captives into quarantine and rehabilitation programs to purge the brainwashed of Communist propaganda.[349] Notwithstanding these precautions, many soldiers, if not drawn to Communism, understood and even sympathized with Tito's cause; yet only a few defected to the Partisans before Mussolini's fall.

The hardships that the Italian soldiers faced were manifold, but after fiercely fought skirmishes they could return to the safety of their forts. Life as a Partisan was infinitely worse. Deprived of the comforts of home, the guerrillas felt like hunted dogs scavenging for food and shelter. Although convinced of ultimate victory, they knew that they faced heavy odds. The Italian adversary was formidable and possessed a decided advantage in numbers and firepower. Equally plaguing, the Partisans often sensed that they were aliens in their own land, for the Communist message fell on deaf ears in the countryside, where the peasants mostly belonged to Catholic par-

ties and feared losing their small plots of land to Bolshevik collec-
tivization. But when the Partisans attacked Italian garrisons, and the
troops retaliated by blowing up houses, shooting hostages, and placing people in concentration camps, the peasants were caught in a
deadly crossfire. To avoid Italian persecution, many went into hiding where they were persuaded, or constrained, to join Partisan
ranks.[350] Robotti's brutality backfired by causing many to opt for the
Partisans as the lesser of two evils.[351]

How many Partisans did the Italians face? Roatta estimated
12,000, including many intellectuals, professors, and medics, flanked
by 20-30,000 partially armed and part-time combatants. Robotti
reckoned the number to be 10,000 active guerrillas, while the historian Ferenc puts the figure at half that.[352]

Under heavy siege from the Partisans, the Italian authorities, very
late in the day—March 1942—tolerated the birth of the Slovene
Alliance, a semi-clandestine organization composed of leaders of
the Popular party and their national/liberal allies. Belatedly, they
realized that failure to profit from the anti-Communism of these
conservative parties would result in the loss of an influential force
in the province that could serve as an important intermediary between the government and population at large. On the other hand,
it was clear that the Slovene Alliance was merely feigning collaboration with Italy and intended to function as a "shadow government"
under men like Natlačen and his military adjutant, Leon Rupnik,
whose purpose was to reanimate the idea of independence and form
an embryo national army that would turn on the Italian occupier as
soon as he began to falter.[353] Grazioli reported that Archbishop
Rožman, for one, was ready for a concrete and energetic collaboration. But Rožman was unable to rally the Alliance to break with the
Slovenes in the government-in-exile in London and their sympathizers in Ljubljana, a step required by the Italian military. The majority
of the popular and national liberal parties preferred to stay in limbo
and wait on events. Robotti was right in expressing serious doubts
about the loyalty of Catholics and national-liberals.[354]

By July 1942 both town and country had become thoroughly
estranged from Fascist Italy. Marco Natlačen, the Consulta presi-

dent, was the only important figure to join Archbishop Rožman in
the anti-Communist crusade. For this decision he paid with his life
when cut down by Partisan bullets on 13 October 1942. In reprisal,
Grazioli ordered a mixed squad of Blackshirts and police to massacre twenty-four Slovene political prisoners.[355]

At their wit's end in quelling insurgency, Robotti and Grazioli
were still very reluctant to recruit Slovenes as military auxiliaries. In
late April the High Commissioner declared that enrollment of armed
Slovenes was "inadmissible for questions of prestige," a view shared
by Robotti.[356] But as the XI Army Corps general was preparing for
a grand offensive against the Partisans, he agreed to consider a plan
proposed in June by General Rupnik that would create a network
of collaborators and informants along with Slovene
counterinsurgency formations to be led by former Yugoslav officers. Even this limited program was fraught with danger. The moderate Slovene classes had lost confidence in Italy's ability to put down
the Partisans, and the anti-Communists held back because of the
military's generally hostile attitude. These negative judgments grew
out of a basic anti-Italianism that had forged a unity among Slovenes
of all classes and political loyalties. Anticipating an Allied victory,
they obstructed the occupier or feigned apathy. Hardly a Slovene
passed on useful information to the Italian command, and those who
did were promptly cut down by the OF. No wonder that Robotti
was reluctant to accept Slovene military assistance.[357]

In July Robotti finally yielded to military necessity. To support
his struggling troops, he formed a Voluntary Anti-Communist Militia (MVAC), whose core consisted of the Slovene Legion, the fighting arm of the Peoples party. In October local vigilante squads
sprang into action, searching houses and arresting suspects in
Ljubljana.[358] The Storm Guards, if not adding many numbers, provided a strident pro-Fascist voice. But the Guards' influence had
already been greatly reduced when their top man, Lambert Ehrlich,
was assassinated by Partisans on 27 May. To protect their leaders
against Partisan counter-terror, young anti-Communist toughs
formed "legions of death." Finally there were the Četniks. Under
the titular command of the Pan-Serb Mihailović, who stood for a

reconstituted Yugoslavia, they had an uneasy relationship with the other patriotic Slovenes. Out of these disparate groups, 4,000 MVAC volunteers were mustered up for Italian service and divided in units of approximately 200, attached to XI Army Corps formations throughout the Province of Ljubljana. By August 1943, their numbers reached 6,000; the majority were refugees from German Slovenia or Croatians.[359] Monsignor Rožman urged the Italians to create protective "village guards" under Slovene command in rural areas as well as a "Corps of Secret Police" for Ljubljana. General Roatta acted on the suggestion and expressed pleasure over the archbishop's lively role in leading "civilization and religion" in the crusade against Bolshevism.[360]

The MVAC formations, rather than acting to protect a traditional way of life, resembled goon squads. Insubordinate and rowdy, they performed poorly in their baptism of fire and ransacked the countryside during the *rastrellamenti*. Even General Roatta was dismayed by their savagery.[361] Since Robotti had estranged the anti-Communist urban middle classes and peasant yeomanry, he had to settle for rightist fanatics, bullies, refugees running away from the Germans, and aimless youth brutalized by the war.

Embarrassed by the inability of his legions to finish off insurgency in Slovenia, Mussolini told General Roatta on 23 May: "You have all the power. I will give you the troops. Extirpate the plague." Roatta asked again for total control over the police forces. "Of course," the Duce replied. "Everything." After reflecting that the best enemy is a dead enemy, Mussolini exhorted his commanders to round up and shoot hostages at will and intern 20–30,000 of the highly suspect in Slovenia.[362] This gave Roatta the opening to extend the criteria of internments to cover, "for example, students."[363] Robotti, in turn, flouting Grazioli, immediately issued the order that placed all public security forces, including the Questura, under military authority.[364] In this spirit Roatta plotted a grand maneuver: "At whatever cost Italian domination and prestige must be restored, even if all Slovenes have to be shot and Slovenia destroyed." In battle zones, he implored, deny the Partisans shoes by impounding them from tanners![365] A careful preparation for the upcoming attack was "already in the works," Roatta confided to Pietromarchi; "30,000 Slovenes would be taken away."[366]

Responding to Robotti's requests,[367] General Roatta sent large contingents from Montenegro and Herzegovina, bringing the XI Army Corps' force to 70,000. In early July Robotti prepared for the ultimate sweep against the Partisans. Having in hand Mussolini's open-ended directive to pursue unrestrained counterinsurgency in an expansive "abnormal zone,"[368] the XI Army Corps commander overlooked whatever restraints Roatta posited in his 7 April memorandum and ordered his army to "suppress without pity not only the guilty but also suspects, and to intern all men of fighting age who seemed to be following in the footsteps of the rebels."[369] "The dwellings from which emanate offenses to the authority and troops—the homes in which are found arms, munitions, explosives, and war materiel—and those in which the owners have voluntarily given hospitality to the 'rebels' . . . *must be inexorably destroyed.* The above measure does *not* only apply in the zones where the mobile troops operate, *but in the entire province of Ljubljana.*"[370]

The Slovene people were duly warned when Robotti and Grazioli posted a proclamation on 15 July that read in part: All local trains would be suppressed and people forbidden within a kilometer of the railroads. Those who bore arms or showed hostility toward Italian authorities would be shot; a similar fate would befall "men of fighting age no matter their attitude who are found in combat zones without a justifiable motive." All homes that contained the implements of war or hosted "rebels" would be "razed to the ground."[371] Robotti and Grazioli had leaflets dropped from the air inviting "rebels" to return home and hand in their arms in exchange for their lives.[372] This was put in form of a proclamation on 17 September when Robotti and Grazioli declared that the lives of rebels would be spared and their property would not be confiscated if they surrendered before a pending battle.[373] After sealing the leaky frontier with Fiume and Croatia to deprive the Partisans in Slovenia outside assistance and escape routes, Robotti set off on the 16th against an enemy of about 2,500 to 3,000 men in a hostile countryside.

Despite his resolve to train élite and mobile guerrilla fighters who would stealthily pursue the enemy, Robotti made his preparations with no effort of concealment. His plan of attack bristled with graphs, troop deployments, and maps—the same old book of fixed movements and heavily laden supply trains. When the artillery roared to announce the campaign, any element of surprise was lost. In serried ranks the troops lurched forward into empty spaces. General Pièche observed: "This is a ridiculous farce that resembles the memorable deeds of the Bourbon militia." Pietromarchi added: "We have to rid ourselves of the 2nd Army. Otherwise, we will end with stupidity and dishonor."[374]

In the heat of the campaign, Mussolini addressed his top military officers on 31 July:

> All our original optimism and good treatment of the Slovenes have been dashed by the German attack on the Soviet Union, which has induced them to declare their solidarity with the Russians. I wonder if our policy was wise. One can say only that it was ingenuous . . . I think that it would be better to pass from a friendly manner to strong-arm methods . . . At issue is our prestige. I do not fear the word. I am convinced that we must meet the "terror" of the partisans with iron and fire. The depiction of Italians as sentimentalists incapable of being tough when necessary must cease . . . This population will never love us.[375]

Mussolini, like Robotti, was no booster of the MVAC, and collaborators were only a cut above Partisans.[376]

The Duce's combativeness was vitiated by a warning. No reinforcements would be available for the Balkan theater since they were needed in North Africa and at home. Actually, for the Duce Yugoslavia had become a backwater that merely inflicted wear and tear on the soldiers and ate up supplies needed elsewhere. "Let us not worry about the economic plight of the population. They have willed it on themselves! Let them take the consequences... I am not opposed to the mass transfer of populations."[377]

Immediately afterwards the Duce addressed a public rally in Gorizia, where he admonished the Slovenes to note the stern face of Rome. "Those who do not lay down their weapons and nourish unhealthy dreams will be completely annihilated; their belongings and houses will literally be razed to the ground."[378] Impetuous and determined, Mussolini implicitly waved aside men like Grazioli, who was only "pro-Slovene" insofar as he had attempted to Italianize the native population. Instead, the Duce endorsed the culture of hate and war on the Slovene people that already had been waged with halting effectiveness by the Italian High Commissioner of Ljubljana Province and the commander of the XI Army Corps. During a meeting of officers under his command held at Kočevke on 2 August, Robotti, not to be outdone by the Duce, hastened to strike further fear in Slovene hearts: "I intend to make the zones behind the front safe for a five-year-old Italian child . . . Every useful severe measure must be fully applied."[379]

If Robotti unrelentingly pursued repression, his mopping-up expedition sputtered.[380] Although the Italian troops inflicted heavy casualties on the Partisans and demoralized the population, many insurgents managed to slip through the Italian ring, regroup, and reoccupy territory around the abandoned fortresses. Grazioli attributed the half-success to Robotti's unimaginative tactics of engaging stodgy large columns against a mobile enemy. Worse still, in his view, was the indiscriminate destruction, for Italian attacks were preceded by heavy artillery barrages and air strikes that made no distinction between civilian and rebel.[381]

The long campaign wound up in November, with the Italian command reporting 1,053 Partisans killed in combat, 1,381 captured, and 1,236 shot.[382] Between January and December of 1942, the XI Army Corps suffered 678 dead, 111 dispersed, and 1114 wounded.[383]

Robotti was a frustrated and angry warrior. His prestige as general of an imperial army had been compromised by Slovene scorn for Italian military virtues, his "altruism" unappreciated. "Fascism and its representatives, organs of government and troops, have sincerely extended a hand to the Slav people, who have rejected it."

Rather than kowtow, the Slovenes struck back, which prompted this response from Robotti: "No false pity for the treacherous assassins of our soldiers." In the middle of a *rastrellamento* in August that hardly turned up any "suspects," Robotti raged: "You're killing too few!"[384]

Convinced that the Italian imperialist cause was just, Robotti castigated Rome for a lack of support: few Italians fluent in the Slovene tongue had been supplied to spread the conqueror's message, and negligible help was received from Grazioli's police in stifling Communist propaganda. Furthermore, the Questura had failed to submit names of those to be shot in reprisal for Partisan killing of Italian soldiers and Slovene collaborators.[385] Although he, Robotti, had received power over the police, they were unwilling to share responsibility in punishing the Partisans. Everything was going wrong: the police performed poorly and his troops were prone to Communist "infection."[386] Robotti shot hostages in retaliation for Partisan butchery of collaborators as if the latter were Italian, but held all Slovenes in such contempt that only reluctantly did he tolerate the existence of the MVAC. Concerned about Italy's reputation, Robotti was equally determined to retrieve his own, which had been besmirched by unrelenting Partisan resistance. His lone answer was to hit back massively. "If necessary I will not hesitate to burn areas where the population feels moral and material solidarity with the rebels. I will adopt exemplary measures of severity that will serve as an admonishment to those who are irreducibly hostile and who take our just reactions for weakness and incapacity."[387] While Robotti thus moved to restore Italian military pride, Grazioli had come around to defining his "Pax Romana" by arrests and internments.

## Hurly-Burly Life in Dalmatia

In Dalmatia Italy inherited a domain of craggy mountains and little arable land. Impoverished peasants barely eked out a living, shepherds and their flocks grazed on rocky terrain, and fishermen cast their nets from a hauntingly beautiful coastline. Dalmatia had not exactly prospered under Yugoslav rule, and whatever economic life existed had been severely disrupted by war and the Italian occupation. Public services had broken down, unemployment was widespread, and hunger stalked a land wanting in primary necessities. Into this bleak scene entered Athos Bartolucci, former federal secretary of the Fascist party in Zara, appointed on 15 April 1941 as civil commissioner for the annexed Dalmatian zones. Greeted by hammer-and-sickle wall posters and Croatian irredentist propaganda, he went to work quickly by closing down all national Yugoslav organizations and purging "undesirable" functionaries from the administration. But perhaps because Bartolucci received a bad report card from a fellow Fascist, Inspector Giorgio Suppiej,[388] he was soon removed in favor of Giuseppe Bastianini, a Fascist of the first hour. Placed under the authority of Mussolini, Bastianini received the more exalted title of governor (governatore) on 18 May and established his headquarters in Zara. On the same day the notorious Fascist Temistocle Testa was named prefect of the province of Fiume, which had been enlarged beyond the wildest fantasies of Gabriele D'Annunzio. Dalmatia was divided into three provinces headed by Fascist prefects: Vezio Orazi in Zara, Paolo Zerbino in Spalato, and Francesco Sforzolini Scassellati in Cattaro.

Bastianini presided over a land inhabited by about 280,000 Croats, 90,000 Serbs, and from 4,000 to 5,000 Italians. Escorting him was a cohort of Fascists who not only alienated the local Croats but irritated the handful of their Italian compatriots living in Zara by bureaucratic posturing and an obvious disdain of local customs. At first Bastianini did little to encourage former Italian residents of Dalmatia, who had fled to the mainland after Yugoslavia was founded in 1919, to return home. Contrary to every expectation, after the Pact of Rome of 18 May the condition of Italian Dalmatians had deteriorated. Thanks to the jagged final territorial delineation, most of their land holdings on the islands of Brazza and Lesina or in the interior ended up as part of Croatia, which placed them at the mercy of an unsympathetic government in Zagreb.

Armed with a sheaf of Fascist reforms, the energetic Bastianini built on the Italianization program initiated by Bartolucci. This program held that Fascist Italy was finally in a position to eradicate the anti-Italian memories of the Habsburg Empire and the ex-Yugoslav regime that had practically stamped out the heritage of *La Serenissima Venezia*. The task of constructing Italian civilization from the ground up did not daunt Bastianini. He issued decrees that affected every aspect of social, economic, and political life in the annexed territory. Strict censorship was applied to the press and radio. Although use of the local language was permitted, Italian was made mandatory in both government business and in the telegraph and radio services. Government employees and teachers were required to speak Italian to keep their jobs; few were so qualified. Bilingualism was allowed in official correspondence, but communication between government bureaus had to be carried on in Italian. Croatian names of streets, districts, and villages were changed to Italian. All existing political associations and institutions not affiliated with the Fascist party were dissolved. Cultural and sporting clubs were liable to suspension and their goods confiscated. The school system, with the exception of the elementary grades and Catholic institutions, were singled out for special attention: "We inculcate in [the students] that which the millennia of civilization have given to our culture."[389] Stipends were set aside for trustworthy Dalmatians to study in Italy, taken advantage of by 52 Italians and 211 Croats and Serbs.[390]

On 12 April 1942 Bastianini summarized his views in a speech at Zara: "Those who do not wish that their spirit drink at the pure fountains of Virgil, Horace, and Dante, who would feel humiliated to become a part of that community which gave Volta, Petrarch and D'Annunzio, Michelangelo and Raphael, St. Francis and St. Benedict, need only to take the shortest road that leads to the frontier. Here Rome rules—language, science, and morality. The Lion of Saint Mark has returned, armed."[391] Bastianini's message was unmistakable: Italianize or emigrate.

The economy was brought under Italian control by currency manipulations that benefited the mainland at the expense of the local population. The lira was introduced as the sole legal tender of trade. Branches of Italian banks proliferated and Italian firms expropriated many Yugoslav enterprises: coal and bauxite mines, cement plants, electric power, chemical and aluminum factories, shipping, fish processors, banks, and insurance companies. The Institute for Industrial Reconstruction (Istituto per la Ricostruzione Industriale— IRI) seized control of the French electrical and chemical firm La Dalmatienne.[392] Bastianini issued a fiat to take over the promising network of farmers' cooperatives initiated by the Yugoslav government on the pretext of defending it from anti-Italian subversion. By this measure Bastianini gave himself the authority to dispossess the peasants of their lands unhampered by any legal constraints.

To overcome unemployment—and not incidentally, to glorify the imperium, Bastianini launched a comprehensive program of public works, reclamation projects, and road construction. Since trained personnel were in short supply and only limited funds were available, he faced major obstacles. True, thousands of Yugoslavs found work in these projects, but his major purpose, particularly in the reclamation efforts, was to clear areas for Italian settlers and their families. An exchange rate that favored the national treasury at the expense of Dalmatia hampered his efforts to generate an economic takeoff. To prevent Dalmatia from becoming a parasite of the mainland, Bastianini encouraged private investment. But venture capital was scarce and progress limited to small-scale enterprises in the more heavily populated towns along the coastline. A spiraling cost of living reduced the population to near penury.

Bastianini and the financiers in Italy were not fully responsible for Dalmatia's stagnation. The boundary makers in the Palazzo Chigi broke up a natural economic unity by fashioning a frontier that left important coal mines, water sources, and cement deposits in Croatia, while placing manufacturing facilities on the Italian side. Nature added to these man-made woes. The barren soil and defiant landscape resisted economic progress. Many isolated communes in the interior were unable to secure essential services, while the towns dotting the craggy coastline, cut off from each other by overhanging peaks, were thrown on their own devices. Handicapped by potholed roads and antiquated communications, and ringed by formidable mountains on three sides, Dalmatia survived like an island that lived by sea trade. This reality was made especially stark by Croatia's disposition to boycott trade with the Italian enclave as retaliation for annexation. The distance between Zara and Cattaro, broken by swaths of Croatian land, stymied coherent government as well. The combined factors of a tactless imperial rule, impassible topography, and a paucity of resources doomed Dalmatia to existence as a ward of the mainland for the necessities of life. Italy, however, itself short of provisions and financial wherewithal, was in no position to nourish its unhappy province.

Bastianini was determined to reform Dalmatian administration from top to bottom. A purge of "undesirable elements," i.e., all those native inhabitants hostile to Italy, had top priority. His problem was partially solved when many Serb and Croatian ex-Yugoslav bureaucrats took flight; in addition, he expelled or jailed approximately 4,000 deemed disloyal or potential 5th columnists, which included railroad workers, hospital attendants, and doctors.[393] Croat and Serb lawyers, notaries, pharmacists, and artists were proscribed. On 7 July Bastianini sent 700 "suspect civilians"—Serbs, Croatians, Communists, Jews, and criminals—for internment to Italy.[394]

There was the question of Italian citizenship. Under Bastianini's restrictive definition, citizens of Yugoslavia who had been born in annexed Dalmatia, or who had proven residency, or who had not been born in Dalmatia but had lived there for at least fifteen years and spoke fluent Italian, were eligible for citizenship. Would there be many takers? The immediate problem was to staff the school system. But since Bastianini had discharged so many "unreliable" teachers, and since there were so few Dalmatian Italians to replace them, he pleaded to Rome for a significant number fluent in Croatian. By the beginning of the fall semester, 741 elementary teachers, 93 for intermediate classical and jurisprudence study, and 32 principals would be needed.[395] The Minister of Education, Giuseppe Bottai, was at his wit's end trying to fulfill this request.[396]

Bastianini did not neglect ecclesiastical affairs. To eliminate the "ferociously anti-Italian" episcopal districts in Dalmatia, he placed them under the jurisdiction of the closely Italian-monitored archbishop of Zara. Italian became the required language for the rites of baptism, marriage, and death; prayers were to be conducted at the end of the sermons blessing the king of Italy.[397] The Slav peoples of Dalmatia, reduced to second-class status, greeted their Italian tormentors and their Italianization programs with marked indifference.

Italy's grandiose plans were immediately imperiled by a widespread breakdown of the administrative apparatus, due to the shortage of trained personnel that followed the purge of Yugoslav "undesirables." Troubles erupting in neighboring Croatia harried Bastianini too. Croatian officials, he wrote, were inefficient and debauched, and hardly lifted a finger to check the Ustaša violence that incited local Serbs to strike back.[398] The governor chastised Rome for permitting the reestablishment of Croatian authority in the demilitarized zones. He wondered why Italian troops should be ordered "to stand by inactive in the face of such acts carried out under their very eyes."[399] More dangerous still, the uneasy peace in Dalmatia was disrupted by a Partisan armed uprising that broke out in the latter part of July 1941 in Lika, just across the eastern border, which threatened to touch off insurrection in Dalmatia itself.

Bastianini took to his bunker. The Croats make war on the Serbs, impede commerce, and sponsor strikes in Spalato, he complained. Scratch a Dalmatian Croat and you find an irredentist, a Communist, or both. Enraged by Ustaša criminal acts against them, the Serbs strike back at them but don't attack the Italian military. The 2nd Army intervenes only to safeguard installations and railway lines. What about security and public order? Commercial activity is snarled by strikes, and Partisans disrupt daily life undeterred by an undermanned police force. Both Serbs and Croats defy Italy.[400] In his panic, Bastianini begged Ciano to seal Dalmatia off from external threats by allowing him to advance the "line of vigilance" to the outer rim of the demilitarized area and grant the military untrammeled liberty of action against a force "of about 10,000 "rebels.""[401] Since the NDH had already become a German fief, Bastianini pointed out, Croatian protests could be ignored.[402]

The Dalmatian governor drew other ominous conclusions. Attracted by the Marxist message, the native inhabitants of his province were driven by a partly rebellious, partly barbarian instinct.[403] The Communists, by insinuating themselves in Croatian and Serb movements, had worked to bury their ethnic differences in the higher purpose of expelling the Roman civilizer.[404] Bastianini perceived the embryo of a functioning Yugoslav Communist movement rooted in Spalato and Cattaro and orchestrated by Moscow.[405] By resolute action he was able to crush a Communist insurgency during the summer led by workers in Spalato and Sebenico.

Bastianini's belief that Croats and Serbs were already conspiring against Italy during the summer months of 1941 was sheer imagination; he was on firmer ground in pointing out that Croats hated Italy. Indeed, Zagreb had a field day stirring up irredentist passion. Doubtless, the boundaries of Dalmatia, having been drawn up by outlaw occupiers bent on blocking national unity, were unjust. The Ustaša was no less angry at Italy than the mainstream Croat. This so-called spiritual kin of Fascist Italy maligned Bastianini's Fascist government, beat up Serbs, and picked fights with Italians. Nazi and Gestapo agents—Coselschi estimated 2,000—were no less a plague by telling everybody that Germany would deliver Italian-occupied Dalmatia to Croatia once the Allies had been crushed. The small knot of Dalmatian Italians braced for the worst.

By fall 1941 Bastianini's Italianization programs had barely left a mark. Instead of presiding over a smooth transition from ex-Yugoslav "barbarism" to Italian Fascist civilization, the governor encountered insurrection. He replied with a flurry of repressive orders based on Mussolini's proclamations of 3 and 18 May. On 11 October the death penalty was decreed for membership in Communist and other subversive organizations, civil disobedience, and other ill-defined abuses.[406] To discourage dissidence Bastianini rounded up hostages and legitimized reprisals.[407] To keep the factories humming, he promised to break strikes ruthlessly and fire or jail refractory workers. Frustrated by the "silence" [omertà] of the population, Bastianini resorted to arbitrary household searches for hidden weapons and suspected Communists. Curfews were imposed and Fascist squads sent around to enforce them.

As protests increased against his regime, Bastianini beseeched Rome for additional police powers to crack down on the "troublemakers." On 28 October Mussolini granted him jurisdiction over a special tribunal that expanded the definition of criminality and re-inforced punishment. Those who threatened the integrity of the state, who belonged to subversive "armed bands," and who committed violent acts against Italian military and civilian personnel were subject to the death penalty. Jail sentences were meted out to those participating in conspiracies against the state, strikes, and worker slowdowns. The same fate befell people caught with illegal firearms and who spread false information.[408]

To maintain peace and enforce the civilian administration's edicts, the governor disposed of the forces of public order: the gendarmerie, financial guards, border police, and Blackshirt militia. A large part of the XVIII Army Corps was deployed in Dalmatia to firm up the governor's authority. To strengthen his security forces, Bastianini procured units from the "Milano" Squads and two Fascist "M" battalions. Such preoccupation with force did not cause Bastianini to neglect his imperial mission. "I will win over this population not just by oral promises but by the reality of civilizing political and social policies of Rome and our Fascist state."[409]

On 19 January 1942 the Duce defined Dalmatia, Slovenia, and Croatian territory garrisoned by the Italian armed forces as military "zones of operation."[410] The civilian forces of public order would be placed under military authority. For Bastianini, to have the laws of war applied to Dalmatia was both embarrassing and an infringement on his power, for the annexed areas were supposed to be part of a safe and secure metropolitan Italy under civilian authority, not a "battle zone" or a no-man's-land subject to military law, as in the Italian-occupied areas of Bosnia and Herzegovina.[411]

Not surprisingly, General Quirino Armellini, commander of the XVIII Army Corps, whose headquarters were in Spalato, was pleased to learn that Mussolini regarded annexed Dalmatia as a "zone of operation" under his direct authority. Bastianini, on the other hand, complained bitterly to the Duce over his loss of power. Pietromarchi records his discontent:

Yesterday the Duce met with Bastianini and Buffarini-Guidi. He received them very coldly. Bastianini was determined to resign.

He spoke with his usual passion, highlighting the things he had accomplished, the peace he obtained, the responsibilities he took by having the rebels executed. Why deprive him of all power? "It is not appropriate to have the military authority guard public order," he said. "Why?" asked the Duce. "Because they say that you are a clown." "Who?" "The Commander of the 149th infantry." Buffarini-Guidi, moving anxiously his enormous body, then asked Bastianini why he interpreted the decree as something against him. "Shut up," Bastianini answered. "I don't let anybody make fun of me."[412]

Mussolini backed down on the 24th by restoring the forces of public order to civilian authority, but only in Dalmatia, not Slovenia.[413] Bastianini, however, barely had time to breathe when, surprised by Mussolini's flip-flop, Armellini took exception over having to perform police functions at the governor's whim and informed Bastianini of his discontent. Tempers flared. Bastianini demanded that he have the authority to deploy regular troops alongside the public security forces in military operations against the insurgents. But Armellini, aiming to defend the military prerogative in supervising counterinsurgency, intended to limit Bastianini to the police function of maintaining public order.[414] *Déjà vu*, the same kind of dispute as in Slovenia between Grazioli and Robotti.

The governor was not amiss in pointing to unresolved logistical problems and faulty troop deployment. Defense of Dalmatia was needlessly complicated by unwieldy organization: he sat in Zara and the XVIII Army Corps resided in distant Spalato. Far from his eye, Bastianini observed, the army floundered in serious military error. Units were sporadically released for search and destroy missions and ordered back to barracks located in areas far from the Communist-infested cities and troubled borderlands. This hardly provided security to a harassed population or relief for an overworked police force.[415]

In spring 1942 Armellini admitted the need for reform. He was served by unruly subordinates bearing conflicting orders, he had no interpreter, no reliable translators, and no effective intelligence service. The garrisons strung out on the Dalmatian frontier were isolated, short of food and provisions, and vulnerable to attack. Roads were heaped up by snow or rendered unsafe by Partisan incursions. In defiance of the prefects, who annoyed him by ordering around the troops that garrisoned local military posts, Armellini wanted to close down the remote command posts and pull back soldiers for retraining as a mobile fighting force.[416]

Bastianini reacted in disbelief. Denuded of outposts, Dalmatia would become a Partisan playground.[417] If it were up to the governor, he would reinforce the lightly manned and isolated forts by building a "Chinese Wall" of garrisons along the frontier to seal Dalmatia off from Partisan infiltration.[418] But since Armellini dithered and scattered his troops about "indifferently,"[419] Bastianini would go over his head by appealing directly to Roatta: "Together, you and I" will find a solution to prevent Partisans fleeing the 2nd Army's *rastrellamenti* in neighboring Croatia from deluging Dalmatia.[420] The governor played on three themes that resonated loud and clear in Rome: Armellini had underrated the Communist menace, was delinquent in providing defense, and seemed unaware that Italian prestige would be shattered if Dalmatia fell to the insurgents.[421] For his part, Armellini dismissed Bastianini as a hothead who overestimated the Partisan threat.[422]

On 26 May in broad daylight the Partisans cut down the prefect of Zara, Vezio Orazi. In the spirit of Mussolini's speech a week before glorifying the squads and their motto "*me ne frego,*" Bastianini swiftly ordered ruthless reprisals. Three hundred and fifty Blackshirts reinforced by an "M" battalion torched 80 houses, shot 12 Communists, and tore up the countryside.[423] Bastianini boasted to Mussolini that the border population had been favorably impressed by the swift and successful operation in areas where the "rebels" had previously moved about freely. "I am pleased that the Black Shirts . . . have revealed the same spirit of the squads of yesteryear; we have shown the enemies of Fascism that here squad methods are seriously applied . . . They [the Blackshirts] are the only ones capable of breaking Communism and its guerrillas wherever they are."[424] Further harsh measures ensued. On 7 June Bastianini ordered the roundup of hostages among Partisan family members, restricted the movement of the population, compiled lists of suspected persons, halted provisions to areas crowded with suspected rebels, and decreed that all sympathizers be shot.[425]

In this overheated environment, Blackshirt gangs stormed and sacked the synagogue of Spalato in mid June, spreading terror in the neighborhood until finally brought to order by the Carabinieri.[426] Another raid netted 700 so-called Communists whom Bastianini ticketed for the concentration camp of Melàda.[427] Internment of Partisan families was designed to cut off the "rebels" from their supplies and therefore to isolate them. In a report to Mussolini in early July, Bastianini blustered over yet another "meritorious" punitive expedition under his leadership. In such actions of "disinfection" there were many enemy casualties and few Italian losses. Proudly he reported the arrest of all insurgent families in Dalmatia.[428] In a hardly veiled criticism of Armellini, Bastianini boasted that the Blackshirts carried out their missions with much more dispatch than the ponderous military in areas "infested" with Partisans.[429] Once the insurgents had been rooted out, Bastianini was convinced that offers of clemency and conciliation would persuade them to lay down their arms and return home.[430]

Armellini was greatly exercised over Bastianini's employment of unsavory Blackshirts.[431] In his view the squadrista mentality provoked rebellion and disgraced Italy.[432] He deplored their incendiary attack on a Jewish synagogue—looked on with tacit approval by the local police—and reported that the Fascist culprits harassed the military sent to quell the violence.[433] (Armellini did admit that certain military personnel participated in the destruction and looting of Jewish property.[434]) "No one denies the existence of the sun—that sqadrismo saved Italy. But the ambience of 1919-20-21-22 in Italy is not the ambience of 1941–1942 in Dalmatia. The venerated system of the club and castor oil that was employed then no longer serves a useful purpose now."[435]

To overcome Armellini's "negligence," Bastianini set up a military cabinet under his own authority to direct repression. To remedy a shortage of troops, he supplemented the existing security forces—Carabinieri, border guards, and police—with an anti-Communist militia, whose first volunteers were Orthodox Serbs later joined by Croatian Catholics.[436] The potential advantages, in his mind, were great: local recruits who knew the terrain, the nature of the resistance, and the language the Partisans spoke. But the recruitment bar was set high; a militia member must loyally accept Dalmatia as Italian and be militantly anti-Communist. The governor would reciprocate by providing volunteers supplies, family protection against reprisals, and land expropriated from "undesirable elements."

Armellini was dismayed by the governor's energetic invasion of the military sphere. He wrote off Bastianini's gubernatorial military cabinet as a reckless power grab and warned him to keep his hands off the Carabinieri.[437] Bastianini's fighting force consisted of a "dysfunctional and dangerous" motley array of police agents and anti-Communist volunteers, organized by a pseudo-military cabinet under a bogus commander in the person of the governor.[438] Having two armies, two heads, and two systems dissipated cohesion, squandered energy, and sent mixed signals. He, Armellini, should be the unchallenged military czar of Dalmatia.[439]

The two men carried their quarrel beyond military deployment and strategy and the nature of the threat facing them into the dangerous realm of politics. Bastianini argued that insurgents pouring into Dalmatia from Italian-occupied Croatia upset a natural domestic tranquility, while Armellini held that insurgency erupted from within—an outgrowth of wrong-headed policy. Instead of winning over the population with benign rule, Armellini mentioned, the governor inspired hate by brutal repression.[440] Indeed, in his view, Bastianini was part of the problem.[441] It was ridiculous for him to claim that "behind the weak and insecure façade, the heart of Dalmatia beats in harmony with the heart of the mother country."[442] Worse still, Armellini suggested darkly, Italy had committed a radical error in creating a Blackshirt Italian government in Dalmatia.[443]

His resigned views on the flawed nature of Italian imperialism veered toward anti-Fascism. Small wonder that he, a skeptic, and Bastianini, a first-wave romantic Fascist, sparred like pugilists in a ring.

As was his wont, Bastianini took his case against Armellini directly to the Duce, claiming that he was incompetent and that the squads moved far more aggressively than the military's lumbering legions.[444] This was the last straw for the commander of the XVIII Army Corps. A further exchange of vituperative letters between the two men ensued in which the normal civilities were completely ignored. Roatta tried to prevent an explosion, but nothing could stop Bastianini from bringing the dispute to a head by an extraordinarily vitriolic denunciation dated 15 July 1942:

> As long as I am in my position and you are in yours, the reciprocal attributes are: the civil authority, with all its organs, are under my orders and the military authority with its assigned troops are yours. I carry out the administrative policy and you fight the war. To put it bluntly: I do not like polemics and to engage in such before the enemy disgusts me. For the past two months, the province of Zadar has been infested with rebels. I was assured that the situation would be re-established within a few days. I requested you to bring the territory of the province of Zadar back to normality, adopting such criteria and measures of action that you desired, provided the objective was attained. Such a request did not exceed my mission, and I desired to give it maximum weight . . . you consider the government of Dalmatia a thing that has no reason for existence and that it should be abolished and be turned over to the command of troops, which come and go, depart and return in Italian Dalmatia . . . It would not be useful for Italy—if your very apparent mode of reasoning were to be applied—because it would demonstrate to the Allies and our enemies that Italy had to turn to the military government in order to maintain itself in Dalmatia. Nevertheless, as long as there is a governorship of Dalmatia, do me the favor of letting it carry out its work in peace. I am not one of your subordinates or one you merely tolerate. I have been serv-

ing my country and my leader in peace and war for a quarter
of a century. I am more inclined towards action than polemics.
To every one of my entreaties, requests, or opinions, from the
very first days that I met you and received you with cordiality,
you have opposed with difficulties, contrariness, and polemics.
I operate in my field, in the sphere assigned to me by the Duce
and by law. I ask you to cooperate in yours, to attack the rebel
formations that are raiding the territory of Zadar [Zara] from
one end to the other.[445]

Bastianini followed up with a letter to Roatta, rebuking Armellini
for his argumentative temperament and lack of respect toward a
governor holding equal rank.[446] Bastianini's secretary, Egidio Ortona,
noted in his diary:

What happened today can be defined as the complete break with
the military authorities ... From now on a harsh and bitter skir-
mish has opened with drawn swords in which the governor is
ready to take the worst consequences and the military will not
distinguish themselves in tenderness.[447]

Bastianini's poisoned arrows hit an already wounded warrior,[448]
for Armellini's belated admission that Dalmatia's security was indeed
imperiled by a stepped-up Partisan insurgency exposed him to the
governor's charge that he was a lightweight with flawed judgment.
Moreover, by questioning Italy's imperial mission, Armellini had
broken ranks with his military peers, which deprived him of protection against the Fascist chain of command. Roatta prepared to
abandon him as "a Badoglio man,"[449] and for this was severely rebuked by his understudy General Giacomo Zanussi, the assistant
chief of staff of the 2nd Army, who accused him of failing to stand
up for a general "of the caliber and valor of Armellini."[450] Without
further ado, the Duce swung the axe. Armellini would go. Mussolini
really had no choice, for obliging Bastianini to resign instead of dis-
missing Armellini would have been an admission that the Fascist
regime in Dalmatia had failed. General Umberto Spigo took over

the XVIII Army Corps on 8 August and Armellini was assigned other duties in Italy.[451]

In frustration, Roatta uttered: "Don't we cut a fine figure! To have no courage, that is our problem."[452] General Zanussi reflected: "The disagreement between Bastianini and Armellini, which I had often called to Roatta's attention, counseling him to request, Solomon-like, the removal of both, and which he had sought to heal, ended, as it had to end, with the sudden recall of the commander of the army corps . . . which the governor, pressuring Rome, had intrigued for and obtained without Roatta knowing anything about it."[453]

In a conclave held in Rome on 1 August, Bastianini tried to bring his victory home by urging Cavallero to set up a unified command headquartered in Zara, where the XVIII Army Corps could be carefully supervised by the governor of Dalmatia.[454] Roatta sidetracked this proposal by dwelling on the impropriety of Blackshirt violence, which reflected poorly on Bastianini's ability to manage Italy's counterinsurgency. Cavallero picked up the cue by placing the "M" battalions and Fascist squads under the XVIII Army Corps command, adding that the army would hold primary responsibility for the defense of Dalmatia. This fully satisfied Roatta, who was ready to reach "a gentleman's agreement" with Bastianini confirming that a "united front" of all military branches and forces of public order existed under the command of the 2nd Army as spelled out in Mussolini's edict of 19 January.[455] Bastianini was left with a Pyrrhic victory. Unable to reap military profit from Armellini's dismissal, he ended up where he had started, as constable of public order.[456]

As fall approached Bastianini sank ever deeper in insurgent turbulence. In despair he wrote that Partisans hacked away at convoys, cut communications, raided supply depots, blew up aqueducts, and ambushed solitary soldiers without retribution. The Croatian population stared indifferently during Italian ceremonies, while Communist propaganda found fertile ground among a people fed up with confiscations and harassment. The mounting insurgency, coupled with Italian military slothfulness, he lamented, foretold imminent disaster. The troops, holed up in isolated fortresses, allowed the "rebels" to intimidate the loyal inhabitants by selective assassination of suspected collaborators. Out of fear of Partisan reprisals workers stayed home. The economy was paralyzed. Although defiantly affirming that the final residue of Yugoslav officialdom had been extinguished, he failed to mention that local administration had practically ceased to exist.[457] Having allegedly sighted a vast number of enemy submarines, Bastianini was convinced that Allied troops were poised to land on the Dalmatian beaches in an invasion coordinated with Partisans, who were supposedly massed on the frontier. The military, he held, was culpable for underestimating Partisan strength and neglect of shoreline defenses.[458] He demanded reinforcements.

Roatta replied with a series of "it is not exact that . . . ," which did not exactly refute the veracity of Bastianini's reports, but added up to the opinion that "rebel" attacks were on a small scale, sporadic, and on the way to rapid elimination.[459] Still, Roatta, referring to Mussolini's statement of 31 July, encouraged the governor to extend his punitive edicts by confiscating immovable property as well as personal belongings of rebels, their accomplices, and sympathizers.[460] Cavallero, aware that Bastianini held Mussolini's ear, hoped to dodge the Duce's expected bullet by sending Bastianini an additional division in mid October. But, as Ortona realized, this was only a stopgap measure that would hardly staunch the rising Partisan threat.[461] It never crossed Bastianini's mind that the root cause of insurrection in Dalmatia was neither Partisan activity nor the military's incompetence in handling it, but an imperialism infused with Fascist "reforms" that had alienated the overwhelmingly Slav majority of Dalmatia from day one of the Italian occupation. Unmoved by a Marxism that prescribed class warfare and a future Proletarian wonderland, many Dalmatian Croats were eventually drawn to Tito's standards because the Partisans, much more convincingly than the Ustaša regime, were organizing a resistance to liberate Dalmatia from imperial Italy.

From his bastion in Dalmatia, Bastianini ruled like a miniature Duce. Supported by a fanatical following, he promulgated

Italianization programs to no avail. Seemingly unaware of the bankruptcy of his imperial policies, Bastianini wrote in November, a few months before his departure, that without Italian colonizers, "our political and military expansion would have only a provisional character."[462] His Dalmatian *civiltà italiana* implied the exact opposite of a pluralistic society. Contemptuous of multicultural diversity, Bastianini demanded the obliteration of the historical memory and civilizations of the native peoples under his rule.[463]

# Chapter V

# Friends and Enemies

Roatta's Counterinsurgency
Musical Chairs with the Četniks
Operation *Trio*
Partisan-Free Montenegro
Stressed Out by "Allies"

*Roatta's Counterinsurgency*

On an inspection tour, just before taking charge of the 2nd Army on 19 January 1942, General Mario Roatta discovered how untidy the Italian occupation in Yugoslavia was. Feuds between the Italian civilian authorities and 2nd Army commanders raged without letup in Slovenia and Dalmatia. In the 2nd and 3rd zones a hodge-podge of ethnic groups and diverse religions defied uniform treatment. Ustaša violence and the NDH authorities obstructed the 2nd Army at every turn. An endless train of military and civilian representatives from Rome, Berlin, and Zagreb crowded into army headquarters at Sušak dispensing advice, lodging complaints, and competing for power and influence. Četniks darted in and out of the far-flung command posts seeking equipment and favored treatment.

Nor did order prevail in the strictly military sphere. Troops huddled in forts in the craggy mountains of the Lika region were under siege by Partisan forces, Tito roamed freely in eastern Bosnia, the Italian army had unleashed a major crackdown in Ljubljana, and no one could predict when or where the Partisans would strike next. Confusion reigned in the command centers. There were no Axis joint chiefs of staff in the Anglo-American mold to provide a framework for systematic planning and oversight of agreed-upon strategy. Meetings between the Axis generals were ad hoc and irregular, with every detail subject to negotiation. Each Axis partner fought its own anti-insurgent war and negotiated behind the other's back with both friend and foe. The suspicion and uncertainty that dominated life between the two Axis Powers gave the Croats and Četniks space in which to conduct their own deadly struggle.

When General Roatta took up his position as commander of the 2nd Army, he realized that to suppress the Partisans and their hidden networks throughout Yugoslavia, he would have to work out a coherent and flexible military policy. Thanks to the liberty of action afforded him by the 2nd Army's privileged position in the chain of command (it answered to the chief of staff rather than to the Supreme Command), Roatta would not be under the direct thumb of his rival, General Ugo Cavallero, Mussolini's current military favorite in Rome. Nor was he subjected to close scrutiny by the Duce. Preoccupied by events on other fronts, Mussolini paid only sporadic attention to the Balkan theater until forced to do so by Hitler when an Allied invasion of the Balkans appeared imminent in early 1943.

Roatta believed that a thorough and efficient suppression of rebellion could not proceed until unity of command had been achieved by placing the civilian public security forces at the disposal of the 2nd Army.[464] But he had to make his way carefully. Sudden and sweeping moves against the civilian Fascist overlords might inspire Mussolini to extra vigilance in protecting their prerogatives against military encroachment. In the long run, however, nothing would stop Roatta from usurping the police functions of Italian civilian authority in the annexed territories. Moreover, in his determination to establish untrammeled military domination in areas declared "zones of military operation," Roatta would not hesitate to infringe upon the sovereignty of the NDH in Italian-occupied Croatia. Mussolini, he gambled, would support strong-armed and decisive military leadership over less competent Fascist underlings and intractable allies in Zagreb.

From the military standpoint, Roatta pondered two options. The first involved wide-ranging troop movements to hold the vast expanses conquered and occupied by his predecessor, General Vittorio Ambrosio. Yet Ambrosio had undertaken this expansionist program without sufficient reinforcements of trained and seasoned troops, a firm understanding with the Četniks, or an agreeable German ally. Overextended and spread too thinly, his troops were not infrequently cut off and encircled. Failing correctives to these problems, Roatta adopted a second course: the protection of strategic points and important cities to reinforce the key forts, "similar to medieval castles,"[465] to be placed along pivotal railroads and lines of communication. Remote outposts would be abandoned and the rugged terrain and wastelands left to the Partisans. Italy would thereby be spared heavy losses and wear and tear of its equipment. The consolidated troops would be retrained as a mobile force to conduct hardhitting offenses against the Partisans.

At the outset of the Italian occupation, no particular defense measures were taken. The troops filed in expecting easy duty in comfortable barracks and pleasant company in popular cafes and bars. But in July 1941 the peaceful spring was shattered. Outbreaks of insurgency by the Partisan enemy caught the troops unprepared and bewildered by the unorthodox tactics employed. Dispersed throughout the countryside in isolated pockets, the Italians were killed singly and in groups. Without the benefit of helicopters to locate the enemy, their regiments, trained for conventional warfare, frequently fought ghost battles. When confronted by superior numbers or firepower, the guerrillas took to the hills or retreated to their

villages, hid their weapons, and blended in with civilians till the occupying forces left for their barracks. On 6 January 1942 Ciano noted:
"Our public-relations officer with the second army in Croatia sends
bad news on the situation and on the morale of the troops. Some
units permitted themselves to be captured without firing a shot."[466]

General Roatta quickly discovered that the Italian military,
weaned on the trench warfare and defined fronts of World War I,
was unable to cope with a wholly different type of conflict in Yugoslavia. Commanders in the field were "indescribably confused"
by guerrilla tactics and did not adjust easily to Partisan hit-and-run
behavior.[467] Their troops were locked up in the forts and sallied forth
against the guerrillas—who sometimes posed as civilians—only
when superiority in numbers and weaponry assured the success of
mass operations in open fields. While such *rastrellamenti* exacted a
heavy toll on the enemy, withdrawal to the safety of the forts enabled the Partisans to stream back into the countryside.

If, in the eyes of the High Command, the Italian foot soldiers
stationed in the Balkans for occupation duty lacked sufficient mettle,
it was certainly not their fault alone. Rigidity and backwardness in
the military hierarchy worked their way from the top down, and the
officer class was filled with nitpickers and martinets. Furthermore,
Yugoslavia was not the posting for Italy's crack divisions, and the
second-line soldier suffered confusion over whether he was serving as an imperial mercenary or defender of the motherland. Frequently he was unaware that his country was involved in a war of
aggression, or that he was imposing hardship on defenseless and
innocent people. Fighting a guerrilla war that involved repression
of civilians eventually brutalized the mind and impoverished the
spirit, which rendered the troops susceptible to committing atrocities no less dismaying than those of the Fascist battalions.

Aware of the sinking morale, General Ambrosio had already
pointed out that the Italian soldiers lacked the "indomitable will to
annihilate the adversary." There was "a crisis of combative will."[468]
Some Italian soldiers, puzzled by duty in remote mountainous regions, concluded that they were caught in an "unjust" war; others,
demoralized by beastly weather and mediocre provisions, longed to

quit and go home; a few, susceptible to Communist propaganda, lost the will to fight an opponent bravely defending his land against an imperial invader.[469] Hundreds deserted and became hospital orderlies and cooks in Partisan units.[470] The majority of officers and troops, however, fought bravely out of patriotism, pride, and a sense of duty, if not from deep conviction. The threat of a firing squad and other lesser but humiliating punishments for desertion or talking back also served as powerful reminders to carry on. It was the Fascist units that showed élan and an aggressive spirit in pursuing Partisans or carrying out reprisals and executions. If Roatta was never a champion of "squadrismo," he, like the Blackshirts and generals the world over, scorned the hang-dog attitude, defeatism, and failure of nerve that defined more than a handful of Italian soldiers in Yugoslavia.

In an effort to recover the initiative by clarifying and unifying all phases of military operations, General Roatta crafted a comprehensive new program. This appeared in the form of a printed pamphlet, Circular 3C, which was distributed among his commanders on 1 March 1942.[471] The program called for novel tactics and maneuvers by smaller units in commando-style action against a mobile and unseen enemy. Roatta's handbook bristled with didactic instructions on how to upgrade fighting skills.

High on Roatta's agenda was to extinguish the opprobrious notion, "bono italiano." That many good-natured soldiers should mingle easily with the local inhabitants whom they were supposed to oppress annoyed many an Italian commander.[472] Mussolini, offended by the "excessive exaltation" of the Slavs displayed by the Italian troops, noted that this attitude betrayed a failure to "feel" the war. In lacking the certainty of victory, the conqueror had lost the respect of the enemy.[473] Roatta expounded on this theme. Lassitude, sloppy deportment, and friendly contact with the conquered peoples must yield to a "forbidding face" and a steely determination to destroy the enemy. The nature of guerrilla warfare, characterized by booby-traps and ambushes, did not admit repose or carelessness. Under his direction, the 2nd Army reinforced the existing program of indoctrination by inculcating in the troops the notion that the enemy "rebel" defiled human values. The struggle was reduced to one between "civilization" and "barbarism," the redoubtable standard-bearer of Rome pitted against the enemy "bandit." If victorious, the infidel "Bolshevik" would plunder and burn the homeland in the style of Attila the Hun.[474]

There was an important unstated assumption in Roatta's thinking that was shared by many of his commanders. Stung by caustic German criticism that the Italian soldiers lacked the will to crush rebellion, many Italian generals—no lovers of the Wehrmacht—were determined to prove that they were their equals in cruelty and perseverance. The vanquished Balkan peoples must be taught to fear and respect the Roman legionnaire no less than they did the Teutonic warrior. Generals like Roatta hungered to be esteemed as imperial marshals who magnanimously dispensed justice to beaten and reverential subjects as in the days of ancient Rome. The tranquility of the docile would be observed, but those who sullied Italian prestige or the honor of the military could expect "exemplary" punishment.

Roatta went out of his way to point out that Italy was involved in "abnormal" warfare with insurgents, where the traditional rules of engagement had given way to lawlessness. The entire Italian-occupied territory, he declared, was a battlefield; the soldiers faced not only criminal "bandits," but also secretly armed and malevolent bystanders anxious to waylay unsuspecting troops at every turn. Save for a handful of collaborators, the enemy was everyone and the front everywhere. All civilians were potential "rebels." In this climate, civilian and insurgent, male and female, parent and child, were indistinguishable as potential killers of Italian troops. This was no job for untrained and squeamish civilian Italian functionaries, Roatta maintained; the military should have a free hand to crush any sign of rebelliousness and crack down on disrespectful behavior on the part of the indigenous population.

Before Roatta's tenure at the 2nd Army, General Ambrosio had already adopted the linguistic usage employed in Italian memoranda on counterinsurgency by decreeing on 23 October 1941 that "captured rebels are to be immediately shot."[475] A "rebel" was a "bandit" who fell outside laws protecting war prisoners. Clandestine activists, people suspected of giving support to the resistance, and unarmed populations with no known political allegiance were to be brought before the firing squad (*passare per le armi*).

Armed with this precedent, Roatta wrote a long chapter in his 3C pamphlet on counterinsurgency strategy to provide security for the troops against civilian sabotage. His list of punishments for a multitude of transgressions was long and detailed. In locations deemed "abnormal" (imminent or actual war zones), males between sixteen and sixty were liable to internment. To intimidate the population, hostages in territories of operation would be rounded up among social groups and professionals deemed "dangerous." "Treacherous aggressions" against Italian military and civilians justified the taking of hostages, who would be shot in reprisal if the "bandits" who had escaped refused to come forward and admit their "crimes" within 48 hours. In areas declared war zones, Roatta gave his commanders a free hand. And not to worry about the consequences: "*Let it be understood that excessive reactions, undertaken in good faith, will never be prosecuted.*" In this environment of hate, there would be no taking of prisoners. "The treatment dealt the rebels ought not to be synthesized by the formula 'tooth for a tooth' but by a 'head for a tooth.'"[476]

Roatta reserved his greatest fury for the Partisans who were disrupting life in the annexed areas. To uproot rebellion, he proclaimed: intern family members, sympathizers, and all males absent from their homes without a clear motive; reduce ration cards of all those suspected of collaboration with the "rebels."[477] Roatta inserted new clauses in the original 3C publication by means of Order 7000, issued on 7 April. In areas of ongoing operations, all men of fighting age, with or without arms, captured in the immediate vicinity of rebel action, or in zones of military operation, and all men and women who do not live in those areas, will be arrested for interrogation or interned. During military operations, if circumstances dictated, a commander should not hesitate to clear out and intern civilians singly, by family, in groups, or in entire villages. But here Roatta issued a word of caution: "Inconsiderate and useless destruction" must be avoided. Villages should be razed and individuals shot only when proof was provided of participation or connivance in insurgency. Desist from the destruction of churches, schools, and hospitals, he exhorted his commanders, reminding them that local populations were often constrained by Partisans to provide shelter and provisions against their will and not infrequently were told to abandon their dwellings.

Appendix "B" of this circular 7000 reads: "Rebels caught with arms will be immediately shot on the spot." Exceptions were made for the wounded, minors under eighteen, and women who would be dispatched to ordinary tribunals for judgment.[478] Roatta specifically instructed that Appendix "B" not be inserted in the 3C document and ordered his commanders to inform their troops of its contents orally. The Slovene historian Tone Ferenc speculates that Roatta excluded Appendix "B" from the official printed record because he knew it constituted a flagrant violation of international law.[479]

As Italy's efforts to suppress the Partisans flagged, Roatta on 1 December 1942 issued a broader version of his earlier 3C counterinsurgency pamphlet. Among the new provisions, he decreed that hostages drawn from the "suspect part" of the population should include "the upper classes," who would pay with their lives if Italian soldiers experienced "treacherous aggressions." Roatta gave his commanders license to confiscate farm animals and destroy villages of those who gave aid and comfort to insurgents attacking military installations and transportation facilities. Inhabitants near areas where sabotage had been verified would be declared accomplices subject to internment. Homesteads used by snipers or containing explosives or weapons, or which belonged to Partisans or those sympathetic to their cause, merited destruction. But once again Roatta inserted a word of caution: outright pillaging of houses, including those earmarked for destruction, "*must be impeded with preventive measures and, if necessary, with draconian repressions.*"[480]

In January 1943, in preparation for a large German-planned expedition dubbed Operation *Weiss*, Roatta issued orders that all males eighteen and over should be shot at once if found in operation zones; all other civilians rounded up in these areas were to be arrested and sent to concentration camps and their houses burnt to the ground.[481] The brutality evidenced in Roatta's writings on repression exposes an unashamed denial of justice and respect for the occupied peoples of Yugoslavia.

Mussolini found little to criticize in the 2nd Army's ruthless counterinsurgency programs. He certainly favored them over the assimilation ideas of his Fascist governors. But he seemed in the main to be a passive spectator in Rome who only directly intervened in Yugoslavia on the spur of the moment to posture or to grab headlines, as in his 31 July 1942 speech. Counterinsurgency was not a program Mussolini worked out in Rome and delivered to Sušak for implementation. He merely rubber-stamped Roatta's codification and expansion of the 2nd Army's on-going repression of the Yugoslav peoples.

If Roatta needed an example of repression to copy, he had no further to look than the example set by the Germans, who had already acquainted the Balkan peoples with brutish occupation. Enmeshed in the strife that engulfed Serbia in fall 1941, General Wilhelm List, commander of the German Army Southeast, ordered his troops to intern all men, kill resisters, and drive women and children off the land and into the mountains. To deny the insurgents food supplies, General List was prepared to reduce their providers, the Serb people, to starvation. The approach of General Franz Böhme, the German commander in Serbia, was no different. All men were to be arrested and interned in newly constructed prisons or concentration camps; women and children were to be driven from their homes; villages were to be burned and livestock confiscated. He made sure that there was always a plentiful hostage pool available to fulfill the promised ratio of 100 Serbs shot for every German killed.[482]

## Musical Chairs with the Četniks

When General Roatta first arrived in January 1942 as commander of the 2nd Army, he was prepared to follow the edict of Rome to destroy the Partisans in cooperation with the NDH. The Hitler-Mussolini partnership and the existing ties between the

Croatian and German officers worked against any other policy.[483] But Roatta was no ordinary general who carried out orders to suit a given political line; he was a cold realist who knew how to dodge them when circumstances required. Based on the example of the Greek campaign, he quickly realized that Italy's military was not up to the task of vast sweeps against a formidable Partisan foe. Instead of relying solely on force, Roatta would achieve mastery over Croatia by deal-making with the Četniks. This notion, however, ran counter to existing policy in Rome. Pietromarchi held that since the Četniks were enemies of the Axis, there should be no political negotiations with them.[484] Ambrosio, however, as army chief of staff, was prepared to give Roatta leeway. In "struggling to the bitter end" against the Partisans, he advised, cooperate with the Četniks, but "*avoid negotiations*" and any binding commitments. Respect the NDH as an ally but contain Ustaša disorder.[485] Knowing how to profit from Ambrosio's ambiguous orders, and ready to add Četnik units to his own forces, Roatta was the right man to extract Italy from a precarious military situation.

As a splintered organization under the sway of self-reliant warlords and civilian notables, the Četnik movement was no easy ally, and Mihailović, their titular leader, was hardly a pillar of support. By promoting Mihailović to general and war minister in January 1942, the Yugoslav government-in-exile made him doyen among Četnik leaders. His following, in turn, looked up to him as a charismatic figure who could provide moral guidance. The Italians were aware of Mihailović's pro-Allied views and did not trust him. By bestowing money and weapons on local Četnik leaders, they hoped to wean them from their remote chieftain. As loyal subordinates dependent on the 2nd Army, the Četniks could choose to fight or be neutral. The bottom line was that they must not fire on Italian troops. Angry Serbs who had survived the Ustaša roundups provided a harvest for Roatta's recruiting agents.

But there was a fatal flaw in the developing Četnik-Italian partnership. Under pressure from Rome, the Italian commanders felt obliged to accord their Croatian "ally" formal respect and weapons deliveries. Rather than fighting Partisans, however, the Croats lost no time in training their acquired Italian guns on Orthodox Serbs. Having hoped to establish a privileged relationship with the 2nd Army, the Četnik leaders concluded from this that every agreement they reached with Italian military commanders would be tenuous.

The principal Italian ally among the Četniks in the Dinaric Alps and Lika sector was the Orthodox cleric Momčilo Djujić, "the occult head of the entire Serb movement in the area,"[486] who organized a strong movement of about 3,000 warriors. A commanding figure who sported a huge beard, Djujić was said to have three loves in life: "wine, women, and war."[487] He was personally courageous but not easy to get along with. As an Orthodox zealot, he detested Communists and Ustaša alike and hoped to discredit them both. By refusing to recognize Croatian sovereignty, he intended to disrupt ties between Rome and Zagreb. In territory where Djujić's authority over the local Serb community was unquestioned, no Croat dared challenge him.[488] By April 1942 he was conducting raids alongside the Italians against several Partisan-controlled villages.[489]

However, Serb relations with the Italians were strained because General Paolo Berardi, commander of the "Sassari" division around Knin, was required to stay on an even keel with the local Croatian prefect, David Sinčić. When Berardi attempted to broker agreements between the NDH and Četniks, Djujić, instead of negotiating with Croatians, periodically abducted them. A further display of independence came on 5 October 1942 when, during a round of toasts, Djujić informed Berardi that his primary loyalty lay with King Alexander, who happened to be a declared enemy of Italy. General Berardi considered arresting him, but, since he was dependent on Djujić, swept the incident under the rug. Because Rome in its wisdom insisted on benevolence toward the NDH, Berardi had the far more taxing job of finding common ground with the clearly anti-Italian Sinčić.

In eastern Bosnia—German-occupied territory—there emerged Major Ježdimir Dangić, a former gendarme and exemplar of a Serb headman who would negotiate with all sides and bind himself to no one in his determination to avenge Ustaša outrages. After many turnabouts Dangić finally sought a collaborationist settlement that would restore the rights of the Serb civilian population. The Germans initially showed interest, for Dangić, an avid Pan-Serb, was allegedly the long hand of Nedić (who also was in touch with Mihailović), but, bending to the wishes of Zagreb, avoided binding agreements with him. Eventually, the Germans realized, Serbia would be able through Dangić to exploit the disturbances in Bosnia to its own advantage. Berlin would not tolerate the emergence of a Great Serbia under either Nedić or the Četnik leader Mihailović.[490] Dangić did not neglect the Italians. One of his representatives suggested to General Dalmazzo that the NDH's authority in eastern Bosnia be replaced by the 2nd Army supported by Serbs.[491] Roatta, no more interested than the Germans in a "Great Serbia," explored cooperation with Dangić as a politically useful partner with a strong following, but was aware that the Germans had the inside track.[492] The tenuous Italian connection with the mercurial Dangić was severed when the Germans arrested him in mid-April 1942.

The chief Serb nationalist spokesmen in Herzegovina, the notable Dobroslav Jevdjević and Colonel Ilija Trifunović, were the most solid Italian allies. In October 1941 they made their initial contact with Italian army commanders, asking for protection against Ustaša raids and for the 2nd Army's occupation of Bosnia and Herzegovina. But Cavallero ordered that these contacts be broken off.[493] They would be resumed the following year by General Roatta. Although the 2nd Army occasionally applied pressure on the two Četnik leaders to cooperate with local Croatian forces, they had only to go through the motions, since it was common knowledge that the Italian military itself barely tolerated the NDH. That does not mean that the two Serb leaders were incapable of flitting between enemy and ally. They carried on talks with the Partisans, but these were desultory and short-lived, and they also approached the Germans, but were rebuffed.[494]

Trifunović was a colorful figure, a "famous invalid of the war," considered by his following as a Serb Garibaldi.[495] Perhaps more than any other Četnik leader, Jevdjević, a former member of the Yugoslav parliament, lawyer, and large landowner, did most to rescue his fellow Orthodox from the roving Ustaša bands. Of portly figure and bluff manner, which concealed the most tortuous of minds,[496] Jevdjević bartered military support to the Italians in exchange for food to ward off famine.[497] Eventually, in cooperation with General Roatta, he would organize a sizeable Četnik militia to fight side by side with the 2nd Army against the Partisans.

The Germans were appalled by what they saw. In the words of Glaise von Horstenau, Četniks "were parading in every village occupied by the Italians fully armed . . . In Herzegovina it has even come to the point where the Italians actually handed over a Croatian military column to the Četniks. Croatian `independence' is being trodden under foot."[498] Chafing over the loss of initiative to the clever Roatta, the Germans insisted on forcible action against insurgents of all stripes. But Roatta refused to fire on the Četniks. Apart from the "inelegance" of such a gesture, this would produce an immediate fusion between them and the Partisans that would imperil Italy's strung-out garrisons. Roatta walked a tightrope. He talked in riddles with the Germans and held off Rome with persuasively cynical logic. As price for cooperation, he wrote Ambrosio, the Četniks would say, "Now pay us." If Italy did not yield the required coinage, the armed and seasoned Četniks, "flushed with success," would turn against their Italian ally. Roatta's solution was to support them against the Partisans, but not too much. And, needing no prompting from Ambrosio, he would avoid any political commitments with Četnik leaders. Why not enjoy the sport of the two rival insurgent movements "slaughtering each other"?[499] Some Četnik units were hostile, Roatta admitted, but he did not want to drive them into Partisan arms by treating them like "rebels."[500] No more than Ambrosio, or Armellini—or most of the Italian generals—did Roatta favor an independent Croatia. Instead of cooperating with an essentially anti-Italian regime in Zagreb, he preferred a 2nd Army occupation of the Balkans as enemy territory till the Axis could dictate a final peace settlement, which was Mussolini's long-range plan. Roatta had no scruples over making generous promises to the various ethnic groups that might not be kept later.

The Palazzo Chigi sensed that Roatta's understandings with the Četniks were out of line with Mussolini's wishes. For the diplomatic experts the entrepreneurial Italian general was too clever by half.

Jevdjević had ties with Mihailović, whose head was filled with ideas of a Great Serbia, and enemy submarines were supposedly delivering substantial supplies to the Četniks. Pietromarchi noted: "We should revise our policy toward the Četniks, who, while feigning to fight against Croatia, in reality nourish a bloody war against us to reconstruct Yugoslavia."[501] A copy of Mihailović's political platform of December 1941, which Pietromarchi believed to be authentic, fell into his hands.[502] In this statement Mihailović, claiming to be aligned with Britain, America, and the Soviet Union, declared war against the hereditary enemies Italy and Germany. The eye-opener was his unabashed call for "a grand Serbia ethnically distinct" that carried the same connotation of ethnic cleansing against Muslims and Croatians as the Ustaša program against Orthodox Serbs and Jews. His proposed boundaries reached far beyond the original Yugoslavia to include Italian areas, Trieste, Gorizia, Istria, as well as Austrian Carinthia and northern Albania—claims no less extravagant than Pavelić's "reborn" Croatia. Both of these chauvinistic programs cut deeply into Italian territory and "vital living spaces." Small wonder that Pietromarchi cast a jaundiced eye on collaboration with Mihailović-style Četniks.

In retrospect Mihailović's ultimate purposes are not easy to fathom. Between 1940 and 1943 he wavered between resurrection of "Yugoslavia," based on authoritarian principles that allowed certain rights to ethnic Croats as well as tolerance toward Muslims, and a radical version of a Great Serbia similar to the manifesto that Pietromarchi had obtained. Mihailović's views often reflected the constantly shifting coalition of forces supporting him. After he moved to Montenegro in mid-1942, he had to take into account the more intransigent Montenegrins who, in their notorious intolerance, aimed for a racially pure and enlarged Serbia.[503]

## Operation Trio

In January 1942 the 2nd Army seemed to be on the verge of cutting its losses by withdrawing troops from outlying areas in Croatia. Reluctantly, Pietromarchi agreed. Operations in the third zone had already cost inordinate amounts of blood, money, and energy on the part of underachieving troops. But the second zone was another matter. There, the Duce opined, the 2nd Army should settle in to prevent any further German penetration into the Italian side of the demarcation line. To signal Zagreb that Italy was there to stay, Mussolini favored reduction of Croatian forts and the removal of the Ustaša.[504] But would the Germans abide by these plans?

After suppressing the Partisans in Serbia in November 1941, the Wehrmacht in January planned an expedition to crush all resistance in eastern Bosnia. To trap the insurgents, the Germans intended to occupy the mountain passes while having the 2nd Army close off escape routes leading southward. But the Italians neither had faith in the new battle plan nor forces available for large-scale operations.[505] By their reckoning, the German armies had been too thinned out and the NDH was too inefficient and "incapable" of a large-scale operation.[506] Moreover, the season could hardly be worse. Since the mountain passes were blocked by snow, the troops, enjoying little maneuverability, would be subject to Partisan sniper attacks.

Glaise, too, was beset by worries. If the Italians, flanked by Četniks, arrived on the German side of the demarcation line before the Croats moved in, the "peace and security" of territory already pacified would be upset.[507] But there was no need for concern; the 2nd Army did not appear. Roatta maliciously reported that the Germans requisitioned skis and mountain shoes, then impressed local men "off the streets and in coffee houses to clear snow from the roads."[508] Eventually the German expedition against the Partisans fizzled out.[509] Tito managed to escape and set up headquarters in relative safety at Foča on the 25th.

Undaunted, the Wehrmacht pressed on. General Keitel wrote Cavallero on 4 February that he intended to "burn out" the insurgents in Axis-occupied Yugoslavia. There would be no more talk of agreements with Četniks or Partisans, only resolve to consolidate the Croatian state. The Italian endeavor to seek ties with the Četniks he wrote off as cowardice. But here differences emerged between Berlin and the German Command Southeast. Having only a skeletal force, the Wehrmacht generals were not averse to seeking out Četniks; the Wilhelmstrasse, on the other hand, standing firmly behind the NDH, forbade them from doing so. The German strategic military purpose was to secure the important Maribor-Zagreb-Belgrade-Salonika line of communication that carried supplies to General Rommel's Africa Korps against insurgent incursions.

The Italians were not happy. The 2nd Army's hope to leave a permanent footprint in Croatia had already been foiled by Germany's domination of the country's economy. Now they were faced by a joint German-Croatian determination to keep them on their side of the demarcation line. Pietromarchi was offended by the German battle plan because it required the 2nd Army to chase the "rebels" from the German zone in eastern Bosnia to the Italian side of the demarcation line. After retaking forts the Germans had lost, the Italian military would be obliged to restore them to the Wehrmacht's command.[510] Worst of all, according to Pietromarchi, if Germans were allowed to dictate field strategy, domination of Croatia would be theirs by the favor of a docile subaltern.[511] Count Volpi's comment: "Italy is to be the cat's paw."[512]

Italian suspicion of the Germans was met by German disgust. Holding that Italian methods fanned rather than suppressed revolt, the Wehrmacht moved to keep the 2nd Army out of eastern Bosnia. In view of the "avarice, which is characteristic of our allies," wrote Glaise, additional Italian troops "will cause more difficulties for the government in Zagreb" and "affect our economic interests in the country." The German Commander Southeast reported that "the Italian attitude toward the insurgent movement makes a lasting success of the German efforts doubtful. The inactivity of the Italians against the insurgents until now, the obvious denial of Italian help during the current operations in Croatia . . . are responsible for the continued increase in the number of insurgents."[513] Since the Wehrmacht was undermanned and short of equipment, however, it sorely needed Italian help to suppress rebellion in eastern Bosnia.

In a tense atmosphere the Italian generals met their German counterparts on 2 March 1942 in Abbazia near Fiume to draw up Operation *Trio*. The Croatian general Vladimir Laxa joined the talks the following day. Instead of undertaking operations simultaneously in eastern and western Bosnia as originally proposed by German General Walter Kuntze, the Italians succeeded in splitting the expedition into two phases. German forces would, with the help of the Croats, first mop up eastern Bosnia in operations around Sarajevo and Banja Luka and, in the second phase, would eventually reoccupy the vast stretches of the upper Drina valley.[514] Once again the Italians were asked to cut off the Partisan retreat on their side of the demarcation line. Since the Germans seemed determined to limit Italian intervention in eastern Bosnia, General Ambrosio raised objections. Against the wishes of the Croats and Germans, he pushed through a motion that gave the 2nd Army the right to garrison troops and police territory freed of insurgency "for an indeterminate time." Rome, he supposed, would make sure that the "*spazio vitale*" would become a diplomatic "effective reality."[515] Italy's allies could reasonably ask: was Italy's top priority defeat of the Partisans or seizure of eastern Bosnia? Ambrosio then proceeded to advance Cavallero's request that the action be carried out under Italian overall command. The Germans yielded, but insisted that General Paul Bader be given control of field operations. The Italians reciprocated by agreeing to shun the Četniks.[516] The target date was set for 15 April.

Italy's negotiating partners were displeased. The German commanders bristled over having to make concessions to the do-nothing Italians and were frustrated by Berlin's reluctance to support them in challenging Ambrosio's battle plan modifications. But, as Glaise realized, the Wehrmacht was not strong enough to undertake expeditions against insurgency on their side of the demarcation line without Italian military assistance.[517] The Croats were unhappy because the Axis expedition that was supposed to clear out the insurgents for a restoration of Zagreb's political authority in eastern Bosnia stood to be compromised by a possible Italian move into Sarajevo, the palladium of the Muslim world in the Balkans. Fully aware of Roatta's pro-Četnik proclivities, the Croats feared that their already mangled sovereignty would disappear altogether.[518]

The Axis military summit reassembled in Zagreb on 28–29 March. Roatta pushed the date of attack to 20 April. The "oily" Italian general, as Glaise depicted him, informed the Germans that he would cooperate with rather than disown the Četniks as promised in the Abbazia agreement three weeks earlier.[519] First take on the Communists, then the Četniks, Roatta reasoned, not both at the same time. Moreover, he pointed out to his German colleagues the importance of cooperating with the Četniks in their zone to preserve a unity among them. Since the Četniks in Herzegovina were friendly to Italy, they could be persuaded to work on their compatriots in eastern Bosnia (German-occupied territory) to line up behind the Axis Powers and come to a modus vivendi with Croatian authority—or stay neutral. If treated as an enemy, the Bosnian Četniks would go over to the Partisans, and the Axis would be faced by a united insurgent movement.[520]

Roatta had more surprises up his sleeve. He told the Germans that Vjekoslav Vrančić, the Croatian representative to the 2nd Army, was authorized by Pavelić to offer the following: the NDH would provide the Četniks in Herzegovina with weapons to fight the Partisans and defend the Croatian border against Montenegro. Such offers, however, would not be extended to the Četniks in Bosnia, for, according to Vrančić, they were under the influence of Nedić, the Pan-Serb holding power in Belgrade.[521] For Roatta this represented a breakthrough, since the NDH was prepared to come to terms with the Orthodox Serbs in Herzegovina.[522] General Laxa, although admitting that talks between Croats and Četniks had taken place, declared himself unaware of Vrančić's initiative, and Kvaternik the elder dismissed the notion that arming any Četnik or obtaining Serb neutrality had ever crossed the Poglavnik's mind. For him the Četniks were no different from the Partisans, both being "mortal enemies of Germans and Italians."[523] Noticing that the NDH no longer spoke in one voice, Roatta easily pushed through the abrogation of No. 10 of the Abbazia Protocol prohibiting negotiations with the Četniks.[524] General Bader put on a brave face by telling the Italians that if the Axis forces acted against the Bosnian Četniks of Dangić, trouble would brew in Serbia.[525] But inwardly he seethed over Roatta's facile tongue and nearly broke off Operation *Trio* in disgust.[526]

To bring his point home, Roatta wrote General Bader three days later in his usual didactic manner: "It is not suitable to abandon immediately the possibility of dividing the Četniks from the Communists; it is not suitable to redouble . . . the number of our adversaries; one cannot initiate operations by beginning to shoot people who do not oppose us and in part are fighting our enemies at our side . . . You negotiate with the Četniks in Bosnia, I will handle them in Herzegovina."[527] Since there was no love lost among any of the protagonists, Roatta, with a foot in each camp, intended to be the mastermind of Axis strategy.[528]

The fly in the ointment was the Croats. Of all involved in Yugoslavia, Roatta abided them the least. Back in January he prepared to tell them:

> Sirs, we and you have in mind an important question: *to win the war.* In winning it, everything will be adjusted. In losing it, you will lose not only independence but probably your own skins. This being the case, do me the favor of an understanding: don't oppose us, don't offer us passive resistance or provoke quarrels, and don't sow discord. Collaborate with us loyally and with wide vision and decisively overlook all the little inevitable tensions that arise from living together. Along the same lines, do the favor of allowing your people, already floundering in confusion, to live. We want as little trouble in the Balkans as possible. We want to disabuse the people of the idea that we are here to support a government hated by a great part of the populace.[529]

To quiet Pietromarchi's alarm over his Četnik policy, Roatta declared his intention of incorporating the Croats into the 2nd Army in a "comradely" spirit.[530] But however cleverly Roatta maneuvered, he could do nothing to assuage Croatian anger. Zagreb perceived, not incorrectly, an Italian attempt to separate eastern Bosnia from the NDH, either to reward the Četniks or for annexation to Dalmatia.[531] (Zagreb also suspected that the Germans, through

Dangić, were preparing to hand eastern Bosnia to Nedić.) But since Roatta had adroitly sidetracked the Germans, he could ignore Croatian protests with impunity. The constant bickering that was the way of life between the Italians and Croats was taking a dangerous turn, for both seemed more intent on occupying eastern Bosnia before the other than in combining their forces to fight the Partisans.[532]

On how to conduct the campaign Roatta was much more direct: all men caught with weapons would be immediately shot and all suspects interned. His German counterpart General Bader uncharacteristically pondered a general amnesty, but was easily won over by Roatta's counterinsurgency logic.[533] Based on the success of the severe German crackdown on Serbia the previous October, Bader was not one to shrink from harsh reprisals to pacify eastern Bosnia.[534] With Bader neutralized, Roatta lectured the Croatian General Vladimir Laxa: "We, the Germans, and the Croats fight Communism. We also fight part of the Četniks. But one should take note that some Četniks fight not against the Axis but only against you Croats. It behooves you therefore temporarily to forget your difficulties with these Četniks and allow us to improve our rapport with them so that we can distance them from the Communists."[535]

When General Bader fell in with Roatta's views on the Četnik question,[536] he found himself in good company among his own soldiers. Led by Glaise, his commanders had held secret talks with some Serb warriors.[537] As opposed to the Nazis, they were offended by Ustaša barbarism, but, rather than taking strong measures, uttered only gentle reproofs to old Habsburg comrades in Croatian uniforms. Like the Italian military, however, the German field commanders thought that Ustaša terror, by provoking Serb retaliation, was weakening, not strengthening, the authority of the NDH, which, in any event, they held in contempt. General Bader and his staff firmly believed that the inefficient and "clumsy" NDH was incapable of keeping the peace in areas the Wehrmacht had pacified, especially the Croatian gendarmes, who plundered and attacked Serbs rather than upholding the public order.[538] Contrary to the Nazi diplomats in Zagreb and Berlin, who advocated unflinching war against both insurgent movements, the German army thought the Četniks might be a reliable partner in the campaign against the Partisans. In compliance with the Führer's order to shore up the Zagreb regime, the OKW satisfied the Croats by ordering General Bader to abstain from further contacts with the Četniks. Although urging the Italians to do likewise, Bader closed an eye while his commanders lined up Četnik leaders, who have "in cooperation with the German Wehrmacht performed better than the Croatian units."[539] But he did this with less finesse than Roatta and on a much smaller scale. And Bader was periodically overruled by the OKW. Whereas Roatta was a political general to his Italian bone and artfully dodged orders from Rome when it suited his purposes, his German counterparts were, in the main, apolitical technicians who faithfully obeyed orders. Stepping around Mussolini was, of course, a far less risky business than challenging the Führer.

General Bader's flip-flop complicated Roatta's military tasks. So did Rome. Seeking clarification, the Supreme Command asked Ciano on 3 April for guidance on the Četnik question, but the foreign minister demurred, which meant that the 2nd Army would continue to utilize Četnik units. This was in line with Cavallero's momentary willingness to allow limited assistance to the Četniks under certain restrictive conditions. At this point the OKW, distrustful of Roatta, bypassed Ciano by urging Cavallero directly to consider all insurgents as enemies of the Axis.[540] Cavallero caved in and duly instructed Roatta to toe the German line,[541] which momentarily placated Bader. Thanks to Berlin's determination to wage war indiscriminately against both insurgent movements, Roatta's scheme to advance Italian interests in eastern Bosnia through cooperation with the Četniks edged toward failure.[542]

But Roatta was not to be denied. Instead of carrying out Cavallero's orders, which would guarantee high casualties and force him to play second fiddle to the Wehrmacht, he delayed in completing his preparations to meet important deadlines set by the Germans. Claiming lack of transport, bad weather, and impassable roads, he repeatedly postponed the jumping-off date. There were, to be sure, sound military reasons for this. Ever since taking up his command in January, Roatta had been busy freeing isolated Italian garrisons that the Partisans had encircled in mountainous regions of Lika, an operation not completed until April.[543] Meanwhile, he tiptoed around the orders from Rome by keeping in touch with the Četnik "enemy." These endless delays over the launching of Operation *Trio* allowed the Partisans time to prepare themselves for the Axis offensive.

Roatta held off the Croats by telling Pavelić on 13 April that lining up Četniks to fight the Partisans meant "chloroforming" them. Bending to Roatta's pressure, Pavelić finally acquiesced in Italian use of the Četniks in Herzegovina. But the Poglavnik chastised the Germans for negotiating with eastern Bosnian Četniks. Their leader, the "drunkard" Dangić, was an avowed pan-Serb who desired to attach Bosnia to Serbia.[544] Roatta, in turn, observed that General Bader, on the orders of the OKW, refused to negotiate with the Četniks in Bosnia—a big mistake in his opinion, for the Wehrmacht, already short of troops, desperately needed allies. Unable to keep all these balls in the air, Roatta in frustration criticized both Croats and Četniks for approaching each other;[545] in turn, Berlin and Zagreb found him to be an elusive ally.

If Roatta constantly denigrated Croat military reliability and performance (as did the Wehrmacht generals), he did the same with the Germans for bragging about having "twenty divisions" at the ready instead of only six mobile battalions. Testily he yielded to Bader the right to handle the Četnik problem in eastern Bosnia,[546] mainly because there were hardly any Italian troops there. "We are always second," Pietromarchi glumly observed. "Our army of 220,000 has not been in the position even of holding territory beyond the demarcation line. It is evident that our military organization is deficient."[547]

In the end there was to be no real Italian contribution to the first stage of *Trio*. Before the Italians had manned their battle stations, General Bader, annoyed by their dawdling, suddenly informed Roatta on 18 April that he had to move quickly to relieve the Croatian garrison under heavy siege in Rogatica.[548] The Wehrmacht surged forward against the Partisans, accompanied by bedraggled units of Croatian Domobrani and undisciplined Ustaša. On 20 April Bader informed his superiors: "Joint German-Italian operation miscarried due to absence of Italians."[549]

Doubtless, the Germans and Croats were determined to safeguard mineral and industrial interests in eastern Bosnia from Italian encroachment.[550] On the sly Glaise and Bader met on 19–20 April with the Croats Lorković, General Prpić, and Kvaternik, Jr. to forestall an Italian advance into Sarajevo.[551] They resorted to dissimulation by telling the Italians that direct negotiations between the Croats and Četniks had resulted in improved security in eastern Bosnia, and that the Partisans had been successfully cleaned up and order entirely restored—this a mere six days after asking for a speedup in Italian preparations and forty-eight hours after telling them that the Croatian situation in Rogatica was desperate.[552] Undaunted, the Italian General Ettore De Blasio asserted that Italy had the right to occupy eastern Bosnia, kick out the Croats, and take over the political power.[553]

It was already too late for the Italians. In clear defiance of General Bader, Pavelić on 30 March hurried his Ustaša chieftain Juraj Frančetić from Sarajevo into eastern Bosnia to "pacify" the area— that is, to crush the Četnik forces of Dangić, with whom the Germans were still negotiating, before the Italians crossed the demarcation line. Entire Četnik units, pinched between the Ustaša and the Partisans, who directed their fire on them rather than on each other, were shattered in the crossfire. The Četniks lost power in eastern and central Bosnia, the Ustaša moved into the towns where they could slaughter Serbs at their leisure, and the Partisans melted into the countryside.[554] While Zagreb crowed over having subjugated eastern Bosnia, Ambrosio concluded on 25 April that the Germans were determined to keep the 2nd Army out of their side of the demarcation line so that they could seduce the Četniks from the Italians in the framework of a Serb-annexed eastern Bosnia.[555]

So as not to be shut out, the Italians accelerated their movements. The "Taurinense" division reached Sarajevo between 20–25 April, but was kept on the outskirts of the city by German command (General Bader was in charge of field operations on the German side of the demarcation line). Rogatica was taken without a fight on the 27th, and the combined Axis armies reached the right bank of the Drina River on the 30th, which wound up *Trio* I. The Italians blamed the Germans for pursuing political goals at their expense. Instead of synchronizing the attacking forces to encircle the Partisans, General Bader had changed his battle plan in mid-stream to minimize the Italian presence in eastern Bosnia, which allowed the Partisans to escape the pincers movement.[556] The Axis seethed in distrust.

*Trio* II, launched on 7 May, targeted Partisan strongholds at Foča and Kalinovik. Tactical command had shifted from Bader to Roatta, and now the shoe was on the other foot: the Germans, in pursuit of the Partisans, were poised to cross the demarcation line to the Italian side where they decidedly would not be welcome. The Italians blamed the Wehrmacht for deliberately slowing down so that they would have to absorb the brunt of the fighting, and contrasted their own mobility and speed with German sluggishness and outmoded battle tactics.[557]

Despite the many fissures and mutual recriminations, the Axis armies wound up the last stage of the campaign on 15 May. The Germans and Croats cleared the Partisans from eastern Bosnia to the demarcation line, and the Italians swept the Partisans out of Herzegovina. Important roads bearing German supplies to the Wehrmacht in North Africa had been secured against Partisan incursions.[558] Roatta believed that the Italian troops had acquitted themselves well.[559] During the second stage of *Trio* they received unexpected help from the Četniks, who, having regrouped after the earlier reverses, combined forces with the Montenegrin Nationalists and hit the weakened Partisans with blows that turned a dogged retreat into what appeared to be a rout. Still, many Partisan units managed to escape to the Sandžak and across the Drina into Montenegro; others blended back into the civil population.

According to the Italian record, during Operation *Trio* the Partisans suffered 1,720 dead, 821 wounded, and 600 taken prisoner, while the 2nd Army sustained 220 dead, 556 wounded, and 173 unaccounted for. The German losses were considerably lighter: 11

dead, 15 wounded, and one lost.[560] Italian losses were bound to be higher since they had committed a larger force to the campaign than the Germans did. Still, if these Italian figures are correct, they tell us that the 2nd Army was not unjustified in claiming that the Germans, in the aim of keeping the Italians at arm's-length from areas deemed of high strategic and economic interest to themselves, had successfully saddled Italy with major combat duty against the Partisans during Operation *Trio*.

Just as the Italian offensive had finally swung into high gear, General Ambrosio concluded during the latter part of April that the 2nd Army, short on manpower and equipment, had better trim its forces in the nether reaches of Croatia and withdraw to the "natural frontier" of Dalmatia—along the crest of the Dinaric mountain range—as conceived by Mussolini on 28 December 1941.[561] Roatta accordingly withdrew from most of the 3rd zone by the middle of May, leaving only Karlovac and areas in the 2nd heavily defended.[562] The Germans were alarmed over the suddenly created vacuum about which they had not been forewarned[563] and which they knew the Partisans would be able to exploit, while the Croats were elated over re-establishing a presence south of the demarcation line. But would they be able to get there before the Partisans? This Italian gift to Zagreb was followed by Rome's determination to reduce the financial burden on the Croatian government caused by Italy's military occupation. Mussolini, reported Pietromarchi, "is of the opinion that we must avoid suffocating Croatia, which owes its birth to Italy."[564]

In another momentous development, on 2 May the 2nd Army was removed from supervision by the Army General Staff. Together with the other military arms—the Navy and Air Force—it was reconstituted as the High Command of the Armed Forces in Slovenia and Dalmatia (Supersloda) and placed under the direct orders of the Supreme Command. General Ambrosio, as chief of the army general staff, was thereby taken out of the Balkan military chain of command, which left Roatta at the mercy of his archenemy Cavallero. (To avoid confusion the term 2nd Army instead of Supersloda will be used, as previously, throughout this text.)

## Partisan-Free Montenegro

During the first half of 1942, the Italian task of crushing Partisan resistance in Montenegro was relatively easy. The Germans were not there to harry them and no Croats were around to throw up roadblocks. A large number of Montenegrin warriors flocked to their banners, and the Partisans had already been routed, their ranks debilitated by internecine conflict. Many former Partisan sympathizers, alienated by the radical Communist propaganda in 1941, were driven into watchful waiting or reached new homes in the various nationalist organizations sprouting up throughout the country. The Partisans continued to wage a Red Terror in Montenegro against "class enemies" and collaborators of all shades, which did not bode well for transforming a hardcore few into a mass movement. After the shattering defeats administered by Operation *Trio,* the Partisans who remained in Montenegro took to the forests or hid in caves. But these setbacks and miscalculations did not kill the spirit; the Partisan leadership vowed to make a triumphant return.

In spite of the Italian victories, General Pirzio Biroli knew that his forces alone would not suffice to keep Montenegro under firm control. The Montenegrin separatists by themselves formed far too weak a base on which to build a puppet regime. Instead of ruling over Montenegro as a satellite, Pirzio Biroli took the next best step by surrounding himself, contrary to the December restraining order from Rome, with people willing to support him against the Partisans: Montenegrin warlords, Partisan apostates, and Četniks. Dubbed Nationalists, the Četnik allies of Mihailović in Montenegro moved in behind the retreating Partisans and proceeded to allocate turf. In early February 1942, they formed a National Committee that eventually served as a liaison with the Italians.

Pietromarchi was troubled. Pirzio Biroli, he felt, was carried away by the same "romantic illusion" as King Victor Emmanuel in believing that Montenegro could be set up as a separate entity. The hard lesson of the previous July had already been forgotten: the so-called constituent assembly dominated by "separatists" had fallen like a house of cards. "Montenegrins feel themselves as Serbs and wish to remain so."[565]

On 6 March Pirzio Biroli and the Montenegrin Nationalists signed an agreement to coordinate a struggle against the Communists.[566] A few months later he presided over a meeting to celebrate Italo-Montenegrin unity with headmen arriving "bearded, armed to the teeth, and wearing fezzes embellished with skulls."[567] They were a colorful lot with checkered histories. Major Pavle Djurišić, who participated in the July 1941 uprising, defected and sought out the Italians; he eventually became an ally of Mihailović. Strong and athletic, he had the appearance of a mystic, with flowing hair and a Nazarene beard—a type reminiscent of Garibaldi.[568] As proof of loyalty, he declared himself disposed to deliver his family as hostages to the Italian military.[569] There was no love lost between him and elements of the Muslim population who, as auxiliaries of the Italian troops, had ransacked Orthodox villages during the suppression of the Montenegrin revolt the previous year.

Colonel Bajo Stanišić was another key player. Having fought against Serbia during the Great War, he became a militant Communist after Yugoslavia's collapse. Reduced to starvation, he stalked the Nationalists and was eventually welcomed by the Italian army. Like many of his ilk, he was ready "to throw himself in anyone's arms."[570] A Pan-Serb reputed to be a ferocious warrior, Stanišić delighted in the ethnic cleansing in Montenegro and Herzegovina.[571] Krsto Popović, the leader of the separatists, and hence closest to the Italians, was out of the Mihailović loop but cooperated more or less with the Montenegrin Četnik chieftains. Of this group only Popović can be considered an out-and-out collaborator. Like Četniks elsewhere, the Montenegrin warriors accommodated themselves to Italian rule to gain an important ally in the fight against the Partisans. Their hearts, however, lay with the Allies, not from political affinity but as potential liberators.

Italo-Montenegrin cooperation was clinched on 24 July when Blažo Djukanović, who emerged as the head of the National Committee, and Pirzio Biroli signed a final agreement that sanctioned the formation of the Montenegrin Flying Detachments, with arms and supplies provided by Italy. The country was divided up. Popović presided over the districts of Cettigne and Antivari and a small part of Nikšić; Stanišić oversaw the rest of Nikšić and the districts of Savnik, Danilov Grad, and Podgorica; and Djurišić supervised the rest. The Sandžak remained under the authority of Pirzio Biroli. By tacit agreement the Monenegrins patrolled the rural areas, while the Italians garrisoned the towns and safeguarded communications.[572] By fall 1942 Montenegro's Nationalist men, who numbered in the thousands, had erected a parallel occupation and police force, enabling the Italians to siphon off troops for more turbulent areas in neighboring Albania. Still, the Italian military, determined eventually to be the only player on the Montenegrin field, was not blind to the possibility of exhausting the Nationalists by encouraging them to spend their energies pursuing the Partisans. But there was fear in the Palazzo Chigi that Pirzio Biroli had shown bad judgment and unsteady nerves in handing so much power in the heart of Montenegro to the likes of unreliable people like Djurišić, who, it suspected, marched to the orders of the pro-British Mihailović.[573]

Pirzio Biroli, however, was so thrilled over his newly recruited allies that he wanted to show them off to Mussolini in Rome. Cavallero turned down the idea for fear of creating a flap with Francesco Jacomoni, the lieutenant-governor of Albania, who thirsted to be the Italian empire-builder in the lower Balkans and looked on Pirzio Biroli as a deadly competitor. Pietromarchi had only nasty things to say about Jacomoni but, though he considered Pirzio Biroli a political lightweight, admired his presence: "Notwithstanding his age, [Pirzio Biroli] is in full vigor, massive, tall, and without a grey hair. With steady eye and a pistol he hits a matchbox at thirty meters."[574]

The Italian-Nationalist partnership held sway in Montenegro except for a precarious Partisan footing in the mixed Orthodox-Muslim border region to the east.[575] In the spring Mihailović slipped into northern Montenegro with his small force to link up with the victorious Nationalist warriors. Having shown their muscle in dealing the Partisans an almost mortal blow, the Nationalists were able to impose on Mihailović their "peace" agreements with the occupying Italian forces.

Pirzio Biroli presided over a Montenegro parceled out among unruly Nationalist headmen who were bound to him by medieval-style oaths of fealty grounded on the common goal of defeating the Partisans. Once that threat had subsided, the Montenegrin clansmen resumed their age-old jockeying for power and constructed strongly fortified camps against each other. The prefect in Cattaro, long a bitter critic of Pirzio Biroli for his failure to crush every scintilla of Montenegrin independence, was outraged that he should hand over authority to such an unreliable crowd.[576] Clearly Pirzio Biroli had built up a ramshackle and unsteady edifice. He was further harried by the intrigues of Jacomoni, who furtively sponsored Muslim raids into Montenegro to carve out additional territory that would enlarge an already outsized Albania.[577]

Freed from Italian constraints, the Nationalists, particularly the formations under Djurišić, roamed deeply into the Sandžak on revenge missions to ravage Croatian civilian and Muslim communities. The scaled-down XIV Army Corps was hardly in a position to discipline the strongly entrenched Nationalist warlords, despite a certain leverage provided by Italian control over the ports through which food passed to relieve starvation in the countryside. But Pirzio Biroli, who in July 1941 had employed Albanian Muslim auxiliary formations to aid in the suppression of insurgency, made no move to restrain the indispensable Nationalist ally.[578] Nor did he obstruct their roundups of suspected Communists and tribal rivals branded as "favoreggiatori" [fellow travelers]. Anyone who so much as sympathized with the Partisans was relentlessly hunted down. Montenegrin jails were crammed with innocent people who lingered for months on end without trial and in abominable conditions.[579] Pirzio Biroli furthermore ordered the collection of hostages liable to be shot. He set a high price on the heads of the most dangerous Communist leaders and richly rewarded any Četnik leader apprehending them. The total number of Montenegrins interned under his command has not been decisively determined. The Yugoslav Commission on War Crimes estimates 26,387, while the well-informed Stephen Clissold arrives at the much lower figure of 10,000.[580]

## *Stressed Out by "Allies"*

T he Croats were "allies" in name only. The Italian alliance with the NDH stood as a phony construct devised by Fascist ideologues in Rome. Pavelić, weakened by an ongoing backlash over his dependency on Italy, clung to the Duce because he did not want to be reduced to a simple German *Gauleiter*. The two sides were constantly locked in competition over control of Bosnia and Herzegovina.

During the spring Pavelić, to appease the Italians, softened his treatment of the Orthodox Serbs, urging that they escape outright massacre by converting to Catholicism. He also opened up half-hearted negotiations with various Četnik leaders. The Poglavnik undertook these gestures in the face of opposition on the part of his most fanatical followers. Some Četnik commanders, hoping to recover from their military setbacks, were prepared to cooperate with the Croats against the Partisans. To receive desperately needed ammunition, the forbidden phrase "Croatian sovereignty" was occasionally uttered, but in entirely bad faith. No Serb would ever accord Zagreb the slightest official legitimacy, especially to Vrančić, a principal interlocutor and "a 100 percent Croatian Ustaša man."[581] Roatta was of no use as a middleman because trust between him and the Croats was non-existent.[582] Since neither side had the slightest illusion that old scores could readily be settled, no paper, signed or unsigned, was taken seriously. In this atmosphere of distrust, nothing, it seemed, could stop the unending cycle of violence between the Croats and Orthodox Serbs.

In mid-1942 resentment in Zagreb against Italy, spawned by the loss of Dalmatia, threatened to envelop the Poglavnik's inner circle. Just as the 2nd Army belittled the Croats, so did agents of the NDH describe Italian soldiers as cowards, double-crossing allies, and lackeys of the Četniks. As seen from Zagreb, not only did the Italian military infringe upon Croatian sovereignty, not only was Bosnia sliding to the Četniks in complicity with the 2nd Army, but the Croatian treasury was groaning under the financial burden of sustaining Italy's military occupation. The Croatian civil commissioner attached to the 2nd Army, Dr. Nikola Ružinović, reported that, "under the patronage" of the Italians, the Četniks had destroyed "Croatian elements" east of the Neretva river.[583]

The Croats did their best to elude this stark Italian imperialism, but Rome held them to the onerous provisions of the one-sided economic agreements of 27 October 1941. Pietromarchi, ignoring Croatian protests over having to feed the 2nd Army, dismissed their cries for mercy as a cover for the ulterior motive of downsizing Italian troops in western Bosnia and Herzegovina.[584] But in June 1942 he admitted that the 2nd Army was bleeding the country, a viewpoint shared by Mussolini.

Just as the Italian army lived off the Croatian land, so did Rome attempt to dominate the Croatian economy. Count Volpi led a group of financial and electrical impresarios bearing plans for Italian economic exploitation of the resources in Yugoslavia. The quasi-state monopolies IRI and AMMI (Azienda Minerali Metallici Italiani), eyeing the rich primary materials such as lead, zinc, and chrome, also attempted to establish a foothold. Since the financiers realized that the underwriting of industrial development was far beyond Italy's means, they strove to establish a monopoly over primary materials, forestry lands, and agricultural exports, the latter of which, however, had the drawback of competing with large landholding interests in Italy. Certain Italian banks set up joint enterprises with their Croatian counterparts, and public works projects abounded.[585]

Italian economic imperialism was, however, on the whole hampered by a shortage of resources and trained personnel. The group of businessmen and state functionaries that arrived in Zagreb to do business flaunted an inefficient and flabby "Fascist Corporatism." Though benefiting from a protected market at home, the Italian oligarchy implemented a self-defeating autarchy that discouraged entrepreneurial spirit. The financial know-how and economic resources needed for an imaginative and comprehensive imperialist drive in the Balkans were clearly wanting. Disjointed planning and ad hoc improvisation gave way before the insuperable obstacles posed by an inhospitable economic environment in Yugoslavia, which lacked infrastructure, a docile and trained workforce, and efficient transportation. And a land torn by fratricide and guerrilla warfare did not make for attractive investment.

Italy also had its share of outlaw entrepreneurs who sucked the local economy dry, unhindered by any watchdog in Rome. Free-wheeling personalities like Temistocle Testa, the prefect in Fiume, and Undersecretary of the Interior Buffarini-Guidi made a fortune in black marketing and contraband operations that robbed the Croatian state blind. To facilitate forestry exploitation, the Palazzo Chigi convoked a meeting of financial and industrial tycoons in January:

> The exploitation of the forestry lands will be entrusted to Italian firms that will act according to the directives and under the vigilance of the forestry militia. The Croatian government will be asked to stipulate appropriate conventions: *if it does not adhere to our requests we will proceed to exploit these lands on our own.*[586]

On a much smaller scale, members of the military with insider information engaged in smuggling and thievery—common practices of occupation armies the world over—that further undermined the already fragile Croatian economy. This exercise in spoliation caused further corruption in the Ustaša state's already venal administration.

Volpi and his partners, though willing to engage in joint ventures with the Germans, did not receive much reciprocation from either Berlin or Zagreb. The Germans wanted it all, and the Poglavnik dashed Italy's protectorate ambitions by signing economic agreements with the Third Reich that established joint monopolies over the manufacture of chemicals and explosives. No matter how much pressure Rome applied through the press and in the desultory economic meetings between the experts of both sides, the NDH refused to loosen ties with Berlin by granting the Italians any significant economic privileges.[587] A worrisome development occurred when Pavelić, meeting with Hitler on 23 September 1942, revealed his preference for German military equipment and know-how over Italian. He was promised the hardware but was told that, as Germany had no political interest in Croatia, he must cultivate good relations with Italy—another Führer crumb for Mussolini. That was a safe position for Berlin to take, since Italian influence in Zagreb was in rapid decline.

However much Rome feared growing German influence in Zagreb, the reality that the 2nd Army was overstretched had to be faced. In fact garrison posts in the outlying areas had already been evacuated.[588] Pietromarchi put his finger on the problem: "In my opinion the 2nd Army has assumed a task beyond its competency, that of garrisoning territory as well as performing policing and administrative duties. Those tasks have caused [the 2nd Army] to divide its forces, which results in weakness and immobility. By doing this the [2nd Army] has played the game of the adversary who, save in some sectors, is capable, thanks to the scarce cohesion of its forces, only of sudden attacks on isolated units. All this has worn down our forces, diminished their prestige, and prevented us from obtaining any political result." The time had come for a policy reversal. Italian occupation should be reduced further to a few strategic posts. Let the Croats exercise the police power and man the forts and we will see how far they get, Pietromarchi reflected. Inevitably they will wear themselves out fighting a guerrilla war. "The Croats will invoke our help," he predicted. "At that moment we will have them at our mercy."[589]

This was the kind of subterfuge that made sense to Roatta. Cavallero gave the signal to change course, which was pretty much an acknowledgment of a fait accompli.[590] Roatta proceeded to sign a landmark accord with Pavelić on 19 June in which Italy promised to withdraw its garrisons from the 3rd zone and yield civilian and police power to the NDH in the 2nd. Even in those communities where the Italian garrisons remained, the NDH would have the authority to suppress all activities against public order and ensure the safety of people and property. The 2nd Army was obliged to build up the Croatian Domobrani in the evacuated areas and broker understandings between the NDH and the Četniks. Italy demanded that in the lands to be evacuated the Croats uphold the engagements already in place and refrain from reprisals against the

Serbs.[591] Superseding the 29 August 1941 accords,[592] the 19 June
agreements represented a kiss of death to an Italian protectorate
over Croatia.

There was, however, no feeling of diplomatic triumph in Zagreb.
Although sovereignty was recovered in the 2nd and 3rd zones, the
Orthodox enemy gained a legal title to exist as a state within a state.
In promising to uphold Italy's engagements with the Orthodox
Serbs,[593] the NDH was legally bound to allow them to form Četnik
and MVAC units. And there was Roatta still to be reckoned with,
for nothing would stop him from arming Četniks, a declared enemy of the state. In Zagreb's view, the Italian general was abetting
Serb Orthodox bands to avenge themselves on Croats instead of
fighting Partisans. Dissatisfied with Roatta's facile explanation that
the Četnik problem would vanish once the Partisans were defeated,[594] the Croats were further chagrined on learning that Roatta
had weakened the advantages conceded to Zagreb in the 19 June
accords by "clarifications" that amounted to an Italian veto over any
Croatian move. Furthermore, Roatta reserved the right to reoccupy
territory in case of any renewed outbreak of violence.[595]

The Četniks felt betrayed. Now they would be required to acknowledge Croatian sovereignty in areas earmarked for a Great
Serbia. They were also unhappy over the prospect of an Italian withdrawal to the Adriatic, for that would breathe new life into Ustaša
activity and expose them to renewed Partisan attacks. *Tant pis*,
thought the Palazzo Chigi, which had long been disturbed by the
Četniks' contacts with the British. Reliance on them, felt
Pietromarchi, had "reduced the 2nd Army to a Corps of Voluntary
Troops"[596] Forgotten by the generals in Yugoslavia, according to
the Fascist vulgate, was Italy's obligation to protect the NDH against
Pan-Serb aspirations.[597]

If there was support for the NDH in Rome, there was none at
Sušak. Before General Ambrosio left to take up the army command
in Rome, he wrote the Supreme Command that any military cooperation with the NDH suggested that "we are in Croatia exclusively
to favor this hateful Ustaša regime and its excesses."[598] Roatta added
that Zagreb was poised to undertake "a second edition" of the previ-

ous summer's persecutions.[599] In sum, he regarded the NDH as a cancer on the Croatian body politic and the Ustaša as a band of half-witted racists estranged from the rest of the population.[600]

In spite of what had been put to paper, Rome was hard pressed to make definitive decisions: should Italy continue occupation of Croatia or retreat to the coast? Ciano, for one, concerned over the mounting disorders in Slovenia and Dalmatia, was relieved that forces from Croatia's interior would be released to deal with them.[601] Pietromarchi, on the other hand, was worried that the Germans would profit from the Italian pullback by expanding already established beachheads on the Italian side of the demarcation line. Yet, frustrated that the 2nd Army had conducted politics that favored the "enemy" and estranged the "ally," Pietromarchi comprehended the necessity of a military withdrawal, and concluded: "With such a military organization it is not possible to actuate an imperial policy."[602]

In placing their bets on the NDH "ally," Mussolini and Pietromarchi were fully au courant of the terrible Ustaša-run Holocaust machinery working overtime in Croatia and the unpopularity of the Pavelić regime among the Croatian people. The Italian secretary of the Legation in Zagreb, Raimondo Giustiniani, reported on 12 May—in a missive read by Mussolini—that of 40,000 Jews in Croatia, only 6,000 remained, some languishing in concentration camps, others laboring in agricultural settlements. Giustiniani added that the Ustaša regime's violent racism and anti-Jewish measures were coldly received by the Croatian people, while the far better-organized ethnic Germans happily seized Jewish economic assets and property.[603] Pietromarchi was horrified over such criminality. Yet he still implored Roatta to "create harmony" with "Ustaša formations" to win over Croatian public opinion.[604] He counted on a pro-Italian faction led by Pavelić and seconded by Minister of the Economy Vladimir Košak, who were persuading Italy to build up a collaboration between the Ustaša and Blackshirts that would offset the inefficiencies of the 2nd Army and block the intrusion of the Gestapo into Croatian domestic affairs. Pietromarchi hoped to engineer the appointment of Carabinieri General Giuseppe Pièche to clean up the mess in Zagreb.[605]

Pavelić never had the slightest intention of opting for the Italians at the expense of the Germans. Pietromarchi's failure to appreciate this reality obscured the harsh truth that the 19 June accords with Croatia were, from the Italian standpoint, deeply flawed. They rested on the fallacious assumption that the NDH would be able to move into the abandoned areas with a capable administration and strong military force. Equally shaky was Zagreb's promise to protect strategic railroads and conciliate the Orthodox Serbs. When the Croatian authorities trudged into the abandoned areas totally ill-equipped to tackle the myriad problems and threats facing them, they beseeched the Italians to postpone their departure[606] (as Pietromarchi predicted), which left the NDH shamefaced and the 2nd Army's perception of Croatian incompetence vindicated. No longer did the Croats insist that the Italian troops depart; it was the 2nd Army, answering high strategic necessity, that decided to pull them back, which would leave the local Serb population defenseless. Under a mandate from Rome to utilize Croatian troops,[607] the 2nd Army in September made arrangements with the NDH to create an "Ustaša territorial militia," which immediately triggered the protest of Italian commanders, one of whom pointed out the "dangers for us, because the Croats are our enemies."[608] In the village of Foča, where the Croats had replaced the Italians, the Ustaša, instead of engaging in talks with the Četniks, attacked them and shot prisoners. The Četniks were not slow to reply in the same coin.[609]

Italy undermined its own standing in Croatia by habitually appointing party incompetents to manage the Stefani press and supervise the spread of propaganda. Success in influencing Croatian radio and movies was practically nil.[610] Rome had no answer to the anti-Italian agitation in Dalmatia promoted by highly placed Croats under the leadership of foreign minister Mladen Lorković. Most disconcerting were intercepted messages indicating an agreement between some officers of the Croatian army and Partisans in Herzegovina for the purpose of annihilating Četnik units organized by Italy.[611]

Having thoroughly alienated both the Axis occupying armies, the NDH enjoyed sympathy outside the country of no one save Mussolini, Hitler, and the zealots surrounding them. The German military in Croatia was quite disabused of the regime and its countless savage repressions. An undisciplined army and daily inefficiency diminished popular support to a handful of fanatical Ustaša and spun the country into economic decline. In despair, Glaise mulled over Maček as an alternative to Pavelić to gain the allegiance of the Croatian "silent majority." This was anathema to the Italians. From the perspective of Rome Maček was staunchly anti-Fascist and an incorrigible Dalmatian irredentist.

Above all, the German generals, especially those of Austrian origin still bewitched by Habsburg memories, resented the intrusion of the scorned Italy in their *Grossdeutschraum*. Since they regarded the Italians as not much better than tin soldiers, it did not cross their minds to cooperate with the 2nd Army in imposing a commonly worked-out reform program on Zagreb. Had it been up to them, the German generals would simply have established a military dictatorship and sent the Italians packing. In accordance with Hitler's proclivity to take the elder Kvaternik's word that the Croats were not "Slav" but descended from the Goths,[612] the Wehrmacht generals were ready to organize a peasant/soldier society as a source of agricultural production for Germany and as a bulwark against Communism.[613] But Hitler would not reverse the policy that he had laid down in July 1941: endorsement of the Pavelić regime and its extermination of Orthodox Serbs and Jews.[614] The 2nd Army was not predisposed to an open airing of views either, since the Italian generals suspected that behind every German word lay conspiracy engineered with the NDH to override their "rights." Beyond suspicion lay a common outlook independently arrived at: Croatia warranted no less than an imposed military dictatorship.

In Yugoslavia, Italy's "Pact of Steel" with Germany had transmuted into a cold war. "Comradely" military discussions in the Balkans were constantly hampered by double-talk, concealment, suspicion, and derision. Top-level Germans in Croatia—Kasche, Löhr, and Glaise von Horstenau—compiled a long list of grievances

H. James Burgwyn

against the 2nd Army that included fostering "mistrust" of Croats, hatching plans to "eliminate" the NDH's independence, conniving with the Četniks to occupy key titanium and armaments factories, and encouraging Croats to ignore recruitment into the army. Worst of all, the 2nd Army "had done nothing" to defend the Sarajevo-Mostar railroad from Partisan attacks.[615]

Roatta's clever persiflage, which constantly plagued the Germans, could not prevent the powerful Axis ally from encroaching upon Italian prerogatives. A choice example of this came when the Germans swept into the Croatian port of Ploče on the Italian side of the demarcation line to upgrade shipyard facilities and build a navigable water-link to the Neretva River, where bauxite was loaded up for shipment to Germany. Capital poured in while the infamous Todt agency, the German arm charged with requisitioning labor in occupied territories, supplied workers to facilitate access for the Göring Werke to rich bauxite mines and forestry land in the hinterland. The Italians only learned of the operation on 7 April 1942.

When the Partisans attacked the shipyards in early May, the Croatian Black Legion of Colonel Frančetić, urged on by the Germans, attempted to take over civil power in the Ploče area.[616] That move violated the accords between Croatia and Italy forbidding the presence of the Croatian military in the 2nd zone. General Giuseppe Amico, the commander of the "Marche" division, peremptorily told the Ustaša to leave, while General Dalmazzo looked askance at a burgeoning Ustaša-German military collaboration in the Mostar region that would alienate Jevdjević, thereby reopening Herzegovina to Partisan penetration.[617] But Roatta himself had partially abrogated that agreement. Needing German assistance in shipping provisions for his troops in the Mostar area, as well as raw materials to feed Italian factories in Cattaro, he signed an accord with the Germans on 28 May 1942 that temporarily suspended Italian authority in Mostar.[618]

Caught off balance by the Croatian move into the region, Roatta hastened to repair the damage. He finally prevailed on Pavelić to order Frančetić and his legions out. Pietromarchi chaired an important meeting in Rome between Germans and Italians to find a so-

168

lution. Italy, it was decided, would provide the dredgers to construct the port facilities and assure security, while the Germans and Croats would build the connecting roads and rail service.[619] The Italian minister of public works, Giuseppe Gorla, alleged in his memoirs that he tried to prevent delivery of the expensive dredgers and bring the German reclamation work to a halt, but that Mussolini, succumbing to Göring's pressure, failed to back him up.[620] Since the Germans easily could have rented port facilities at Spalato, their determination to construct one at Ploče revealed their intent to hew out a niche on the Adriatic.[621] Pietromarchi traced the German decision to build the port with Todt labor to Berlin: "It was not a question of a peripheral policy of pro-Austrian elements [Kasche and von Horstenau] who wish to undermine our position in Croatia but a directive from the center [Berlin]."[622] A further indignity occurred when the Germans established a consulate in Dubrovnik against bitter Italian protests. Provided a listening post on the Adriatic, the Gestapo spread rumors that Germany supported a Croatian annexation of Dalmatia.[623] The Italians reeled from these rapidly developing German intrusions. For two generations they had prevented a hostile *Drang nach Osten* from reaching the Adriatic, only to find their Axis ally hoisting flags in both Ploče and Dubrovnik.[624]

The incident at Ploče was only one example of German penetration. Fleets of advisers, financial agents, and SS men engulfed Croatia. The *Südosteuropa Gesellschaft*, active in Yugoslavia before the war, blanketed the country's economy to exploit primary materials that would feed the German war industry.[625] The far less endowed Italian financiers, arriving late in the day, ended up practically empty-handed. A propaganda line spread by German "agitators" and "spies" that contrasted Italian slothfulness with the German work ethic and discipline further shook the Italians.

Neither Axis partner was able to devise a viable solution regarding the Croatian government. Both were pulled down by its unpopularity, corruption, and violence. Major responsibility for reform as spelled out by existing treaties lay with Italy. But as Italian power waned, the responsibility fell to the Germans, who agreed with the Italians that without a thorough overhaul of the Croatian state and a clean sweep of the Ustaša, victory over the Partisans would be a pipe dream.

Hitler, however, would not listen to his top military advisers in Yugoslavia. Unmoved by Ustaša atrocities, he joined Mussolini as Pavelić's guardian angel. By declaring Croatian "sovereignty" untouchable, the Führer ignored every suggestion that questioned the Poglavnik's monopoly on power. Since there was also the Duce's ego to stroke, Hitler would not modify the official German pose that Croatia was Italy's business. This was ridiculous. The Germans had done nothing to lift the demarcation line—which had originally been devised as a temporary measure to keep the Axis armies separated—that prevented Italy from taking over Croatian eastern Bosnia, a situation bitterly resented by the 2nd Army. In fact, economic predators accompanied by German-trained Domobrani were already swarming into Italian-occupied western Bosnia and Herzegovina. But Hitler's promise to respect Croatia as Italy's *spazio vitale* sufficed for the Duce and his foreign office. They could not face the reality that the Führer was not a man of his word.

# Chapter VI

# Četniks, Jews, and Partisans

Unsteady Friend and Resolute Foe
Odd Man Out
Political Fallout
Italy Saves the Jews
The Beginning of the End

*Unsteady Friend and Resolute Foe*

T he major Italian summer expedition in 1942 was Operation
*Velebit,* launched on 16 July, whose primary purpose was to
create a security zone beyond the Dalmatian frontier against Partisan incursions and raids on the railroad linking Fiume and Spalato,
essential for the transport of military equipment and food to
Dalmatia. The fighting was fierce and marked by atrocities. In order
to assure the security of the Dalmatian frontier, the 2nd Army attempted to create a buffer zone free of Partisans through scorched-
earth measures that would deny them "every possibility of life in

areas [that Italy] occupied."[626] Responding to the burning and pillaging of villages, the Partisans shot, captured, and wounded Italian soldiers. Mussolini retaliated by instructing the 2nd Army to
utilize the "law of reprisal" that condoned the shooting of Partisan prisoners.[627]

As for the fighting, the Italian troops acquitted themselves reasonably well, but there were worries in Rome over discipline in the
ranks. The Minister of Communications, Giovanni Host Venturi,
told Mussolini: "Things are heating up; if this continues, the 2nd
Army will become bolshevized. There are officers who would take
pleasure in throwing their stripes in the faces of their commanders." Mussolini replied: "I told Roatta that since he had assumed
command, the situation has not stabilized but deteriorated." Host
Venturi countered: "You have replied with kind words."
Pietromarchi, who recorded Host Venturi's version of this conversation, remarked on the Duce's reluctance to criticize Roatta or to
undertake any initiative. Pietromarchi gloomily recorded small episodes that he thought were representative of the worsening situation, e.g., a major, whose unit had been ambushed by the Partisans
and captured, "fell in a swoon" and "was spat at." Bastianini, recognizing the volatile situation, constantly implored Rome for more
troops and pressed Mussolini to visit Spalato. "To be shot?" wondered Pietromarchi, who in the next breath advocated that Roatta
be replaced by General Gastone Gambara.[628]

Besides plotting military strategy, Roatta as usual expended much
time balancing conflicting aims of his so-called allies, who threatened to upset his major goal of maintaining the Italian upper hand.
He was particularly annoyed by the onerous chore Rome had imposed on him of bringing together the Orthodox and Croats to
operate harmoniously on the side of Italy. Equally vexing was the
presence of Croatian "legionnaire divisions" under German command. The politics undermining military unity distracted him from
full concentration on field operations. Still, the Axis coalition held
together well enough to establish a rough-and-ready order in Bosnia
and Herzegovina by the end of summer 1942. In cleared areas the
Četniks quickly established de facto political authority. New recruits

and many Partisan deserters filled the ranks.[629] Just after the Italians had reiterated their intention to withdraw from wide swaths of Croatian territory, which upset the Četniks, the uneasy partnership managed with the indispensable help of the Wehrmacht to deliver the Partisans a series of reversals.

With so many areas cleared of the Partisans, Mihailović was given rare opportunity to assemble the widely dispersed Četnik forces under a unified command. Most of the Serbs loyal to his movement agreed on certain fundamentals. They wanted to restore Yugoslavia, but strove to set markings around territory approximating "Greater Serbia" within a resurrected multi-ethnic kingdom; this implied a forced migration of Croats and Muslims from the expanded "homogeneous" Serb core. The other ethnic groups of former Yugoslavia would be invited to participate in a "federal" scheme in which Serb predominance would be unquestioned. The urge to punish the Croatian and Muslim "instigators" of the April 1941 treason (the collapse of Yugoslav resistance against the Axis Powers) and to avenge Ustaša culprits responsible for the mass killing of Orthodox Serbs simmered beneath written declarations.

Under the banner of Serb chauvinism, Mihailović convened a meeting of Četnik leaders in the neighborhood of Pustopolje on 22 July, where he denounced the German-dominated Nedić regime in Belgrade, foreswore collaboration with the Germans, and branded the NDH a mortal enemy. According to one of Mihailović's spokesmen, who delivered a speech to Četnik leaders in nearby Trebinje on the 23rd, Mihailović had declared that "Serb territories must be purged of all Catholics and Muslims. Here only Serbs can live. We will throw them out and annihilate them all, without exception and without pity."[630]

Mihailović's hold over the motley crew of Četnik leaders, most of whom were *prečani* Serbs, hardly went beyond strident nationalistic sloganeering. As autonomous warriors, they regarded him as no more than a useful father figure to legitimize their position in the eyes of the population since he represented the king and the Allies.[631] Hence the Četniks fought or rested at their convenience, not at his command. Since Mihailović was having trouble convincing his officers to adhere to a common battle plan, they tended to choose their own enemy from among Partisans, Muslims, or Croats. Many Četnik farmer-warriors, on the other hand, were simple apolitical villagers and clansmen who, welcoming the Italians as defenders of their homeland against the depredations of the Ustaša, merely wanted to be left alone by both Croats and Partisans. But as time passed, the barbarity of guerrilla warfare worked to the advantage of the politically minded *prečani* and Montenegrin leaders, who saw Mihailović as a messiah leading them to the promised land of an ethnically cleansed Great Serbia. At the moment of triumph, however, their greatest weaknesses were revealed. Lack of discipline among the commanders was rife. The territorial levies, bound to land and village, frequently refused to march outside their own districts.

As opposed to the Četniks, who were inclined to save their own lives by taking a grandstand view of the action, the Partisans, even with their fortunes at a low ebb, promised a struggle without quarter. Beyond the hardened fighters under Tito's direct command, they did not comprise a unified force but were scattered about the country—from Slovenia to Montenegro—operating independently of one another. Resistance took a variety of forms. In rural districts Partisan guerrilla bands skirmished with the Italian "forces of order," while in urban areas their activity was more clandestine and devoted to the spread of propaganda. Since he was penned up in a massif on the Montenegro-Herzegovina border, Tito frequently lost touch with these far-flung guerrilla operations. While reorganizing his politically indoctrinated veterans into assault brigades, the Partisan leader made a momentous decision. To rally Muslims and Croats to his core of predominantly Serbs, he began a "long-march" on 23 June from Montenegro to western Bosnia, a more central area from which to organize and coordinate the disparate Partisan movement. His trek over some 200 miles lasted the entire summer along a route that followed the border between the German and Italian zones through practically uninhabitable territory.

During their journey the Partisans alienated large portions of the peasantry by torching Četnik villages and carrying out executions of "class enemies." Constantly short of supplies, they pillaged farms and carried away the livestock of peasants who declined to supply them with weapons and food. The population was given a choice to align with them or be branded as collaborators opposed to "the will of the people."[632] Communist leaders made a serious mistake by heralding radical revolutionary measures. The Četniks were thereby enabled to brand Marxism as an alien ideology that threatened the small holdings and lifestyle of the independent-minded yeomanry residing in the lands of Yugoslavia. Partisan strength was further drained by a loss of followers who, sensing defeat, defected to the victorious Četniks. Yet Tito in late autumn was able to claw his way into the little market town of Bihać in northwest Bosnia, where he established the seat of the "People's Liberation Movement." After his arrival, the mood began to change. Affected by the traumas of defeat and massacre, the Serbs living in western Bosnia warmed up to the Partisans' cause.

The voluntary Italian retreats from outposts in Bosnia and Herzegovina were a godsend to the Partisans. In the newly created open spaces Tito was confident that he could take the measure of the Četniks in any one-on-one fight. Since he placed a higher premium on winning power at their expense than on defeating the occupier, he seldom descended from the safe mountain redoubts into the cities or rich lowlands of the NDH to duel with the Axis forces head-on.

In stark contrast to the stay-at-home Četniks, the Partisans were ready to travel far afield as mobile units under the discipline of tough-minded commanders. While the Četnik recruits rested in their huts between skirmishes, the Partisans became hardened warriors through constant exposure to combat and privation. When the battle passed on to other regions, the Četniks were prone to abandon their units, whereas the Partisan shock troops obediently pursued the enemy in far-flung areas or retreated in good order. The Četnik bands and their warlord leaders more and more resembled marauders bent on booty and the massacre of ethnic enemies. The Partisans, on the other hand, spurred by righteousness, were able to regroup as a more effective fighting force after suffering catastrophic losses.

Given a moment of repose, the Communist leadership began to change its line from uncompromising Marxist-Leninism and "revolution" to one of brotherhood, ethnic solidarity, and a common patriotic struggle to free the country from foreign domination. Just as important were newly adopted battle tactics. Reminiscent of Oliver Cromwell's New Model Army, "Proletarian brigades" and "shock troops" were formed and led by political commissars to supervise the political education of raw recruits attracted to the new Communist party line. The Partisan "comrades" were greeted as protectors by the decimated Serbs and were welcomed by the Catholics and Muslims, whom they defended from retaliation by Orthodox warriors. Gradually Croats, sickened by the Ustaša bloodbath, enlisted in Partisan ranks, since the Serb Communist leadership was careful not to blame the entire Croatian population for the sins of the few. The Partisans were the lone political force in Yugoslavia that refused to recruit on a religious basis and who always appeared to be on the side of the underdog–those fighting for their lives and livelihood against exploiters, exterminators, and invaders. At the Bihać Congress, held on 26 November 1942, it was announced that the People's Liberation Movement was a broadly based expression of patriotism rather than an instrument of Communist revolution.[633]

Throughout all these Partisan peregrinations, the Italians had no effective intelligence service tracking Tito's military forays. Informants were few. Captured propaganda pamphlets described Partisan aims, but the movement remained a phantom force that struck at unexpected moments. "Our war," reported General Giovanni Esposito, "is a war without a zone behind the front . . . we punch in the dark."[634] If anything, the Palazzo Chigi was immersed in a deeper fog over the nature of the movement. Pietromarchi wrote in June: "one of the Montenegrin rebels, a certain Tito, a Jew . . . "[635]

As far as the Italians were concerned, their patchwork cooperation with the Četniks in the war against the Partisans was proving useful in areas under the 2nd Army's control. By protecting the Serbs from further persecution, the Italians were able to restore a food supply in what was a poor and infertile area. They also provided the harassed Serbs with a blanket of physical protection against both

Partisan and Ustaša marauders, which influenced the mass of the small holders not to challenge the occupation authorities. Their warlike leaders utilized the Italian connection to secure arms for use against domestic rivals—and eventually against the Italians themselves.

To coordinate their policies and thrash out differences, Četnik leaders and Italian generals met frequently. Forthright talk alternated with dissimulation. A key figure was the supposed Italian ally Jevdjević, who was known to be answerable to Mihailović. Jevdjević had not been altogether standoffish with the hated Croats, and he did not neglect the Germans, although they had arrested his mother, sister, wife, and mother-in-law![636] Jevdjević even deigned to address Muslims, whom he viewed as religious recreants deserving the worst.

On 9 and 10 September Jevdjević and the renowned Trifunović proposed to Roatta that the Italians and Četniks conduct a large-scale operation against the Partisans in northern Dalmatia and Lika, to originate in mountainous western Bosnia, the seat of Tito's hideout. Roatta appeared to be receptive, but was told by the Supreme Command that he must first seek Zagreb's approval and allow Croatian troops to participate in the operation.[637] He met with Pavelić on the 19th and predictably discovered that he did not warm to the idea of Četnik participation in military operations on Croatian soil.[638]

The two Četnik leaders met again with Roatta on 21 September. Trifunović insisted that he, not Mihailović, was in charge in Bosnia and Herzegovina. He had the cheek to say that Serbs living there were so in debt to Italian largesse that they would ignore any order from "The Old Man" to turn on their benefactors.[639] His comrade Jevdjević promised to respect Croatian sovereignty, but that probably skipped by Roatta since he himself chafed under such an obligation. Perhaps General Dalmazzo was a bit naive regarding Četnik loyalty, but not General Roatta, who knew exactly what they were up to. Privy to intercepted communications whose code had been cracked by Italian and German cryptologists, he knew that the Četniks stood for extreme Pan-Serb nationalism and claimed boundaries that would snuff out the *spazio vitale*. Holding in his hands a report of the Pustopolje meeting, Roatta was under no illusion that, if push came to shove, Jevdjević would answer to Mihailović rather than to him. In fact, by appealing for Italian support of a postwar reconstruction of Yugoslavia, Trifunović was predicting that Serbia would be enlarged to include Bosnia, Herzegovina, and Montenegro. Mihailović and his following, he admitted, were being pressured by the exiled ex-King Peter and the British to intensify guerrilla war against the Axis. But Mihailović, according to Jevdjević, would move against Italy only in the distant future, "when the Russians entered Budapest, and the English Sofia."[640]

Refusing to be drawn into any written political commitment, Roatta countered by informing Trifunović and Jevdjević that Italy would not tolerate the Četniks' postwar aims; he insisted that they fight for "exclusively anti-Communist ends" and eschew "any sort of political activity of an anti-Croat nature."[641] Roatta was aware of Četnik ties to Nedić—something admitted to by the two Serb leaders[642]—although it was unclear to the Italian general how closely Mihailović was in touch with the Quisling Serb ruler.[643] He tried to delineate areas and adapt Axis policy to given circumstances by having the Germans collaborate with Nedić in Serbia and the Italians with the Četniks in Croatia.[644] But none of Roatta's straight talk would deter the Četnik leaders from pursuing a "pure" and expansive Serb state, and he was unable to extract a promise from them to refrain from harming Muslim and Croat civilians.[645] There was obviously growing distrust between Roatta and the Četniks. Trifunović resented Roatta's suspicion of Četnik motives, while the Italian commander was unhappy over Četnik ties with Mihailović and reports of unruly Serb behavior.[646] But he would stop the Croats from pitting them against him.[647]

In yet another meeting with Roatta on 5 December, Jevdjević consulted his crystal ball. In case of an Axis defeat, the Croatian state would disintegrate. The Četniks alone would not be able to reestablish law and order. If the 2nd Army lent a hand, no Serb would object to Italy's keeping Croatian-populated Dalmatia. Roatta made clear that he would not be drawn into any discussion posited on an unfavorable outcome of the war.[648] Undeterred, Jevdjević reported Mihailović as having said: "The days of the Axis are numbered." To avoid capitulation and the Axis stigma, Italian troops should join the Četniks to defeat the Partisans and bar the Soviets from the Balkans. In a friendly Adriatic neighborhood, Italy would pose as *primus inter pares*. Far from Roatta's view, however, Mihailović, in a decidedly anti-Italian *tour d'horizon*, had just outlined a newly constituted Yugoslavia that pointedly would deny Italy the smallest foothold in Dalmatia.[649]

Roatta, doubtless, suspected that Mihailović was treacherous and would desert Italy in a heartbeat. Nonetheless, as long as Četniks continued fighting the Communist enemy, they would be useful allies. However much Pietromarchi wrung his hands over this, the Italian general had Mussolini's grudging approval to cooperate with Trifunović's formations.[650] Estimates vary greatly as to the number of Četnik warriors in the Italian zone of occupation. Jevdjević contended that he had 28,000 followers; Italian sources claim a growth from 11,000 in late summer 1942 to 20,000 at the beginning of 1943.[651]

*Odd Man Out*

Among the religious groups in Yugoslavia, the Muslim population was perhaps the most defenseless, having only a few armed bands to protect their communities from the many enemies surrounding them. They were particularly hated by the Serb Orthodox, for whom they were reminders of the despised Turkish rule. In Bosnia, Herzegovina, and the Sandžak, centuries of religious and political Christian-Muslim antagonism had been exacerbated during the First World War when many Bosnian Muslims joined the Austro-Hungarian armies, whose soldiers subjected Serbs to a fearful occupation.

The Muslim community was cleaved by divisions. In April 1941 many Muslims declared loyalty to their new Croatian masters, relieved to be left off Pavelić's list of religious groups to be liquidated. Over time other Muslims sought refuge in the ranks of the Partisans. In the zone of Mostar, a group of intellectuals under the guidance of Dr. Ismet Popovac intended to form an army with Četnik support in order to realize an independent Bosnia-Herzegovina. But the Muslims of Sarajevo, lead by the cleric Medzilisa, who likewise aimed at an independent Bosnia, renounced collaboration with the Serb Orthodox. Still another group denounced the Croats and sought the protection of Italy. A strange competition over the Muslims ensued between the two nominal allies, Croatia and Italy. Aware that Mihailović was more conciliatory toward Muslims than were his followers, Roatta tried to arrange a communal truce by bringing together the Italian ally Jevdjević with Ismet Popovac and Mustafa Pašić from Mostar. But these contacts could not prevail against relentless Orthodox hostility.

To broaden his support, Roatta pondered an alignment between Croats and Muslims equipped and supported by the 2nd Army. Such a coalition could be employed as a useful pawn on the Balkan chessboard to checkmate the Montenegrin Nationalists in the Sandžak and to combat the Partisans. But his successor General Robotti did not take up this idea because of his low opinion of Muslim fighting ability. The few Muslim units in the MVAC had not acquitted themselves well, fleeing to the Partisans at the first shot. But having less faith than Roatta in the staying power and loyalty of the Četniks, Robotti sought to use the Muslims as a counterweight against them.[652] In his negative judgment of Muslims Robotti was not alone. "By nature," wrote Roberto Ducci, head of the Croatian desk in the Palazzo Chigi, they "gravitate toward the strongest . . . The Muslims are not good fighters."[653] This was hardly surprising, since the Italians had provided the Muslims with shoddy equipment and barely lifted a finger to defend their communities from rampaging Četniks. Actually, the Italians did not have the means to outfit and train Muslim units properly, and they were in too deep with the Četniks to reverse themselves. With vastly more money and equipment, the Germans succeeded in luring the Muslims.[654] Whatever Italian-created Muslim militia existed in the Sandžak and Herzegovina broke up in spring 1943.[655]

Following a punishing Ustaša attack on Serbs in Foča, Četnik armed formations spilled into Italian-evacuated areas in Herzegovina to wreak vengeance on their Croatian enemies during late summer 1942.[656] In September Jevdjevič provided the Mostar Muslims a chance to redeem themselves from a "history of crimes without precedent perpetrated against Serbs" by collaboration with the Četniks.[657] But when Roatta decided to arm Muslim and Croatian anti-Partisan formations, Jevdjević came under strong attack from his following.[658] To recapture his standing, he condoned the burning of villages and massacre of over five hundred Croats and Muslims in operations around Prozor. With Major Djurišić in charge, a Četnik raid in the Sandžak and southeastern Bosnia during the first two months of 1943 netted, according to one historian, 10,000 Muslim dead.[659] In desperation the Muslims of Mostar asked the Italians for protection against these Četnik outrages and on one occasion asked the Italian government to annex Bosnia.[660] In happier times the Italians might have taken this up, but, since they were withdrawing, they could do nothing to protect the Muslims from the ravaging Četnik bands who moved in behind them. Irritated by the religious violence, the Italians did not have the strength to restrain all involved. When having to choose, they perforce came down on the side of the far larger and more formidable Serbs.

## Political Fallout

On 12 August General Dalmazzo undertook Operation *Albia* against the Partisans operating in the mountains south of Spalato. On the same day, General Umberto Spigo, commander of the XVIII Army Corps, which was charged with the defense of Dalmatia, moved to block any Partisan retreat. Requesting the authority to destroy houses and villages, he ticketed vast cross-sections of the population for internment. Roatta overruled his commander: "One cannot do all this. Spoke with the chief of the XVIII Army Corps; destruction limited to those houses participating in offenses against us and those that are rebel-owned."[661] The Duke of Spoleto's informant wrote of widespread burning of Serb villages by Italian troops and of glaringly contradictory policy: "In some places we propitiate Serbs and alienate Croats; elsewhere it is the reverse."[662]

Within weeks General Dalmazzo succeeded in administering a sharp defeat of the Partisans. According to his probably inflated body count, his troops killed 962 of the enemy while losing only seventeen of their own.[663] Roatta congratulated Dalmazzo on his victory, but continued to grapple with the thankless task of coordinating unreliable Četnik units and undisciplined Croatian army formations who hated each other no less vehemently than they did the Partisan enemy.

On 5 October General Ugo Santovito, who had replaced General Dalmazzo as commander of the VI Army Corps, launched *Alfa*, whose aim was to eliminate Partisans from the Mostar-Posučje-Prozor triangle and to safeguard German bauxite and lignite deposits located in the basins of Mostar and Livno against Partisan raids.[664] The Četnik insurgents, however, refused to cooperate. If in the German zone they signed agreements with the Poglavnik's forces, in the Italian they categorically refused, or merely feigned, collaboration with the NDH. To the dismay of the Italians, the Četniks preferred to skirt the Partisans in order to wreak vengeance on Croats and Muslims, which cost them the support of the countryside. MVAC units got out of hand by shooting innocent people and indiscriminately burning houses. The behavior of Fascist Blackshirts, no less deplorable, issued from slightly different motives. Whereas Serbs were moved mainly by revenge, the Blackshirts burnt and pillaged as sport. Even the prototypical Fascist Governor Bastianini was made sufficiently uneasy by the surge in violence to demand the repatriation of the "Vespri" brigade, while General Spigo, equally alarmed, concluded that the Squad units under his command, save the "M" battalion, should be sent home.[665]

The Italians in both Rome and Croatia had no answer for the unpredictably shifting tides of war. During the summer it seemed that the Partisans were on the run, but in early fall they reappeared everywhere. *Rastrellamenti* by the Axis in general proved frustrating. Fugitive peregrinations of the Partisans and their narrow escapes from Axis-devised culs-de-sac would be followed up by renewed infiltration into territory the Italians had voluntarily abandoned as they slowly made their way to the coastal areas. Periodically the Italians turned around to recapture towns and hamlets, but these could not be securely held because of the vastness of the territory and the small number of troops available for occupation duty. If the Italian troops rarely gave ground—retreats were preplanned—at no time did they preside over a pacified countryside.

Against this murky background, Italian illusions of imperial power took a long time to die. Raffaele Casertano, Rome's minister in Zagreb, typified this escapist attitude; he only faced reality when a German takeover appeared imminent. To prevent the crumbling NDH from falling into Teutonic hands, Italy must, he exhorted in late October, move quickly to establish a protectorate. A simple chore—the Germans would gracefully excuse themselves and the Croats would submit. The 2nd Army's task, according to Casertano, was no more difficult: to establish law and order by annihilating the Partisans. The head of the Fascist delegation in Croatia, Carlo Balestra di Mottola, made a similar recommendation on 2 November to the party secretary in Rome, Aldo Vidussoni. Striking a more realistic note, General Pièche, the Carabinieri commander sent to the Balkans to coordinate Italian intelligence operations, and the noted journalist Solari Bozzi, chief of the Stefani office in Zagreb, reported that Ustaša massacres deprived the regime of moral credibility,[666] but these were ignored by a Rome clinging to the NDH till the last drop of Ustaša blood.

As the hold of Italian troops over much of Croatia slipped rapidly, their influence in Zagreb weakened by the day. Sušak was awash with rumors of an imminent coup d'état against Pavelić inspired by German sympathizers in his cabinet. But it was Pavelić, in early October, who engineered a changing of the guard by removing two outspokenly pro-Germans, father Slavko and son Eugenio ("Dido") Kvaternik, from his government.[667] The Italians, not surprisingly, were relieved. Months before Volpi had told Mussolini: "The son is a stinker, a sadist responsible for making rivers of blood flow; unfortunately those massacred bear in a certain way our signature."[668] The German generals agreed. Glaise thought that the old marshal had mismanaged the Croatian army, and "Dido," as head of the police, had created chaos in German-occupied territory by

his persecution of the Serbs, which merely fed the Partisan uprising.[669] But turning in his police badge did not stop "Dido," as head
of the Ustaša clique, from scouring the countryside for Orthodox
Serbs to kill. Still, the Germans were able to establish a firmer grip
on the NDH. When the post of commanding general of German
troops in Croatia was created on 1 November 1942, Glaise looked
forward to a thorough overhaul of the Croatian military.

The Italians anticipated a more loyal "ally" following the cabinet reshuffle, but were let down, for Pavelić quite successfully continued to play the two Axis Powers off against each other. Resent-
ful of the Wehrmacht's prestige in Zagreb, the Italians, who distrusted Glaise's professed disenchantment with the German-ori-
ented Croatian officer class, recoiled against any further major
change in Zagreb for fear that the Germans would benefit more
than they.

In fall 1942, despite hard-hitting Partisan counterattacks, the
Palazzo Chigi once again importuned Roatta to break off from
Četnik leaders.[670] Pavelić likewise inundated the 2nd Army commander with protests over Italy's unwillingness to stop Četnik massacres of Croatian Catholics.[671] Confidence in Roatta's judgment was
further questioned when Radio London announced that Pop Djujić,
a stalwart Italian confederate, had been decorated for services rendered to the Yugoslav government-in-exile.[672] The negative Croatian
view of the Četniks was reinforced by the censorious voices of the
Holy See, the Grand Mufti of Jerusalem, the German ambassador
in Rome, and the NDH, all of whom were exercised by Četnik violence against Catholics and Muslims. The Nazis in particular were
pressuring Rome to end the modus vivendi between the Italian army
and the Četniks.[673]

Without question incidents of Četnik indiscipline and transgressions against Croatian communities were on the rise.[674] A staunch
supporter like General Dalmazzo remarked on their unrestrained
violence and faithless politics,[675] while General Spigo acknowledged
that many Četniks under his command were recalcitrant and undisciplined.[676] Although having sent the usual haughty denials to NDH
officials of any major Četnik wrongdoing, Roatta asked the V Army

Corps commander to look into allegations of MVAC excesses.[677] Information that Četniks were defecting to the Partisans in large numbers might have spelled finis to Roatta's confidence in the Orthodox ally.

In what appeared to be a decided change of course, Roatta told Pavelić in mid October that he would bridle Četnik revenge on the Croatian population and order his corps commanders to collaborate with the NDH as a member of the Axis and an ally of Italy.[678] Untrustworthy units and those guilty of outrages against the Croatian people would be disarmed. "Attitudes that induce one to think that such and such a command, great or small, can, for example, be 'pro-Serb,' while others are 'pro-Croatian,' cannot be tolerated."[679] Such an unequivocal declaration of loyalty to Zagreb further narrowed his maneuverability with the Četniks.[680]

As the Italian forces contracted and the military vacuum widened, Roatta, as noted above, resorted to arming Muslims. By some ruse he got Jevdjević formally to agree to this. But keeping the Partisans at bay by this frenetic diplomacy was an exercise in futility, and reliance on the NDH was fast eroding.[681] Since the Ustaša and Domobrani heartily disliked each other,[682] Roatta was unable to coordinate them to act against the Partisans. Many Domobrani soldiers occupying forts abandoned by the Italians left for home or defected to the Partisans with their Italian equipment.[683] Faced by such dysfunctional allies, Roatta did not hesitate to turn over areas evacuated by Italian troops to Četniks rather than to Croats. No matter what he promised Zagreb, Roatta relied mainly on Četniks to hold the outer ring for his retreating troops.[684]

## *Italy Saves the Jews*

As Croatian Jews forced to take flight from the Ustaša round-ups in Zagreb, Ivo Herzer and his family, Jewish residents of Zagreb, found themselves in the town of Gospić, where they were afforded protection by common Italian soldiers. After many vicissitudes the family ended up in Cirquenizza [Crkvenica], which had been placed under Italian political authority. Protected by the tricolor, they were untouchable. While the Germans looked on in stony silence, the Italian soldiers winked at their captive brood. To keep the Germans off their backs and the Jews in their hands, the Italians devised clever excuses for inaction. One day General Roatta showed up to tell the Jews that they had been concentrated in a camp to make it easier for the army to protect them. Roatta, Herzer reminisces, wanted to "put all of us aboard a submarine so that we could disappear from view for the immediate future."[685]

During the summer of 1941, needing no encouragement from the Germans, the Ustaša drove more than two-thirds of about 38,000 Croatian Jews into concentration camps.[686] The few who escaped desperately sought refuge behind Italian lines. "Dido" Kvaternik demanded that the 2nd Army return all male Jews "who without our permission were sent by Italian authority to Cirquenizza."[687] The 2nd Army was in a quandary. As in the case of the desperate Orthodox Serbs, the Italians were prepared to protect the persecuted Jews; on the other hand, they lacked the resources—food and shelter—to take in the vast number of refugees fleeing the Ustaša. The Jews could not be sent to Italy, including the annexed areas, since they had been denied the right to obtain visas by an Italian law passed in August 1939.[688]

In March 1942 Pietromarchi came across information on the unspeakable Ustaša horrors visited on the Jews of Mostar by the Ustaša: "Of this regression, which dishonors humanity, we are in debt to the country of culture, to Germany."[689] But his friend Bastianini was not yet so moved. He either expelled or denied asylum to an undetermined number of Jews (as well as countless Orthodox Serbs fleeing the Ustaša and any Croat suspected of irredentism) and sent approximately 1,000 foreign Jews to Italy for internment.[690] Like a housekeeper cleaning out the trash, he wanted to drive the untidy Jewish refugees back into Croatia, where, as everyone knew, they would be greeted by the Ustaša with torture and death.[691] Bastianini was particularly diligent in rigorously applying the mainland racial laws to the Jewish community in Dalmatia, regardless of their "pertinenza."[692]

On 7 July Bastianini wrote Roatta that the "undesirable" Jews of Spalato should be turned out.[693] Pietromarchi showed a kindness absent in the Dalmatian governor: "Handing them [the Jews] over means to condemn them to extermination. Italy and the Army must avoid the shame of making themselves accomplices in such wickedness."[694] General Roatta agreed: "We have guaranteed [the Jews] a certain protection and have resisted Croatian pressure to deport them to a concentration camp. It is my opinion that if Jews who have fled to annexed Dalmatia were to be consigned to the Croatians, they would be interned at Jasenovac with the well-known consequences."[695]

As hands-on observers of Ustaša atrocities against the Orthodox Serbs, the Italians were not surprised that Jews should be victims too. The Poglavnik's oft-repeated offer to provide Jews "refuge" in concentration camps if they renounced their fixed assets was common knowledge. But for long the Italians had only a dim awareness that the Croat authorities were actually handing them over to the Germans. During an Italian-German lunch at the headquarters of the "Murge" division, a representative of the Todt organization let the news slip that the Italians were expected to cooperate in this grisly business. The commander, General Paride Negri, stated: "Oh no, that is totally impossible, because the deportation of Jews goes against the honor of the Italian army."[696]

The fate of the Jews seemed sealed when Germany and Croatia signed an agreement on 24 July by which the NDH would turn over Jews to the Nazis in Croatia, including those in the 2nd zone occupied by Italian troops. The next month the Ustaša and the Nazis signed an agreement whereby Croatia would pay thirty marks to the Germans per Jewish head transported to the Reich's concentration camps.

On 18 August 1942 the Germans officially opened a campaign to enlist Italy in the roundup of the Jews. The Minister of State at the German embassy in Rome, Prince Otto von Bismarck, delivered a telegram from von Ribbentrop, requesting that the Palazzo Chigi have the 2nd Army arrange for a transfer of Jews in Italian-occupied territory to German hands. There could be no doubt re-

garding German intentions. That the word "annihilation" in the
original was crossed out in favor of "dispersion and elimination"
did not obfuscate their purpose.[697] The vicissitudes of the Jews on
Croatian territory now became an integral part of Italy's formal
diplomatic relations with Germany.

The officials in the Palazzo Chigi were united in the resolve to
avoid complicity in the German Holocaust. In the expectation that
Mussolini would be as horrified as they by the German demand, they
drew up a memorandum for him summarizing Bismarck's note and
emphasizing the clear reference to the "dispersion and elimination"
of the Jews. To their consternation, instead of rejecting Bismarck's
note, Mussolini wrote the words *"nulla osta"* on the Italian summary—that is, he had no objection to condemning the Jews in the
Italian zone to death.[698] In the absence of any other instruction,
*"nulla osta"* was a typical bureaucratic phrase which allowed the necessary authority receiving the order a certain latitude in enforcing
it. Hence, one can argue that Mussolini, to avoid responsibility, had
left Roatta leeway in carrying out Bismarck's request. Pietromarchi,
on the other hand, believed that there was no ambiguity: "The Duce
has ordered the surrender to the Germans of the Jews who find
themselves in Croatian territory occupied by us."[699]

Pietromarchi lost no time in sabotaging this order. "I sent for
Castellani, who serves as liaison with the 2nd Army, and agreed with
him on the ways to avoid surrendering those Jews to the Germans
who have placed themselves under the protection of our flag."[700]
Lest there be any doubt on the 2nd Army's view, Roatta told
Pietromarchi that delivery of the Jews "is out of the question. They
have placed themselves under our authority. The Croats have asked
us to give them back. I naturally opposed it with a flat refusal. They
said that they would then have to ask the Germans. Now there's an
order from the Duce."[701] Neither man needed prompting to hold
off the Germans—as well as the Duce—by proceeding "without
any undue haste" on the Jewish question.[702]

Pietromarchi and Roatta were now in agreement to circumvent
the Germans and Croats without making their lack of cooperation
look like a defiance of the Third Reich. For perhaps the one and

only time Rome and Sušak worked in complete harmony. It is astonishing that these two men who advocated different policies in Yugoslavia—the one favoring Četniks and the other Pavelić—could so easily agree. Hardly a known humanitarian, Roatta, in protecting both Jews and Serbs from the merciless NDH, had in hand a convenient pretext for reminding both Germans and Croats that he alone was in charge of Italian-occupied territory. Pietromarchi, though revealing a greater sense of moral outrage over the plight of the Jews than the hard-boiled Roatta, acted inconsistently, being constrained to uphold official policy that called for support of the hangman's regime in Zagreb as the legitimate government of Croatia and faithful offspring of Fascist Italy.

On 31 August Roatta took pleasure in informing the Croats that they would not be able to touch anyone who had found Italian protection,[703] and proceeded to moralize: "I asked this Croatian commissioner general to exercise a sense of humanity—from which it is not impossible that he is completely disassociated—to take an immediate interest in the question and intervene with those authorities to bring a halt to a state of things that, independently of every other consideration, can lead to a serious disturbance of the public order."[704] On another occasion he demanded that Croatian authority intervene in Dubrovnik to avoid further abuses against the Jews.[705] For Roatta, handing over Jews would betray promises; his credibility with the Četniks was at stake.

> My own point of view is that consigning the Jews to the Germans or the Croatians would end in practice by harming our prestige because, even if only tactically, we have put them under our protection and because it would cause grave repercussions among the armed voluntary *Četnik* militia who might be induced to believe one day they too might be given over to the Ustaši.[706]

Rather than bend to the dictates of Germany, which would have meant compliance to the Third Reich's hegemony in Croatia, the Italians held to their golden rule as laid down by General Ambrosio on 7 September. No one seeking care and protection under the Italian tricolor would be discriminated against or turned away because of religion or race. For Roatta to honor this pledge required finesse. Bad blood ran deep between him and Cavallero, who feared that the 2nd Army commander was angling for his job. Roatta, in turn, suspected that "friends" in Rome were waiting for the chance to portray him as a rebel who did not obey orders. The phrase "Let him [Roatta] slip on the customary banana peel," was making the rounds at the Supreme Command.[707] Fortunately for Roatta Mussolini was either sick or out of Rome for much of the fall. In the absence of the Duce, Cavallero faded into the shadows.

In spite of relentless German pressure, the Italians continued to feint and dodge. Pietromarchi commented on 14 October: "They [the Germans] have repeatedly asked that their order to hand over the Croatian Jews be honored, but have learned that the 2nd Army has not received instructions in this sense."[708] Four days later: "While the Balkans are being put to fire and smoke Hitler has asked us for the nth time to deliver the Jews concentrated in the 2nd zone occupied by us . . . We have again given an evasive answer."[709] Pavelić, however, warmed hearts in Berlin by telling Hitler that wherever Croat authority existed, "the Jewish question would be resolved."[710] But he had no idea what to do about Roatta's dissembling. Instructions had been received from Rome, Roatta told Pavelić, to prepare Jews in the 2nd zone for delivery to the Germans, but added that he did not know whether the Wehrmacht was authorized to receive them![711]

Meanwhile, officials at the Palazzo Chigi searched for the right formula for deception. Five drafts later, at the end of October, one was finally found. Orders were sent to the General Staff to arrest and place in special camps the approximately 2,500 Jews living in the area of Italian occupation, where their origin and citizenship would be tabulated. Distinctions were to be made: Jews who were Croatian would be consigned to Zagreb; those bearing Italian citizenship would be placed under Italian protection.[712] Their internment would hopefully satisfy the Germans, who argued that Jews at liberty were either spies in the pay of Communists or represented a threat to the public order.

On receiving these instructions, the Italian military commanders were outraged. Colonel Zanussi thought that collecting Jews in camps was a prelude to handing them over to the Nazis via the Croatians.[713] Colonel Amodio was distressed by what he deemed a dishonorable mimicry of "the German system." The Croats were given an unexpected opportunity to divert hatred from themselves to Italy.[714] When the roundups commenced, rumors spread that Italy had buckled to German pressure. The Croats gleefully pointed out that Italy was not the civilized country of Roman legend but a German vassal unable to resist Nazi pressure.[715] Fearing imminent delivery to the Ustaša, many Jews gave way to despair and recrimination and a few committed suicide. General Roatta hastened to Porto Re [Kraljevice] on 27 November to assure his assembled guests that they had no grounds for fear. No Italian or Jew in Croatia was aware of the Palazzo Chigi's real intentions.

The masters of deception in Rome had misled the 2nd Army because they were involved in a complicated maneuver that required the utmost secrecy. By ordering that Jews be gathered up and placed in camps, they would be able to tell the Germans that the Army was taking "practical steps" toward a plan that would end with the extradition of their captives. Yet they were aware that Mussolini could, at his whim, ruin the work of obstruction and delay.

Mussolini's confidant, the peripatetic and well-heeled troubleshooter Carabinieri General Giuseppe Pièche—who moved with equal ease in military, diplomatic, and Fascist circles—joined the crowd of stonewallers. He informed the Foreign Ministry in a memorandum that received the stamp "seen by the Duce" that " . . . the Croatian Jews who were deported from the German-occupied territories of the West were 'liquidated' by poisonous gas in the railroad cars in which they were locked."[716] Pièche warned that the Italian army should avoid "soiling its hands" by handing over Jews on their territories to the Croats. The Vatican weighed in by admonishing Italy not to deliver Jews to the NDH. The secret was out in Rome that Jews handed to Croats would eventually land in Nazi death camps.

A decisive turn came during General Roatta's visit to Rome on 17 November, where he met with Mussolini and Cavallero. Roatta argued that betrayal of the Jews would undermine confidence in Italy on the part of the Četnik ally, which was still needed in the fight against the Partisans. Mussolini seemed to abrogate his "nulla osta" by suggesting that all Jews in Italian-occupied territory would find safety if willing to forfeit property possessed in Croatia.[717] However, fearful of affronting Germany, Mussolini would not allow any Jews to be transferred to Italy.[718]

Now what to do about the Germans? While trying to assure them that everything possible was being done to comply with their wishes, the Italians put a deft spin on the delays. Before one Jew could be turned over, much work had to be done. The army had to catalogue, count, and establish the original province of every Jew under its jurisdiction. Establishing legal status was an arduous and time-consuming business. Who were residents and who were refugees? What was the origin of citizenship? There was no end of practical problems to be resolved, too—a lack of trucks, gas shortages, and camps yet to be built.

Finally all the Jews were collected at Porto Re, supposedly ready for shipment. And there they stayed. During this period Nazi luminaries descended on Rome—Göring, Ribbentrop, and Himmler, among others—to exert further pressure on the Italians. Only Mussolini gave way in March, promising to ship the Jews held in Italian custody to Trieste, where the Germans could pick them up. "Italy must not become the protector of the Jews," he declared.[719] Generals Robotti and Pirzio Biroli countered by reminding the Duce that Četnik confidence in Italy would vanish following such a move. Bastianini, who as under-secretary had supposedly undergone a complete turnabout—he bragged later that Ribbentrop had branded him "an honorary Jew" (no one in Yugoslavia would ever have described him as "an honorary Slav")—drove home the main point: "We know the fate that awaits the Jews who are deported by the Germans. They are gassed. All of them—women, old men, and children. We will have no part in such atrocities. And you, Duce, must not allow it. Are you prepared to take this responsibil-

ity on yourself?"[720] Mussolini sought to elude von Ribbentrop's
nagging by a ruse. Because of Partisan activity, he advised Robotti:
"Say that we have no means of transport to take them [the Jews]
to Trieste."[721] Not for the first time had Mussolini been unwilling
to take responsibility. Pietromarchi spoke for Rome when he observed that the Germans were desperately trying to implicate Italy
in their brutal policies.[722]

Since by the end of March the 2nd Army was on its way home
and could no longer offer the Jews protection in Croatia, the officials at the Palazzo Chigi decided to send the 2,661 "internees" to
the island of Arbe [Rab], where they would be out of reach of the
Croats and Germans.[723] General Robotti, Roatta's successor as 2nd
Army commander, pointed out logistical problems: the camp at Arbe
lacked electricity, barracks, and food supplies; however, he eventually yielded to Rome's entreaties.[724] Robotti did not seem to mind
that the thousands of Slovenes huddled there suffered grievously
from these same deficiencies. He shared with the other Italian commanders the notion that declared enemies who had been rounded
up deserved brutal internment, but that *rastrellamenti* in the name of
a racial principle was not in keeping with Italian *civiltà*. Thus on Arbe
Jews were "guests" who would enjoy rudimentary amenities, while
Slovenes, as "criminals," were condemned to suffer and perish.[725]

The transfer of Jews began in May and ended in July. By September 1943 the number interned had reached 3,577. As opposed
to the Slovenes, who daily died from malnutrition, the Jews received
barely adequate food and shelter. When Italy surrendered, luckily
for them the Partisans arrived before the Germans. Some, like
Herzer and his family, found their way to the Italian mainland and
safety; except for the elderly and children, a large majority volun-
teered to fight for the Partisans from brigades already organized in
the Arbe barracks. Eighty percent of the Yugoslav Jews who fled
the Italian-occupied zones were saved.[726]

There is another not so happy side of the story. Many Jews,
seeking refuge in either Italian-occupied territory or in Italian-annexed provinces in Yugoslavia, were denied entry, or, having ille-
gally slipped across the frontier, were summarily deported if caught.

Temistocle Testa, the prefect of Fiume, surpassed Bastianini's record in denying Jews sanctuary and expelling those captured—approximately 800 between July 1941 and May 1942. The Ustaša was there to provide them with the customary homecoming.[727] The Italian commander Renato Coturri of the V Army Corps stationed in Fiume composed memoranda on the "cunning Jew." General Dalmazzo, who abided persecuted Serbs, forbade contact between his men and "Jewish elements."[728]

No question, the Italians had major logistical problems sheltering refugees of all kinds. Paranoid rulers like Bastianini were sure that these bedraggled people posed a threat to security and the maintenance of public order—much like the police and society look on the homeless in our own day. If refugee Jews arrived in Dalmatia penniless, they were condemned to a miserable existence and rarely knew from one moment to the next if they would be caught and deported. The Italian military often appeared to be unfeeling and insensitive to their plight. According to one eyewitness report, 7,000 Italian soldiers watched in silence while 500 Ustaša marched 700 Jews through the Croatian town of Gospić. Many other similar incidents of Italian indifference can be cited. Indeed, Italian troops have acquired a reputation for venality and laxness, particularly when compared to the more disciplined Wehrmacht. Hence it is no surprise to learn that many officers and soldiers saved Jews as part of a commercial transaction, accepting gifts and bribery in exchange for safe transit and protection. But not a few Italians, who knew that Jews thrown back to Ustaša territory meant deportation and death, were moved by compassion to hold out a helping hand. For yet others, the enjoyment of slapping the Croatian "allies" in the face by denying them "their" Jews was irresistible.

Before General Ambrosio issued his 7 September proclamation, Mussolini ordered the Italians to respect the political sovereignty of the Croatian government in areas they garrisoned. This non-intervention decree allowed the Ustaša to dispatch Jews to concentration camps at will under the noses of the Italian troops. For several months after September 1941, Jews, along with the persecuted Orthodox Serbs, were able to enjoy Italian protection on Croatian territory—

until the 17 June 1942 Italo-Croatian agreement, which restored political authority to the NDH in many Italian-occupied areas in Croatia. After that Jews were once again exposed to Ustaša roundups.

When all is said and done, Italy stands out as the lone country among Third Reich satellites that rejected German demands regarding Jews of Italian citizenry residing in other countries. Furthermore, only the Italians extended protection to non-Italian Jews found in territory where the tricolor flew.[729]

## The Beginning of the End

November 1942 was a disastrous month for the Italian armies fighting on far-flung fronts. The Allies landed unopposed in North Africa on 12 November; Tobruk fell the day after, which marked the loss of Cirenaica to the enemy. On the 20th Mussolini unrealistically promised Roatta an additional 20,000 troops and funds to equip and train half a million Croats to meet the threat.[730] He also vowed to sack Grazioli and Bastianini. Roatta, who considered these two Fascist commissars a hindrance to military operations, surprisingly pointed out that peremptory dismissal would make a bad impression. The Duce made no further move.[731]

Lacking clear directives from Rome, Roatta had to make hard and unpleasant decisions. Anticipating further losses of Italian troops to protect the mainland, he agreed to a unified command of Italian, German, and Croatian military forces, but left the Wehrmacht in the lurch by withdrawing troops from key areas under Partisan attack in Jajce and Banja Luka.[732] Roatta's aim was to tighten the defenses around Italian Dalmatia against a Partisan force, estimated to number 20,000, with troops falling back from the interior, accompanied by whatever Četniks were still with them. But such a precipitous retreat left many Serb villages on the perimeter exposed to Partisan reprisals. Many Orthodox fled before the Partisan advance and took refuge in Knin, where they began to turn on their Italian protectors. Since Bastianini refused to admit any more Serbs in his province, the army was faced with the unpalatable prospect of having to abandon them to Partisan vengeance.

To check the Partisan onslaught, Croats and Serbs frantically cobbled together plans to coordinate a resistance, but these quickly fell apart because of long-standing hostility. Both sides blamed the Italians for their sorry plight: the NDH for handing over fortresses to the Serbs, the Četniks for kowtowing to the Croats. While the Domobrani were amply supplied with German war materiel, the Četniks ended up starved of needed weapons.[733] (Still, they received ten times more arms from the 2nd Army than they did from British airdrops.[734]) Taking advantage of the mounting confusion, the Partisans ever more boldly blew up bridges and derailed trains. "These rebels pullulate like vermin on a decomposing organism," reflected Pietromarchi.[735]

Having to pare down his own forces for defense of the homeland, Roatta prepared to dig in on the Dalmatian beachhead. There was a defeatist strain in his memoranda that spoke of a desire to flee the Balkan mess in the realization that his country's days were numbered. In a round of meetings in Rome during mid-November, Roatta told General Löhr that he lacked the strength to wipe out the guerrillas; he could only make their life miserable by destroying winter quarters and supply bases.[736] Italy's Balkan empire had turned into a chimera. Military headquarters wrestled with the daunting task of moving large numbers of troops widely dispersed in inhospitable terrain to the coastal areas, mainly by means of donkeys. Disengagement of the troops trapped in countless military and political coils was also no easy matter. Troop morale wavered. Roatta admitted: "The units were *poor in quality* by age and training; *tired* because of heavy duty for months without the possibility of rations; *insufficient* in number."[737] Added to disarray in the ranks, the Italians not infrequently yielded to German and Četnik pressure to turn around for yet another punitive anti-Partisan expedition. By permitting progress toward the Dalmatian ports to slow to a crawl, the Italians courted disaster in the months ahead. When the year 1943 turned, they allowed themselves against their better judgment to be drawn into German-planned *rastrellamenti* against the Partisans that were larger in scale that any undertaken previously during the Axis occupation of Yugoslavia.

The partition of Yugoslavia, 1941–1945.

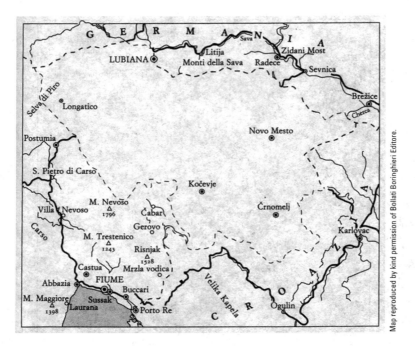

*above*
Slovenia, spring 1942.

*right*
Dalmatia, 1941–1943.

Montenegro.

Mussolini, Hitler, and Galeazzo Ciano meet on a train in 1941.

Ciano *(left)* and Joachim von Ribbentrop in 1941.

Draža Mihailović in 1937 as Yugoslav military attaché to Prague.

Mussolini and Ante Pavelić, the Poglavnik of Croatia, in Rome in 1941.

*above*

Pavelić *(left)* and Ciano sign the Italian-
Croatian agreement of 1941.

*left*

Mihailović at Ravna Gora,
where he established his headquarters
in May 1941.

Cardinal Alojzije Stepinac.

*left*

A partisan fighter from Plevija captured by Italian Alpine troops.

*below*

Italian artillery from the "Belluno" regiment firing near Plevija.

Buildings on fire in the streets of a town overtaken by Italian army units.

*left*
General Mario Robotti, commander of the 11th
Army Corps, 1941–1942.

*below*
Ante Pavelić *(left)* and Slavko Kvaternik in Venice in
May 1941 to sign the border agreement for the NDH
(Croatian State).

*right*
General Vittorio Ambrosio, commander of
the Italian 2nd Army and later Chief of Staff.

*left*
General Mario Roatta, commander of the
Italian 2nd Army following Ambrosio.

*right*
Giuseppe Bastianini, governor of Dalmatia and later
undersecretary of foreign affairs in 1943.

*above*
General Ugo Cavallero
on the Yugoslav front in
April 1941.

*right*
Atrocities and
propaganda: Italian
soldiers castrated by
partisans.

*above*
Hanging of a partisan woman accused of having participated in the castration of the soldiers in Nikšić in May 1942.

*left*
Mussolini *(right)*, with General Pirzio Biroli, tours the Greek front on March 18, 1941.

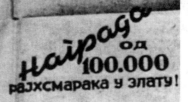

**награда од 100.000 рајхсмарака у злату!**

100.000 Рајхсмарака у злату добиће онај који доведе жива или мртва вођу банди Дражу Михаиловића.

Овај злочинац бацио је земљу у највећу несрећу. Отупавши од развратног живота, уобразио је он да је позван да „ослободи" народ. Као енглески плаћеник, овај смешни хвалисавац није ништа друго радио већ утирао пут бољшевизму и тиме помагао да се униште сва национална добра која су народу од вајкада била висока и света.

Он је тиме пореметио мир сељака и грађанина, упропастио имање, добро

па и живот хиљадама људи, а земљу бацио у неописиву беду и невољу.

Стога је овај опасни бандит у земљи уцењен са 100.000 Рајхсмарака у злату.

Онај који докаже да је овог злочинца учинио безопасним или га преда најближој немачкој власти не само што ће добити награду од 100.000 Рајхсмарака у злату, него ће тим извршити једно национално дело јер ће ослободити народ и отаџбину од бича нечовечног крвавог терора.

Врховни Заповедник

German poster offering a 100,000 reich mark reward for the capture of Mihailović, "dead or alive."

*above*
King Peter visits with President Roosevelt in June 1942 seeking U.S. support for Mihailović.

*below*
Josip Broz ("Tito") *(center)* with his staff.

Mihailović in handcuffs in 1946 awaiting trial, where he would be condemned to death and executed by the new Communist regime.

# Chapter VII

# Operation *Weiss*

Planning Operation *Weiss*
Diplomatic Byplay between Rome and Berlin
Italy and *Weiss* II
Croatian Wake-Up Call
The Italian Military and the Četniks
Solemn Truths

*Planning Operation Weiss*

D uring the course of 1943, stresses in the anti-guerrilla front
of Germany, Italy, and Croatia grew worse. Unfavorable outside events aggravated the centrifugal pressures of the Axis alliance.
The German defeat at Stalingrad and the Anglo-American landing
in North Africa marked a turning point of the war and exposed Italy
to an Allied invasion. Self-defense took precedence over Axis cooperation. To protect the mainland, the Supreme Command was
poised to call home major units from Yugoslavia while leaving the

rest to hold the coastal belt on the Adriatic. Evacuation of the Balkans seemed imminent. But the Italians were loath to sacrifice their *spazio vitale*. And they were aghast at the thought of the Germans taking advantage of their country's declining war fortunes by moving into territory abandoned by the 2nd Army.

The Germans calculated quite differently. The sudden threat of an Allied front somewhere along the Aegean or Adriatic coasts made it imperative to stamp out insurgency throughout the Balkans. Aware of British contacts with both Četniks and Partisans, Berlin feared that they would come together in a major uprising synchronized with an Allied amphibious operation. To maintain the outer perimeter of the fortress Fatherland, the Germans intended to throw back the invading forces. First the interior needed to be secured. Transportation systems, communication networks, and vital mineral deposits were constantly subjected to Partisan attack. Tito's forces had already disrupted important links connecting Belgrade, Vienna, and Salonika to the Adriatic ports of Spalato, Fiume, and Trieste. Through these arteries, in lieu of dangerous sea routes patrolled by the ever-vigilant Royal Navy, Germany sent large supplies of materiel to the African front.

While scanning the waters for the anticipated invasion, the Germans devised Operation *Weiss* to inflict a mortal blow on both Partisans and Četniks. In crushing insurgency, a secondary aim would be achieved—stabilization of the tottering Croatian state. But if Tito's forces had by this time superseded its bitter rival as the most formidable foe, Hitler, fixated on Mihailović, seemed the last to know. An unspoken German purpose was to wrest Croatia from Italian hands. In Berlin's view, Italy had become an uncertain ally on the verge of defeat. Mussolini appeared more and more a shadowy and infirm figure floundering in mounting opposition led by the king with strong military support. Since the Germans were already anticipating an overthrow of the Duce and the downfall of Fascism, it was not too far-fetched for them to suspect a cabal of Italian military officers searching for a way out of the Axis alliance. During more halcyon days, when Mussolini was in top trim and military optimism in Rome waxed strong, the 2nd Army was, from the German perspective, at best a prickly partner, at worst impudently anti-German. With Italy's military fortunes now in a free fall, Berlin viewed the behavior of the 2nd Army, particularly its continued utilization of the Četniks, as treacherous.

As German patience with the Italians ran thin, their litany of complaints piled high: the Italians dallied with the Četniks, fought the Partisans half-heartedly, and abandoned fortresses without prior discussion or notification. Hitler had already made clear his position on the Četniks by posing the question of their disarmament in latter December 1942.[738] Since Marshal Cavallero "adhered without reserve" to the Führer's point of view,[739] the Germans anticipated that Italy would disarm valuable allies without further fuss. They would make the decisions and instruct the Italians in the art of amiable compliance.[740]

Pietromarchi shared these German views. Italy, he felt, should not bank on a policy based on the "ineluctable eventuality" of a Četnik defection when the Allies landed in the Balkans.[741] Germany's flagging confidence in Italy's ability to manage its own house was, in his opinion, crucial. To reimpose obedience on the 2nd Army, "Italy must assert itself" by removal of the pro-Četnik warrior/politicians in Yugoslavia.[742]

In Sušak the 2nd Army commanders groused over German leadership and Wehrmacht conduct of the war. They sized up General Löhr as a stodgy air force general and thought that further resources expended in faraway Croatia were resources thrown away. Additional *rastrellamenti* in remote regions would tie up troops needed for homeland defense against an imminent Allied invasion. General Roatta accordingly outlined a plan on 22 November for a more restricted deployment of the 2nd Army.[743] In addition to distant outposts abandoned the previous year, his commanders began to undertake other pullbacks to strengthen key centers like Knin, Drniš, and the mountain ranges defending Spalato and Zara. Next would be a withdrawal from the outer regions of Herzegovina to protect the areas around Ploča and Metković. Concentrated in more compact and defensible areas, the troops, worn out by months of constant fighting without leave or rotation, would be able to rest and recuperate.

In the second half of December, the Germans formally apprised Rome of Operation *Weiss*. In disregard of the 2nd Army, the Germans, in their endeavor to stamp out insurgency, intended to campaign in western Bosnia, which happened to be located on the Italian side of the demarcation line. Instructed by Hitler, the OKW informed Cavallero that General Alexander Löhr would assume command of the Axis forces in the Balkans: Greece, Dalmatia, Croatia, and Montenegro. Cavallero insisted on parity in command and received it, but grudgingly.[744] It was a typical Axis military arrangement by which Italian subordination, if not committed to print, was confirmed by the existing situation. Löhr took charge of *Weiss* while Roatta acted as backseat driver. No matter how much the 2nd Army commanders sought to retain a modicum of independence, they could not, as 1943 turned, avoid the reality that Italy had finally and definitively been forced to assume the position of Germany's subaltern in the Yugoslav war theater.

The Italian generals Cavallero, Ambrosio, Roatta, Dalmazzo, and Pirzio Biroli, together with General Löhr, assembled in Rome for a series of meetings on 3–4 January. It was agreed that the Wehrmacht would set off south of Zagreb-Karlovac, and southwest from Banja Luka toward Montenegro, while Italian troops moved from their bases in northern and central Dalmatia to protect the German right flank.[745] Somewhere between them they would find and annihilate "the Partisan State."

Cavallero announced that Operation *Weiss*, besides cleaning up Partisans, should "confine and then disarm" the Četniks. This view was vigorously opposed by Roatta, who wanted to protect his "white marble." Drawing Četniks to Italy by favored treatment would mean weaning them from the faraway English. In more private sessions among the Italians, backbiting prevailed. Roatta told Pietromarchi that if Četniks were disarmed, he would step down. "Perhaps this is the only way available to escape an inextricable situation," Pietromarchi noted."[746] Pirzio Biroli, in turn, lambasted Ciano for supporting Germany's decision to disarm the Četniks. Pietromarchi countered by pointing out that it was Cavallero and the Germans who had laid down this law, not the Palazzo Chigi. Pirzio Biroli "has shouldered our ministry with responsibility for this outcome."[747]

During a break in the formal military meetings, the Italian generals had an audience with Mussolini, where Operation *Weiss* was reviewed. After the first phase, to be carried out by Italy and Germany, five thousand Montenegrins would join the Četniks in Herzegovina to block Tito's escape, a plan strongly urged by Pirzio Biroli: "I will have my head cut off if the only prisoners rounded up will not be taken by my Montenegrins. They know how to find the enemy. They are people who fight with hate." To prove Montenegrin loyalty, Pirzio Biroli offered himself as a hostage. "Believe me," he boasted, "I will go into Croatia and clear out all the rebels."[748] Mussolini replied that the Četnik question would be revisited.[749]

Cavallero proceeded to distort the views of his generals by telling General Löhr (perhaps to deceive him) that "we will no longer deliver arms to the Četniks," that Pirzio Biroli would collaborate in action against them, and that Roatta no longer would support his auxiliaries.[750] Notwithstanding Cavallero's misrepresentations to the Germans, he, prompted by Roatta, prevailed on Mussolini to overlook Ciano's skepticism of the "precarious and dangerous" understandings with the Četniks.[751] That the Četniks harbored Great Serb ideas was no mystery to the generals, but they were not bothered by this so long as the Četniks fought the Partisans.

Roatta met with German generals on 9–10 January. If Löhr remained silent on the Četnik question, Glaise, in an aside to the Italian general, admitted that it would be foolish not to utilize them against the Partisans.[752] (Indeed, certain German units on the local level were delivering weapons and supplies to the Četniks.[753]) Satisfied on that score, Roatta proceeded to acquaint his interlocutors with the Italian method of dealing with the native population. Males from fifteen to fifty caught in zones thought to be sympathetic to the Partisans would be interned, and suspected civilians would be shot or hung and their houses destroyed.[754] This hardly shocked the Germans, who, by order of Hitler, were deep in plans to purge hostile peoples and consign all Orthodox males of fighting age to concentration camps.[755] But some protested. Glaise pointed out to

Löhr in a letter dated 4 January that to declare peremptorily the civil population enemies, simply because they lived in Partisan-controlled or military combat areas, was a draconian measure. Like other German officers before him, he recognized that most people living outside Wehrmacht-dominated areas, their lives daily imperiled by marauding bands, had, perforce, to seek out local insurgent leaders for protection.[756]

Since Italian troops were already on the move toward the coast, and Operation *Weiss* was to be launched in the dead of winter, Roatta wrote it off as a harebrained scheme. But the Germans were not to be denied. They brought Ciano around to their military plans and enjoined Cavallero not to withdraw but to reoccupy the 3rd zone. Cavallero obliged by promising the troops.[757] Operation *Weiss* would go forward. When rebuked by his camp adjutant, Colonel Giacomo Zanussi, for failing to stand up to the Germans, Roatta lamely replied: "Orders were orders."[758] Hardly concealing his dark pessimism, he told Ciano that to carry out "the German plan of extermination we need a great many more troops than both we and Germany can afford."[759] Both Ambrosio and Roatta laughed at the idea of Croats defending aqueducts and hydroelectric plants from Partisan attacks,[760] and they certainly had no interest in protecting the German bauxite mines around Mostar. Their sole purpose was to keep the Wehrmacht out of the region.[761]

On 15 January, three days before the scheduled launching of Operation *Weiss*, the Supreme Command reiterated its intention of withdrawing troops to the Dinaric Alps, an idea Mussolini had broached as far back as 28 December 1941 and reformulated on 31 July 1942. Roatta, as we have seen, had already undertaken retreats. Pietromarchi was not unopposed to a withdrawal, but wanted to be sure that the defense lines from Romania to Italy through the Balkans were deep enough to allow for the cargoes bearing indispensable oil.[762]

Like Roatta, General Ambrosio had no qualms about disengaging Italian troops from Croatia's outer regions. But as usual no timetable was set. Operation *Weiss* tied them up and, as Ambrosio pointed out, "political interferences" in Rome (Hitler's pressure on

Mussolini) caused considerable delays. The two Italian generals sought to profit from this by rushing Četniks into the Italian-evacuated zones before the major body of the Italian troops headed toward Dalmatia. The Italians had fallen between two stools: they neither ceased to participate in the German-masterminded sweeps nor simply got out of the 3rd and 2nd zones. Their reluctance to hand over Italian-occupied territory to German and Croat "allies" slowed the evacuation of the interior to a snail's pace.

When Roatta sped up arms deliveries to the Četniks,[763] Ciano concluded that Rome had lost control over the 2nd Army commander.[764] Because Ciano intensely disliked Cavallero, he would bypass him and ask the Croats to persuade Berlin to apply pressure on the errant Italian commander. But Roatta undercut this maneuver by prevailing on General Löhr to accept a limited engagement of Četniks in predetermined sectors.[765] In this he again indirectly received the support of Glaise, who on frequent occasions had himself sought OKW permission to approach the Četniks. Armed with Mussolini's concurrence on the Četnik question, Roatta was finally in a position to tell Pavelić without diplomatic circumlocution that he would employ Četnik formations in the upcoming campaign and "orient himself" to their disarmament in an undefined future.[766] But much to his embarrassment, Četniks in some places had seized power at the expense of the hapless Croats without notifying the Italian command.[767] Roatta persisted in cooperating with the unreliable Četniks, not because he believed in their loyalty but because the Axis did not have enough troops to carry out the "German plan of extermination" against them.[768]

If Roatta and Cavallero differed on the Četnik question, they were in agreement that not one German foot should step into Herzegovina. Moreover, no Italian troops should be employed for garrison duty in areas "pacified" by the Germans in the 3rd zone. Having set these conditions, Cavallero authorized the inclusion of Pirzio Biroli's "volunteers" from Montenegro for operations in Croatia,[769] and Roatta released the "Lombardia," "Re," and "Sassari" divisions, as well as about 6,000 Četnik auxiliaries from the Lika region and northern Dalmatia for the upcoming campaign.[770] To

fend off the Germans, Roatta reiterated his divide-and-rule stratagem: instead of taking on Četniks and Partisans at the same time,
pit them against each other and dispose of the survivors.[771] History
was repeating itself: the same differences between Italian and German purposes and policies that vitiated the planning for Operation
*Trio* persisted to cripple Operation *Weiss*. And worse was to come.

As opposed to the earlier undermanned expeditions, the Germans assembled five divisions, which jumped off on 20 January with
the above-mentioned Italians and the 369th Croat division to pacify
the entire area from south of Zagreb to the Montenegrin border—
some 65,000 troops pitted against 20,000 Partisans.

Roatta intended to foist the brunt of the fighting on the Četniks,
guessing that such a policy would further widen the gap between
Tito and Mihailović.[772] But in so doing, the Italians alienated many
Četnik leaders, including Mihailović, by subordinating them to the
2nd Army's command. As a result of endless misunderstandings,
troops moved around aimlessly or failed to arrive at their assigned
battle stations. The Germans made clear their intention of sending
two divisions into Herzegovina to disarm Italian-organized Četniks
concentrated there and replace them with their own garrisons.[773]
Pietromarchi concluded that the 2nd Army, in spite of having "thirty
divisions or so as compared to Germany's ten," had allowed the
Wehrmacht to dictate military policy and take "control over the
entire peninsula."[774]

During latter January, in a move that offended no one save the
Germans, Cavallero was dismissed from the Supreme Command
and replaced by General Ambrosio. General Roatta was removed
as commander of the 2nd Army and sent to Sicily. (At the end of
May, he was appointed chief of the army staff.) Roatta's days had
long been numbered. Relegated to Cavallero's doghouse, he had
no support from Pietromarchi either. Count Giuseppe Volpi, an
ambitious financial and industrial mogul who had easy access to
Mussolini, told the Duce that the 2nd Army should be placed in
the hands of a general "less bookish . . . and more aggressive" than
General Roatta.[775] But Mussolini suddenly revoked the order to
dismiss him from the Yugoslav command. "With Roatta or with-

out," reflected Pietromarchi, "the prestige of the 2nd Army has hit bottom."[776] The backstage maneuvering, however, was far from finished. Acting on the wishes of Bastianini, who was barely on speaking terms with Roatta, the king gave the word that the Italian commander was to be removed from Sušak. The deed was done on 1 February. General Robotti, of Slovenian fame, was handed the 2nd Army command on the 5th. Pietromarchi lamented: "The 2nd Army has been given over to incompetence."[777]

Other major changes soon followed. Ciano was discharged from the Foreign Ministry and posted at Vatican City as ambassador to the Holy See. Pietromarchi was sorry to see his boss go: "Ciano is a generous man, has a very noble heart and an extraordinarily fast intelligence. He is a brilliant stylist, good conversationalist, and has a Tuscan wit. He is faithful in friendships and deprecates those who let him down."[778] Mussolini took over foreign policy and appointed Bastianini undersecretary of state.

The overhaul of the cabinet occurred against a background of ominous events that propelled the country toward the abyss: heavy German defeats on the Soviet front, staggering Italian losses in the Mediterranean, irreversible Axis setbacks in North Africa, massive Allied air bombardments of Italian cities, and Mussolini's nagging health issues. Defeatism was in the air, and Ciano's appointment to the Vatican seemed to presage a separate peace, as did the mission of the American representative Myron Taylor to the Holy See. But Mussolini's cabinet reshuffle had nothing to do with peace or contacts with the enemy. He wanted a more disciplined team to tighten up the country for protracted conflict over the long haul. And he wanted time for inducing Hitler to abandon his hopeless crusade against the Soviet Union. A truce with Stalin would enable the Axis to focus on the Mediterranean, where the Anglo-Americans could be finished off before they had a chance to launch an invasion of the Italian Peninsula.

Once Ambrosio had replaced Cavallero, the Germans' "Quisling" at the Supreme Command, the Italian military team in Yugoslavia could afford to be less accommodating to its Axis partner, which reduced the friction between Rome and Sušak. The Italians were at one in questioning the German strategy to pursue Balkan guerrillas relentlessly across the breadth of Italy's "zones of occupation." The united front was established just in time. In early February General Walter Warlimont, deputy chief of the Wehrmacht's operations staff, expressing the most earnest wishes of the Führer, stepped up pressure on Ambrosio to reoccupy territory in the 3rd zone and to disarm the Četniks during the current *Weiss* operation. The Italian general replied that he had no reserves available to move in behind the Germans—indeed the 2nd Army was poised to abandon the 3rd zone completely. The Partisans should be defeated with the help of the Četniks, who would be disarmed in a nebulous future, "with circumspection, not in haste."[779]

General Robotti needed no persuasion in carrying out Ambrosio's directives. He considered the German battle plan "stupid" and resented the dispersion of Italian forces.[780] At a meeting in Belgrade on 8 February, he told General Löhr that, "because the region was perfectly tranquil," future operations in Herzegovina (in the Italian-occupied zone) were unnecessary. Therefore Operation *Weiss* should be scrapped. The Četniks would be disarmed, but only "at a propitious moment."[781] Why, he wrote Rome, should Italy tolerate the absurdity of an action that could only be characterized as a betrayal of the Četniks?[782] Löhr raised no objection; neither could Ambassador Kasche, for, as he admitted, the Wehrmacht itself had established contact with Četniks loyal to Germany.[783] Robotti took a break from military statecraft to chastise his commanders for falling down on reprisals. "It is absolutely inadmissible to leave unpunished acts of piracy committed by the Partisans"; such conduct should be followed up by *"immediate and energetic"* repression by every conceivable means.[784] The Germans held up their end in this first stage of the campaign by arresting 2,010 men and 350 women suspects and, in addition, interning in the camp at Semlino 490 men and 283 women.[785]

Notwithstanding Robotti's determination to avoid costly engagements with either Tito or Mihailović, military operations in mid-February took a nasty turn for the Italians when the Partisans captured the town of Prozor in the Neretva river valley, destroyed a small Četnik contingent there, and shattered elements of the widely dispersed "Murge" division holed up in isolated forts.[786] The battle was vicious. The Partisans shot captured officers, wounded prisoners, and all captives of the 259th regiment except for the drivers, who were needed to transport the munitions and wounded.[787] The Italians lost 2,300 men.[788] A large cache of supplies fell into the hands of the attacking Partisans, who were now poised for an assault on Mihailović's bastion in Herzegovina.[789]

## Diplomatic Byplay Between Rome and Berlin

Aware that Ambrosio and Bastianini were more restrained in following Germany's lead than their predecessors Cavallero and Ciano, Hitler sent Mussolini a sarcastic letter on 16 February that dwelled on his vacillation and Italian disingenuousness. "If a landing takes place tomorrow, Duce, anywhere in the Balkans, then Communists, followers of Mihailović and all the other irregulars will be in accord on one thing: launching an immediate attack on the German or Italian armed forces (as the case may be) in support of the enemy landings." To avoid a surprise attack by an Anglo-Saxon landing in the Balkans, the Führer continued, the Axis must "disarm both the Communists and the Četniks and 'neutralize' the whole area." Otherwise "revolt would break out, in the event of invasion, and all communications with Greece would be cut. The German divisions in the region would then have to fight the rebels—Communist and Četnik—and Italian troops will be unable singlehandedly, to stave off an invasion of the Peloponnese or the Adriatic."[790]

In two clear-headed memoranda to Mussolini, Ambrosio delivered a synopsis of Italian policy:

As to an attack against the Balkans, we think that the lack of suitable ports on the Western coastline, the impenetrable nature of the hinterland, and the distance from the principle objective—the Romanian oilfields—could lead the enemy to act against Salonica with the view to occupying Crete and the Archipelago . . . *it suffices to state that it is absolutely necessary for us to withdraw our forces from less important fronts (Croatia), to increase the garrisons of the islands, to build up a reserve in the mother country, to bring up the strength* the Western and Eastern Alpine frontiers. In addition we cannot contribute to a strategic reserve in the Balkan peninsula . . . The Germans must . . . decide to grant Italian requests for material to put the defense of their coasts and those of Greece in order; and facilitate as soon as possible the disengagement of Italian divisions operating in Croatia, permitting their withdrawal to the coast to a line enabling them to hold the key points there [Zara, Sebenico, Ragusa, Cattaro] . . . These troops in the Balkan peninsula must be set up as a strategic reserve. Mobile forces should be sent to Greece giving added flexibility, and also to watch the approaches to Salonika.[791]

When Ambrosio was appointed supreme commander, Mussolini told him: "The cycle of Cavallero is closed. What do you intend to do"? Ambrosio replied: "I intend to put my foot down against the Germans." Mussolini: "Very good. I will help you."[792] Ambrosio now seemed to go one step further, stating that "the Germans must change their operational objectives and must come to our aid, and help us, *otherwise we shall not be obliged to follow them in their erroneous conduct of the war.*"[793]

Aware of Ambrosio's diffidence and fearful that the recent changing of the guard in Rome presaged an Italian separate peace, German mandarins hastened to Rome to keep Mussolini in the war and re-establish Italian subordination in the Axis. In a series of meetings at the end of February, Ribbentrop and General Warlimont spelled out Hitler's grave concerns to an Italian delegation consisting of Mussolini, Bastianini, and Ambrosio. The Führer anticipated an Allied invasion in the Balkans and demanded the extirpation of the Četniks, who, in his opinion, were under the command of insurgency's premier leader, Mihailović, the sycophant of the British General Staff.[794] Mussolini discounted an Allied landing and pondered a solution of the Četnik problem. Mihailović was a bitter foe, he admitted, but "eight thousand Četniks in Herzegovina give Italy more help than two or three divisions, especially since they are such specialists in guerrilla warfare."[795] No question the Italians downplayed the numbers of Četniks in their employ and wrongly insisted that they were disciplined and closely supervised.[796]

Mimicking Roatta, Bastianini snapped: "Let them [the Četniks and Partisans] destroy each other."[797] In a swipe at Operation *Weiss*, he declared that vast sweeps did not work. Upon conclusion of every mopping-up exercise, the "rebels" would pop up everywhere from cleverly concealed places. Frustrated by counterinsurgency failures, Bastianini sought to reconsider everything "from top to bottom." One way or the other, the Axis Powers had to extricate themselves from a deepening military morass.[798] Since in this period of Italy's declining military fortunes it was no longer fashionable to expound on Fascist themes of imperial conquest, Bastianini, to counter the enemy's propaganda that the Allied Powers were fighting on the side of the angels, showcased a "New European Order." This concept had the purpose of convincing the occupied and Tripartite countries of Nazi Europe that they were participating as free peoples in a fruitful collaboration with the Axis Powers. Mussolini, however, displayed little interest in Bastianini's ruse, and, not surprisingly, Hitler none at all. Ambrosio achieved a Pyrrhic victory in having the Germans put off a final showdown with the Četniks to a misty future.[799] Only in this limited sense was Pietromarchi correct when remarking that, for the first time, the Italians had looked the Germans squarely in the eye and held firmly to a position.[800] General Warlimont would suffer Italian views on the Četniks if the 2nd Army deferred further troop withdrawals.[801]

Mussolini, the 2nd Army, and the Palazzo Chigi agreed on another important point: Italy could no longer cope with rebellion in Yugoslavia. The Duce confessed to Ribbentrop: "No effective methods of combating the partisans had yet been found. The German and Italian regular troops were not up to guerrilla warfare. This method of warfare was highly uncongenial, involved heavy losses, and had so far brought inadequate results."[802] Tortured semantics over the Četniks aside, the fundamental differences between Rome and Berlin were merely papered over. The Germans expected the Italians to do as they were told in rooting out insurgency the German way. Not daring to criticize the Duce for his wavering, Ribbentrop disgustedly concluded that the Italian officers were singularly ill-adapted to fight an ideologically Fascist war.[803]

## Italy and Weiss II

Following the end of *Weiss* I on 15 February, the Germans launched *Weiss* II against the Partisans on the 20th during the joyless Italian experience at Prozor.[804] To prevent the Partisans from crossing the Neretva, the Germans assigned Italy the task of blocking them from the south. The Italians saw things differently. General Robotti was testy with the Germans for stubbornly pressing on without taking account of the dispersion of his forces. And the situation in Herzegovina had dissolved into utter confusion. The Četnik leaders could not decide whether to resist or comply with Italian orders; Mihailović strove to mold a semblance of unity among his warlords, which conflicted with Italian efforts to bring them under the 2nd Army's control; and the Germans divided their worries between Četniks and Partisans around Mostar, which created differing objectives between the Axis partners.

By the end of February, fed up with Italian dillydallying, the Germans decided to proceed with *Weiss* II on their own. As the Četniks in Herzegovina shifted their attention from the Partisans to face the imminent German threat, Tito's legions in early March marshaled their forces for a breakthrough across the Neretva to Herzegovina in the direction of Montenegro. The odds were long, but fortune smiled on them when a large portion of the 2,000–5,000 Četniks in their way unexpectedly broke and ran during the early weeks of March. In a "biblical exodus" during this final stage of *Weiss* II, the Partisans escaped the Axis pincers movement.[805]

When Tito's shock troops broke out of a pocket north of the Neretva through Četnik lines, they proved their military superiority over the insurgent rivals.[806] But the victory was not theirs alone. Just when the Četniks appeared to have them bottled up, the Germans, arriving from Serbia, suddenly fell on their exposed flank. Surprised by the attack, the Četniks fell back in disorder and lost many men and large quantities of equipment, which gave the Partisans enough time to escape.[807] And the Italians were hardly blameless. To steer the Axis ally away from Mostar on Italy's side of the demarcation line—and from any contact with the Herzegovinian Četniks—Robotti, acting on the orders of Mussolini, implored Löhr to halt his advance at a line running north of the city.[808] This complicated the Wehrmacht's encirclement plans by leaving open a corridor through which the Partisans could escape. Upsetting the Germans' battle plan did not prevent the Italians from reproaching them for "tardy advances" and "unexpected" retreats.[809]

Actually, the Četniks had brought about their own downfall by ignoring Italian orders in Herzegovina. Moreover, the Montenegrin Nationalists, by deploying their forces independently of the Italian "Taurinense" division, opened up a gap between them.[810] When the smoke cleared from the Battle of the Neretva, the Partisans had gained a decisive advantage over the Četniks in their civil war in Yugoslavia—an unwelcome outcome of Operation *Weiss* from the Italian standpoint.

Tito had conducted a virtuoso performance. He was able to administer a crushing defeat on the Četniks and he had escaped the Germans mainly through a diplomacy contrived to delay their advance while his forces prepared for maneuver and recuperation.[811] In early March Tito sent a high-level delegation to German headquarters in Sarajevo for the purpose of arranging a temporary ceasefire. Here they hoped to discuss an exchange of prisoners and to avoid further punishing reprisals by gaining recognition of the Partisans as a belligerent force. Further, in an offer exceeding anything proposed by the Četniks, Partisan representatives expressed a readiness to oppose by force any attempted Allied landing on the Adriatic coast.[812] Owning up only to prisoner exchange negotiations, the Partisans had long kept these comprehensive proposals carefully concealed for fear of being exposed to the charge of collaboration they had levied against the Četniks. Tito showed that when faced with destruction, he, too, could bow to *force majeure*.

If Tito had accommodated to Hitler's major objective—the liquidation of the Četniks—his essay in diplomacy with the Germans

was short-lived. Ribbentrop, told by Hitler that "one does not negotiate with the rebels, one shoots them," abruptly ordered an end
to the talks with the Partisans on 29 March. Tito, meanwhile, having made Četnik destruction top priority, issued orders to shoot
every captured officer "without mercy."[813]

*Weiss* II had not only misfired militarily, it had ruined the 2nd
Army's plan to withdraw to the "15 January" line. Instead of an
orderly retreat, Italian troops were widely dispersed and exhausted
by the Wehrmacht's constantly shifting battle plans; instead of regulated deployment, troop strength had been dangerously thinned out
by orders from Rome to send weapons and units back across the
Adriatic for homeland defense. Rather than having Četniks move
into Italian-abandoned fortresses in the Lika area, Partisans competed with Croats in taking them over. And the Partisans had not
suffered a knockout blow on the Neretva River; on the contrary, they
were reassembling, replenished by rest and the acquisition of captured heavy weapons. Their morale had soared while the Italian
troops only wanted to go home. The future of Italian Dalmatia
trembled in the balance.

*Croatian Wake Up Call*

In early 1943 the Palazzo Chigi began to face certain truths regarding the NDH.[814] The "Croats indulge themselves in
irredentism against Italy for Dalmatia," Pietromarchi noted.[815] Foreign Minister Mladen Lorković, who headed an "untrustworthy" and
distinctly anti-Italian clique, he held, was involved in a plot to take
over the government supported by Germany's representatives in
Zagreb. To steady Pavelić in power, Lorković should be silenced.
In this spirit Mussolini asked Hitler to give the Poglavnik a personal
boost,[816] as if he were more beholden to Italy than to Germany.
When the NDH upbraided the 2nd Army for fathering a Serb revolt, Pietromarchi began to assume a more balanced position by
asking the Croatians "to appreciate that many Serbs fight with maximum intransigence against Communism." But instead of pursuing
this thought, Pietromarchi backtracked: "There is no doubt . . . that

the policy of the 2nd Army accelerates the crisis. It is reconstituting a real Serb army. It is clear that Croatia cannot tolerate it." Yet, Pietromarchi sensed the military's predicament: "The 2nd Army is a prisoner of these Četniks; they are the only prop in this situation, like the Barbarians armed by Rome who were its support and danger. Neither with them nor without them."[817]

Worried over losing complete control in Zagreb, Mussolini in mid-February summoned Casertano to Rome and asked him: "Is Pavelić master of the situation? Does he have a firm grip on the reins?" Pavelić, Casertano answered, had distanced himself from the Rome accords and did nothing to prod his following to take up a pro-Italian course. The brittle NDH construct was tottering, he continued; German penetration had eviscerated Croatian independence; and the Ustaša regime, manifesting a primitive and violent mentality, was turning on Italy.

Casertano had photographed the NDH accurately. The Croatian regime would be content to serve Germany as a satellite on the Slovak model. The basis of the Poglavnik's program, as Casertano noted, lay in the extermination of the Orthodox, of whom, he estimated, 400,000 had been slaughtered and 100,000 forcibly converted to Catholicism. Mussolini replied: "I will not forgive Pavelić for having bestowed on us an additional charge of war on his territory by a clearly impolitic obstinacy of suppressing two million Orthodox."[818] Mussolini wanted Pavelić to be informed that "I am always his friend and a friend of an independent Croatia. But he should refrain from war against the Orthodox, not only for reasons of humanity, but because it is an error, a grave error, if he—as I believe—wants Croatia to live and his regime not to perish."[819]

The Duce did not hesitate to fling this view at Ribbentrop: "The idea of the Croatian government to annihilate the Serb minority is absurd . . . This is the policy of the Ustaša."[820] Furthermore, the Poglavnik should stifle irredentism and cease flitting between Italy and Germany. In instructions sent to Casertano, he revealed: "I am convinced that Dalmatia cannot live in this manner; it must be reunited . . . We are going to fight the war till the end."[821] In an Axis "peace," the Duce would cast the Poglavnik aside and make an expanded Dalmatia Italian.

Defying Italy, Pavelić stonewalled the Duce's complaints over the persecutions of the Orthodox, shoved off on others Croatia's pro-German proclivities, and discounted the importance of the irredentists in his government. Casertano concluded that Pavelić faced "a clique of pig-headed and bloody megalomaniacs . . . who turn him against Italy."[822]

The political crisis in Zagreb was coming to a head. Lorković accused Casertano of singling him out personally as a scapegoat for everything that had gone badly between Rome and Zagreb, while the Croatian head of legation in Rome, Stijepo Perić, complained that Italian machinations to overthrow a minister in Zagreb impinged on Croatian sovereignty and must cease. Pietromarchi counted on Pavelić to stand against such provocation,[823] but found little hope there since Lorković, with the help of Kasche and Glaise von Horstenau, held the Poglavnik to an anti-Italian course.

Submerged in this nest of anti-Italian vipers, Mussolini instructed Casertano to bring the Croats to book over their "pendular" policy and irredentist propaganda. Casertano seized the initiative by plotting to have Lorković cashiered.[824] Pietromarchi despaired of this "scabrous" business because, as Pavelić admitted, the Germans were masters in Zagreb, not Italy. Finally the gloves came off. Casertano dressed down Kasche and Glaise for the lack of military collaboration between the Ustaša and the 2nd Army, for Croatian irredentism, and for German support of a Croatian navy that would pose as a direct challenge to Italy's domination of the Adriatic.[825] Glaise did not shrink from voicing his unwavering support of Croatia's claim to Dalmatia. The conflict between Italy and the German "Austro-Croats" was out in the open, an "ineluctable" phenomenon in the "Central European game."[826] Bastianini concluded there was nothing else to do but "throw Lorković into the sea,"[827] while Pietromarchi took out his frustrations on Casertano, whose "confused and noisy" policies merely reinforced the German hold on Croatia.[828]

To the delight of the Italians, Pavelić removed Lorković from the foreign ministry at the end of April. He was replaced by Mile Budak, a heartless Serb-killer, which added further proof that Pavelić was involved in a shabby power struggle among practitioners of a vicious Ustaša ideology in which political principle and diplomatic loyalty were noteworthy by their absence.

Pietromarchi was fully aware that a disagreeable gang dominated Zagreb. But instead of cleaning house by advocating straight-out regime change, he wanted to sweep criticism under the rug for fear of provoking an open breach with the Germans.[829] In Pietromarchi's view, the more Germany's domination over Croatia was publicly displayed, the heavier the blow to Italian prestige. There the matter rested. Mussolini made no further effort to bring Pavelić to reason, and the Palazzo Chigi continued to treat him as a Croatian martyr of the Italian cause rather than as a debauched Serb-hater and blatant opportunist milking both Rome and Berlin to save himself in a war already lost.

The German threat afflicted the Italians like a punishing nightmare. The head of Ciano's cabinet, Blasco Lanza d'Ajeta, reported to Rome that the Germans aimed to acquire all territory that formerly belonged to the Habsburg Empire, including Fiume, Gorizia, and Istria.[830] General Pièche's reports revealed the Italian defensive reflex against further German encroachment on Italian rights in Yugoslavia. Casertano reported on German "enslavement" of Croatia,[831] but, owing to a dearth of financial resources and military shortages of all kinds, Italy could do little. Pietromarchi saw Italian prestige and credit in Zagreb plummet because the 2nd Army could not provide the Croats 100,000 rifles and 25,000 overcoats; Italy looked on helpless while the Germans "took over the country."[832] An unsigned memorandum in the Palazzo Chigi reflected ruefully that the Croatian Domobrani, 30,000 strong, danced to the German tune rather than the Italian. Actually, the Wehrmacht's discipline went for naught, for the Domobrani continued to display cowardice and lack of discipline that made the Četniks by comparison look like tenacious Prussian grenadiers. Still, the threat to Italy was real. The German High Command reassembled Croats, who

had fought on the Eastern front, to move into Italian-occupied territory behind the Wehrmacht and chase away the Četniks. To keep
some semblance of equilibrium between Berlin and Rome, Pavelić
asked that Italy equip a 6,000-man Croatian force for use by the 2nd
Army. But since the Italians had neither the equipment nor the language skills to accomplish even that humble undertaking, they
stalled, much to the discomfort of Zagreb.[833]

Contrary to Italian perceptions, German policy in Croatia was
neither coherent nor unified, owing to a growing rift between the
Nazis and the officers of the Wehrmacht. The generals believed that
radical changes would have to be made in Zagreb if Partisan insurgency were to be brought under control.[834] As long as Pavelić held
office, Glaise reckoned, nothing would be done to weed out corruption, end Ustaša violence, and bring about military and bureaucratic reform, which proved that German influence was anything
but decisive.[835] For no lack of trying, Glaise had been unable to bring
Pavelić to the realization that Croatia should not be regarded a national state but a state of nationalities. Italy, according to Glaise, bore
chief responsibility for the doggerel regime by imposing a "clique
of rootless émigrés" led by the Poglavnik himself on the Croatian
body politic in a "flawed experiment."[836] General Löhr was no less
critical. Viewing the Ustaša as a "played out piano," he pushed for
a drastic solution: removal of Pavelić from power and recall of
Kasche, the fiercely radical Nazi minister in Zagreb, who, "as an
ideologue, does not see the reality." When Löhr pointed to the Ustaša
as a "putrid abscess" on the state organism of Croatia,"[837] the German general read a page out of Roatta's notebook. Oddly, it was
the "non-political" Löhr who seemed ready to press reforms on
Hitler, an implacably Pavelić loyalist, whereas Glaise, less willing to
stir up trouble in Berlin and aware that a German military regime
in Zagreb was not feasible unless the Wehrmacht received large
reinforcements, was resigned to stumbling along.[838]

Since Hitler stood solidly behind his Nazi emissaries who were
working hand-in-glove with the Poglavnik and his Ustaša following,
the German generals showed daring in proffering such opinions. As
opposed to both the Italian and German military, Hitler was not in

the least troubled by Ustaša massacres. Since it was he, not Mussolini, who stood between Pavelić and political oblivion, the Wehrmacht officers had to maintain correct relations with the Poglavnik and abide the fiction that Croatia lived in Italy's sphere. Glaise manfully undertook reform of the Croatian military, but, since Pavelić still retained a modicum of sovereignty, he did not have an entirely free hand. Feeling the sand slipping through his fingers, General Lüters noted that the Croatian army was "a living weapons arsenal of the Communists."[839] The average Croatian soldier, a draftee one day, a deserter the next, barely went through the motions of war. The Italians and Germans never tired of depicting the Croats as poor fighters and cowards, but the truth was simpler: they had no motive to fight. For them, the Axis had long ago lost its sheen.

While the Germans obeyed their Führer, Mussolini's minions in the Palazzo Chigi clung to the Rome-Berlin-Zagreb triangle. From their perspective the messy business in Croatia had grown out of a misunderstanding between Rome and Berlin. Hence the remedy need not require a painful reappraisal but merely smoother cooperation between the Italian and German diplomatic representatives in Zagreb. Confidence reestablished, the two sides would eschew military initiatives without prior discussion. Eureka! The Italian hold on Croatia would be restored and everything set right between Rome and Berlin.[840] While famine hung over the country exacerbating political disarray, the Palazzo Chigi did nothing other than rely on Berlin.

Behind this official posturing, Pietromarchi knew better; it was time for Italy to abandon Croatia. Mussolini's lack of focus concerned him. Instead of worrying over the particulars of political intrigues in Zagreb and what drove the Germans forward in Croatia, held Pietromarchi, the Duce should attend to the "flames threatening to engulf our house."[841] "This unawareness of the danger," Pietromarchi concluded, "represents the worst of all worlds. Since nothing can be done to fight the malady, one is seized by acute agony."[842] Pietromarchi was quite aware that the Germans cared not a whit for Italy's living spaces; Croatia was already their satellite. But his private thoughts did not alter the reality that Mussolini was still *il Duce*. Empire-building, therefore, must continue. Short of a diplomatic revolution, there were only the Teutonic masters of imperialism to revive the dying dream of an Italian imperium in the Balkans.

## The Italian Military and the Četniks

During the initial phase of Operation *Weiss*, the Četniks severely tried Italian patience. In the key Dinaric areas, defined as the Gračac-Knin-Derniš sector, Pop [Father] Djujić, long a stalwart Italian ally, held strong positions. Nonetheless his men were surprised and defeated by a determined Partisan force and yielded Gračac. Italian troops recovered the lost ground in dogged counter-attacks, but the battle revealed shortcomings and faltering morale in Četnik ranks. Mihailović blamed their failures on the "perversity" of Roatta and Pirzio Biroli. However, dependent on the 2nd Army for arms and equipment, he had no choice but to tell Jevdjević to conceal Četnik ill feelings from their Italian paymasters. The Montenegrin Nationalist Pavle Djurišić, who was supposed to make a contribution to Operation *Weiss*, caused the Italians no end of embarrassment by diverting his troops for a rampage through the Sandžak and southwest Bosnia, slaughtering thousands of Muslims including women and children.[843]

The Četniks began to question ultimate victory over a more resolute and better organized enemy confidently "riding the wave of the future" and to doubt themselves when comrades fell away or defected to Tito. As warriors inspired by bards recounting the glories of Serb martyrdom and sacrifice, they were torn between a visceral impulse to defy the odds and fight, and Mihailović's imperative to avoid extermination by desisting from insurgency against the Axis. Absent a strong hand from Mihailović, certain Četnik units frequently did not observe the same restraint toward each other in settling old scores.

The Četniks certainly felt ambivalence toward the Italians. They appreciated the protection and help afforded them by the 2nd Army, but did not hold Italian troops in high esteem and resented the shedding of Serb blood to save Italian lives. Rather than fight as auxilia-ries, the Četniks preferred to form their own units and would an-swer to Mihailović, if anyone, rather than to Italy. Depending on locale and circumstance, they struck deals with the Italian military but sometimes broke them, owing to a loss of confidence in Italy's steadfastness. The Officers resented having to move around accord-ing to Italy's battlefield needs. After a series of crisscrossings and contradictory orders, Montenegrin Četniks under the command of Stanišić appeared in Mostar, where they were imperiled by the Ger-mans. The Četniks were invariably reluctant to stray far from their native villages. A sharp reduction of Italian weapons coming their way was hardly a morale booster.

In spite of these strains, it was clear that the Četniks wanted to destroy the Partisans, a basic Italian objective as well; however, the Četniks would go to war against the Italians if they were to get in the way of a Great Serbia. The Officers, in general, could not help but notice that Italy's doomsday in Yugoslavia was fast approach-ing after the military reverses of late 1942 on other fronts. The wind was blowing strongly in favor of the Allies. By early 1943 the Ital-ians had practically completed the abandonment of the 3rd zone, were dismantling fortresses in the 2nd, and thinning them out in the Croatian demilitarized zones along the coast and in back of Italian Dalmatia. Četnik families were exposed to Partisan reprisals, and renewed Ustaša onslaughts further contributed to a loss of morale. Since the 2nd Army was subject to contradictory pressures imposed on them by Germans, Croatians, and Rome, the Četniks asked: will we be disarmed, sent home, used as auxiliaries, or armed and equipped as independent units? Or will the Italians yield to German pressure and turn on us?

The Italian commanders, for their part, strove to orchestrate the "illegal" Četnik formations and the Serbs fighting in the MVAC as auxiliaries in a common endeavor to defeat the Partisans and keep the Germans out of their backyard in Croatia. There was no uni-form approach, since much depended on the personality and de-termination of each Italian commander who, subject to conflicting pressures, was afforded a certain leeway. If he chose to cooperate with the local Četniks, he could do so without hesitation, for his superiors in the 2nd Army command were generally supportive and stood as a buffer against disapproval or punishment from the higher-ups in Rome. The Italian commanders could only be sure that the 30,000 Serbs belonging to the MVAC,[844] and therefore under direct Italian command, could be kept in line. Serb swaggering, however, offended them. Intercepted radio messages among Četnik commanders in late 1942 and early 1943 revealed Serb deprecation of Italy and boastful talk of disarming Italian troops and seizing their arms.[845]

Whether the Četniks fought poorly or robustly, they appeared, from the Italian standpoint, more and more like mercenaries. As long as money and supplies flowed, they could be counted on to stay the course, but if the Italian faucet should run dry, they would desert or change sides. In their distrust, the Italians contrived to supervise the Officers carefully by keeping their forces fragmented and denied a unified command over detachments drawn from Montenegro, Herzegovina, and Bosnia.[846] During a six-month period in 1942 the Italians delivered the Četniks about 30,000 rifles, but released no mountain artillery, mortars, or machine guns—weapons that really mattered.[847] In skirmishes with the Partisans, the Četniks were clearly outgunned. Still, although aware that they consisted of often unruly and poorly trained groups, General Roatta assigned them the crucial role of stopping the main body of Tito's battle-hardened shock troops in order to spare his own soldiers.[848] No matter how much Četnik inconstancy and indiscipline harried the Italians, no matter how much Italian weakness and lack of will disturbed the Četniks, the two sides in the end were prepared to overlook each other's shortcomings in the knowledge that they were doomed to succeed or fail together.

On 3–4 March Ambrosio met in Rome with Robotti, the commander of the 2nd Army, and Pirzio Biroli, the military governor of Montenegro, to pass on the decisions Cavallero had arrived at with the Germans. Hitler no longer would hear of Italian objections and, in view of a possible Allied landing in the Balkans, "considered the Četniks absolutely as future enemies to be disarmed or exterminated . . . immediately after operation *Weiss*."[849] Pirzio Biroli took exception to this formula. If the Montenegrin nationalist forces were to be disarmed, "All Montenegro would go up in flames." As monarchists, they "have faith in us . . . Mihailović does not obey London. It is an error to believe so." Furthermore, "The Germans make every blunder and kill logic."[850] Robotti made the point that "every Četnik disarmed signifies the loss of two men: one loses an ally and obtains an enemy." Any attempt to disarm the Četniks would provoke a violent reaction. Why should their fate be debated in Rome while German field commanders were cooperating with them in the Neretva valley?[851] The Četniks should be exploited to the maximum and disarmed, not immediately following Operation *Weiss* but after the Partisans had been completely destroyed, which was still a long way off.[852]

Ambrosio confided to his agitated commander: "Poor Robotti. I see that you have a pained expression. I know very well your displeasure over German intransigence; I appreciate and share your reasons, but we were compromised in the last meeting in Germany (Cavallero) when we gave our known promise." (That is, Četnik disarmament would begin right after Operation *Weiss*.) Neither could Mussolini understand the great German urgency to disarm the Četniks. As long as the Axis Powers held out in Tunisia, an English landing in the Balkans—Hitler's obsession—"for now" was "neither easy nor immediate," which made the German plan to pursue Mihailović through Mostar and thence to Montenegro a madcap adventure. Robotti took leave of the Duce bearing the following advice: "Keep the heavily armed and slowly moving troops in the barracks and train Italian Četniks to fight in the woods and off well-worn tracks."[853]

Deadlocked in irresolution, Ambrosio decided to let the Četnik question rest in the laps of the 2nd Army commanders. They reciprocated by promising to keep the Četnik forces under tighter control.[854] But no stone would be left unturned in preventing Germans from entering areas evacuated by Italian troops. The 2nd Army still dreamed of a capacious Croatian home looked after by reliable Serb housekeepers who would stop the Teutonic barbarians and their

Ustaša allies at the gates. This illusion, however, gave way to despair. An 11 March note of the Supreme Command admitted:

> Our troops are worn out. The reasons of a political order to-day no longer have value. As long as we feared a strong German hegemony in Europe, it was logical to stay in Croatia and Greece to impede the Germans from installing themselves in the Adriatic. But now this danger no longer exists. The threat to Germany no longer comes from us but from the enemy who now dictates matters in the Balkans. The armed struggle against insurrection is too onerous and lacks adequate compensation; the final outcome favors the Germans, because they and they alone can stop an invasion.[855]

In an unwonted display of defiance, Mussolini informed Hitler on 8 March that only after the "Partisans ceased to be a dangerous armed movement" would arms deliveries to the Četniks be halted.[856] The German forces, too, he reminded the Führer, had cooperated with the Četniks in conducting joint operations in the upper Neretva area.[857] Indeed, during February and March, the German commanders, in spite of Hitler's unambiguous position, had established their own contacts with them.[858] General Löhr wrote on 14 March: "It is especially necessary to state that temporary shoulder-to-shoulder fighting with the Četniks in certain areas against the Partisans was a necessary evil which had to be accepted, because the fight against both groups at the same time would not have permitted the destruction of either."[859] Roatta and Robotti could not have put it better. Moreover, after the heavy defeats at the hands of the Partisans in March, the Četniks, desperately hanging on in Herzegovina, sought out the Germans.[860] As early as 23 February Jevdjević had secured their help in defending eastern Herzegovina against the Partisans. On another occasion, by agreeing not to cross the Neretva, the Germans promised to avoid contact with Četnik troops.[861] Other negotiations produced a series of mutual hands-off agreements that resulted in the surrender of some Četnik arms to the German military authorities.[862] The emphasis, to be sure, was on disarmament rather than military assistance. Before Mussolini's fall German contacts with the Četniks were sporadic, localized, and far more limited in scope than the Italian.

*Solemn Truths*

The German commanders fundamentally agreed with the Italian thesis that a decisive military victory over insurgency was a mirage and that political means should be employed to divide and conquer the two insurgent forces. But this concordance of views was not matched by mutual trust. A breakdown in communication resulted partly from accident but mostly from suspicion. The Germans, who counted on a continued Italian presence in the 2nd zone, complained bitterly when the Italians broke camp without forewarning them. The Croats, as good toadies, egged them on to further accusations and made their own in Rome. The Italians were annoyed by Hitler's relentless hostility toward the Četniks and confused by the willingness of some German field commanders to cooperate with them.[863] Worse still, the Germans tore up the demarcation line and tramped into Herzegovina—Italian turf—where the Wehrmacht disarmed Četniks, who had been supplied and given moral support by the 2nd Army, and where, as General Robotti kept insisting, tranquility already prevailed.[864]

The consequence of this breakdown in Axis cooperation was that each participant in the guerrilla war proceeded on his own with varying degrees of success and failure. The Partisans persuaded the Germans to relax their pursuit so that they could focus on the Četniks. The Germans, ignoring Italian opposition, likewise concentrated on the Četniks, but since they took refuge in Italian-occupied territory, the Wehrmacht did not have complete liberty to act. The Italians failed to keep the Germans out of Herzegovina, but got some measure of perverse revenge by forcing them to take a roundabout route so that the Wehrmacht would not pass through Mostar in Herzegovina. That prevented the Germans from springing the trap on the Partisans after dealing the Četniks a punishing blow, which left *Weiss* II a semi-success. As a result of these German detours, the mauled and fatigued Partisans, surmounting innumerable hardships and fearful losses, were able to escape by crossing the Neretva River for the relative safety of eastern Bosnia and Montenegro.[865] But they continued to be battered by fierce Italian attacks.[866] The Četniks were hardly the beneficiaries, since the Italian VI Army Corps showed them studied indifference by undertaking unannounced withdrawals from the Sandžak and key Montenegrin towns, which exposed them to further sharp Partisan attacks.[867]

Still, the 2nd Army baulked at disarming the Četniks, as proposed by the Germans—Četniks whose blood was sacrificed in the anti-Communist cause. The Italian commanders were sure that there were fundamentally irreducible differences in world outlook between Partisans and Četniks. If asked to pinpoint the greater threat, the 2nd Army would unequivocally single out the Partisans who, answerable to Moscow, favored Bolshevik conquest of the Balkans that would touch off Communist revolution in Italy. The Četniks, looking to London for supplies and moral support, yearned to create a Great Serbia under a restored Karageorgević kingdom, which, if spelling the end of the Italian *spazio vitale* in the Balkans, represented a far lesser threat to Italian national interests and the integrity of the country. The Četniks had no real bone to pick with Italy, but would fight the Partisans to the death. What would happen to the motherland should the Soviets sweep into the Balkans? Hence, Sušak concluded, partnership with the Četniks should continue.

While the Axis Powers circled each other suspiciously, the Partisans and Četniks proceeded to fight a desperate civil war in which Tito seized the upper hand. Thanks to their pronounced differences on the Četnik question, the Axis Powers in Yugoslavia found themselves working at cross-purposes in Operations *Weiss* I and II. To clean out the remaining nests of insurgency, the Germans devised Operation *Schwartz*, to be launched on 17 May in Montenegro and the Sandžak. This time the German juggernaut would proceed unhampered by Italian vacillation and backstairs deals with the insurgent Četniks.

# Chapter VIII

# End of the *Spazio Vitale*

Mihailović's Dilemma
Relentless German Pressure
Operation *Schwartz*
The Četniks Abandoned
Agony in Slovenia
Last Act in Dalmatia

*Mihailović's Dilemma*

As the year 1943 turned, Mihailović was deep in a grandiose plan to destroy the Partisan forces. But if in an upbeat mood over his existing position vis-à-vis Tito's "proletarian shock troops," Mihailović found himself in a fix everywhere else. Everyone had overestimated his strength and importance. The Italians saw him as a means of keeping their imperialist dreams alive, while the British expected great things of him against the Axis Powers. If Mihailović had been free to choose, he certainly would have preferred alliance with the British for the obvious reason that they were both locked with Serbia in a desperate struggle against the country's mortal enemies, Germany and Italy, and London was the home of Mihailović's political masters in the Yugoslav government-in-exile. His enemies, on the other hand, singled him out for destruction: the Partisans because they viewed the Četniks as a formidable rival with a favored position in London, and the Germans because they regarded the Četniks, who were tied to the Allies, as the most dangerous insurgent movement.

Mihailović's position was indeed precarious. His Italian ally showed clear signs of exhaustion, and Tito's Partisans, much better disciplined and organized than his own following, were gaining center-stage in Yugoslav insurgency. Owing to the severe military setbacks the Četniks endured in January at the hands of the Partisans, Mihailović was reeling from the criticisms of his subordinates, embittered by the lack of Italian support, and fearful of an imminent German penetration into Herzegovina and Montenegro.

Mihailović, it was obvious, was no diplomat. He was a merely an officer whose readiness for combat had been tempered by the recent military tragedies of his country. Hence it was not improbable that Mihailović would have a falling-out with the British agent Colonel William S. Bailey, who found him in his mountain fastness in late February 1943. Hardly a greater contrast can be found in diplomatic parley—a rough-hewn warrior in dialogue with an upper-class British officer sent to enlist Četniks in imperial grand strategy. Bailey reproached Mihailović for making no real effort to dynamite the bridges connecting the German road from Belgrade to Salonika, which bore supplies for the Wehrmacht in North Africa. It was unfathomable to him that Mihailović could not patch up his dispute with the Partisans in the life-and-death struggle against the Axis Powers.

Bitterly and indiscreetly, his tongue loosened by too much plum brandy, Mihailović lashed back at Bailey: his enemies were the Communists, the Ustaša, and the Muslims, in that order. When he had dealt with them, it would be the turn of the Germans and the Italians. Since he had received only two air sorties and three tons of supplies from Britain, its material assistance was pitiful.[868] In the back of Mihailović's mind lurked the suspicion that if required by Realpolitik, "Perfidious Albion" would throw him and Serbia to the wolves. He was particularly irked by the BBC's newly found proclivity to portray Tito's movement as an indomitable insurgent force in the country.

The flare-up with Bailey hastened Mihailović's fall from favor with Churchill's government.[869] In defense of the British, short of a Balkan landing there was little they could do to extricate Mihailović from Operation *Weiss*. But Mihailović glossed over this reality, and the British never clearly explained their constraints nor displayed any comprehension of the tremendous obstacles facing him. Rather, they conveyed the impression that he was not doing enough. It should have been obvious that Mihailović was barely able to elude capture and was lacking the weapons needed to conduct successful sabotage against heavily defended railroad lines and communication posts—precisely what London expected of him. Particularly unnerving to Mihailović was the British presumption that he had committed an unpardonable sin for failing to link up with the Partisans and carry on against the Germans. It was fine, in his view, for the British to ponder a "popular front" with the mortal Titoist enemy, for such a maneuver did not imperil London, but it did imply more massive German reprisals against his people and further Communist gains at his expense. So when invited to fall in with British strategy in the Balkans, Mihailović in the future would feign a rapprochement with the Partisans in order to prevent a break in the wire to London.[870] Mesmerized by the memory of Salonika, on whose beaches the French and British had made an ill-conceived landing in 1915, Mihailović wanted to preserve his forces until the Allies arrived—this time, he hoped, in far greater strength. Until then he would fall back on the Italians as his first line of defense against the expected Partisan onslaught to destroy his movement.

Since Mihailović's command center was constantly shifting and always remote, he was hard put to maintain even the shadow of unity contrived at Pustopolj in July 1942 among the disparate group of Četnik commanders. There were serious symptoms of political malaise, which raised questions as to whether the movement would ever be capable of becoming anything more than an agglomeration of Serb nationalist bands loosely tied together by their anti-Communist sympathies and a nominal allegiance to King Peter. Fragmented by local interests, their outlook shaped by tribal and regional politics, the Četniks posed problems for Mihailović. The Montenegrin contingent was particularly obstreperous. In an atmosphere crackling with holy war—against Communists, Muslims, and Croats—Montenegrin delegates emerged from a meeting in latter November 1942 advocating a backwoods patriarchy and a Četnik dictatorship that would primarily benefit the Orthodox. A subordinate place could be found for Croats and Slovenes, but none for Muslims.

Mihailović had a different view. To widen his net beyond Serbs, he was able to persuade some Muslims enrolled in the Ustaša and living in northern Herzegovina and the Sandžak to join his ranks.[871] But this effort to develop an army "to liberate the sacred soil of the country," whatever the political and religious orientation of its members, did not sit well with the signature Muslim haters among his Serb following. Furthermore, having only a small number of combatants under his direct command, Mihailović, despite his position as war minister in the Yugoslav government-in-exile, lacked a strong power base to stand against independent-minded Montenegrin warriors seeking to control the destinies of the Četnik movement. Unlike the commissars who imposed unity on Partisan ranks, Mihailović did not have a cadre of disciplined and loyal political agents. Since during the latter part of 1942 his headquarters were located in Montenegro, he was unable to control the vengeance the fanatics periodically visited on Muslim communities. Rather, he had to adapt to them one way or the other, employing whatever persuasion and moral authority he had.

As for the Italians, there is no question that Mihailović resented them as inveterate enemies of Yugoslavia and, more recently, as imperialist invaders. But since not one Italian soldier had stepped on the soil of "Old Serbia," current experience outweighed historical memory. As compared to the cruel German oppressors, who had committed heinous crimes against the Serb people, the Italians protected and gave comfort to the *prečani* brethren trapped in Croatia. On one occasion Mihailović stated: "Today everyone is aware that the Italians have spilt much blood in saving us from Ustaša and Muslim outrages. The many Serbs and Montenegrins who have escaped abuse for having the good fortune of Italian protection will back up what I have said."[872] But he was under heavy pressure from subordinates who, having lost confidence in the Italians, began to suggest an open break with them.[873]

As a necessary price for bringing Trifunović and Jevdjević into his fold, Mihailović tolerated their agreements with Italian commanders. So as not to compromise himself completely in the eyes of the English, he avoided any face-to-face meeting with representatives of the 2nd Army. He would simply outsmart them: "We are determined to deceive the Italians in order to reach our goals. Since they are astute, we must be more astute still."[874]

Mihailović's idea was to fight a parallel war with Italy against the common Communist adversary. With luck, if the German ship went down, Italy would abandon the Axis and join the Serbs in "fighting the Communists to the death."[875] Besides, the trickle of provisions and equipment offered by the Italians seemed like manna from heaven compared to Britain's minuscule number of air drops.[876] But whatever pro-Italian thoughts Mihailović expressed, these were in truth sentiments of despair. Feeling unappreciated by the British, outshone by the more resolute Partisans, and pursued by the Germans, Mihailović reached out to the 2nd Army through his agents as the only possible hope to save him from his many enemies.

*Relentless German Pressure*

The Italians and Germans met at Klessheim 7–10 April, where they renewed discussion on the many problems they faced. To counterbalance the recent Allied Atlantic Charter declaration, Italian Undersecretary Bastianini persevered in trying to gain German approval of his version of an "Axis New Order." Simultaneously, he undertook a new diplomatic initiative. The idea was for

a war-weary Italy to rally the Axis satellites—Hungary, Romania, and
Finland—for a compromise peace under the aegis of Italy. Such
diplomatic pressure, it was optimistically imagined, would induce
Hitler to wind up the campaign in the East by signing a truce with
the Soviet Union. Bastianini's maneuver, however, upset the Germans, who took every independent Italian peace gesture as a prelude to withdrawal from the war. Moreover, Berlin wanted no "New
Order" that respected the rights of satellite nations and occupied
peoples; the Nazis could only live in spheres where dissidents and
racial enemies had been totally subdued or annihilated. Italian hopes
to escape invasion and a crushing defeat were dashed when Hitler
refused to contemplate any separate peace with the Soviet Union.
This spelt finis to Bastianini's idea of a progressive Axis "New Order," a notion that had replaced more grandiose visions like an Italian "Mediterranean New Order," which had more in common with
Hitler's ideas than anything found in the Atlantic Charter. It was a
mark of Bastianini's delusion—or desperation—that he could advance Italy as the political brains or conscience of the Axis.[877]

On the military front, Ambrosio sought to obtain a firm German commitment to hold the Tunisian bridgehead and send reinforcements to the Italian mainland in the expectation of an imminent Allied invasion. But the Germans, in their mounting distrust
of the Italians, would be bound to nothing, fearing that an Italian
political collapse would be followed by the loss of precious military equipment to the enemy. As for the Balkans, the Italians restated
their intention of withdrawing troops from the 2nd zone for deployment on the 15 January line to facilitate passage to the mainland. The Germans insisted that no evacuation be undertaken until
their troops arrived, so that the Partisans would be denied the chance
to scamper in first. In a surprising reversal the Italians agreed.[878]

Pietromarchi was dismayed at the prospect of delaying the withdrawal of Italian troops. Ambrosio, however, felt that there was no
real urgency in bringing them home, for defense of Italy required
tanks and artillery, and the 2nd Army was deficient in both.[879] Hence
his readiness to suspend the withdrawal of troops specified in the
15 January order till the Germans and Croats had arrived.

When Robotti flared in anger over this Italian submission to Germany's will, Ambrosio simply rewrote the Klessheim agreements by divorcing any Italian withdrawal from the 2nd zone from movement of German troops into the vacated forts.[880] This unilateralism hardly obscured an unpleasant reality. Rapidly dwindling military strength left the Italians no alternative but to retreat and no time to thwart the Germans and Croats by first installing the Četnik ally in the abandoned territory. Frustrated by his predicament, Robotti sharply reminded the Germans that any occupation of Mostar would be entirely provisional and that they dare not near the Adriatic coast.[881]

Ever since the Italian cabinet reshuffle of February, followed by the fall of Tunis to the Allied forces in May, the Germans perceived marked changes in the tone of Italian diplomacy. While Ciano had endeavored to please the NDH, Bastianini, Glaise complained, did not hide his hatred of the Croats and hardly concealed his desire to have himself and Kasche recalled.[882] The Germans were taking the lead in Yugoslavia because the Führer, consumed by worry over a possible cave-in of the Fascist government in Rome, was bracing himself for a "traitorous" defection from the war. Like the Četniks he wanted to destroy, Hitler anticipated an imminent Allied landing in the Balkans, which, in his mind, made them a far greater threat to Germany than the Partisans. He seemed not to be aware that Britain was already shifting gears by favoring Tito over Mihailović. Hitler revealed his true intentions in a meeting with Pavelić on 27 April 1943.[883] In offering German protection to the NDH, he no longer would maintain his own fiction in Zagreb that Yugoslavia lay in Italy's sphere of interest. Enmeshed in a prolonged "agony of the regime," the Italian military had quite obviously fallen out of Hitler's strategic equations.[884] In a caustic letter to the Duce dated 19 May, the Führer denigrated the 2nd Army, lampooned the Italian military effort, and chastised Pirzio Biroli for supposedly secreting Mihailović to a safe hideaway. The Supreme Command, Hitler's litany continued, obstructed "disinfection" of the Četniks and "sabotaged" the agreements reached on operations aimed at crushing insurgency. The Italian authorities defiantly protected the Četnik bands but, attached to their treacherous allies, failed to keep the Communists out of Montenegro. Adding to the disgrace, isolated and cut off Italian units begged for German relief.[885] Hardly a more scornful indictment has ever passed between one ally and another.

Mussolini's response was not long in coming. In a letter sent on the 22nd he reminded Hitler that the Četnik bands would be disarmed only after the defeat of the Partisans. Since Operation *Weiss* had not led to any decisive results—the Communists having escaped the net—"the necessary conditions . . . for proceeding to disarm the Četnik formations are thus lacking."[886] The Duce none too gently chided the Germans for acting without forewarning the 2nd Army, and he would not fault the Italian military for the current imbroglio over the Četniks.

## Operation Schwartz

After a long period of relative tranquility, Montenegro, filled with Partisan warriors who had escaped across the Neretva River in March 1943, turned into a hotly contested battleground. While Germans chased Četniks, the latter and the Partisans crisscrossed, fought each other, and scurried to elude the pursuing Axis forces. The Italian troops, substantially reduced, struggled to take up their positions against a Partisan force that had crossed the river Drina into the Sandžak. In the Durmitor region the Partisans overran Italian forts and made off with a large cache of arms, which enabled them to recruit more men for their armies.[887] A battalion of the "Ferrara" division defending the road to Nikšič was overwhelmed; 400 troops fell and 500 more were taken prisoner.[888] Pietromarchi chalked up this disaster to the military's having appointed mediocre talent to command posts.[889] The Četniks, with portions of the "Taurinense" division manning the Drina line were defeated by the Partisans during the first half of April.[890] That Tito's small force of 7,000 could so effectively hold off the much larger Italian formations was to be explained, Pietromarchi supposed, by the latter's "lack of aggressive spirit and initiative."[891] Stunned by the sudden deterioration in their position, the Italians became more amenable to German military assistance in eastern Montenegro, the Sandžak, and along the Albanian frontier.

After the poor Četnik military performance around Nevesinje, their "gem" in Herzegovina, and the humiliating fact that many Montenegrin units who, having crossed over there, broke and ran to protect their own homelands during the April campaign, the Italians began to modify their view that the Četniks were fighting "valorously" at their side. The Italians wavered between keeping the Četniks fragmented to prevent a potential move against the 2nd Army and forging a coherent striking force to fight the Partisans, which ultimately would benefit Mihailović rather than themselves.

Robotti met General Löhr on 5 May to discuss the disposition of the 200,000-odd German, Italian, Bulgarian, and Croatian troops forming to launch Operation *Schwartz* against approximately 19,000 Partisans. The purpose of the expedition was to protect the bauxite mines in Herzegovina and the lead and chromium ore lodes in the southern parts of Serbia, Kosovo, and Macedonia from the Partisans and Četniks. Those resistance movements, if not destroyed, would be driven deep into the mountains far from the coast where the Allies were expected to land. The Germans refrained from informing the Italians of their intention to disarm the Četniks and Montenegrin Nationalists, unilaterally if need be.[892] This concealment was by order of the Führer, who, under the impression that the Partisan forces had been broken, considered Mihailović his chief remaining enemy in the area.[893] Whatever motive Hitler had to protect the persona of the Duce was overridden by what he deemed a paramount strategic necessity. Reliance was placed on the Ustaša, Muslim SS units, and German trained anti-guerrilla mountain forces to kill off the Četniks, seize Mihailović and his staff in Montenegro, and destroy the remnants of Tito's forces.

By agreement with the Supreme Command,[894] German units entered the Sandžak and eastern Montenegro, where they began to seize possession of the telegraph lines and the railroads, which diminished the 2nd Army's fighting capacities and its power to resist Partisan attacks. To the further dismay of the Italian soldiers, the

Germans fanned out to disarm and arrest Četniks. Thousands were rounded up and packed off to work camps in Germany—or they scattered to the woods. Mihailović managed to escape into western Serbia. By thus flouting the 2nd Army, Pietromarchi observed, the Germans had inflicted deep wounds on Italian prestige.[895]

The impotent Italians could only express dismay. "Our troops have already tranquilized Herzegovina," remarked the astonished commander of the VI Army Corps, General Sandro Piazzoni. By their "sudden, inopportune, and impolitic disarmament" of the Četniks, the Germans had destroyed the Italian peace and rekindled ethnic strife.[896] Pirzio Biroli stood by helplessly while the Germans rounded up his comrades-in-arms, unable to obtain their release.[897] In this situation of "abnormality," could he ever face General Löhr again? General Robotti defiantly circulated an order that forbade the passage of Wehrmacht troops toward the coastal zones. As long as the Četniks fought against the Partisans in Herzegovina and Montenegro, he, for one, would postpone their disarmament indefinitely.[898] Hearing the alarm bells in the field loud and clear, the Supreme Command was put on notice to remove the German hand from the Četniks in Italian-occupied territory.

On 19 May, when General Rintelen, the German military representative in Rome, complained about a lack of Italian cooperation in the Balkan theater, Ambrosio retorted: "In practice your troops act independently . . . regarding Montenegro we cannot speak now of disarmament of the Nationalists if we do not wish to augment the rebellion by 100 percent."[899] He informed the OKW through General Efisio Marras, the Italian military attaché in Berlin, that unless the Germans ceased throwing their weight around, Italy would "answer force with force."[900] Such tough talk between the military commanders on both sides was not common. But nothing could conceal the dysfunctional Axis partnership. The Germans were certain that the Italians were not militarily capable of defending Bosnia, Herzegovina, and the Sandžak from Partisan attacks, while the Italians were no less sure that their ally intended to take possession of their *spazio vitale*. The official line in Berlin had always been that Italy was an equal partner in the alliance, but in the formidable expeditions of 1943 this pretense was discarded.

Having broken up the Četniks, the Germans concentrated on the Partisans. Despite the appallingly difficult mountain terrain, they almost succeeded in trapping them. During the first days of June, the indefatigable Partisans, exhibiting great courage, managed to extricate themselves by crossing a narrow gorge and climbing steep mountains raked by Stuka dive-bombers, which marked their great success at the Sutjeska River. By the end of the month they had found a refuge in the uplands of eastern Bosnia.[901] Having once again saved thousands of wounded from sure death at the hands of the enemy, the Partisans proved to the Yugoslav peoples that they were capable of enormous sacrifice for the national cause in a back-breaking guerrilla war against powerful and pitiless invaders. They simply would not quit. During this perilous journey, Captain William Deakin, a personal friend of Prime Minister Churchill, parachuted into Tito's headquarters. Based on his reports, which described Mihailović's dithering and his unwillingness to strike hard against the occupiers, Churchill prepared to support the Partisans as the more determined insurgent force fighting the Axis. The British cast Tito as the star of Yugoslav resistance and relegated Mihailović to a bit part. Hence an ironic turn of events in the aftermath of Operation *Schwartz*: The Partisans, who had barely survived the battle, emerged strengthened thanks to offstage help from London.

The Italians billed Operation *Schwartz*, which was wound up in the middle of June, a success, although they suffered 2,106 soldiers dead, wounded, or missing.[902] The Germans knew otherwise, for Tito was still at large. The Partisans lost more heavily, perhaps thirty-five per cent of their troops.[903] Montenegro remained under Italian occupation until the fatal days of September. Both Axis partners behaved brutally toward captured prisoners and the Montenegrin population. One Italian soldier noted that there was destruction everywhere: "This war is continually degenerating to ever lower depths and we can no longer see it as a war between civilized peoples."[904]

## The Četniks Abandoned

At the end of April, approximately 22,000–23,000 Serb warriors purportedly were fighting for Italy.[905] This was an unreliable figure, however, for many were going over to the Partisans or had abandoned the struggle. Without guidance or food, the Četniks were on the run, chased by the Germans and reeling from sharp battles with the Partisans. Where the Četniks were not clearly defeated they were widely dispersed, which baffled the Officers trying to keep track of their scattered following. A lack of discipline and organizational disarray continued to bedevil the Italians. To break out of isolation, certain leaders in their desperation took up negotiations with their German assailants, who were pleased to take advantage of the chaos and ethnic strife that had been aggravated by the inconclusive *Schwartz* campaign.[906]

The Germans were handed, free of charge, a divide-and-rule strategy among Četniks losing faith in the 2nd Army. A few lower-ranking Wehrmacht officers were ready to explore German-Četnik collaboration against the Partisans,[907] but were quickly disabused of the idea by an unbending OKW that stood by Hitler's orders to disarm and arrest them. Instead of the Germans, therefore, it was the Partisans who benefited primarily from Četnik war fatigue. Exposed to capture by the Germans, many Četniks passed over to the Partisans, who welcomed the simple guerrilla fighters and shot the officers.

A significant number of Muslims, ground down by the ceaseless attacks against them, also sought a new home in Communist-style ethnic fraternity. But at the same time they were successfully wooed by the Germans, who scored points by sponsoring a trip to Sarajevo by the Grand Mufti of Jerusalem. The Italians rose to meet the challenge. But when they ostentatiously courted the notoriously pro-Axis Grand Mufti, the Serb leader Jevdjević, Italy's staunch ally who hated Muslims, lost face before his rank and file.[908] By bidding for the support of the ancestral enemy, the Italians, in turn, lost credibility with the Orthodox Serbs. Furthermore, the Germans already had a foot in the Muslims' door thanks to their long-standing appeasement of the NDH, the only organized force in Yugo-slavia that had promised to leave them alone. It was a game the Italians could not win. If forced to take a position, the Muslims were inclined to rally to the Germans as the best defense against their sworn Serb foe.[909]

Adding to the Italian humiliation, General Giuseppe Amico of the "Marche" division on 28 May formally yielded Mostar to General Zellner, commander of the German 373rd division, which marked the end of Italian preeminence in the 2nd zone.[910] Mussolini pretended that he had granted the SS "Prinz Eugen" division "temporary" oversight of the bauxite mining area in the vicinity.[911] In a typical put-down of the Italian "enemy," General Zellner, in his greeting to the denizens of Mostar (and the large number of Croatian recruits in the 373rd division), hailed the camaraderie of World War I days between Wilhelmine Germany and Habsburg Austria-Hungary—the empire that had long denied Italy unification.[912] A further ominous development nettled the Italians: the German preference for Muslims over the Orthodox. The Italian "ally" in Zagreb was immensely pleased that its only non-Croatian confederates were streaming into SS units hungering to strike back at the Serbs. Since Pirzio Biroli's bargaining power with General Löhr had shriveled due to the steady withdrawal of Italian armies, he could only fret over these unfolding events.[913]

As the Italians fell back toward the coast (by April they were out of the 3rd zone and held only a few fortresses along the Adriatic littoral), they lost touch with many Četnik allies, which undid their many arrangements and understandings. Things were not at all working according to plan. Instead of garrisoning the forts abandoned by the Italians, the Četniks were being broken up by the relentlessly pursuing Germans.[914]

Worse for the Četniks, Mussolini abruptly ended his faint-hearted support by ordering his military in latter May "to cooperate as quickly as possible with the Germans in the disarmament of the Četnik formations and Nationalist units belonging to Mihailović."[915] Since he was busy trying to convince Hitler that the epicenter of the war should be moved to the Mediterranean by making peace with Stalin, supporting the military's position on the Četniks against the Führer's will in a secondary theater was not worth the risk. Mussolini's directive, however, would not apply to "independent" Četniks—bands in Slovenia and in territory under the command of the V Army Corps. The Četniks of Pop Djujić, who persevered in the Lika area against the Partisans, would also be left alone.[916] But in Herzegovina, in accordance with the Duce's instructions, General Piazzoni on 1 June posted a notice in public places ordering all auxiliary formations under his command to disarm and dissolve themselves on pain of arrest and deferment to an Italian military tribunal.[917] Out of 8,000 Četniks in Herzegovina, only 120 surrendered their arms.[918]

In the Palazzo Chigi Pietromarchi wondered why the Četniks should continue to draw so much attention, since they were in an advanced state of disintegration and boxed up in remote parts of Montenegro and Herzegovina far from the key transportation avenues in the Balkans. High-handed German disarmament of the Četniks admittedly besmirched Italian honor, but nothing, in his view, should obscure the dire necessity of bringing the troops home. In the Balkans, therefore, he felt that Italy would have to hand over all power in Italian-cleared areas to the Wehrmacht.[919]

The beginning of the end of the relationship between the 2nd Army and the Četniks had arrived. Mussolini was glad to be rid of them—and especially their leader—as inveterate enemies of Fascist Italy. In a letter to governor of Dalmatia, Francesco Giunta, he warned: "Indirectly a notice has come to me that you intend to contact Mihailović or one of his delegates. Don't do it. Mihailović is a fierce enemy of Italy and is minister of war of the Yugoslav government in London. To look for contacts with such an individual is dangerous and in any event useless."[920]

Constrained by Mussolini's order, Pirzio Biroli arrived in Salonika on 2 June, hat in hand, to meet with General Löhr. He agreed to a "forced" disarmament of the Četnik bands in Herzegovina and asked for German help in subduing the formations of Djurišić in Montenegro. The separatists, and the forces of Stanišić, proven anti-Partisans, would be left alone. Löhr replied that he would await clarification on the separatists but expressed doubts regarding Stanišić, a solid Mihailović man. The German commander, however, less rigid than Hitler, accommodated Pirzio Biroli on the Četnik question elsewhere. In Lika and the Italian annexed areas, disarmament would be suspended until the Partisans were defeated; the Četniks in the Dinaric region would be disarmed "progressively."[921]   Although he endured military and political pressure on all sides, Pirzio Biroli, because of his dependency on the Montenegrin Nationalists, refused to give them over. Once the Axis had wound up the campaign against the Partisans, he would rearm "his" Četniks. For Pietromarchi, Pirzio Biroli lived in a fictional world: "He will recommence to commit the same errors. Experience has instructed nothing."[922]

Pirzio Biroli did not radiate composure. He resented Rome for questioning his use of Montenegrins, worried over losing his favorite Nationalist collaborators, and, when faced with stepped-up Partisan pressure, panicked by calling in the Germans, who quickly disarmed some of his most trusted Četnik warriors. His unsteady nerves did not go unnoticed in Rome.[923] On 1 July 1943 Pirzio Biroli was withdrawn and replaced by General Curio Barbasetti di Prun.

At the worst possible moment the Italians had shot themselves in the foot.[924] In spite of the volume of complaints sent to Rome by the Italian commanders in the field over rough and arbitrary German behavior toward the Orthodox, they themselves, by order of the Duce, had begun to disarm Četniks in the Mostar region and across the swath of Croatian territory still held, albeit sporadically and on a small scale. After the Germans had disarmed the elite Četnik troops of Major Djurišić in Montenegro, the Italians followed suit, save for the handful of separatists free of any taint of Mihailović, but they had only limited success in disarming other units in Herzegovina.[925] As was often the case, orders from Rome in some areas were promptly and efficiently obeyed, in others simply disregarded. An Italian flying squad swooped down and placed Jevdjević under house arrest.[926] Not surprisingly, the followers of Jevdjević were greatly distressed and his lieutenants had no choice but to flee as fugitives from justice. An essential pillar upholding Četnik confidence in Italy had been removed. "Disarmament" provoked consternation in the ranks and implied an Italian readiness to leave the Četniks at the mercy of the Partisans.[927]

In the Dinaric region, Pop Djujić, who had long cooperated with the Italians, saw his position slip following the Supreme Command's decision to undertake the disarmament of his formations. But General Francesco Giangrieco, commander of the "Zara" division in the sector of Knin, baulked at doing anything that would deprive him of his eyes and ears. Dismayed at the prospect of double-crossing loyal allies, Giangrieco asked to be replaced.[928] He was not alone in his discontent. Like many commanders in the field, he felt compromised by the order of high authority in Rome to disarm Četnik formations. Not only would they resist or vanish, but the order exacerbated the already treacherous business of disentangling the Italian troops from a complicated network of local agreements and tacit understandings as they prepared to leave Croatia. Small wonder that Djujić would take this as Italian betrayal, but he was already used to exhausting his troops in battle, insufficiently supplied and equipped by his paymasters. Like Četniks everywhere he held that Italy, with its empire-building fixations, was an enemy after all. Why spill more blood in a hopeless cause? The Četnik meltdown had begun.

The position of Mihailović was not enviable either. The British threatened to abandon him unless he cooperated with the Partisans rather than attacking them. Defiantly, he radioed his following: "Accord with the Communists is impossible."[929] This left Mihailović no option but to soldier on with the Italians, because "we have common enemies."[930] Meanwhile, according to an Italian report, Mihailović revised his program in July by advocating a Yugoslav confederation rather than a resurgent Greater Serbia. He did not want the Partisans to be the lone beneficiary of a Yugoslav plan that the Allies found more attractive than the Serb chauvinist alternative. According to his latest scheme, minorities would be transferred to regions of their origin. The Muslim, once again, was the odd man out: he must either convert to Orthodoxy or leave.[931]

Abandoned by the British, large numbers of Četniks clung to the Italians, many of whom ignored the order from Rome to disarm them. Indeed, the Italians frequently helped the Četniks to escape the German dragnets by providing hiding places, or took them along on the march to the Adriatic. As things turned out, the Supreme Command, though formally standing by its orders for the 2nd Army to disarm the Četniks, looked the other way as implementation faded in a smokescreen of studied indifference and blasé disobedience.[932]

In shame, Italians stole away from their areas of occupation. The Swastika flew unchallenged in Bosnia and Herzegovina. The Italian intention to disarm the Četniks played into the hands of the Partisans by fueling their propaganda mill: the anti-Communist collaborating "lackeys" had sold themselves to the occupier and now must flee to escape the Axis. Whatever bands of Četniks had survived Operation *Schwartz* in Herzegovina were more or less isolated in a no-man's-land of craggy mountains between the German and Italian lines.[933]

But like the Partisans, Mihailović was capable of amazing resilience. By the end of June he was back in the bastion of inner Serbia, soon branching out again into eastern Bosnia, Herzegovina, and Montenegro, with the backbone of his movement functioning once more. But the serious reverses suffered by the Četniks in Herzegovina and Montenegro between mid-March and June 1943 ruined Mihailović's plan, in force since the previous June, to ensure his survival by utilizing Italian protection and support. He had no time to cobble together a unified movement capable of dealing with both the Ustaša and Partisans before the Allied landing, expected to come in a month or two.[934]

On 10 July, the day of the Allied invasion of Sicily, Robotti ordered all units to intensify vigilance and prepare for possible hostilities against the Četniks.[935] Immediately afterward the 2nd Army was informed that Mihailović had instructed the Četniks to abstain from action against Italy, "also in the case of an Italian collapse."[936] Still, Ambrosio, following Mussolini's directive, scotched proposals on 12 July coming in from the field for a reorganization of the Četnik units. Rather, he ordered that they be dissolved in Herzegovina, the Dinaric region, and in Lika.[937] At Feltre, on the

19th, encountering no protest from Mussolini, Hitler reiterated his hard-line position on the Četniks, notwithstanding the recruitment drive of the Germans among Serbs disarmed by the Italians and disabused of Mihailović. In contrast, Mihailović, although poised to take advantage of an Allied landing, still intended to keep the lines open to the Italians.[938]

After Mussolini's fall the Četniks prayed for a peace settlement between Italy and Britain—a forlorn hope in view of Badoglio's announcement that the war would continue. The Četniks asked themselves: should they compel the Italians to hand over their weapons before the Germans and Partisans arrived, or should they persuade their old comrades to change sides and align with them as an ally of Britain? Expecting Italian capitulation, Mihailović issued instructions calling on his subordinates to prepare for attacks against the 2nd Army garrisons that gave no sign of either surrender or fence-jumping to the Allies. The Italians answered in kind. Regardless of the momentous events taking place in Italy, the 2nd Army continued to track down Četniks. Mihailović was in desperate straits. Instead of invading the Balkans, the Allies had landed in Sicily.

When General Badoglio issued highly ambiguous instructions to the Italian army to fire on Germans only when attacked, he invited confusion and impotence. Lacking strong leadership and straightforward directives from Rome, the 2nd Army was in no shape to turn around and join either the Partisans to fight the former German ally or the Četnik associate for combat against Tito. They had to fend for themselves individually. In this mayhem an ironic reversal took place. The Germans, previously bent on Mihailović's destruction, now approached him for cooperation against the Partisans.

While the Četnik leader struggled to keep his resistance alive, his lieutenants, who had been most dependent on the 2nd Army, scattered to the winds. To avoid a 2nd Army gaol, Jevdjević expatiated on Mihailović's hostility to Italians. But then he turned around and promised certain Croats that he would participate in mixed commissions from which Italy would be excluded.[939] Eventually he landed in Slovenia, where, openly collaborating with the Germans, he was repudiated by Mihailović. In the closing months of the war, the Italian Četnik ally in the Lika region, Pop Djujić, combined his forces with Jevdjević in a desperate and successful effort to reach Trieste before the Partisans closed in. Fearing that the British would hand them over to Tito, they hid outside Naples. Djujić eventually emigrated to the United States and lived in California, while Jevdjević found protection under the British at Salerno. Pavle Djurišić, the Montenegrin leader, having surrendered to the Germans in the spring, was taken to Austria as a prisoner of war. In August he escaped and rejoined Mihailović. In early 1945, trying to lead some Četnik units toward Italy, Djurišić tried to slip through a Ustaša ring but was caught and executed.[940] Djukanović, Stanišić, and their retinue were caught and killed by the Partisans in the monastery of Ostrog in October 1943, which caused a complete collapse of the Četnik leadership in Montenegro. Mihailović fought on against his multiple enemies. Ignored by the British, who had cast their lot with Tito, he eventually was caught by the Partisans and brought to trial. No one doubted the ultimate outcome in a decision rendered by a Communist kangaroo court. Mihailović was shot in 1946 as a traitor.

### Agony in Slovenia

Edgy over increasingly brazen Partisan behavior in Slovenia, Mussolini in early October 1942 ordered the 2nd Army to undertake tough countermeasures.[941] The fault, he concluded, lay with Grazioli for stirring up controversy with the XI Army Corps. Hereafter Slovenia would be treated as a "zone of operation."[942] That left the High Commissioner with not much to do save the everyday administration of the province, which had been reduced to a minimum since Italy only controlled the capital and a few pockets in the countryside.[943] The Italianization programs had long ago languished, and the Fascist organizations were reduced to a mere shadow.

The record of the Italian military was not much better. The XI Army Corps' drawn-out expedition against the Partisans (which included MVAC forces and a contingent of the Ustaša), launched with much fanfare in July 1942, ended inconclusively at the end of

November. General Robotti's campaign was severely hampered by the departure of units for other fronts, and the troops were worn down by endless fighting without rotation or leave. The Partisans, although suffering many casualties, survived as a coherent fighting force, while the MVAC, burdened with antiquated equipment, descended into criminality. Carabinieri commander Amedeo Tommasini reported that MVAC units had committed "abuses of every kind" during their searches,[944] while the Fascist Giovanni Domenis wondered why the MVAC should subject so many people to prolonged tenure in jails awaiting interrogation. Countless arrests, he noted, had seriously disrupted business in Ljubljana.[945]

Thrown against the Partisan enemy, the undisciplined Ustaša units simply broke and ran. Nor did the Fascists hold up their end. Robotti lambasted the "Nizza" battalion for poor training, lack of discipline, and spoliation of women. He urged that the "XXXI" legion be broken up and placed directly under army command. Since the Fascist lieutenant, General Montagna, was a troublemaker whose intrigues sapped army morale, the less seen of him the better. Robotti pleaded with Roatta to send him reinforcements.[946] Pointing out that there were plenty of troops (40,000 in Slovenia, which meant one Italian soldier for every eight Slovenes), Roatta, having none to spare, merely lavished him with praise.[947]

The Grazioli-Robotti duo carried repression to its miserable end. Pondering different approaches, Grazioli wrote that the Slovenes could be completely destroyed, transferred, or the worst elements weeded out to create a basis for a "profitable and loyal collaboration first and possibility of assimilation next, which, however, only with time can be realized." In his opinion, "the total or partial transfer of the population will be difficult to execute during the course of the war."[948] To deflect Slovene hatred of Italy, Roatta slyly suggested to Robotti that he set up the MVAC to take the hostages and conduct the reprisals.[949] But Robotti was crippled by a dearth of trustworthy informants.

As a result of the incessant military expeditions, much of the countryside lay in ruins. Transportation, disrupted by Partisan raids and countless Italian checkpoints, came to a standstill. To block

Partisan inroads from Croatia, the Italian military had closed the frontiers. The result was punishing autarchy and a pauperized labor class. General Robotti strode through a besieged city, whose semi-deserted streets were traversed by small clusters of bedraggled women, children, and the elderly. The lack of male youths was striking. More than three denizens congregating together was forbidden, a 5:00 p.m. curfew imposed, and pedestrians, encountering countless checkpoints, were forced to take time-consuming detours. The Italian soldiers, confronted by the dangers of abduction and sniper fire, bore weapons during leave hours on streets and in cafes; officers were surrounded by escorts on the open road and avoided dangerous pedestrian walkways.[950] Catholics and patriots emerged from watchful waiting to join battle against Italy on the side of the Partisans, which made for more retaliatory crackdowns. On 21 December the Carabinieri and Blackshirts arrested 252 suspects in Ljubljana; in another roundup a week later 289 more were taken into custody.[951] Grazioli's Pax Romana was turning into a gigantic Italian internment camp.

True to Roatta's 3C memorandum, General Robotti fought a fierce war against the Partisans. As Partisan attacks intensified in both strength and savagery, so did Italian military retaliation. Late in the day, however, Robotti tried to curb counterinsurgency excesses. Massive internments could not be carried out because of irreparable harm inflicted on the economy and because there was not enough space in Italy to house those rounded up.[952] He informed his commanders: "From now on reprisals are aimed at *safeguarding the honest population* against the savage crimes of the brigand Communists of the OF . . . and never against 'hostages' properly identified, that is, elements immune from indictment."[953] Admitting that the guiltless had been abused, he wrote: "One must never strike out blindly."[954] It took a long time for Robotti to learn a hard lesson: that the "rebels" hit the houses of collaborators "to incite our reprisals, with the evident purpose, beyond ridding themselves of ideological adversaries, of conducting a savage and perfidious form of propaganda against us."[955]

Having set in motion the long cycle of death and decay across "la provincia di Lubiana," Robotti sacrificed the chance of gaining allies among the vast Catholic "silent majority" who were as alarmed as he at the prospect of a Communist takeover. In the atmosphere of contempt toward Slovenes that Robotti engendered among his troops, pompous officers like General Taddeo Orlando could issue an order requiring all civilians to doff their hats and salute Italian sentries and officers passing by.[956] Robotti's heavy-handed repression fell on both "rebels" and civilians, and his sweeps devastated the countryside. He reduced villages to smoking ruins, blew up houses suspected as Partisan hideouts, and absconded with property and farm animals. Shards of buildings looked over a landscape of debris that evoked images of the Russian front. In winter the rubble lay sealed under a blanket of snow as thousands of Slovene villagers eked out an existence in war-damaged homes.

In a December 1942 graveyard peace, General Gastone Gambara replaced Robotti as commander of the XI Army Corps in Slovenia. More amiable, though no less determined to pursue the Partisans, Gambara took gingerly steps to appease the Slovenian population by dismantling the barbed wire, reopening the city, and easing up on reprisals.[957] Gambara held his troops out of police activity and explored areas of collaboration with Slovene nationalist organizations. Common ground was provided by the need of protecting themselves against vindictive Germans. Drawing on a confidential contact in Luca Pietromarchi, Gambara obtained a special fund to undertake new initiatives for the pacification of the province.[958] In the field he moved to devise a more effective strategy against the Partisans by training special forces, hoping to infuse them with the spirit of the *arditi*,[959] who, it was said, had challenged Austro-Hungarian machine-guns in World War I with grenades in both hands and a knife in clenched teeth.

Gambara initially remarked: "Logical and opportune that concentration camps do not signify fattening-up camps. Sick individual=quiet individual."[960] The next day he reflected more soberly: "The wasted appearance of those released from Arbe is truly remarkable." But they need not worry. "Supersloda for some time has been improving the conditions of the camp. It should be observed that the improprieties have practically been eliminated."[961] Gambara recommended the release of Catholics and anti-Communists from the Arbe camp.[962] But that was a treacherous business. "Shameless and dark swindlers" tried to extort large sums of money by volunteering as middlemen to mediate the release of prisoners.[963] Corruption abounded in the administration of the military's concentration camps.

At the beginning of 1943, many internees arrived home undernourished and sick,[964] which exacerbated Slovene hatred of Italy. The MVAC heartlessly wrote off clemencies and releases.[965] As if sensing a settlement of accounts at the end of the war, Lieutenant Colonel Ermanno Rossi, chief of staff of the "Isonzo" division, wrote a telling missive: "For obvious reasons it would be convenient if, in the transcripts or other reports regarding the death of rebels, the civil authorities were not given the term 'shot' or 'executed,' but instead given the generic term 'in an encounter with our troops the rebel . . . so and so . . . was killed . . . in such and such a location.'"[966] In early July Robotti, now 2nd Army Commander, hastened to empty the camps, especially of "those not deemed dangerous—women, children, and the elderly."[967]

Whether Gambara's military stratagems worked during the early months of 1943 to "normalize" civilian life and roll back Partisan insurgency is still subject to debate.[968] Italian military reports did emphasize a decided drop in insurgency.[969] If the intensity of guerrilla warfare relaxed, it was probably due to a Partisan awareness that Italy's occupation of Slovenia was fast drawing to a close. A much more serious German threat loomed in its place. Resources had to be husbanded and strength preserved for that day of reckoning. But there was no letup in Partisan anti-Italian proclamations aimed at isolating the MVAC volunteers. To win over fence-sitting Catholics, disgruntled Slovenian Četniks, and "absentee" patriots, the Partisans cast a widened propaganda net by declaring freedom of thought and religious choice that caught the attention of patriots and moderates of all shades who were ready to come out in the open against the hated Italian oppressor. The Italians reported that such propa-

ganda elicited a muted response from a population that preferred
the existing social order and the authority of the parish priests.[970]

In April-May Gambara's optimism was jarred by a recrudescence
of Partisan insurgency,[971] directed mainly against the railroads.[972]
There was no letup in the ferocity of the XI Army Corps' response.
Italian reaction, wrote a Carabinieri commander, is reduced to burning and destruction of villages previously occupied by the rebels.[973]
Gambara was only yielding on the question of reprisals. Responding to Robotti's reminder to keep them in check, he told his subordinates that "one must never strike out blindly."[974] In early July an
Italian commander proposed that negotiations with Partisans be
instituted to explore an exchange of prisoners and medical equipment.[975] "All captured rebels . . . will be shot," was Gambara's reply. "Deal with them this way: What do you want? Give yourselves
up . . . and then we will talk."[976] Outraged by Partisan massacre of
Italian prisoners in Herzegovina, Robotti reconfirmed the Italian
position that rebels under no circumstance would be granted belligerent rights and treated as equals. Engage the rebels to discover
their deployments, then reply "with our aviation in the most massive way possible."[977]

On 10 May Grazioli was finally given the title of prefect, but
he presided over an Italian-ruled province despised by the Slovenes.
His only achievement seems to have been a much better rapport with
Gambara than he had had with Robotti.[978] Grazioli's petition to have
the laws of the mainland extended to the province of Ljubljana was
denied by higher authority in Rome. He enjoined the Interior Ministry to place the justice tribunals under his authority, but they remained in the military's jurisdiction. Nor did he have more luck in
wresting control of the concentration camps from the XI Army
Corps command.[979]

During May what there was of collaboration fell away and defections and desertions thinned out the ranks of the MVAC.
Grazioli was forced to admit: "These Partisans have maneuvered
magnificently and have known how to 'disengage' from our battalions any time they wished. And this . . . *gives me great pain*."[980] On
15 June Grazioli was nominated prefect of Catania and replaced by

Giuseppe Lombrassa as prefect of Ljubljana province. Six weeks later the Duce fell from power. Grazioli hastened after him to Salò, where he served as prefect of three different cities, ultimately being captured by Italian Partisans and shot. The departure of the Fascists, however, did not result in the cessation of *rastrellamenti*. The military conducted vigorous sweeps up to 10 August 1943 that caused more deaths and more dynamited houses.

During the counterinsurgency campaigns in the "Province of Ljubljana," 85 Italian officers and 1,115 soldiers died, 131 officers and 1,843 soldiers were wounded, and three officers and 282 soldiers were unaccounted for. Exchange of prisoners was rare.[981]

Tabulating accurately the number of Slovenes whom the Italians interned and killed is no easy chore. Grazioli admitted in January 1943 that approximate figures were hard to come by on the number of Slovenes interned. The official Italian military documents, unfortunately, yield no precise figures either.[982] But there are credible estimates. Grazioli noted in August 1942 that 10,000 Slovenes had been interned.[983] Capogreco, a meticulous researcher, estimates that, all told, during twenty-nine months of occupation the Italians interned about 25,000 people, nearly 7.5% of the Slovene population of Ljubljana province;[984] this figure was corroborated by Ferenc,[985] a careful Slovene scholar who has devoted a lifetime of research to the Axis occupation of his country. Fifteen hundred innocent people died on the island of Arbe from hunger, privation, and lack of medical care.[986] In the Gonars camp, which included a large number of former Yugoslav soldiers, 420 succumbed to malnutrition and brutal treatment.[987]

Ferenc calculates that the Italian army executed 1,569 Slovenes, a figure that does not take into account those condemned to death by the military tribunal of war in Ljubljana. Provided with large numbers of arrested Slovenes, the military tribunals worked overtime. Of 80 Slovenes sentenced to die, 51 were killed while the rest had their sentences commuted to life imprisonment. During Robotti's time in Slovenia, 136 hostages were put to death; Gambara was responsible for the execution of ten.[988]

Grazioli, who had started out with the lofty ambition of intro-
ducing the Slovene population to Fascist civilization, was critical of
Robotti for sabotaging his Italianization programs with mindless
repression. A power struggle between the two ensued over control
of the police and military operations. When insurgency got out of
hand, Mussolini gave Robotti full power to combat insurgency. Discredited, Grazioli retrieved his tattered Fascist credentials by abandoning Slovene assimilation for repression à la Robotti. This signified the end of his "parallel government" idea—a Fascist Italian
imperium superimposed over subordinate and dutiful Slovenes.

## Last Act in Dalmatia

Francesco Giunta came to the Italian province of Dalmatia on
18 February 1943 to pick up the pieces left by his predecessor, Bastianini, who headed for his new job as undersecretary in the
Palazzo Chigi. Giunta's situation was not enviable, for the initiative
had definitely passed to the Partisans. Under pressure from the 2nd
Army, he surrendered the governor's military cabinet to one of
Robotti's favored generals.[989] Still, he was ready to instigate a fight
with the 2nd Army over control of the forces of public order.
Giunta initially arrived as a mollifying reformer who would issue
pardons, weed out politically appointed wastrels, and mend fences
with the estranged military. He realized that grave mistakes had been
made by superimposing Italian structures and institutions where they
did not suit local conditions. Bullies had been sent over, as well as
"prevaricating and blackmailing functionaries, police agents no better
than thieves, swindlers, trafficking and impulsive fascists, and edu-
cators hardly worthy of the name."[990] The highly placed hoarded
scarce goods in an economy wracked by chronic unemployment and
stagnant business.

When the Partisans cut down Italians and Croatian collaborators, Giunta, claiming that the troops in Dalmatia acted like "wild
boars" in hunting down the enemy, asked Rome for "mobile" military reinforcements.[991] Moving ahead on his own, he ordered the
public security forces to undertake reprisals that included intern-

ments, seizure of hostages, and executions publicly staged to intimidate a hostile population. For every telephone pole cut down, three hostages would be shot! Reacting to some beastly mutilations of Italian soldiers killed, he decreed: "For every one of us two of them."[992] Giunta wrote his prefect in Spalato Paolo Zerbino: "You must arrange a series of ferocious and inexorable reprisals." Any less a reply to Partisan "outrages" would be cowardly. People living in areas along telegraph and telephone lines "must be reduced to starvation."[993]

However, Giunta's fierce measures boomeranged because the populace displayed greater defiance than ever and more youth took to the hills. The Communists quickly exploited the Italian excesses by gathering in the angry runaways to swell their numbers, which enabled them to step up ambushes and killings. This, in turn, provoked further Italian retaliation. Taking no note of this, Giunta proudly wrote Mussolini that reprisals had become a routine integrated in the governance of the province and bearing rich dividends in restored public order. On a visit to Cattaro, Giunta noted that his civilizing mission was misunderstood by those "rascals" in England and America who define themselves as the keepers of civilization—"with a small 'c.'"[994] Like many of his ilk, Giunta frequently measured success by body counts, houses burned, and numbers interned, which precluded objective evaluation of unbridled counterinsurgency.[995]

To explain the mounting chaos, Giunta found an easy scapegoat: the harried XVIII Army Corps under the command of General Spigo, who was charged with the military defense of Dalmatia. Giunta complained that Spigo's troops arrested people roughly and undertook ill-conceived house searches, which fostered further acts of violence. The appropriate civilian authorities should handle the job, he said. Like Bastianini, Giunta criticized the military for closing down fortresses in order to consolidate and retrain the troops for offensive expeditions. Giunta held that such thinning out enabled the Partisans to slip through the defense perimeters and set up 5th column networks in the cities. Robotti hastened to Zara on 21 June to discuss the rationale behind Spigo's troop deployments, but walked into a governor's office filled with acrimony. Giunta fumed over Spigo's abandonment of forts, the poor performance of the division "Bergamo," the vulnerability of Spalato, and the flagging spirits of his troops. Robotti explained why smaller forts were being abandoned: instead of hunkering down in fixed positions, the army needed more mobility for search and destroy missions.[996]

To divert attention from his own ineffectiveness, General Spigo pointed out that counterinsurgency à la Giunta was exacerbating the Partisan problem.[997] Like most Italian commanders who favored orderly repression, Spigo took exception to senseless Fascist violence, such as beating people for their failure to salute the swaggering *squadristi*. He blamed Giunta for supervising raids that caused heavy peripheral damage and artillery bombardments from both land and sea that indiscriminately destroyed private dwellings and property instead of hitting buildings known to house insurgent leaders. In the same breath Spigo criticized the governor for trusting local clerics and overlooking Catholic seminaries serving as storehouses for bombs and munitions. The public security forces interned people by the thousands and then incomprehensibly released them, he added.

Like his predecessor, General Armellini, Spigo suggested that the ultimate failure in Italian empire-building lay in Fascism. Political intolerance, he wrote Robotti, drives the population against Italian rule without distinction of religion, political perspective, social standing, and ethnicity. To reduce tension, "our political activity" must be "progressively demobilized."[998] Instead of attracting anti-Communists in a common cause, the Fascists, by their disreputable behavior, disport themselves as brutal imperialists. According to one of Spigo's generals, the effort to Italianize Dalmatia was a "colossal mystification."[999] Robotti handed on the essentials of Spigo's letter under his own name to Governor Giunta,[1000] who himself was not unaware of Fascist excesses. In an ugly incident that occurred when the Squads again comported themselves like thugs, Giunta admitted the "shameful conduct and lack of political sense by the directors of the Federation of Spalato."[1001]

The man who inspired General Spigo's greatest wrath was the Fascist prefect of Spalato, Paolo Zerbino, whom he accused of obstructing his operations, arrogating power, and relentless back-biting.[1002] Matters came to a head in a dispute over an agent of SIM, who was arrested and beaten up by Zerbino's police.[1003] The larger issue centered on the Četniks: Spigo was negotiating with local leaders when suddenly Zerbino interned them. The two proceeded to blacken each other in correspondence to Robotti, which created an irreparable breach between them.[1004]

Robotti convened a meeting on 12 July to thrash out differences between Giunta and Spigo. Giunta wondered why 200,000 soldiers could not halt the Partisans and remarked: "The troops lack bite."[1005] After suggesting that the governor had been misled by Zerbino, Robotti moved to cut short the same kind of debilitating confrontation of the previous year that spelt the ruin of Armellini. His means of conflict resolution was to sacrifice his own commander: Spigo should be replaced. Since the governor was untouchable, Robotti placed blame on the "black spirit" of Spalato and his local acolytes, and suggested that he, too, be cashiered. (Zerbino eventually followed Mussolini to Salò and was shot by the Partisans at Dongo.) Anticipating that Giunta would protect Zerbino, Robotti resignedly proposed that "His Excellency" in Rome [Roatta] intervene with the appropriate measures that "would enable us to work more tranquilly, even if imposing on us greater responsibility"; that is, let us command the public security forces.[1006] Like Roatta, Robotti practiced political legerdemain, but did not have the savoir-faire to bring about in Dalmatia what Roatta had been able to obtain for him in Slovenia: undisputed domination over the forces of public order.

After the many heated exchanges, General Spigo finally got the "Bergamo" moving against the Partisans, but Robotti was not wrong when he observed: "The rebels do what they want."[1007]

In this twilight era of empire-building, the Italians were snarling at each other just as fiercely and desperately as they were hunting down Partisans, burning villages, and interning civilians. No less than the discredited Fascists, the soldiers took out their frustration on the Slav peoples of Dalmatia. In spite of his finger-pointing at

Giunta's excesses, General Piazzoni relentlessly undertook *rastrellamenti* in Dalmatia during July that netted 14 executed Partisans and the internment of 833 people, while General Spigo, cooperating with a German unit, shot 25 captured "rebels" after a successful surprise attack.[1008] As for the Dalmatian governor, Pietromarchi remarked: "Exactly what is the policy of Giunta is hard to divine. He passes from excessive indulgence to excessive severity. He thinks to free himself of every responsibility for ruthless *decisions* by passing them on to the prefects; in the same way, he intends to guarantee the security of Dalmatia by loading on Supersloda the job of making tough decisions."[1009]

On 6 August 1943 Rome abolished the Governorship of Dalmatia, which left the military complete power over the province. After Italy's capitulation in September, the Partisans and Germans competed with each other in moving in to take control and disarm, or shoot, helpless Italian troops and civilians.

A most telling proof of the failure on the part of the Dalmatian governors to Italianize the Slav population was the ghastly internment camp set up on the island of Melàda. Opened for business on 30 June 1942, the camp by August hosted 2,337 inmates. As of 25 November 1942, 442 of about 2,000 had lost their lives from malnutrition, malaria, and tuberculosis.[1010] The Catholic bishop of Sebenico, Girolamo Mileta, moved by the grisly conditions, high mortality rates, and the internment of family members—not excluding children—for the crime of "flight into the woods," protested to Bastianini.[1011] But the governor would admit no wrong.[1012] Nor did he exhibit much humanity. If the "*favoreggiatori*"—the clear majority of the population—was reduced to bare survival, wrote the governor, they would have no extra food to hand on to the Partisans[1013]

# Chapter IX

# Italy's Götterdämmerung in Yugoslavia

The 2nd Army: A Balance Sheet
The Četnik Ally
The Partisan Enemy
Roatta, Robotti, Ambrosio
Chinks in the 2nd Army's Armor
War Crimes and Counterinsurgency
*Bravo Italiano* and *Cattivo Tedesco?*
Diehards in the Palazzo Chigi
Finis to Mussolini's Empire-Building

*The 2nd Army: A Balance Sheet*

Of all the Italian empire-builders in Yugoslavia, the military was the least enthusiastic. As reluctant and cynical warriors, they were quite aware of their own shortcomings and despaired over quick reform, realizing that they were confronted by a determined enemy who enjoyed the aid and support of the countryside. Yet, if Mussolini had set the 2nd Army a task it could not fulfill, the generals did not flinch in doing their duty. As traditional romantic nationalists more loyal to the king than to the Duce, they found the idea of empire congenial. But not in the Balkans. It was the wrong place at the wrong time, for Italian armies were already heavily committed elsewhere. Overextended, the Supreme Command provided the 2nd Army with scant resources and inferior troops for wearying expeditions in the remote mountain areas of Croatia. If Rome had sent the 2nd Army half a million more seasoned soldiers trained to fight a guerrilla war, the commanders undoubtedly would have been cheerleaders, urging on Italian expansion in the Balkans.

At first the military seemed little inclined to venture beyond the outer perimeter of the annexed territories defined by the Dinaric mountain range. The troops expected no more than light occupation duty. But Ustaša violence, which tore civil life asunder, disrupted the Italian "peace" by immersing the troops in ethnic politics and warfare. Then it was the turn of the Partisans, who disseminated propaganda and conducted sporadic hit-and-run raids. In response, the generals tore down Communist posters, undertook patrols, and erected checkpoints. But cosmetics did not suffice. Instead of encountering a handful of "terrorists," the Italian troops, after the German invasion of the Soviet Union, woke up to find homegrown warriors with ever-widening popular support. Lacking the resources of an organized state, the Partisans employed novel guerrilla tactics that baffled the occupier. Gamely, the Italian troops marched into the far corners of Croatia to quell the disorder. Circumstances, therefore, rather than a foreordained program of conquest, had driven the 2nd Army forward. The generals were not unhappy to advance the prestige of their country on the points of their bayonets. Perhaps their honor, which had been stained in other war theaters, could be retrieved in the Balkans.

In a land filled with Italian-haters, lukewarm friends, and so-called allies, the 2nd Army confronted a bewildering state of affairs. The Partisans represented only a small percentage of the population; the Croatian people, though hostile, refrained from taking up

arms against the Italian military because their government was diplomatically in league with Rome; and the Orthodox Serbs, hounded
by the Ustaša, sought out the troops for protection. Throughout
Croatia the Army exhibited unusual concern for Serbs battered by
Ustaša violence. Many of the Orthodox population singly and by
village owed their survival to Italian protection.

The 7 September 1941 declaration by General Ambrosio was
the benchmark of Italy's record of assistance to persecuted peoples.
The 2nd Army felt obliged to rescue and provide safety for those
who fought bravely as allies against the common Partisan enemy or
were running from Ustaša cutthroats. The Jews provided a special
case. That Italian soldiers afforded shelter to runaway Jews from the
German death squads stands as a shining example of bravery and
honor and a stirring chapter in the unrelieved suffering of the Holocaust experience. True, the Italian rescue was prompted by a variety of motives beyond humanitarian impulse: rank opportunism, an
assertion of Italian pride, and defiance toward the overbearing
Germans. Yet, whatever the reasons, the Italian military took risks
in sabotaging the Führer's direct order to round up Jews for deportation to the dreaded death camps in Eastern Europe.

Whatever humanitarianism one finds in the 2nd Army's treatment of the violated peoples in Croatia vanishes in the annexed areas
of Slovenia and Dalmatia. Whereas the Serbs in Croatia beseeched
the Italians for protection, the Slovenes and Dalmatian Croats
greeted them with hostility. When rebellion surged, the 2nd Army
replied with counterinsurgency. Unrestrained military brutality had
supplanted the Fascist lordly manner. Not much effort was made
to distinguish between Partisans, *favoreggiatori*, or blameless civilians.

During latter September 1941, Mussolini authorized the military to take possession of the demarcation zone. The commanders
in the field demanded and received political authority in the areas
they occupied. Faced by lawless Ustaša and determined Partisans,
the undermanned 2nd Army hired Četniks to assist them in quelling the disorder. Opportunistically the commanders pitted them
against the Partisans to reduce wear and tear on their own troops.
They anticipated that these two irreconcilable adversaries would

exhaust each other and eventually be crushed. Mainly the handiwork of General Mario Roatta, this strategy ultimately made sense to the Supreme Command. Should such collaboration with the Četniks land Italy in controversies with Germans and Croats, so be it. But the results were mixed. After much wheeling and dealing, the Italian commanders ended up with no friends among the two "allies" and one shaky ally among the enemies. If the Italian military did not anticipate compensation from the Jews for sheltering them, it expected loyalty and assistance from the Četniks in return for protection from the Ustaša. However, this mutually advantageous quid pro quo rarely turned into sustained mutual confidence, primarily because Mussolini was determined to honor the Italian alliance with the NDH.

During 1942, the surge in Partisan activity, an ever more intrusive Wehrmacht, a hostile NDH, and disjointed Četnik support imposed a job of pacification on the 2nd Army that dampened the spirits of the most enterprising military commanders. Zagreb cried out at the massive infringement on its sovereignty resulting from the 2nd Army's obvious preference for Serb Orthodox over Roman Catholic Croats. Rome reacted by ordering Sušak to restore civilian authority to the NDH. When the Ustaša danced in the streets, and the Orthodox accused the 2nd Army of prevarication, the Italian commanders fumed over the blow to their prestige. The purpose of crushing insurgency got lost in a swirl of political maneuver. Clever makeshift combinations among conflicting forces could not offset endemic military weakness, and the fantasy of empire without military effort metamorphosed into the nightmare of a Partisan ascendancy over the insurgent movement. The Italian troops had to pull out. On the slow but inevitable withdrawal to the 15 January 1943 line, they beat off the Partisans assisted by still loyal Četniks, who had nowhere else to turn. When the balance of war in Europe began to shift against the Axis Powers, the generals knew that Rome would order many units under their command for posting in the Peninsula to counter the inevitable Allied invasion. But they were loath to have their pride hurt further by leaving the abandoned areas to either the Germans or the so-called Croatian ally.

So they frequently did an about-face and fought in the forlorn hope that the ground could be held till the Četniks arrived to relieve them.

Needing no encouragement from the NDH, the Wehrmacht hastened to move into the voids left by the retreating Italians. As Italy tottered toward defeat, the Germans threw off the mask of loyal ally, supporting Croatian irredentism in Italian Dalmatia and breaking in on Italy's *spazio vitale* by ill-concealed domination of the Croatian government and economy. Operations *Weiss* and *Schwartz* took the Germans deep into Italian-occupied Croatia and into Montenegro, where they unilaterally disarmed the Četniks, who had been organized by General Pirzio Biroli. An Italian onlooker wrote, "we were left to bow before the fait accompli."[1014]

By 1943, whatever spirit existed among the Italian troops had been drained during the long and exhausting battle. Still, Italy's generals persisted. Mussolini's fall did not occasion much soul-searching, for the 2nd Army pursued counterinsurgency as if by rote. The dazed Italian troops fought half-heartedly, wanting to abandon the desolate Balkan front lines for home. But they followed orders and stayed in the lines with few defections before the Armistice. Throughout the occupation period the 2nd Army doggedly carried out its military assignments in an ethnic morass of religious clashes and ideological divisions.

After the Italian surrender, thousands of the troops were marooned in the Balkans without clear and timely directives from Rome. The Germans closed in for the kill, with the disorganized and bewildered Italian troops able to offer only sporadic resistance. On 9 September General Robotti slipped away by boat and eventually made it to Italy, while General Gambara surrendered to the Germans without a fight at his headquarters in Sušak. At their leisure the Germans disarmed, shot, or sent their prisoners to forced labor in the Third Reich in contempt of the rudimentary tenets of international law. With escape routes to Italy closed off, many troops avoided capture and Ustaša vengeance by joining the Partisans. The newly formed Garibaldi division participated in the resistance against Nazi imperialism and earned the undying gratitude of the Partisans who, the day before, had regarded Italians as deadly enemies.

## The Četnik Ally

Much in the story of Italy's military occupation of Yugoslavia is told in the 2nd Army's agreements with the Četniks in the crucible of battle against the Partisans. From the beginning, as the Italians never tired in pointing out, the Četniks were a troubling and contentious ally. They stubbornly adhered to their own agenda, aligned with the pro-Ally Mihailović, and projected a Pan-Serb future that negated an Italian *spazio vitale*. But unlike Hitler, the Italians never regarded the Četniks as a more serious threat to the Axis than the Partisans. Machiavelli had his day as the Italian High Command double-talked, feinted, and quietly subverted Axis military joint planning to impede German-planned *rastrellamenti* and political machinations in Croatia that threatened to impinge on Italian interests and destroy the lone Četnik ally.

While the 2nd Army snarled at the Pavelić regime for its incompetence and pro-German favoritism, it continued under duress from Rome to respect the formalities of the alliance—the parades, political ceremonies, and arms deliveries. The Četniks put up with this because they had reached a dead end and because there was a pattern of reciprocal advantage that had stood the test of time. Early on, the Italian soldiers had protected Serbs from Ustaša atrocities, and later the Italian commanders and Četnik leaders had engaged in a series of military agreements based on the common endeavor to destroy the Partisans. In spite of all the betrayals and vicissitudes experienced by both sides, these agreements held up reasonably well during most of the Italian occupation of Yugoslavia.

During 1943, when the Germans bore down on the Italians to disarm the Četniks, the 2nd Army was thrown into turmoil. Under Hitler's relentless pressure, Mussolini finally gave way—Ambrosio following suit—by ordering Sušak to comply with German wishes. Četnik confidence in Italy vanished as the troops in the field reluctantly did their duty or pretended to carry out unwelcome orders. Riven by many inner disputes, the Četniks began to disintegrate. Instead of exhibiting self-sacrifice for nationhood or any other high-minded purpose, they acted like xenophobic Serb nationalists bent on ethnic cleansing or mercenaries interested only in plunder and revenge. But in this twilight of occupation, the Italian troops let down their only allies. In disarming Serb formations, they exposed the Četniks to vengeance on the part of their many enemies. The Carabinieri General Pièche, a man of "undeniable experience and purity,"[1015] who had adopted the pro-Serb thesis of the 2nd Army, noted that, in disarming Četniks who had fought for Italy, the military had breached its own honor code.[1016]

During the unhappy finale the 2nd Army was most ungracious toward its onetime Četnik partner, having assumed an attitude of moral superiority. One must be familiar with the dark corners of the Balkan mentality, announced a high-level post-mortem military report. Very few Italians "are in a position to abstract themselves from the sensitivity of the Latin spirit to appreciate the enormous difficulties that prevent us from falling to the level of this [Balkan] mentality that luxuriates in intrigue, scorns sentiment, bows before force, makes a passion of politics, and thrills in confounding adversaries."[1017]

The 2nd Army had committed a multitude of "errors," continued the report. Former Yugoslav officers should not have been allowed to form their own bands. Without direct Italian supervision, they were able to spread a virulent Pan-Serbism and flout Italian authority. Involvement with the Četniks in the crusade against Communism closed Italian eyes to Serb abuses, massacres, and hatred of the NDH. Italian good will "placed us in difficult situations with the Croatian state and above all with German military authority, which believes that we are to a certain extent dominated by the Četniks."[1018] The lesson was clear: the Germans were right in saying that the Četniks should have been integrated in units with Muslims and Croats under direct Italian command. But one can reasonably ask whether the Italian army, in full retreat, was capable of smoothly orchestrating a mixed force of ancient and bitter enemies.

Robotti endorsed this "military eyes only" report, which through back channels had reached the Palazzo Chigi. Pietromarchi commented: "Its importance lies in the fact that these self-evident observations, which habitually have been made by us, are finally given expression by the 2nd Army."[1019] Bastianini annotated: "In fact, in Dalmatia I had placed them [the ex-Yugoslav officers] under Italian command. Of this error [allowing ex-Yugoslav officers to form their own bands] I had drawn the attention of Supersloda, but was not listened to."[1020] The military historian Talpo concludes that "no economic incentive could have given the Italian army the ascendancy over a population that lived by the cult of violence,"[1021] as if Roatta's 3C circular exemplified benign imperialism. Pietromarchi, Bastianini, and Robotti all endorsed the conclusion that the 2nd Army should never have cooperated with the Četniks as an independent force.

Another Italian military report yields further revealing commentary. General Rudolf Lüters, commander of the German forces in Croatia, was praised for keeping both Četniks and Croats under tight control, whereas the Četniks fighting for Italy in Herzegovina were deemed undisciplined and disloyal. As opposed to linear German policy, the report proceeds, the Italo-Četnik condominium fluctuated between breakdown and Croatian manipulation.[1022] Just as revealing is an important VI Army Corps document issued on 1 July 1943, which found that Germany's 6 May 1943 decision to disarm the Četniks behind Italian backs—a move that originally stirred heated protest among the Italian commanders—had been the right one.[1023] That the Italian military displayed pusillanimity toward the German ally—an "ally" against whom they had recorded many a protest for having pushed them around from one end of the Balkans to another—is inescapable. In this unexpected twist, the 2nd Army, on the eve of Fascist Italy's downfall, found itself back on Mussolini's page.

Whether the Četniks deserve the epitaph of reactionary and vengeful clansmen, or whether they should be lionized as true Serb patriots who were betrayed by the Anglo-Americans, depends on one's political perspective. But some facts are indisputable. The Četniks did not unleash the chaos devouring Yugoslavia, and they were far from alone in failing to uphold humane norms in a European continent awash in mass killing. In the Balkans civil life had quite simply ceased to exist. The territories abandoned by the 2nd Army in Croatia, which had enjoyed a primitive peace under its control, lapsed into a protracted free-for-all among foragers and marauding Ustaša that no responsible Četnik or Partisan could bring under control.

Least of all Mihailović. The doughty Serb leader made his mark by refusing to recognize his country's capitulation to the Germans. With barely enough time to flee, Mihailović made his way to the mountain fastness at Ravna Gora and started his resistance from scratch. Having planted his standard of rebellion as an unknown, he had no time and few resources to build up an infrastructure of government and a reliable police force to move in behind the retreating Italians. His vision of an archaic agrarian and patriarchal society in the 19th century Serb peasant state denied him support beyond besieged Orthodox hamlets. Moreover, his potential for community-building in time of war was limited by the lack of a disciplined cadre willing to carry out orders faithfully. Mihailović was not a politician but a soldier, whose attention was devoted to survival first and defeat of the Partisans later.

As opposed to Tito, Mihailović lacked soldiers under his direct command. Notwithstanding an arduous and harsh recruitment program, he was never able to build up a large personal following. Forced to rely on connections and the idea of a Serb resurrection, Mihailović wielded a power more feudal-like than modern; he had perforce to depend on oaths of loyalty that bore limited and easily avoided military obligations particularly when Četnik fortunes began to slide. Without a chain of command everything was negotiable, from party program to troop deployment. Mihailović was therefore unable to exact obedience from the radical and independent-minded Serbs living in Bosnia and Herzegovina, let alone the Montenegrin hotheads. He was as much dependent on them as they were on him.

Mihailović's fluctuating attitude toward the Axis has earned him much criticism, especially by the Partisans, who held that he was an outright collaborator for having avoided battle with the Axis Powers. But Communists too—in Belgium for example, after a brief spell of radical violence—backed off from targeting the Wehrmacht in early 1942 after a German repression almost annihilated the party.[1024]

Mihailović's retreat into watchful waiting, however, played into the hands of the sure-footed Tito, who gained converts by equating "absenteeism" with collaboration. As the leader of a theoretically multi-ethnic Communist movement, Tito portrayed Mihailović among non-Serbs as the bearer of Serbian vengeance and among Serbs as the agent of the British, who were simply exploiting them. The mass of Croatian Catholics and Muslims began to take a harder look at the Partisans, for they saw Mihailović's movement only through the eyes of local Serbian Četniks, who were easily deflected from warfare against the Partisans by vengeful attacks against Muslims and Croats. Powered by a dynamic ideology and the tireless activity of their "popular army," the Partisans contrasted favorably with the Officers, who placed a high premium on saving their own skins for a future life of privilege in a reinstated monarchy. But the clock could not be turned back. The restoration of a rigid class society and an anachronistic dynasty was popular only among Serbs connected with the clique of backward-looking officers in charge of the Četnik movement.

Since many of the Četniks appeared disoriented by the unmitigated savagery of civil war, it is hardly surprising that they would have trafficked with the invader to escape defeat and extermination by the Germans and the Ustaša. Even so, in defiance of overwhelming odds, they frequently stood their ground and fought. Bravery was no Partisan monopoly. In Italian-occupied Croatia only a few Četniks collaborated in the style of the French Vichyites. In German-dominated Serbia the situation was murkier. Hitler was willing to tolerate Nedić as head of a kind of Pétain-type government in Belgrade, but at the same time ordered the Wehrmacht to wipe out Mihailović. That the followers of Nedić and Mihailović, mostly civil servants and gendarmes, constantly shuttled back and forth between the two camps or kept up contacts with both should not lead one to underestimate the differences in political positions between the two men. The Germans never made this mistake. Constantly hounded by the Wehrmacht, Mihailović can hardly be portrayed as a Serb Pétain, and certainly he was no Nedić.

The question of Četnik collaboration is clouded by the hopeless confusion of ethnic and religious warfare in Yugoslavia. The Serb Orthodox peoples simultaneously faced extermination in Bosnia-Herzegovina and civil war against the Partisans within the framework of imperialist invasion and occupation. To defend themselves against the Ustaša—and obtain food and guns for the struggle against the Partisans—the Četniks had nowhere to turn but the 2nd Army. They therefore accommodated to the Italian enemy, made deals with him, and sought his protection and shelter. This reads more like expediency than collaboration. The Partisans had an easier time in acting assertively, for they were not on the front lines of Ustaša bestiality and, once forced out of old Serbia, did not have thousands of women, children, and homes to defend. Hence they were able to avoid some of the excruciatingly painful and immediate choices that bore down on the Četniks, who could either save lives by accommodation or invite immediate destruction by uncompromising resistance. The German massacres in Serbia were a harsh lesson that Mihailović took to heart. And it was hard-headed calculation that prompted the Četniks to duck their heads during the Axis occupation, for they expected that the Allies would land in the Balkans, sweep out the invaders, and hold the ring while they finished off Tito's Communists. The Četniks were, of course, wrong, but so were their sworn German and Partisan enemies. All the combatants in Yugoslavia based policy on the expectation of an Allied landing; all were relieved that such a landing did not occur, save the Četniks.

No matter how justified Mihailović was in avoiding guerrilla war against the Germans, his moves over time made him look more and more like an unabashed Serb chauvinist. Dogged by this reputation, Mihailović failed to overcome his Quisling image and therefore fell behind Tito in the propaganda contest to win the hearts and minds of the Yugoslav peoples. It is an open question whether a more talented conservative leader in the manner of France's General Charles de Gaulle could have prevailed against the imposing forces marshaled against him. Certainly not one who would waffle on the question of resistance. In parleying with the enemy even only for tactical reasons–the very thought of which the French leader found abhorrent—Mihailović besmirched the reputation of his movement as a patriotic force whose aim was to free his country from the Axis yoke.

## The Partisan Enemy

The 2nd Army's primary responsibility during Italy's occupation of Yugoslavia was to suppress Partisan insurgency. This task was not easy, especially after the Germans had chased the Partisans out of Serbia in late fall 1941. They redeployed in Croatia, where Italian opposition was softer and the alignments of war far more tangled. Since Italian reconnaissance was weak or non-existent, the Partisans were able to assemble their forces quickly and achieve temporary superiority for surprise attacks. Capable of audacious but sporadic and fleeting successes, they were, however, up to Mussolini's fall, unable to inflict major defeats on the Italians save in minor skirmishes, the spectacular victory at the Neretva river, and in firefights in Montenegro. And, although the Partisans overran lonely Italian outposts, they were rarely able to storm strongly fortified positions. They infiltrated urban areas but did not take them over. Their employment of hit-and-run tactics, which disrupted Italian communications, was necessitated by the lack of firepower to establish fixed lines of defense.

The Italian military response was hampered by communication breakdowns and overly dispersed garrisons. Not infrequently battlefield strategy was upset by chessboard moves against Croatian and German "allies" that sapped energy and produced confusion in troop deployment. As time wore on and Italian strength fell dangerously below listed fighting capacity, the troops suffered serious local reversals and inordinate loss of equipment. The 1943 spring campaigning in Montenegro showed up Italian performance at its worst, with small pockets of troops, disoriented by mediocre leadership, taking flight or meekly surrendering. This failure of nerve and fighting spirit is fully documented by the Italian generals themselves. Still, on the whole, the troops stayed put wherever they bivouacked and built strong, if haltingly guarded, forts. When they took backward steps, it was for tactical reasons, not because of sustained Partisan offenses. Italian soldiers rarely retreated from enemy pressure but abandoned territory by orders of the Duce and the Supreme Command for coastal defense or home posting to combat an Allied invasion.

But neither did the 2nd Army vanquish the Partisans; they had only moderate success in flushing them from their forest and mountain lairs. No matter how many casualties the Italians inflicted on them, the Partisans usually managed to slip through their fingers and regroup for further raids and ambushes. They occupied much of the rocky countryside, but the Italian tricolor flew in major cities and towns until the surrender in September 1943. Ultimately, the troops of the 2nd Army were overwhelmed by events beyond their control; they could do nothing to arrest the fortunes of war that were shifting in favor of the Allies.

On 1 August 1943, according to a report of the Supreme Command, the Italians had in the Balkans a total of thirty-two divisions and six brigades with approximately 672,000 men. Of these 213,000 were in Greece and Crete, 55,000 in the Aegean Islands, 108,000 in Albania, 71,000 in Montenegro and the Bay of Kotor, and 225,000 in areas under the command of the 2nd Army.[1025] Thus in Yugoslavia alone, counting also the forces in Albanian-held Yugoslav areas, the Italian soldiers numbered about 321,000.[1026] Italian casualties between April 1941 and September 1943 in Yugoslavia are reported as follows: 7,782 dead, 13,010 wounded, and 4,740 missing.[1027] In Montenegro, the Italians suffered 2,849 dead and 2,150 wounded.[1028]

If these figures are correct, they suggest that the 2nd Army losses were not great in number and that mass formations were not continually engaged against the enemy. Fighting was intermittent, a succession of skirmishes and raids. The Italian troops were required to undertake countless long marches that wearied them and wore out equipment, but casualties incurred in the Balkan theater were modest when compared to the devastating toll exacted on other fronts.

One should therefore be careful to avoid crediting the Partisans with "setting Yugoslavia ablaze" against the occupier. They seldom harassed well-fortified Italian and German strongholds and many times searched more assiduously for collaborators (often mere official functionaries) and Četniks to kill. They created problems for the Italians, particularly in Slovenia and Dalmatia, but in Zagreb, Belgrade, and the Dalmatian cities they made little or no headway against the Axis occupation. Open guerrilla combat was limited to the mountains of the hinterland. More than their own exploits, the Partisans owed ultimate victory to the German decision to withdraw from the Balkans following severe reverses on the Eastern Front at the hands of the Soviet armies. Nonetheless, Tito emerged from battle no longer the hunted rebel, but rather the honored ally of the Anglo-Americans.

If the Italian 2nd Army charred the countryside and killed an unknown number of Yugoslavs, the Partisans too left behind a trail of property destroyed and peoples massacred. Communist morality left no room for fine distinctions between collaboration and "absenteeism" to spare the blood of the innocent in this pitiless guerrilla war. The Partisans claimed that if civilians were not on the side of the guerrillas, they ought to be. They should be ready to take over their share of suffering for the common cause by carrying out the reprisals that were the Italian occupier's standard. A terror strategy was devised to provoke Italian retaliation and radicalize the population. According to Edvard Kardelj, an organizer of the Communist uprising in Slovenia:

> We must at all costs push the Croatian as well as the Serb villages into the struggle. Some comrades are afraid of reprisals, and that fear prevents the mobilization of Croat villages. I consider, the reprisals will have the useful result of throwing Croatian villages on the side of Serb villages. In war, we must not be frightened of the destruction of whole villages. Terror will bring about armed action.[1029]

In early 1943 Vladimir Dedijer, editor of the Communist party newspaper, authorized mass murder: "Often the confiscation of property is not a sufficient punishment against regions attached to the Četniks. There are cases when it is necessary to burn whole villages and destroy the populations."[1030] Could Roatta have put it better? Communist justice and Italian military justice were in reality terrifying weapons of a guerrilla warfare that brutalized both sides.

If not featured in Yugoslav sources, Partisan atrocities committed against captured Italian troops were brought to light in the "official" accounts of Loi and Talpo sponsored by the Italian military. Officers and Fascists were regularly shot; common soldiers, however, were not infrequently released. Captivity was harsh, but so were the lives of the Partisans. There was method in this madness, as revealed in one of Bastianini's caustic asides:

> The rebels strip the [captured Italian] officers in the snow, insult them, bring the prisoners together and explain to them that they have been sent by Mussolini to be butchered; that they [the rebels] have come with food to a friendly people, and in front of the soldiers they massacre the officers, who have turned black in the freezing cold. Then they feed the prisoners, give them cigarettes and send them back [to their lines]. It's easy to understand what comments these heroes make and what impressions they spread when they get back.[1031]

When all is said and done, partisan terror in Yugoslavia was reactive rather than initiatory—a weapon employed by the homeland defender against the foreign invader and his collaborators and allies. Apologists of the Italian military hold that the majority of the Yugoslav peoples opposed Communism. That well might be. What is far more certain, however, is that the Italians alienated rather than won over Yugoslavs in the crusade against Communism. Bona fide collaborators could be counted on one hand. The Partisans and the high percentage of non-Communist fence-sitters were understandably outraged by a war imposed on them by imperialist predators. Both Nazi Germany and Fascist Italy brought terror and exploitation. There was an epic quality in the partisan resistance unmatched by the Četniks. Partisan determination to create a just society and ethnic reconciliation made for iron discipline and superhuman self-sacrifice. The vast majority truly believed that they were fighting for the liberation of their country from an exploitative ruling class of reactionaries and Axis invaders. That the Communist regime of Marshal Tito after the war shot countless "bourgeois" enemies, liquidated thousands of rounded-up Četniks, and imposed a resolute dictatorship over the people should not obscure the idealism of many a partisan insurgent.

## Roatta, Robotti, Ambrosio

The Italian army did not lack quick-witted and astute generals. General Mario Roatta was a shrewd and sharp-tongued political operator with diplomatic flair. Unusual in the hide-bound military, Roatta received a command when he was only fifty-five. Having served in military intelligence and as an attaché in Berlin, he moved easily in the corridors of power and absorbed knowledge of the outside world. Much more than the German generals—with the notable exception of Glaise von Horstenau—Roatta understood that politics and warfare in the Balkans were one and the same thing. He was not afraid to speak with brutal honesty and defy wrong-headed authority in Berlin, Zagreb, or Rome. Roatta also knew how to charm Germans and keep a clever antagonist, like General Cavallero, at bay.

Roatta also had to balance the authority of Italy's civilian Fascist rulers in Yugoslavia with military necessity as seen from 2nd Army headquarters at Sušak. As insurgency became stronger, Roatta lobbied in Rome to unify under his command—in both occupied territories and annexed provinces—the forces of public order that originally had lain in the prerogative of civilian authority. It was no easy task for Roatta to talk the recalcitrant Governor Bastianini of Dalmatia, who had powerful ties with Mussolini, into a "gentleman's agreement" that would observe the Duce's edict of 19 January, handing over the forces of public security to military authority.[1032]

Thanks to serious military reverses in Greece and North Africa in 1940, Italy had been reduced to junior partner in the Axis. But occupation of Yugoslavia gave the empire-builders in Rome the idea that they could resuscitate the much-vaunted "parallel war" strategy by conducting autonomous military operations in the Balkan theater. After Germany's rescue of the bogged-down Italians on the Greek front this appeared to be a pipe dream. Roatta, however, was not daunted. To restore military initiative and breathe new life into Italian imperialism, he hoped that the Četniks, who hated the Partisans as much as he, might be coaxed into becoming Italian subalterns in a joint crusade against Communism. Roatta therefore proceeded to accelerate the pace, initially set in motion by his predecessor General Ambrosio, of changing Italian practice—if not official policy—from friendship toward the Zagreb regime to support of their hereditary enemy, the Orthodox Serbs. This was not inconsistent with Mussolini's long-range goal of placing the whole region under an Italian protectorate. It was a question of means. For Roatta, befriending the Četniks was no do-gooder's gesture but an exercise in Realpolitik. He intended to use them both against the Partisans and as a means of assisting him in rolling back German domination in Croatia. They would occupy territory liberated by Axis *rastrellamenti* instead of the pro-German Croatians. Like his fellow commanders, Roatta knew that the Wehrmacht generals sought release from Hitler's repeated oral pledges to respect Italy's long-standing claims in Yugoslavia.

To reduce wear and tear on his own troops, Roatta without scruple pitted Četniks against Partisans. The 2nd Army would have the chore of "mopping up" exhausted Partisans, after which the Četniks, the stalking horse of the British, would be easily disarmed. But there was a catch. In return for their cooperation, the Četniks expected that Italy would look away while they avenged themselves against Muslims and carried out retaliatory raids on Croatian communities. Roatta did not condone such vengeance because of the dismay this caused in Zagreb and Rome. But the warnings he occasionally issued the Četniks to restrain themselves had little effect.

In undertaking the work of pacification, the 2nd Army, led by Roatta, questioned the Duce's endeavor to live or die by Pavelić's dagger. Since the NDH was anti-Italian and a purveyor of chaos, Roatta failed to understand why Mussolini should support such a bungling and antipathetic regime. General Armellini summed up the 2nd Army's view: "These extraordinarily hostile, treacherous, and underhanded people [NDH], whose official friendship [with Italy] facilitates their endeavor of working against us, place us squarely against the population. They nourish a lively irredentism in the population and faith in the liberation of the hated invader. Worse, these people instill hatred in the population toward our system of government. Ustaša provocateurs, by provoking incidents, succeed in exacerbating this hatred."[1033]

Almost every move Roatta made was underscored by the same unrelieved contempt of the Croatian regime—its anti-Italian irredentism, pro-German proclivities, inefficiencies, and mindless slaughter, which greatly complicated his work of pacification. Croatia should not be regarded as an independent state, he wrote, but as a "sick man who has brought himself to the brink of his own grave."[1034] Roatta attributed the success of the "rebels" to political errors committed by Rome in the creation of Croatia and the institution of provinces in Ljubljana, Dalmatia, and Fiume, which "have created disillusion, hope, exhaustion, and disorientation. In addition our behavior has been unpredictable in the sense that after having imparted the appearance of wishing to protect the population against the Ustaša, we have finished up by giving the impression of quasi-support of the selfsame Ustaša."[1035] Whereas the NDH charged that Communism spread because it was compelled to relegate territories in the 2nd and 3rd zones to the authority of the Italians and their Serb cohorts, Roatta pointed out more accurately that insurgency fed on Ustaša violence and Croatian inefficiency and corruption.[1036]

Roatta's overall conception of political events in Yugoslavia was bold and insightful. No matter how the war evolved, he thought, whether the Axis Powers won or lost, the Yugoslav state, like Humpty-Dumpty, could never be put back together owing to the unbridgeable chasm of hatred dividing Croats and Serbs. Whatever fate befell Italy, Roatta foretold, friendship with the Serbs would hold out more advantages for Italy than "peaceful coexistence" with the Italophobe Croats. In the event of an Axis victory, Italy would want the Serbs as an ally to check a German hegemony over the Balkans; the Croats, on the other hand, irredeemably hostile over the loss of Dalmatia to Italy, would, if forced to choose, prefer Berlin to Rome as a protector. Faced with unyielding Fascist and Nazi endorsement of the Pavelić regime, Roatta, with only the 2nd Army behind him, had no chance of transforming Axis policy in Yugoslavia by pursuing a pro-Serb agenda.

As did the Germans and the Četniks, Roatta suspected an Allied landing in the Balkans. How that would play out he did not venture to predict. In spite of his reputation for political skullduggery, there is no evidence to suggest that Roatta contemplated desertion of the Axis ship during his stay in Yugoslavia. He had no known publicly recorded brainstorming session with colleagues on carrying out any diplomatic revolution, and in avoiding subjects of a political nature in discussions with Četnik leaders, he scrupulously followed orders from his military superiors.[1037] No matter what the government in Rome decreed, Roatta would serve it. Like his fellow commanders, he did not foresee the shocking repercussions of his country's regime change and capitulation, which precluded any future role that Italy might play in the Balkans.

Having only Četniks as allies in Yugoslavia, Roatta's hate extended to several groups: Croats, Slovenes, Germans, Communists. But his most detested enemies were the Partisan insurgents. His 3C pamphlet is solid testimony to that. On more than one occasion, however, to stiffen the spirit of his troops, he told them that the Partisans were "overrated" and would ultimately be defeated. How could the Communist "scum of the earth" prevail against Italy's proud imperial legions? But the 2nd Army's slow withdrawals to the coast belied his contrived optimism. Victory would go to "the bandits."

Besides engaging in politics, General Roatta had the no less important task of energizing his lethargic troops for serious fighting. If retrained and furnished with a new combat doctrine, he hoped that they would sally forth against the hardened guerrilla enemy. The problem was that little retraining took place. The officer corps was too inflexible and backward and the troops too demoralized and raw for quick-fix reform. Roatta, with Robotti following him, would rant and rave at the stodginess of their brood, but in the end seemed resigned to serve as caretakers of an army destined to fight with equipment and tactics better suited for World War I.

If General Roatta was a man of his times—a hard-bitten army officer who had few qualms over random killing of the enemy—his appearance belied military bearing. In his pince-nez, he looked more like a schoolmaster than a toughened warrior. Relishing expensive furnishings and high society and flaunting an open marriage, he surrounded himself with beautiful women and threw extravagant parties. Pietromarchi wrote: "Roatta floats around in his yacht and during evenings pours down a shower of roses on his guests in the style of ancient pagans."[1038]

Like many Italian generals, Roatta flourished in Mussolini's Italy. Was he a confirmed Fascist along the lines of Marshal Graziani, who faithfully followed Mussolini to Salò, or was he an opportunist in the style of General Badoglio, who slipped the Duce the knife by heading up the first post-Fascist Italian government after his fall? Roatta was more the self-serving pragmatist than ideologue. At the time he composed the 3C pamphlet on 1 March, he felt besieged by Partisan insurgency, which made him believe that the Italian occupation was precarious. An unexpected uprising had occurred in Montenegro the previous July; Slovenia was awash in rebellion, at least so reported General Robotti; Partisans had trapped and surrounded Italian garrisons in isolated outposts in the Lika area; Bastianini was bombarding him with anxious letters warning of Partisans massing on the Dalmatian frontier; and Tito was rampaging through next-door eastern Bosnia. One can argue that Roatta overreacted in drafting such draconian measures, and perhaps Partisan insurgency in spring 1942 was overrated. But Roatta was responding to a perceived threat that in his mind demanded a massive response by powerful means. He also took his cues from Mussolini, who, after all, was his supreme commander, and who egged him on to be ever more aggressive. Italian generals outdid each other in establishing a reputation for ruthlessness, and General Roatta made sure that he had no peer.[1039]

If not a diehard Fascist, Roatta was an unquestioned nationalist who believed in Italy's imperial mission. He was in the end respectful of the chain of command whose guiding imperative was "orders are orders." If Roatta differed with Mussolini over which Slavs should be considered allies and which defined as the enemy, he never wavered in carrying out the Duce's expressed will to destroy Partisan resistance without pity. In the end Roatta's constant temporizing misfired, and his conduct of the war was politically convoluted. Roatta's reputation has suffered even more because of his overzealous efforts to master insurgency, which involved him in war crimes, a subject to be further discussed below. But in his memoirs Roatta owns up to no moral wrong; he admits only mistaken policy.

Of Italy's 2nd Army commanders, General Robotti was the most faithful executor of Roatta's counterinsurgency program in the Italian "province of Ljubljana." Although not numerous, the Slovenian Partisans spread propaganda in the capital, sniped at Italian troops on patrol duty, conducted raids in the countryside that harried them, and disrupted railroads and supply convoys. Robotti played into their hands by retaliatory overkill, alienating even more the essentially anti-Communist majority of the Slovene population, which was left in a no-man's-land between collaboration and Communism.

When Robotti took over command of the 2nd Army, he assumed the delicate task of moving endangered troops toward the Adriatic shore at least possible cost. Like his predecessor Roatta, he was appalled that the Croats and Germans, rather than the Četniks, were entering territory abandoned by his troops. In the absence of clear directives from Rome, it is surprising that the Italian retreat through areas bristling with Partisan activity and allied ill will did not turn into a rout. But the 2nd Army bravely held together till broken up by Partisans and Germans after Italy's departure from the war.

Since independent newspaper reporters were not allowed in the Balkans, let alone the battle zones, the outside world had only faint knowledge of the violent ethnic warfare and counterinsurgency raging in Yugoslavia. The Vatican was informed of the horrors via reports sent to Rome by ecclesiastical representatives, but kept an official silence until 1943. In July of that year Archbishop Stepinac of Zagreb informed the Papal Nunzio in Rome, Monsignor Francesco Borgoncini, that Italian troops had allowed "religiously schismatic Četniks" to commit atrocities against innocent Catholic Croats. The monsignor let Sušak know of papal displeasure.[1040]

General Robotti handled the Vatican's protest by stoutly defending the behavior of both his troops and Italy's Orthodox allies who, he claimed, were ravaged by Partisan outrages. Here Robotti had a point. Partisans savagely manhandled captured Italian soldiers and massacred those of their own peoples thought to be friendly toward Italians—that is, those not explicitly committed to them. Robotti was careful to cover up Četnik atrocities and claimed that the behavior of his troops was exemplary.[1041] On another occasion Archbishop Stepinac complained of Italian outrages in Herzegovina during Operation *Weiss*. Robotti dismissed these allegations as nationalistic anger on the part of Croats trying to obscure their own terror by pinning blame on Italian troops.[1042]

General Robotti lacked the political sophistication needed to cope with the complicated webs of political intrigue spun by "allies" and enemies alike. For Pietromarchi, he was "one of the most mediocre of our generals."[1043] Stiff-necked and tempestuous, Robotti was an unblushing practitioner of counterinsurgency who, like Armellini and Roatta, had the habit of drawing a distinction between himself, a disciplined and just warrior, and the out-of-control Fascist squads. On 8 May 1943 he reported: "Battalion 'M' acted excessively . . . there was no reason for extending the torching of houses whose dwellers obviously had no sympathy or connection with the partisans . . . Please remind the commander of the 'M' battalion to refrain from these deplorable excesses, which have no other result than to sow hate."[1044]

If Robotti went overboard in brutal treatment of the Communist enemy, he bent over backwards in trying to save thousands of Četnik refugees and their families who had been turned into a scared and half-starving horde fleeing vengeful Partisans. Since the retreating Italian troops could barely provision themselves, he turned to the Croatian authorities, who "should shake themselves from their inertia" to provide food for the Orthodox refugees.[1045] That, of course, was a forlorn hope.

In what amounts to a valedictory to his counterinsurgency, Robotti declared in September:

> I must decisively and firmly insist that one must finally understand that the Italian army is still the most humane of all armies, and that our soldiers are so generous that they often deprive themselves of provisions in favor of the population. I therefore cordially ask that limits be placed on generalizations of our so-called vandalism. These incidents occur sporadically. They are, in truth, understandable consequences of a state of war against an enemy without country or God and the enemy of our ally— as much our enemy as of the Croatian nation and government. This enemy hates the Italian soldier much more and more ferociously than the Italian soldier hates him.[1046]

The unrepentant Robotti was congenitally unable to understand that the Partisans' hated was so great because his troops, no matter how merciful, were the imperial oppressors. To the end he treated the Partisans as barbarians who deserved no mercy.

General Ambrosio typified the outlook and responses of the Italian military in Yugoslavia. During most of the campaign, in spite of Italy's enormous dependency on Germany for all manner of military supplies and equipment, Ambrosio did not hesitate to express dissatisfaction over Germany's high-handed behavior in encroaching on Italy's rights in Croatia. Nor, in the face of German criticism, did he stand against the 2nd Army's use of Četniks to defend the persecuted Serb Orthodox against Ustaša outrages. By February 1943 he had had his fill of the Third Reich. "Our enemy is the German."[1047]

When Ambrosio received his appointment as chief of staff, Pietromarchi was disappointed. Although "a good Pietmontese honest to a fault, he has narrow ideas, without intellectual élan, without enthusiasm, and without creative impulses. He is a man of routine, while what is needed is someone inventive, who transforms passion and faith, and who resuscitates the spirit and shows innovation."[1048]

By July 1943 Ambrosio had begun to sing a different tune. Consonant with Mussolini's directives–and Hitler's wishes—he ordered the dissolution of all the Četnik forces dependent on the 2nd Army. For him the Četniks had become fair-weather friends who followed the Italian command when they could smell victory against the Partisans but deserted in hard times. He pointed out that since the Germans were "irreducibly hostile" to Italy's military collaboration with the Četniks, no stone should be left unturned to "eliminate any further arguments with the Germans."[1049] The man who was prepared to "put his foot down" with Berlin now supinely reconfigured his views to fit German policy. By tortured logic Ambrosio exculpated himself by foisting blame on the Četniks: the Germans were right to disarm them.

## Chinks in the 2nd Army's Armor

The Italian performance on the battlefield was at times heroic and credible, but at best spotty; as every highly placed Italian knew, the 2nd Army failed to adjust to guerrilla warfare. This laid bare long-standing deficiencies on the part of an organization that had remained a law unto itself. The troops were burdened by inadequate supplies and dated weapons. The officer class was an ingrown caste isolated from the rest of Italian society. The senior officer class was overaged, mired in tradition, insulated from Italian society, and immune to technological innovation. The junior officers frequently exhibited élan but little training in modern tactics. Effective reconnaissance, coordinated movement, and prompt response to the Partisans' maneuvers were beyond their grasp.

The top military lords (Ambrosio, Pirzio Biroli, Roatta, and Robotti), aware of the ineffective responses to guerrilla war on the part of their troops, spelled out remedies. They remained stymied, however, by a hidebound military organization. Instead of weed-ing out corruption and dead wood, or undertaking reform from top to bottom, both Rome and Sušak vented frustration on the troops. Dismayed that 230,000 Italian soldiers could not wipe out the thousands of Partisans facing them, Italy's rulers inflicted sarcastic abuse on their men for stupidity and lack of heart. Pietromarchi's comment is typical: "This army of Mussolini is as brutal as it is faint-hearted. Like the rag-tag army of the Bourbon King Francis II, it is a laughingstock."[1050] The equally contemptuous asides of the generals are recorded in this book. But such visceral frustration leaves out of account what appears to be a law of guerrilla warfare: at least a ten-to-one superiority is needed to crush a determined insurgency that expresses the popular will.

The old Italian liberal classes of pre-World War I looked down on the army as a profession and rarely consulted generals on anything save to notify them that war was imminent. During 1916 Foreign Minister Sonnino, despairing of the military's incompetence, dared to place the Albanian command in his own hands, an experiment that was aborted quickly because he knew nothing of military strategy. The Army reciprocated by concealing as much as it could from "nosy" politicians. These were two worlds that rarely intersected. During the Fascist era, the Army's jealous protection of its prerogatives had the salutary effect of keeping the Fascist squads confined to militia duty. The Army welcomed "the First Wave" that suppressed "revolution" in the turbulent years following World War I, but viewed the Blackshirts as an uncouth and rowdy bunch who should stand aside in favor of king and bureaucracy. Mussolini was looked on with a mixture of admiration and contempt. As long as the Duce refrained from invading their precincts, the generals would loyally follow orders or "loyally" subvert them, as in the case of the Četniks. Many of the Italian officers were freemasons, a secret society with a progressive, liberal, and anti-clerical tradition. In a Catholic country ruled by a Fascist government, the military's freemason membership was declared illegal and subversive. But since this law was never enforced against them, the soldiers continued to live in a world of their own largely immune to Fascist influence.

The old values, as found in the code of Italian military honor, preached that an officer was a gentleman. Decorum, courtliness, professional competence, deference, and respect toward both enemy and ally meshed humanity with firmness. World War I destroyed many of these chivalrous attitudes, and guerrilla warfare took care of the rest by turning the imperial Roman civilizer of Italian mythology into the barbarian he accused the guerrilla warrior fighting against him of being. Exaltation of the nation, self-sacrifice, readiness to experience pain, and heroism in combat were other traditional military values appropriated and glorified by Fascists who strove to mold a fragmented Italy into a nation of warriors.

Apart from these shared values, the 2nd Army's attitude toward the regime was ambiguous and variable. Recent Italian scholarship suggests that Italy's commanders in Yugoslavia "worked toward the Duce," meaning that they made a point of anticipating Mussolini's orders and acted in accordance with what they thought Mussolini would do in their place. But if the 2nd Army commanders had been driven primarily by ideology and invariably "worked toward the Duce," they would not have repudiated the Ustaša in favor of the Orthodox Serbs. (Nor would they have given succour to the Jews.) This switch between ally and enemy, undertaken spontaneously, hardly meshed with the ideological underpinnings of Italian imperialism, whose realization, in Mussolini's scheme of things, depended on the alliances forged with Berlin and Zagreb. Moreover, the unceasing military reverses that resulted in increasing Italian dependence on Hitler surely did not bond an essentially anti-German 2nd Army to the person of the Duce. And many soldiers were not eager for an Axis victory. Pavelić once told Glaise that Italian military and civilians regularly drank to an "English" victory in their favorite watering spots.[1051] As long as the king seemed to stand by Mussolini, the army—Fascists, *fiancheggiatori*, the apolitical, or anti-Fascists—would abide him, for any action taken against the regime would have constituted a revolt against the sovereign. If forced to choose, the generals would have opted for the king, for they were, at heart, monarchists, not dyed-in-the-wool Fascists.

As pragmatists, the 2nd Army commanders scorned the Fascist commissars in Yugoslavia, who naively believed that they could make good Italians out of Slavs by schooling them in Roman civilization. The generals knew better. In Yugoslavia there were only inveterate Italian-haters. When insurgency first flared, the 2nd Army flung aside Italian civilian authority and proceeded with the work of repression unimpeded by legal niceties, starry-eyed Fascists, and their bumbling "forces of public order." The ordinary Italian soldier engaged in abominable behavior toward the occupied peoples in Yugoslavia not from any Fascist indoctrination telling him that he represented a "master race," but from duty and the need to get on with the ugly business of putting down an implacable rebellion that enjoyed widespread civilian support.

## War Crimes and Counterinsurgency

Roatta's 3C circular and its updates are incriminating documents whose language defies the general guidelines for the defense of civilians in wartime as spelled out in The Hague Conventions of 1899 and 1907, the law governing conduct during war. The most germane provisions of the Conventions regarding the protection of civilians are as follows. Article 2: "The inhabitants of a territory which has not been occupied, who, on the approach of the enemy, spontaneously take up arms to resist the invading troops without having had time to organize themselves in accordance with Article 1 [in which it is stated that combatants must bear fixed distinctive emblems recognizable at a distance] shall be regarded as belligerents if they carry arms openly and if they respect the laws and customs of war." Article 3: "Armed towns of belligerent parties may consist of combatants and non-combatants. In case of capture by the enemy, both have a right to be treated as prisoners of war." Article 23: "It is especially forbidden to kill or wound treacherously individuals belonging to a hostile nation or army; to kill or wound an enemy who, having laid down his arms, has surrendered..." Article 25: "The attack or bombardment, by whatever means, of towns, villages, dwellings, or buildings which are undefended is prohibited." Article 45: "It is forbidden to compel the inhabitants of occupied territory to swear allegiance to the hostile power." Article 46: "Family honor and rights, the lives of persons, and private property, as well as religious convictions and practice, must be respected." Article 47: "Pillage is formally forbidden." Article 50 states that no general penalty "shall be inflicted upon the population on account of the acts of individuals for which they cannot be regarded as jointly and severally responsible." The Hague Conventions made no provisions for courts authorized to hear such cases; nor did it prescribe penalties to be imposed for violations.

One can argue that the framers of The Hague Conventions codified the usage established between member nations and the requirements of public conscience merely to win public approval for their attempt to "civilize" warfare. In light of the savagery of World War I, one might reasonably wonder whether the emperors, kings, and heads of states who contrived this document really intended to abide by its provisions. But however one might doubt their authenticity when presuming to speak in the name of humanity, their handiwork did provide the beginnings of an international system of law that sought to protect civilians in wartime against the ill-treatment and unnecessary suffering wrought by invading armies. The Hague Conventions were clearly intended to obviate the kinds of punitive measures outlined in General Roatta's 3C handbook.

On the question of legality, defenders of Roatta's counterinsurgency manifestoes hold that his actions should be judged not by The Hague Conventions but by Italian law as defined by Article 8 of the Royal Decree of 8 July 1938, number 1415. This decree declared that the observance of obligations deriving from international law could be suspended toward enemy belligerents who did not adhere to the standards set by the Fascist government.[1052] Armed forces of a hostile state, including militia and volunteers, would be given protection provided that they acted under the orders of a recognized belligerent under responsible leadership, wore distinctive uniforms, bore arms openly, and complied with the laws of war. A certain flexibility was demonstrated by Article 27, which read: "The population of non-occupied territory . . . that sponta-neously take up arms to fight an invading force, without having the time to satisfy the usual requirements, are considered legitimate belligerents provided that they bear arms openly and respect the laws and usages of war."

But here the coverage stops. Italian law gave protection neither to "armed bands" motivated by political ideology nor to "move-ments of organized resistance" unattached to any legally recognized government. In pursuing "unorthodox warfare" against occupying forces and their collaborators, and by failing to wear distinctive in-signia, guerrilla fighters placed themselves outside the law. The Italian government therefore did not feel constrained to obey the clauses of Hague Conventions that pertain to "volunteers" engaged in com-bat. Article 29 of the Italian decree, which defines the "laws of war," holds that "persons not considered legitimate belligerents who per-form acts of hostility will be punished under terms of the penal laws of war," that is, by arbitrary military judgment. Behind this legal spin lay an abiding fear and hostility toward guerrilla warfare that was common among European governments of the day; this attitude influenced the decisions handed down by the Nuremberg Tribunal in the postwar era as well. The guerrilla fighter had become both criminal and coward who rifled corpses and engaged in deception.

Thus it was quite easy for Roatta to take full advantage of the Fascist manual and ignore the protections afforded civilians by The Hague Conventions. By equating "illegitimate" warfare with guer-rilla-style fighting carried out by "bandits" who fight without uni-form, insignias, or for any organized and recognizable govern-ment,[1053] Roatta denied them the protection furnished regular armies of established and recognized sovereign states. War prisoners were now "captives" and Partisans "rebels"; Italians fought "convention-ally," while guerrillas practiced "terrorism."

As the major theoretician of Italian repression, Roatta needed no prodding by Mussolini to be ruthless and unrelenting. He sported a casual disregard for human life that was representative of Italian military bravado. Surprised by the resilience and novel tactics of his Partisan tormentors, Roatta fought a dirty counterinsurgency war designed to crack their resistance. His definition of what constituted an enemy among the Yugoslav peoples was excessively broad and his handling of all suspects was exceptionally cruel—not to mention the fate of death that he held out for proven Partisans. Roatta's fixed policy was to rule with an iron hand in the belief that this would break the will of the Yugoslav peoples to resist.

There was nothing novel in Roatta's punitive measures and dehumanization of the enemy. His predecessor, General Ambrosio, on 23 October 1941 declared that captured rebels were to be immediately shot and their houses burned; in combat areas, "clear out the population and destroy the countryside."[1054] On 30 December he ordered that prisoners were not to be taken, for, he callously noted, "in general they represent a dead weight signifying little or nothing."[1055]

Roatta had no need to convince his own military commanders and civilian Fascist overlords to be merciless in the annexed provinces. In Slovenia, for example, "it was a question of national territory."[1056] Bastianini, Pirzio Biroli, and, particularly, Robotti were other pioneers of repression who on their own initiative had already taken drastic action against people deemed sympathetic to the Partisans. As if not to be outdone, the Carabinieri launched their own searches, arrests, hostage-taking, and internments.[1057] But in Croatia, although Italian commanders applying the 3C memorandum frequently burned and pillaged, this was rarely systematic apart from defined *rastrellamenti* operations. And where the Četniks prevailed, Italian troops were less likely to be involved in firefights against the Partisans. Moreover, many Italian commanders approached the business of repression as a disagreeable chore and exercised a good deal of discretion. General Robotti complained that certain commanders had never heard of the 3C directive.[1058]

The 2nd Army's harsh counterinsurgency took many forms. Denying victuals to the "rebels" was a chief stratagem. If the Italian army suppressed the food supply of the population, or forcibly evacuated farmers and their animals from the war zones, it could deny the insurgents essential provisions. And if the famished "rebels" persisted in requisitioning what few provisions the Italian troops allowed the population to keep, the Partisans would lose their sympathy, and the rebellion would die out.[1059] Any families having ties to the "rebels" would be denied ration cards for all victuals not of primary necessity.[1060]

Equally inhumane were the 2nd Army's wide-ranging destruction of property and atrocities against innocent bystanders. Roatta's orders to intern "suspect" villages and communities and to take hostages among "suspicious" people were invitations to abuse. As the ultimate weapon, Roatta weighed the use of lethal gas. Since the "rebels" were not considered as "belligerents," and therefore stood outside international conventions, he reasoned, it was juridically admissible to administer gas against them. But on this Roatta backed off, citing humanitarian concerns and the impropriety of setting a dangerous precedent.[1061]

Italian counterinsurgency in Croatia took on particular savagery in areas valuable to the security of Italy's annexed territories. General Armellini on 2 August 1942 ordered the "destruction of every possibility of life in territory traversed . . . for the purpose of creating a security zone beyond the Dalmatian boundary by making it uninhabitable for the armed bands."[1062] Talpo justifies this order as reasonable reprisal against "accomplices of illegitimate combatants." Since they did not fight for any lawful government, hardly knew the name of Tito, and represented only a small minority of the population, such people, by his reckoning, were outlaws not deserving coverage by the laws of war.[1063] Talpo's tendency to condone punitive excesses by demonizing and misrepresenting the enemy typifies military rationalization. Pietromarchi had freed himself from such a narrow view somewhat earlier, but only after Mussolini was out of the way. On 18 August 1943, noting that the military's "bestial" reprisals were contrary to international law and the fundamental principles of civilization, he ordered that they be abolished.[1064]

Giacomo Scotti and Luciano Viazzi, in their works on the Italian occupation of Montenegro, cite letters from Italian soldiers detailing wanton violence committed against suspected "Communists." Such Italian retaliation against unarmed civilians not infrequently followed Partisan surprise attacks and atrocities against Italian prisoners; sometimes the vendettas were acts of frustration carried out after *rastrellamenti* yielded only barren results. Military tribunals in Montenegro worked overtime in handing out death sentences to Partisan family members and other innocents even after Tito had left for his "long-march" to western Bosnia. Many an Italian detachment wished to curb Četnik violence but was instructed by the High Command to refrain from intervention in Montenegrin "internal affairs" and "civil war." Any soldier who refused to carry out duty in an execution squad invited a court-martial.[1065] No one can question Četnik brutality against their presumed opponents, but many officers under Pirzio Biroli, if not initiators of such outrages, were at least accomplices by their willingness to consider hostages shot by Montenegrin Nationalists as deserved reprisal for Partisan "disorder."

Scotti and Viazzi make a distinction between Fascist squads who enthusiastically carried out raids and atrocities and the more reluctant and humane Italian foot soldier. This depiction is given credence by the Partisan proclivity to kill captured Fascists and officers and spare the lives of the common troops whenever possible. For logging an unenviable record of mass destruction and wanton killings, particularly on the islands adjacent to the Dalmatian coast, many Carabinieri units did not have clean hands either.[1066] One must bear in mind that the Partisans, too, committed indiscriminate massacre of prisoners, particularly such zealous commanders as Milovan Djilas.

By June 1943 Pietromarchi had become fully aware of the grave damage wrought by Italian reprisals in Slovenia, Dalmatia, Croatia and Montenegro. The Blackshirts had the worst record: "For history one must acknowledge that some 'M' battalions have comported themselves like ill-famed mercenary soldiers. The Partisans are the beneficiaries by recruiting large numbers of a disoriented population deprived of our protection and infuriated by our bestial reprisals."[1067] Nary an Italian general in Yugoslavia disagreed with this assessment of the Blackshirt units.

Under the 2nd Army's watch, internments and concentration camps represent the single most frightening abuse of human life and violation of civilized norms in Italy's campaign against the Partisans. They can be broken down into two major categories: prisoner of war camps supposedly governed by international law and camps reserved for civilian deportees, whose regulations were fixed arbitrarily by Italian military and civilian authority and declared off-limits to inspection by the international Red Cross.

On 8 September 1942 Roatta outlined a comprehensive program of internment for the indigenous peoples living in Slovenia, Fiume, and Dalmatia. "Precautionary" internment was to cover former Yugoslav military personnel and ex-civilian functionaries, individuals suspected of supporting the "rebels," and men of fighting age formerly belonging to rebel formations or absent from their domiciles for no justifiable reason. These groups were to be treated as "prisoners of war." Professionals, students, intellectuals, the unemployed, and people not suspected of harmful activity toward Italy were also taken into "precautionary" custody; they were to be organized into work brigades. Civilians placed under "protective" internment were those fleeing rebel recruitment who sought Italian protection to avoid Partisan reprisals, and those living in rural and isolated areas asking to be taken out of danger. These people, Roatta urged, should be transported to the mainland and provided adequate living conditions.[1068] As Spartaco Capogreco the noted expert on internments points out, the distinctions between "precautionary," "repressive," and "protective" became hopelessly blurred in both policy and application.[1069] In reality, all those interned were oppressed and abused. The War Ministry had no hesitation in employing the term "repressive internment" to cover Communist "bands," people captured in mopping-up operations, and those favoring the Partisan cause.[1070]

Roatta tried to give a legal veneer to his internment edicts by reference to Mussolini's proclamation of 19 November 1942, which decreed that all persons confined in concentration camps were to be subjected to military penal law and jurisdiction.[1071] This actually changed nothing. However much the Italian authorities distributed inmates according to categories such as "precautionary," "repressive," and "protective" internment, everyone in the camps with few exceptions suffered from a lawless regimen.

Massive transfer of Slovenes to internment camps and their replacement by Italian settlers was much talked about among the Italian occupiers. Mussolini on 10 June 1941 spoke of 30,000 Slovenes to be rounded up, held as hostages, or interned, and he lowered the bar to forced population exchanges by affirming that "when ethnicity does not accord with geography, it is the ethnic group that must be moved . . . population exchanges and forced exodus of people are providential, because such transfers result in political frontiers that coincide with racial groups."[1072]

About the same time General Roatta toyed with a somewhat smaller figure of 20,000 Slovenes to be interned, women and children included; they would be replaced by destitute families of fallen Italian soldiers, as in Napoleonic days.[1073] Three months later he gave expression to the same idea.[1074] Before setting down a detailed plan, Roatta sought the counsel of others. Robotti replied that there was no room in his province for large internment camps, and that such a sudden influx of Italians for resettlement would create serious disturbances.[1075] Grazioli pointed out that any comprehensive deportation policy would have invidious repercussions on the economic life of Ljubljana province, while the Interior Ministry noted that since internment camps in Italy were already "saturated" with detainees from Venezia Giulia, Libya, and other occupied territories, there was no more space for additional Slovenes.[1076] Confronted by these practical limitations, Mussolini, typically inconsistent, replied tersely that "civilians of whom mention is made in said note are not to be interned,"[1077] and then lost interest.[1078] For his part, Roatta, for the moment, allowed internments to proceed as defined in his 3C pamphlet, according to the ebb and flow of battle against the Partisans.

Like Robotti, Roatta felt badgered by Vatican missives scolding him for interning in excess of 30,000 Slovenes men, women, and children and subjecting them to deplorable conditions. Only 17,400 were interned, Roatta replied brusquely, of whom 6,075 lived in tents rather than in barracks, but in satisfactory sanitary conditions[1079] —

not exactly the unvarnished truth. The Vatican, he insisted, was swayed by prejudiced local Slovene prelates. "It would be much better if the said local authorities, rather than depicting the concentration camps in dark colors, would persuade the faithful not to support the Partisans, the sworn enemies of civilization and religion, and thus render [the concentration camps] superfluous or, at least, reduced in number."[1080]

To give the lie to Roatta's remarks, Italian medical officers found far too many internees living under tents exposed to the cold and lacking sufficient food and clothing.[1081] A medical colonel noted that many arrived in the camps in poor health. To lighten the load in treating sickness and disease, he advised that the politically innocent be sent home or transferred to other camps.[1082] An in-house 2nd Army report owned up to the barbarism of internment, which formed an integral part of counterinsurgency strategy:

> The interned of every social class and of all ages including those over eighty years of age arrived in camp, for the most part, in deplorable physical condition. Arrested, they saw their houses burned—were told that they would be burned. Owing to their sudden departures, they were often not able to take along much-needed possessions and clothing. The journeys by truck were very long and always undertaken in harsh conditions, such as rebel attacks on the truck columns, followed by time at sea, then life under tents in summer season. All this inflicted great hardships on the living. The internees were not compensated by plentiful provisions, but fed rations that provided not even half of the required calories. It became clear, therefore, that with the onset of cold weather, many internees, in such physical condition, would not be able to survive; in fact, many immediately yielded to the inevitable.[1083]

The camp located on the island of Arbe was particularly noxious. The "almost inhumane" conditions there, wrote one Italian observer, led to death and serious illness.[1084] An Italian in-house report admitted as much. Daily calories for "repressed internees" amounted to 877, for the "protected" who did not work, 1,030; for the "protected" who worked, 1,541. These allocations, the report conceded, fell far short of average need: 1,800 calories for those in "absolute repose," 2,100 for light workers, and 2,400 for full-time labor.[1085] Could a "pro-Italian" Slovene find solace in Italian "protective" internment? Families and friends of those not released harbored resentment over unfair treatment and discrimination.

In spite of strapped finances and limited space, the Italians, according to the International Red Cross, managed to arrest and intern close to 100,000 Slav peoples.[1086] For herding thousands of Yugoslav citizens to their deaths in internment camps that lacked adequate water, food, and medicine, Roatta won the well-deserved sobriquet, "the black beast."[1087] Slovenes and Croats constituted the overwhelming majority in the concentration camps run by the military. It is Capogreco's opinion that they were treated much worse than Italy's other foreign internees, and that their fate did not improve after the fall of Fascism—an opinion not challenged by contemporary Italian military reports.[1088] Among the war crimes committed in Yugoslavia, they were most nakedly revealed in Italy's internment policies.

General Roatta had an excessively broad definition of what constituted an enemy among the Slavs, and his handling of all suspects was exceptionally cruel, let alone the fate he held out for proven Partisans, whom he simply ordered to be shot. On the treatment of internees he wrote a harsh handbook. Even though Roatta felt unencumbered by human values, he made efforts, albeit rarely, to keep counterinsurgency under control. There was, for example, a consultative commission on the rights of war, to which he occasionally sent his edicts for review.[1089]

Roatta tried to lay down the principle that Italian troops should burn only villages known to be Partisan hideouts after removing all civilians incapable of or unwilling to engage in serious guerrilla activity. To curb the exuberance of some of his commanders in utilizing the 3C memorandum as a blank check for destruction, Roatta warned them to avoid "inconsiderate and useless" destruction of houses. Distinguish between dwellings infested with guerrillas, he cautioned, and those abandoned by people seeking refuge from Partisan-forced requisition of food and supplies. Be merciful in relocating people unconnected with rebellion. Take note, he reminded his commanders, that local populations are often constrained by Partisans to provide shelter and provisions against their will and not infrequently are told to abandon their dwellings.[1090] By committing excesses the troops would only provide the enemy an opportunity to describe them as wanton destroyers.[1091]

On another occasion Roatta informed his commanders that irresponsible reprisals were counterproductive. Avoid the destruction of churches, schools, and hospitals, he advised. Troops caught sacking dwellings would be subjected to "draconian repression."

> I repeat . . . that reprisals of a general nature <u>thoughtlessly</u> undertaken give rise to an effect contrary to their purpose. Such thoughtless reprisals eventually place the population between the "anvil" of the rebel and the "hammer" of the Italian. That induces the population to make common cause with the rebels, which is antithetic to our original intentions.[1092]

In mid-1942 Roatta issued clemency measures—*"salva la vita"*—for Partisans who accepted Italian offers of surrender outside combat zones or who had returned home, even if such persons were suspected rebel leaders or directly responsible for "massacres, plunder, and violence."[1093] The Italian commander had abandoned the effort to distinguish between Partisans who carried out "criminal acts" as Communist zealots or did so fearing reprisal on the part of their commanders. Such clemency was also extended to family members held in custody for reprisal purposes. People interned at random could be released at a local commander's discretion.[1094]

Roatta, it is true, was hampered by a lack of funds to undertake an orderly protection of innocent civilians. Nor did he have the administrative apparatus to remove civilians efficiently and humanely from combat zones. He also lacked able translators to interview hostages and suspicious people in order to establish guilt and innocence with greater care. But these mitigating circumstances aside,

Roatta leaned on the principle that the civilian had to prove innocence rather than the military establish guilt. The army, by his reckoning, should exercise the right of belligerents to destroy property
and kill people who interfered with operations. If forced to choose
between protection of civilians and military necessity, what would
any commander have done? To defeat a popularly based insurgency,
Roatta knew that the guerrillas had to be isolated from their grass-
roots support. Only a stringent counterinsurgency policy could accomplish this task.

But Roatta stepped over the bounds by imparting orders to kill
and burn in Yugoslavia that were reminiscent of a Fascist African
"colonizer," or any other old-fashioned Italian imperialist warlord
across the Mediterranean who had massacred native inhabitants and
pillaged their lands. Roatta's were not measured responses to an
admittedly dangerous threat to the Italian occupation. No matter
his exhortations to exercise restraint, he gave his commanders wide
leeway in conducting *rastrellamenti* in any fashion they saw fit in order to extinguish the tiniest hint of dissent.[1095] To conclude that
Roatta's counterinsurgency measures, as defined in the 3C pamphlet
and its updates, amounted to a declaration of war against the people
of Yugoslavia—especially Slovenes—is not far-fetched.

Yet, one must not forget that, in spite of Mussolini's non-intervention edicts, Roatta's 2nd Army often acted to contain the brutal
violence of the Ustaša. General Ambrosio's 7 September 1941 proclamation was the touchstone. The Orthodox population of
Dubrovnik—one example among many—was immensely relieved
when Italian authorities assumed control over the civil administration of the city. No Orthodox community enjoyed such protection
under the regime of either Croats or Germans during the war.[1096]
Roatta did not overlook Četnik violence either. On 20 October 1942
he issued the following stern warning: "I request that Commander
Trifunović be apprised that if Četnik violence against the Croatian
and Muslim population is not immediately stopped, we will halt food
supplies and daily wages to those formations whose members are
perpetrators of the violence. If this criminal situation continues,
more severe measures will be undertaken."[1097] The man in charge

of Italian counterinsurgency was at the same time a peacemaker, but not from any moral scruple or overarching desire to grant Slavs or Jews a better life. Rather, he had the opportunistic purpose of curbing any violence that impeded the imposition of an Italian "peace." Regardless of motive, Roatta and his fellow commanders gave protection to as many as 33,464 civilians,[1098] and that is probably a conservative estimate.

Roatta had a lot else to do besides supervising counterinsurgency, including high-level and risky dealings with German generals, Ustaša representatives, Četnik allies, and his Fascist superiors in Rome. There were also military strategy and the chore of keeping his troops up to fighting speed. But in playing off enemies and allies against each other, Roatta derived only dubious military benefits; worse, by fragmenting Axis unity, he made the 2nd Army the object of suspicion on the part of every armed group in Yugoslavia.

The irony is that had Roatta eschewed politics by scrupulously obeying the edicts of Rome—thus proving himself a firm and steady ally of the Germans and Croats—his military fortunes would temporarily have risen rather than declined. But then he would have had to genuflect before haughty Germans and prostitute himself to the Croatian ally whose sovereignty he was asked to respect. Had Roatta stood by the shameful Ustaša regime, he would have become their accomplice in an appalling massacre of civilians. Instead, because of his "rebellion," the oppressed Orthodox and Jews regarded him as a protector. What other general would have made a personal appearance before the huddled and frightened Jews on 27 November 1942 at Kraljavice [Porto Re] concentration camp assuring them that they had nothing to fear? Can one imagine any German commander making such a gesture? While an international tribunal undoubtedly would have found Roatta guilty of war crimes, a Jewish or Orthodox Serb court very well might have dismissed charges brought against him. Roatta emerges from the Yugoslav debacle with a uniquely mixed reputation as both persecutor and savior.

In the immediate postwar era, the Titoist government compiled a list of Italian soldiers and officers they hoped would be expatriated and tried for war crimes; this was forwarded to the United

Nations Commission on War Crimes. Captured Italian documents and oral testimony were submitted. The victims recounted lurid tales of murder, rape, and thievery. Tito also proceeded to bring charges against suspects who had fallen into Partisan hands after the Italian surrender. Amidst grand ceremony harsh judgments were rendered, Communist-style. But at the United Nations and in the western world silence and non-action prevailed. Once the Cold War had settled in, a common front against Communism required a strong Italian government as ally, not one debilitated by trials of former Fascist hierarchs, "flankers," and military officers who had swung behind the new conservative democratic regime. Hence Rome escaped Tito's requested trials.

## Bravo Italiano and Cattivo Tedesco?

In carrying out counterinsurgency, the 2nd Army bore an image of the Balkan peoples that was anything but flattering. For decades nationalists and Fascists in the Venezia Giulia had developed a body of literature depicting their neighbors as dark and foreboding, their behavior synonymous with lawlessness and immorality. They supposedly lived in rude and gloomy huts or crouched in caves hewn out of barren mountains. Hardly touched by Christian values, went this litany, the Balkan peoples emerged from misty feudalism only to be captured by fanatical, atheistic Communism. Imbued with this obscurantist outlook, the military taught the conscript that he was part of a deadly ideological struggle between Rome and Moscow, which justified a "war without quarter" in defense of the homeland. The Partisan was an immoral creature who did not merit the protections afforded by law and civilization.

How much did these notions actually affect the officers and men of the 2nd Army? Compared to the constant hectoring the Nazis inflicted on the Wehrmacht, Italy's military propaganda was sporadic and lacking the well-defined ideology that shaped the Nazi *Weltanschauung*. Also absent was a powerful and well-organized bureaucracy to impose discipline and conformity. The average Italian soldier, therefore, was not the "political" warrior of Wehrmacht vintage. Nonetheless, the dehumanizing notions that were passed down the military hierarchy undoubtedly weakened the will of the typical Italian soldier to resist carrying out reprisals and the massacre of prisoners.

Hubris looms large in explaining Italian military motive and cruelty. The generals lashed out against anyone who refused to render the respect and obedience owed the conquering Caesar. This, for them, was a major Partisan sin. Exacerbating the insult was the Yugoslav peoples' fear of Germans, the more unpitying and powerful Axis ally. By intensifying its own ruthlessness, the Italian military expected to exact the same respect from the population. Having neither the technological skills and superb equipment of the Wehrmacht nor its certainty of victory, the Italian military was both frustrated and impotent. Violent repression and reprisals were not stimulated, as in the case of the Germans, by cold-hearted triumph over a terror-stricken enemy whose helplessness invited contempt, but an inability to control insurgency. While the German officers, buoyed by a Nazi ideology that emphasized their invincible superiority, hardly questioned orders to shoot and kill without reason—and even reveled in the experience—Italian efforts to intimidate the population into obedience issued more from a stern sense of duty, weakness, and bruised pride than from ideology Fascist-style. The 2nd Army protected Jews and Orthodox Serbs because they sought shelter from the Italian conqueror and thanked him for his humanity. The military cooperated with the Četniks out of urgent necessity, but when the Partisan enemy defied its authority, mocked Italian prestige, and gave no quarter on the battlefield, the 2nd Army retaliated by conducting a vicious campaign of repression against them.

Fear also informed Italian military responses, for sabotage greeted the troops at every turn and insurgents dressed as civilians appeared from every nook and cranny to fire on them. The Italians might perish while on patrol duty, guarding a railway line, or walking down a village street. Often they responded blindly with volleys and artillery barrages that indiscriminately mowed down women and children. Retaliation was often individual, a visceral response to comrades booby-trapped or singly picked off. Where death has become a daily norm, life loses value, and a humanitarian outlook becomes irreconcilable with military necessity—all in the nature of guerrilla warfare, the apotheosis of violence and slaughter.

Ideology played lesser importance in Italian counterinsurgency than it did in German repression. Motivated by a systematically indoctrinated racial hatred, the Teutonic masters of destruction undertook a mass slaughter of enemies thought to be no better than vermin, which had nothing to do with battlefield conditions. *Lebensraum*, anti-Communism, and hatred of the Jews fueled a Nazi conquest that foresaw the absorption of territory but not of conquered peoples, for they were programmed to die in a racial reconstruction of Europe.

Apart from a radical Fascist fringe, there was no talk among Italians of *Herrenvolk*. A blueprint of occupation for Yugoslavia did not exist prior to 6 April 1941, and no master plan to exterminate the Slav peoples was ever drawn up. Mussolini intended to create Italian protectorates and satellites where the populations and nationalities would be mercilessly exploited, but not thrown out or liquidated to make place for the Italian "master race." Projects relative to movements of population, massive transfers, and expulsion were contrived to suppress discontent and rebellion. The "inspiring philosophy" justifying the existence of the Italian internment camps did not include exploitation of labor or working people to death. In fact, enforced idleness was a common complaint of the detainees. The object was rather to cordon off people who were thought to be dangerous and undesirable from their communities, particularly in sensitive zones of military operation, these often being expansively defined. Italian camps for Yugoslavs were on the whole worse than those hosting native Italians. They were dreadful places of confinement where Slavs died in droves from neglect, mistreatment, and malnutrition, but no gas chambers were ever set up to enact an Italian "Final Solution." More prisoners survived than died. Albanians, Greeks, and Yugoslavs, the majority of whom escaped the roundups, were humiliated and reduced to servility and forced labor, but not subject to ethnic cleansing.

The concept of blood-defined "racism," which goes to the heart of the Nazi creed, does not really apply to the Italian occupiers of Yugoslavia; otherwise, they would never have extended a helping hand to Jews and Orthodox Serbs. While Nazi racial ideology provided a biological grounding for anti-Slavism, Italian propagandists in the main refrained from discourse on the Slavs as a racial subspecies. Rather they described Italian "race" in spiritual terms—"una razza dell'anima e dello spirito" (a race of the soul and of the spirit), "Romanità," or as "Latin civilization," which bespoke "a common soul" and a warped sense of cultural superiority. In the Italian northeast during the interwar period, the Fascist government applied assimilation policies aimed at the *italianità* of the Slav peoples. This form of hyper-nationalism was a spiritual expression of *nostra stirpe*.

Spun by a handful of fringe intellectuals who drew on highly selective scientific, cultural, traditional, and ideological traditions of the country, the concept of "race" took on a biological dimension during the Fascist "civilizing missions" in Africa: Libya, Somalia, and Ethiopia. Instead of being given the chance to assimilate like the Slav peoples, Africans, with some exceptions, were subjected to apartheid conditions and discrimination based on the distinction of color. When the Fascist and Nazi regimes formed the Axis, some Italian pseudo-philosophers seeking *italianità* began to expatiate on biological racism—"the law of the blood"—while the more traditionally inclined continued to propound spiritual racism—"*romano-italica.*"[1099] The "Nordicists" vied with the "Mediterraneanists" over whose slant should be recognized as the canon of official Italian racial doctrine. During the war years Mussolini refrained from bestowing primacy on either but rather let them fight it out in books and articles.[1100] As for the Fascist occupiers in Yugoslavia, the crackpot ideas of "biological racism" ran only skin deep. And for the Italian military in general, Darwinian notions of "expand or die" and the "law of survival" made more sense than philosophical speculation on the essence of the Italian "race."

Bastianini and Grazioli, as "idealist" Fascists, were exponents of aggressive assimilation of the Slav peoples whom they were determined to remold as loyal Italians. Their belief in the cultural superiority of Italian *civiltà* was grounded more in chauvinism than in biological racism. When the captive peoples shunned *italianità* by resorting to rebellion, the 2nd Army's answer was simple: outright repression. For all its terrible applications, counterinsurgency was an improvised response to a startling and increasingly unmanageable insurrection. The more unwinnable the war the more ruthless the repression.

How does the German record of atrocities in Yugoslavia compare with the Italian? After the terrible reprisals carried out in October 1941 in Kraljevo and Kragujevac, the pace of violence in Serbia slowed down. Tito had departed and the Germans, having set up a fairly reliable puppet government in Belgrade, were able to withdraw troops from Serbia to feed the furnace on the Eastern Front. When the Partisans swarmed into Bosnia the following year, the Wehrmacht was caught short of troops. Only in early January 1943, when reinforcements arrived, were the Germans able to undertake massive mopping-up operations.

Many German generals began to doubt the wisdom of limitless hostage-taking and mass slaughter. Horrified upon learning that General Böhme intended to bring 650 hostages from Sarajevo for public execution to deter future acts of violence against German troops, Glaise urged the OKW to be cautious in the application of reprisals.[1101] In late 1941, advised by the German ally Milan Nedić that a softer touch was in order, it occurred to Böhme that arbitrary arrests and shootings of Serbs were turning nonparticipants in the rebellion into insurgents, especially those who did not flee before a German punitive expedition. Such people, in their innocence, expected to be left alone rather than rounded up for execution. Showing similar concern, General List ordered that Serbs encountered in operational zones be interned and questioned, as opposed to those captured in battle, who should be sent before the firing squad. For the first time the Germans had officially created a new category, the "innocent" Serb, who, unlike insurgents and "suspects," was not to be shot out of hand. Reprisal victims were henceforth to be defined as people found in the vicinity of guerrilla attacks or villages considered focal points of the insurgency, those deemed suspects as the result of police investigation, and "as a matter of principle *all adult male Jews and Gypsies.*"[1102]

German generals had grudgingly come to an awareness that random shooting and excessive punitive measures against Serbs could be deleterious to peace-keeping and work against the interests of the occupying army. The word "excessive" was subject to interpretation. In German-occupied Croatia lower killing ratios were devised; in agreement with the NDH, ten hostages would be shot for every German soldier killed. But the German commanders, bedeviled by confusion, often issued contradictory instructions. (The constant shuttling in and out of commanders and overlapping jurisdictions were contributing factors.) For example, in March 1942 General Bader issued an order to imprison captured Partisans and deserters, but revoked this measure the following day, which left things as they were: all would be shot. A couple of weeks later he "compromised" by allowing the lives of Partisan deserters who had turned in their weapons to be spared. On 29 May 1942, orders went out to burn only those villages whose inhabitants were associated with insurgency.

Still, the Germans amassed formidable figures: between 1 September 1941 and 12 February 1942, 20,149 hostages were killed. In July, to "dry out" "infected" regions, the Germans contemplated mass movement of peoples into concentration camps, but this idea was dropped owing to a lack of space and troops to supervise large-scale evacuation.[1103] Perhaps these chronic troop shortages help explain why German reprisals, too, gradually began to level off. And, thanks to Hitler's friendship with Pavelić, the Wehrmacht was constrained to treat the non-Partisan Croatian population on their side of the demarcation line with a certain degree of civility. (The Italian commanders were not so inhibited by the Duce's ties with the Poglavnik.) Nonetheless, nothing stopped General Löhr in September from issuing an instruction that condemned to death anyone who had ever been a "rebel"; he followed up the next month with a "life and death" order to "wipe out to the last man" all enemy groups.[1104] Yet, on more than one occasion, the Germans, like the Italians, negotiated prisoner exchanges with the Partisans.

One wonders whether General Roatta had studied German practices in Serbia before jotting down one word in his 3C pamphlet. Certainly the ruthless punitive measures he drafted bore a marked similarity to the orders German generals had issued in Serbia. But they, like their Italian counterparts, from time to time advised caution. This effort on the part of the Axis generals to bring counterinsurgency under some measure of control was made not for humanitarian reasons but because draconian reprisals were driving innocent people into the resistance. German killing ratios were, in general, fixed at a much higher level than the Italian. For example, Bastianini wrote that two or three hostages would be shot for every Italian killed. But there are known instances when out-of-control Italian commanders, Fascists squads, and Carabinieri patrols in punitive raids shot up the countryside, and Pirzio Biroli, for one, spoke of a fifty-to-one death ratio. As for implementation, in the absence of anything resembling precise figures, it appears that German reprisal orders were more systematic, binding, and fiercely carried out than the Italian.[1105]

To be sure, the German commanders had only small leeway, for there was always Hitler, who predictably expected "exemplary" punishment, to be reckoned with. The Wehrmacht generals dared not challenge the Führer's will or be suspected of subverting it. The Italian commanders, on the other hand, sidestepped Mussolini whenever it suited them, for instance, when they openly supported the Četniks against the NDH. Their German counterparts, too, surreptitiously held talks with them but obediently backed off when ordered to do so by Berlin. (Significant deals between Germans and Četniks were struck only after Italy had departed from the war and after the Allies landed in Sicily instead of the Balkans, which transformed the strategic situation in Yugoslavia.) The NDH was another matter. Both the Italian and German generals detested the Ustaša regime and longed to sweep it out of power, but could do nothing because Pavelić enjoyed strong support in both Rome and Berlin. But while the Germans watched Ustaša massacre their enemies, the Italians on occasion shot down Pavelić's men in their acts of violence. Buoyed by his visit with Hitler on 23 September

1942, the Poglavnik became ever more unwilling to curb atrocities when exhorted to do so by both Italian and German commanders in Zagreb.

If the Germans surpassed the Italians in brutality and barbarism in Yugoslavia, their margin was not great, save for one major area. While the Italians ended up giving refuge to most of the Jews who sought their protection, the Germans made sure to shoot or send to death camps every male Jew they could lay their hands on, 17,000 in Serbia alone.[1106]

In the postwar period, the Italian mass media formulated a clear distinction between Italy and Germany with respect to their policies in countries they occupied. Thus the image of "cattivo tedesco," a fanatical warrior capable of every wickedness, was contrasted with the so-called "bravo italiano," the Italian "good guy." Badly outfitted, thrown into a wretched war against his will, the Italian soldier supposedly lent succor to the hungry and dispossessed of the invaded countries, saving many lives of innocent and victimized people. As we have seen, this comparison does not hold water, for the behavior of the *regio esercito* in Yugoslavia was at times as beastly as the Wehrmacht toward the occupied peoples in that country.[1107] In clearing out the Partisans from territory under Italian control, the Italian generals, implementing counterinsurgency according to the dictates of Roatta's 3C pamphlet, waged war on the Yugoslav peoples, especially the Slovenes. The irony is this: through ruthless measures and a willful disregard of the nuances of Yugoslav political life, the Italian commanders drove the Catholic "silent majority" and fence-sitters into the enemy camp. Faced by a spreading revolt, they conducted internments, *rastrellamenti*, and hostage-taking without letup. That internments did not soar beyond the already staggeringly high figures is attributable to Italian chronic inefficiency and inability to build concentration camps fast enough to absorb the military's projected roundups—let alone fulfill what Mussolini had in mind. Only in mass hostage killing—as well as the extermination of Jews—did the 2nd Army fail to keep pace with the more methodical Germans. The "cattivo tedesco" and "bravo italiano" myth held for decades; only recently has it been exposed as a fallacy.[1108]

According to the most recent research, the Yugoslavs lost approximately two million to deaths, expulsions, emigration, and deportation during World War II; war-related deaths were approximately half that figure. The historian Zerjavić estimates that there were 530,000 Serb victims.[1109] It is practically impossible to assess how many the Italians killed or maimed, or the number of houses they destroyed. But it is clear that in areas policed by the Croatian "ally," the hate-filled Ustaša far outdistanced the more detached Italians and less numerous Germans in orchestrated and bloodthirsty violence. In the view of the Italian and German generals—as well as the Military Tribunal at Nuremberg—the Croatian people as a whole were not responsible for Ustaša crimes. Rather, they observed that the atrocities visited on the Orthodox Serbs were the work of a decided minority of the Croatian population, who, in the main, they insisted (much to the discomfort of Rome and Berlin) far preferred Maček to Pavelić.[1110]

Regardless of the number of Yugoslavs the Italians killed, or the mind-boggling massacres of the Germans and the Ustaša, their combined totals in this multidimensional civil war did not come close to the extraordinary slaughters visited by the Yugoslav peoples on each other.

## Diehards in the Palazzo Chigi

As the sand in the Italian hourglass ran out, the mood at the Palazzo Chigi became ever more somber. Roberto Ducci, head of the Croatian desk, glumly predicted that the Italian military would not be able to hold out much longer. The troops were exhausted and lacking in modern automatic rifles, machine guns, and mortars. Without 40,000 to 50,000 additional troops, there was no chance to win back the 2nd zone or Montenegro. "The country, given its characteristic morphology, drinks men as a pad absorbs ink," he observed.[1111] The troops have been worn down and their spirit debilitated by a lack of rotation, twenty-four months without leave, and constant exposure to guerrilla warfare. No offensives can be expected without fresh troops or the release of soldiers locked up in the safety of their forts. The 2nd Army is doomed to yield territory to the Germans, who, without a restraining Italian hand, will disarm Četniks and seize important Adriatic ports. Ustaša massacres of the Orthodox precluded cohesive policy, and Italy's action can only be impromptu and improvised, day by day, zone by zone, claimed Ducci. "It is possible, and it behooves us, to make a 'Serb' policy, a 'Croat' policy, and a 'Muslim policy'" by crafting Italian policy according to the perspectives of each territory and local circumstances. He put forth the following scheme:

> We must pursue very clever political actions—absolutely unprejudiced ones—that do not fail because of instinctive antipathy or preconceptions that hamper existing possibilities. An adroit policy that pits the diverse ethnic and political groups against each other, which are inspired by reciprocal hate, will open up new developments.[1112]

Throughout this era of empire-building in the Balkans, the underlying assumption of the Italian Foreign Office was Italian domination over Yugoslavia. But how was the *spazio vitale* to co-exist with a German *Drang nach Südosten*? Was the NDH more loyal to Rome or Berlin? The Carabinieri trouble-shooter, General Pièche, sent the Foreign Ministry reports on Croatia that contained sharp and fearless reporting. It was an unpardonable mistake, he wrote, for Italy to have supported the minority Pavelić regime and the wretched Ustaša. Workers, peasants, and intellectuals—80 percent of the population—who would never collaborate with the "Ustaša terrorists" hoped that Maček would return to power. All shunned Germans and Italians alike. As Pièche pointed out, the Partisans profited from the economic chaos, and Italy had no chance in competing with the Germans for influence in Zagreb. Still, like Pietromarchi, Pièche excused Pavelić. The Poglavnik had good intentions, was loyal to Italy, but was thwarted by enemies who surrounded him. Behind Pavelić stood the pro-German Kvaterniks, who were poised to step in should he falter. Thanks to German and

Croatian obstruction, Italy did not enjoy a *"spazio vitale"* but a *"spazio mortale."* Since the state of Croatia represented an Italian dead-end, Pièche pondered an alternative: the amalgamation of poverty-ridden Dalmatia and resources-rich Bosnia-Herzegovina placed under an Italian military governorship.[1113] The Italian consul at Sarajevo, Marcello Zuccolin, advanced the same idea.[1114]

As opposed to Bastianini, who considered the Croats as implacable enemies, Pietromarchi, in pursuit of an Italian Balkan empire, singled out the Serbs as "the true enemy" for having their sights set on Bosnia-Herzegovina, Dalmatia, and Montenegro. In his view a strong Croatia under Italian protection would suffice to thwart Pan-Serbism.[1115]

By June 1943 the Palazzo Chigi had become fully apprised of Italy's hopeless military situation. The Navy was unable to defend the Adriatic coast and army units were spread thinly or backed up on the beaches. In some strips of territory the Italian troops enjoyed a depth of only a few kilometers, hardly sufficient to stave off a determined Partisan drive to the sea.

For Pietromarchi, the sorry pass that Italy had reached was the fault of the 2nd Army for having conducted a wrong-headed policy that violated the tenants outlined by the Palazzo Chigi:

The military has not understood the directives of the Ministry of Foreign Affairs when it entrusted them full civilian and military powers in the occupied territories. They should have been the mediators among the nationalities divided by centuries filled with rancor and recent atrocities. An impartial policy, moderate and humane, was needed. But they were not up to it. They allowed themselves to be carried away by local passions. They married the cause of the Serbs and Jews who offered them their women. Ours [Italian troops] preferred the luxuries of commodious quarters over marches, ambushes, and combat. The Army weakened itself in the comforts of the barracks. Today we are without prestige and without strength. The scarcity in the intelligence of our commanders is revealed in the accords they made with the Germans.[1116]

In savaging the 2nd Army, Pietromarchi reveals an unrepentant Fascist perspective:

> The truth is that our policies in Croatia and Montenegro have been impeded by the military command. We have based our frontier policies and Adriatic arrangements on strict agreements with the Ustaša regime and therefore with the Croats. The command of the 2nd Army has taken a clear position against the Croats, has brought a certain number to trial, has condemned them to firing squads, has stripped the Zagreb government of authority, has refused every armed collaboration with the Ustaša, who are kept out of our zones, and has allied with the worst enemies of Croatia—the Serbs—who are armed and left free for unleashing vendettas against Croats and Muslims. [The military] has committed ferocious acts of reprisals by bombarding and burning Croatian villages. It has, in a word, undermined the basis of our policy of alliance, collaboration, and guarantees with the Croatian state. Therefore it is not surprising that the Croats hate us and have nourished the most intransigent irredentism against us. This [2nd Army mistaken policy] has thrown us bound hand and foot to the mercy of the Germans. The latter have adroitly practiced the very policy that the Italian Ministry of Foreign Affairs has always sponsored—unwavering support of the Croats and Muslims. And they [the Germans] have imposed on us the breakup of the Četniks. In such fashion they [the Germans] have diminished us before Croats, Serbs, and Muslims . . . Now they are the masters of the situation and we are at their mercy.[1117]

Pietromarchi overlooked the pent-up force of Croatian nationalism that was of a different nature than that manifested in Ustaša behavior. As long as one Italian soldier remained in Dalmatia, Croatian hatred of Rome would be unappeasable.

Italy's estrangement from "allies" and ultimate isolation in Yugoslavia were worsened by the conflicting aims and rival ambitions within the Axis alliance. These rendered even more helpless an increasingly enfeebled homeland engaged in a last-ditch stand against the powerful Anglo-Americans. Bureaucratic inefficiency and personal backbiting added to the problems. And Ciano's personal likes and animosities left their marks. His clash with Cavallero prevented the Croatian Office from supervising military matters when they affected diplomacy; Cavallero, in turn, had forbidden Roatta and Pirzio Biroli from having contacts with the Foreign Ministry. Given the conflicting purposes, wondered Pietromarchi, how could his office forge unity within the various agencies? The Germans simply stepped in and did what Italy should have done: they supported the Croatian regime and recruited 100,000 Bosnian Muslims. By utilizing his program, concluded Pietromarchi, the Germans denied Italy predominance over Croatia.[1118]

For Pietromarchi there was nowhere to turn but to his country's Teutonic masters. Firmly encamped in the 3rd zone, only they were in a position to assist Italy. By devising a carefully worked out plan, the Axis powers could stop the Partisans well short of the Adriatic shore. In the afterglow of renewed camaraderie, the Germans would suspend their own drive on the Adriatic littoral and—presto—Italy's paper proprietary rights over Croatia would be honored.[1119] This illusion was followed by another: that the Wehrmacht would run to Italy's assistance in clearing out the Partisans from areas lost in Herzegovina and the Lika region.[1120]

During Pietromarchi's odyssey through the war he had few good things to say about Germans, and, as word of the Holocaust spread in Rome, his grudging tolerance turned into horror. "Nobody for centuries will forget this wickedness that will brand the German people forever in infamy."[1121] To prevent further encroachment on Italian spheres, he wanted to "habituate the Germans to a greater respect of our rights."[1122] At the same time he habitually blamed the 2nd Army for allowing such penetration because of inefficiency and unseemly retreats from the Croatian hinterlands. Pietromarchi was a conflicted man. No less than any Italian commander in the Balkan theater did he resent German arrogance. Yet he loyally stood by the Axis and Pavelić's murderous regime both before and after defeat stared Italy in the face.

If Pietromarchi had become disenchanted with Fascism, he remained a firm traditional nationalist who valued unity and independence above all else. To the end he opposed any effort to seek a "diplomatic solution" by signing a separate peace with the Allies.[1123] Pietromarchi considered Italian acceptance of an Allied-dictated "unconditional surrender" ignoble and feared that a sudden regime change would bring about social chaos. Honor and the integrity of the state required that Italy fight to the finish. Since the threat of German retaliation paralyzed initiative, Pietromarchi, like most around him, counted on Mussolini and the king to salvage a modicum of national dignity and the regime's survival. This was the faith of the desperate. Only on 24 July, the day preceding the coup, did Pietromarchi turn decisively against the Duce.[1124]

Many other highly placed Italians found themselves in the same boat. Like him, they were at once imbued with civilized values and held a strong patriotic obligation to defend the country no matter how repugnant the regime. Apart from the question of a separate peace, Dino Grandi had much in common with Pietromarchi. Both were confirmed diplomatic Fascist Realpolitiker and rabid Italian "firsters" who scorned the Third Reich; both, convinced that the economic depression of the thirties had killed liberalism, believed that the *Führerprinzip* best suited Italy.

The real key to the Pietromarchi mystery is in his rally to Catholicism at this time of trouble. Like the Vatican, he had an oppressive fear of Communism; Italy and the church, he felt, should be aligned together to man the last barricades against the atheism borne by the Mongolian hordes from the east. Possessed by this fear, Pietromarchi approved the pope's ratiocinations on the themes of Nazism and Croatia, abided his reticence on the Croatian massacres, and concurred with his view to recruit anyone in sight, the Third Reich included, to hold the line against Stalin. Tito was, as Pietromarchi correctly figured out, Stalin's stalking horse. And he was not alone in believing that the Partisans comprised the advance guard of the Communist drive to the Adriatic and beyond. If not the Partisans, then the Četniks, powered by the idea of a Great Serbia.

Pietromarchi's "Axis of Evil" consisted of Communism and Nazism. For this anti-German Fascist any ideological about-face to democracy was beyond the pale. (He would undertake this only in the totally transformed setting of the postwar era; after being cleared as a war criminal, he served as Italian ambassador to the Soviet Union between 1958 and 1961.) His ideological choices narrowed to one form of authoritarianism or another, Pietromarchi prepared to go down in flames with the Germans in a desperate effort to stave off submersion in a tidal wave of Communism.

For Undersecretary Bastianini, a more diligent worker than his predecessor, Ciano, the greatest obstacle impeding a smooth German-Italian rapport was General Glaise von Horstenau, the saboteur of Italian rights, who, in his view, bore major responsibility for a policy that ran counter to the assurances and directives of the German government. It should have been clear to Bastianini, however, that Glaise was hardly the lone German thwarting the Italians. Like Pietromarchi, Bastianini doggedly strove to elicit reassurances from Berlin that Germany would honor its word that Croatia lay in the Italian sphere, verified by a moratorium on competition with Italy in the economic realm for the duration of the war. If the 2nd Army was unable to train the Domobrani, the Germans should have the courtesy of informing Rome what they had in store for them.[1125] The unfortunate Alfieri was charged with the responsibility of making these views known at the Wilhelmstrasse.

However much the Germans trampled on Italian rights in Yugoslavia or established control over all facets of life in Croatia, and no matter how hopeless the Italian situation in the Balkans had become, the Palazzo Chigi, *officially*, persisted in the pie-in-the-sky belief that reasoned exposition and opportune reminders would persuade the Germans to relinquish their hold on Croatia. (Previously, as we have seen, both Ciano and Pietromarchi revealed in their diaries that they had come to hate and distrust the Germans.) Nobody in the Palazzo Chigi would contemplate a break from Berlin, and nobody admitted on paper that beyond rhetoric there were no grounds for believing that the Germans intended to honor their treaty commitments and oral promises to Italy. Touted as Machiavellians, the Italians in their official correspondence seemed unable to view the world from the German perspective. They neither grasped that Hitler's war aims boiled down to either *Weltmacht* or the Apocalypse, nor did they understand Nazi fanaticism. That Italy would have no leverage in Berlin unless the *regio esercito* reversed its battlefield misfortunes was a truism ignored. Italy's setbacks in North Africa, the debacle in Russia, and the retreat to the ports in Yugoslavia only underlined Italy's subordination to the Third Reich. Given these circumstances, the power brokers in Berlin would not do more than prop up the discredited and tottering Fascist regime to save the face of the Axis toward the outside world.

As is so often the case, fear plus ambition underlay these skewed perceptions at the Palazzo Chigi. Pietromarchi et al. correctly believed that Germany would retaliate if Italy were to cut and run from the Axis alliance. But sitting in their comfortable armchairs in Rome, they refused to concede that empire-building in Yugoslavia had ended up in an unwinnable guerrilla war.[1126] The plan was not at fault they believed; it was the 2nd Army's incompetence that brought about failure.

## Finis to Mussolini's Empire-Building

Italy's search for empire in Yugoslavia was no major Fascist innovation. Italian leaders from Sonnino to Mussolini wanted to tear down the Belgrade regime and open the Balkans to Italian domination. Both meant to do so by *"Italia farà da sè."* As a traditional nationalist who disparaged Slavs, Sonnino was most comfortable surrounded by dynasties and would have been disgusted with Mussolini's unrestrained imperial programs as Italy's answer to Hitler's *Lebensraum* in a Europe dominated by the Axis Powers. Since Mussolini could not alone destroy Yugoslavia, he had to follow Hitler's lead, but he did so without shedding the illusion that a new chapter had opened up in Italy's "parallel war" of imperial conquest unhampered by German rivalry.

The timing could not have been worse. The Duce's troops were bogged down against Greece and his legions could gain no traction in the African desert or in the Russian snow. This was hardly the first time that the Germans had surprised him with a lightning move. When Hitler offered him invasion on a silver platter, he had only loosely drawn up plans with no idea of how to turn the Italian *spazio vitale* into a living reality. Mussolini would improvise as he went along. He was no imperialist micromanager but clearly intended to have his generals and commissars work towards a Fascist imperium. In the absence of a fixed blueprint, much would be guesswork and spontaneous decision-making.

Hitler did much of the work in the treaty-making by taking what he wanted and leaving Italy the rest. Events moved far too quickly for Mussolini to catch up. He had only the gimcrack Pavelić and the rag-tag Ustaša to count on and probably never dreamt that he would be associated with exterminators who, by setting Croatia ablaze, would ruin the dream of an Italian empire. But once Pavelić was set up in power—largely to keep the country out of the hands of the Germans—there was nothing to do but watch as the Poglavnik mercilessly fell on Serbs, Jews, and gypsies. Mussolini had bonded himself with Ustaša madmen. As a confirmed Fascist, he would suffer any authoritarian leader over more moderate voices. The Duce seemed not to grasp the tremendous disadvantages incurred by his unstinting support of the NDH, which did nothing to lessen Croatian resentment of Italy. The Germans had all the material advantages in the competition for control over the country. Above all they had a decided edge in the popularity contest because Hitler chose not to annex any Croatian territory, whereas Italy absorbed a large part of Dalmatia. Pavelić in the end turned out not to be Mussolini's puppet; it was rather the other way around, for Pavelić was able to play on the Duce's fear that he would desert Italy for Germany if not free to carry out ethnic cleansing in Croatia.

Although Mussolini from the beginning bore a grudge against Pavelić for his irredentist sentiments, he did not suspect that the 2nd Army would intervene to give succor to the beleaguered Serbs. He sat in Rome for a long time in silence while military commanders like Ambrosio, Roatta, and Dalmazzo proceeded to change around the terms of war in Yugoslavia. Since, in their view, counterinsurgency alone would not win the day in an overwhelm-ingly hostile environment—and in this they were right—they lined up the Orthodox Serb as an ally in a *mariage de convenence* to face an enemy consisting of Ustaša, Croats, and Slovenes. Thus immersed in Balkan politics, the 2nd Army ignored Mussolini's formal diplo-matic alignments. Instead of acting as a forceful *duce* by bringing the 2nd Army into line, Mussolini prevaricated and vacillated, perhaps sensing that events in Yugoslavia had spun out of his control. As much as any Italian general in Yugoslavia "worked toward the Duce," Mussolini worked toward his generals.

Mussolini never tired of pointing out that the Slovenes, Serbs, and Croats belonged to a primitive civilization that worshipped vio-lence and habitually practiced deceit. Radical Fascists were bent on an outright suppression of Slavs that would turn them into an underclass. On the other hand, Fascist idealists such as Grazioli and Bastianini introduced assimilation policies aimed at elevating them to a higher Roman civilization. On this point Mussolini acted inconsistently. He stripped Grazioli of power and wanted to cash-ier him, but gave Bastianini the authority to utilize troops in his *rastrellamenti*. The governor of Dalmatia was a tough and practi-cal Fascist in tune with Mussolini's conception of empire. In prin-ciple Mussolini believed that many of his Fascist lieutenants in Yu-goslavia, deluded by the mirage of Italianization, were no viable alternative to a military that did not flinch from waging a punish-ing war against the reviled Slavs. In the end it did not much mat-ter, for the so-called idealists, Grazioli and Bastianini, eventually aided and abetted the same kind of ruthless counterinsurgency as practiced by their military counterparts. What would have hap-pened had Mussolini taken up the 2nd Army's pro-Serb policy as his own? The Axis alliance would have been disrupted and the country exposed to invasion. Mussolini, therefore, would not risk an open breach with Hitler.

Pavelić and the Ustaša regarded the 2nd Army's trafficking with the Četniks as treachery. Mussolini did as well. The Führer, on the other hand, regarded Mihailović as a deadlier enemy than Tito and made disarmament of the Četniks the acid test for continued German cooperation. The Duce, however, shrank from disciplining the 2nd Army and closed his eyes to Italo-Četnik military cooperation. But Italy's official policy of alliance with the NDH and support of Pavelić in power remained unaltered, no matter how unpopular the regime or chaotic the conditions of the country. There was no other way that Mussolini could see to ward off Germans, Serbs, and Partisans, each of whom would delight in the expulsion of the unwelcome Italian guest. At bottom, Mussolini was playing for time that would give victory to the Axis. He could then brush aside Pavelić's regime and reconfigure the boundaries of Croatia to suit his imperial purposes.

On one score Mussolini was right. The 2nd Army's flirtation with the Četniks induced the NDH to open the door wider to the Germans. Cavallero agreed with the Duce, but took only gingerly steps to soften the intractability of the 2nd Army, so that Italy continued to be seen in Zagreb as more a Serb partisan than a Croatian ally. At the end of 1942 Hitler lowered the boom. He declared that the chief aim of Operation *Weiss* was the destruction of the Četniks and that the Italians had better comply or else. Mussolini, confronted by the none-too-subtle disobedience of his military, dillydallied till May. Finally, when the Italian retreat to the coast left him no more squirm room, he capitulated to the tough German line vis-à-vis the Četniks. It is hard to see what else he could have done. Since Mussolini did not seriously ponder an early exit from the war and had no leverage in compelling Hitler to make a separate peace on the Eastern Front, he allowed events to take their natural course. Paralyzed by a lack of will, his infatuation with Nietzsche notwithstanding, Mussolini let the 2nd Army write its own obituary. Under the Fascist maestro, Italy's empire-building in Yugoslavia was fated for destruction in a German-style Götterdämmerung.

Ultimate responsibility for the Yugoslav tragedy rests squarely on the shoulders of the two Axis dictators. First, they destroyed Yugoslavia, which, though an authoritarian and Serb-dominated state, was able to keep internal dissidence among the ethnic groups from flaring into open violence by police methods that fell far short of

Communist-style terrorism. Who knows? If Yugoslavia had been left alone, it might have evolved into a pluralistic and democratic society. The Sporazum was a good omen for the future. But the Axis invasion turned this hopeful dream into a nightmare by touching off a vicious cycle of ethnic massacres and mass migrations. Slaughter on such a mass scale had only been seen during the Mongol raids and in the two years following the end of World War I when the peoples of Eastern Europe, in a totally lawless environment created by the sudden collapse of empires, butchered each other in unmitigated fury.

Second, by their invasion of Yugoslavia, the Axis Powers breathed new life into a tiny and unpopular Communist party, which had been languishing underground. Tito emerged to pose as the liberator against the foreign invader. The irony is this: the Partisans were ultimately victorious not as agents of revolution; rather, like the Italians, they gained popularity in the NDH as defenders of Serbs against the Ustaša and its murderous policies. Without this terrible misfortune, the Partisans would have had few recruits, and the Communists never would have come to power. But once the dialectics of civil war had begun to work out their inexorable logic, the disparate and poorly coordinated lieutenants of Mihailović, lacking political finesse and a persuasive program for the future, lost out to the more ruthless Communists, who promised to realize an appealing utopian vision that transcended the parochialism of a Great Serbia. It is sheer speculation to ponder whether a Karageorgević return to power, which Mihailović intended to bring about, would have resulted in a more just and workable government than the harsh regime eventually imposed on the Yugoslav people by Marshal Tito. Regardless of political orientation, one thing is certain. Without an Axis invasion, prewar Yugoslavia, although hardly an enlightened democracy, would have been free of both Communists and Četniks.

Third, by installing Pavelić as Poglavnik, Mussolini became an accomplice of Ustaša terror. Without a restraining hand from Rome, the Italian "puppet" proceeded to enact the "final solution" of the Orthodox Serbs, Jews, and gypsies in Croatia's mixed areas, turning the Balkans into a bloodbath. The 2nd Army alone prevented the

Ustaša from matching the formidable German scorecard. Mussolini occasionally protested against Pavelić's savagery and sanctioned Italian advances into the demilitarized areas—among other things, to curb Ustaša violence. However, he never moved vigorously to bring the Poglavnik's ethnic cleansing to a halt.

The course of events in the Balkans during the dark days of 1941–43 was hardly new to history. Whenever imperialist conquests are answered by the occupied peoples with a popularly based uprising, the invaders typically resort to harsh and punitive counterinsurgency strategies that end in misery. Fascist Italy brought that truism home with a vengeance. During the lawless occupation of Yugoslav lands under Mussolini's leadership, little, if anything, was done to contain random and needless violence. Rather, Mussolini, the Palazzo Chigi, and many 2nd Army commanders flouted every known humanitarian norm, encouraging or provoking actions that surpassed battlefield necessity. The occasional official fiat that prescribed limits or terror usually derived from outright opportunism. Whatever compassion was shown the wretched Balkan peoples was undertaken spontaneously by individual conscience-stricken soldiers and commanders, who acted on their own to halt wholesale Ustaša slaughter of Jews and Orthodox Serbs and to offer sustenance to those not perceived as "rebels."

In pursuit of a Roman imperium that was tenaciously opposed by a spirited resistance, Fascist Italy's empire-builders ended up committing a wide variety of war crimes against both guerilla warriors and civilians across the length and breadth of occupied Yugoslavia. Their short-lived "Empire on the Adriatic," intended to bring a superior Italian civilization to the grateful conquered, instead revealed its basest side.

# Bibliography

## Archival Materials

The following captured German and Italian wartime documents in the National Archives were used. They are in individual rolls that are arranged topically in groups.

Microscopy No. T-821: Collection of Italian Military Records, 1933-1943. Rolls 2, 21, 31, 51, 52, 53, 54, 55, 56, 57, 58, 59, 60, 61, 62, 63, 64, 65, 66, 70, 84, 125, 126, 127, 128, 129,139, 218, 219, 232, 247, 248, 250, 252, 257, 258, 264, 265, 266, 271, 276, 285, 286, 287, 288, 289, 298, 347, 356, 395, 398, 403, 404, 405, 406, 410, 424, 498, 503, 505.
Microscopy No. T-501: Records of German Field Commands Rear Areas, Occupied Territories, and Others: Rolls 260, 264–268.

Italian Military Archives
Fondo M 3. Documents returned to Italy by the Allies after the end of World War II.
Fondo N I-II. Diari storici of the Second World War: 2nd Army: files 235, 724, 993, 1222, 2084. Files consulted from selected Army Corps divisions.

State Archives
Presidenza del Consiglio dei Ministri 1940–1943. I.I.3. 16452. 1–180 (Governatorato della Dalmazia), 36146, 57412.
Graziani Papers
Morgagni Papers

Foreign Ministry Archives
Gabinetto Armistizio-Pace (GABAP):
Croatia: files 28–47
Montenegro: files 48–54
Affari Politici 1931–1945:
Jugoslavia: files 105-107
Pietromarchi Papers and Diary, Turin, Italy.
Archives of the Institute of Military History, Belgrade, Serbia.
Archives of the Slovene Republic, Ljubljana. Slovenia.

## Published Materials

*Akten zur deutschen auswärtigen Politik*, Sieres E (1941–1945), vols. 1–6. Göttingen: Vandenhoeck & Ruprecht, 1969–79.

*Documenti diplomatici italiani*, series IX, 9 vols. Rome: Istituto poligrafico e Zecca dello stato, 1960–1987.

*Documents on German Foreign Policy, 1918–1945*, series D (1937–45), 14 vols., Washington, D.C.: U.S. Government Printing Office, 1949–64.

Mussolini, Benito. *Opera Omnia*, edited by Edoardo and Dulio Susmel, 44 vols. Florence: La Fenice, 1951–78.

*Zbornik documenata i podataka o narodnooslobodila kom ratu jugoslavenskih naroda Jugoslavije*, 14 vols. Belgrade: Military Institute of Belgrade, 1949–1986.

## Selected Bibliography

Amoretti, Gian Nicola. *La vicenda italo-croatia nei documenti di Aimone di Savoia (1941–1943)*. Rapallo: Ypotesis, 1979.

Anderson, Kenneth. "Who Owns the Rules of War?" *The New York Times Magazine* 13 April 2003, 38–43.

Anfuso, Filippo. *Da Palazzo Venezia al Lago di Garda 1936–1945*. Bologna: Cappelli, 1957.

Ansaldo, Giovanni. *Il giornalista di Ciano: diari 1932–1943*. Bologna: Il Mulino, 2000.

Avramov, Smilja. *Genocide in Yugoslavia*. Belgrade: BIGZ, 1995.

Bambara, Gino. *Jugoslavia settebandiere: Guerra senza retrovie nella Jugoslavia occupata (1941–1943)*. Brescia: Vannini, 1988.

Beloff, Nora. *Tito's Flawed Legacy: Yugoslavia & the West since 1939*. Boulder, CO: Westview Press, 1984.

Biagini, Antonello, and Fernando Frattolillo. eds. *Diario Storico del Comando Supremo*. Rome: SME-US, 1985–1999.

Bianchini, S., and F. Privitera. *6 aprile 1941: L'attaco italiano alla Jugoslavia*. Milan: Marzorati, 1993.

Breccia, Alfredo. *Jugoslavia 1939–1941: Diplomazia della neutralità*. Milan: Giuffrè, 1978.

Browning, Christopher S. "The Wehrmacht in Serbia Revisited." In *Crimes of War: Guilt and Denial in the Twentieth Century*, edited by Omer Bartov, Atina Grossmann, and Mary Nolan, 31–40. New York: The New Press, 2002.

Broucek, Peter. *General in Zwielicht: Die Lebenserinnerungen Edmund Glaises von Horstenau.* 3 vols. Vienna: Boehlhaus, 1980, 1983, 1988.

Burgwyn, H. James. *The Legend of the Mutilated Victory: Italy, the Great War, and the Paris Peace Conference, 1915–1919.* Westport CT and London: Greenwood Press, 1993.

———. *Il revisionismo fascista.* Milan: Feltrinelli, 1979.

Capogreco, Carlo Spartaco. *I campi del duce: L'internamento civile nell'Italia fascista (1940–1943).* Turin: Einaudi, 2004.

———. "Una storia rimossa dell'Italia fascista: L'internamento dei civili jugoslavi (1941–1943)." *Studi storici* XLII, no. 1 (January–March 2001): 203–30.

———. *Renicci: Un campo di concentramento in riva al Tevere (1942–1943).* Cosenza: Fondazione Ferramonti, 1998.

Carpi, Daniel. "The Rescue of Jews in the Italian Zone of Occupied Croatia." In *Rescue Attempts During the Holocaust: Proceedings of the Second Yad Vashem International Historical Conference, April 1974,* edited by Yisrael Gutman and Efraim Zuroff, 465–525. Jerusalem: 1977.

Cavallero, Ugo. *Diario 1940–1943,* edited by Giuseppe Bucciante. Rome: Ciarrapico, 1984.

Ciano, Count Galeazzo. *The Ciano Diaries 1939–1943,* edited by Hugh Gibson. Garden City, NY: Doubleday, 1946.

———. *Ciano's Diplomatic Papers.* London: Oldham's Press, 1948.

Clissold, Stephen. *Whirlwind: An Account of Marshal Tito's Rise to Power.* London: Cresset Press, 1949.

Cohen, Philip J. *Serbia's Secret War.* College Park, TX: Texas A&M University Press, 1996.

Collotti, Enzo. *L'Europa nazista: Il progetto di un nuovo ordine europeo (1939-1945).* Florence: Giunti, 2002.

———. "Sul razzismo antislavo." In *Nel nome della razza: Il razzismo nella storia d'Italia, 1870–1945,* edited by A. Burgio, 63–92. Bologna: Il Mulino, 1999.

———. "Penetrazione economica e disgregazione statale: Premesse e conseguenze dell'aggressione nazista alla Jugoslavia." In *The Third Reich and Yugoslavia, 1933-1945.* Belgrade: Institute for Contemporary History, 1977.

———. *Le potenze dell'Asse e la Jugoslavia: Saggi e documenti 1941/1943.* Milan: Feltrinelli, 1974.

Cornwell, John. *Hitler's Pope: The Secret History of Pius XII.* New York: Penguin, 1999.

Creveld, Martin. *Hitler's Strategy, 1940–1941: The Balkan Cue*. Cambridge: Cambridge University Press, 1973.

Cuzzi, Mario. *L'occupazione italiana della Slovenia (1941–1943)*. Rome: SME-US, 1998.

———. "I Balcani, problemi di un'occupazione difficile." In *L'Italia in guerra: Il 3rd anno–1942*, edited by R. H. Rainero and A. Biagini, 343–376. Rome: Commissione italiana di storia militare, 1993.

Dassovich, Mario. *Fronte Jugoslavo 1941–'42*. Udine: Del Bianco, 1999.

———. *Fronte Jugoslavo 1943*. Udine: Del Bianco, 2000.

Deakin, F. W. *The Embattled Mountain*. New York & London: Oxford University Press, 1971.

———. *The Brutal Friendship: Mussolini, Hitler and the Fall of Italian Fascism*. Garden City, NY: Doubleday Anchor Books, 1966.

Dedjer, Vladimir. *Tito*. New York: Simon & Schuster, 1953.

De Felice, Renzo. *Mussolini l'alleato: L'Italia in guerra*. Turin: Einaudi, 1990.

———. *Mussolini il duce: Gli anni del consenso*. Turin: Einaudi, 1974.

Djilas, Alexis. *The Contested Country: Yugoslav Unity and Communist Revolution 1919–1953*. Cambridge MA and London: Harvard University Press, 1991.

Djilas, Milovan. *Memoir of a Revolutionary*. New York: Harcourt Brace Jovanovich, 1973.

———. *Wartime*. New York: Harcourt Brace Jovanovich, 1973.

Falcone, Carlo. *The Silence of Pius XII*. Boston: Little Brown, 1970.

Fattuta, Francesco. *La campagna di Jugoslaia, aprile 1941–settembre 1943*. Campobasso, 1996.

———. "Cronache di guerriglia in Iugoslavia: Parte 2, Gennaio–giugno 1942." In *Studi storico-militari 1993*. Rome: SME, 1996, 245–302.

———. "Cronache di guerriglia in Iugoslavia: Parte 3, luglio-decembre 1942." In *Studi storico-militari 1994*. Rome: SME, 1996, 751–803.

———. "Cronache di guerriglia in Iugoslavia: Parte 4, gennaio-settembre 1943." In *Studi storico-militari 1996*. Rome: SME, 1998, 129–225.

Ferenc, Tone. *"Gospod Visoki Komisar Pravi..." Sosvet za Ljubljansko Pokrajino [Consulta per la Provincia di Lubiana]: Documenti*. Ljubljana: CIP, 2001.

———. *Rab-Arbe-Arbissima: Konfinacije, Racije in Internacije v Lubljanski Pokrajini 1941–1943*. Ljubljana: Inštitut za novejšo zgodovino, 2000.

———. *"Si ammazza troppo poco": Condannati a morte-ostaggi-passati per le armi nella provincia di Lubiana 1941–1943*. Ljubljana: Istituto per la storia moderna, 1999.

————. *La provincia 'italiana' di Lubiana: Documenti 1941–1942.* Udine: Istituto friulano per la storia del movimento di liberazione, 1994.

————. "Le système d'occupation des nazis en Slovénie." In International Conference on the History of the Resistance Movements, *Les systèmes d'occupation en Yougoslavie 1941–1945,* 47–133, Belgrade: Karlovy Vary, 1963.

————. "Gli italiani in Slovenia 1941–1943." In *L'Italia in guerra 1940–1943,* edited by Bruna Micheletti and Pier Paolo Poggio, 155–170. Brescia: Annali della Fondazione "Luigi Micheletti," 1990–91.

Focardi, Filippo, "L'Italia fascista come potenza occupante nel giudizio dell'opinione pubblica italiana: La questione dei criminali di guerra (1943–1948). In *L'Italia fascista potenza occupante: Lo scacchiere balcanico,* edited by Brunello Mantelli, 157–183. Trieste: Qualestoria, June 2002.

————. "'Bravo italiano' e 'cattivo tedesco': Riflessioni sulla genesi di due immagini incrociate." In *Storia e memoria,* 55–83. Genoa: Istituto storico della resistenza in Liguria, 1996.

Gobetti, Eric. "Da Marsiglia a Zagabria: Ante Pavelić e il movimento ustaša in Italia (1929–1941)." In *L'Italia fascista potenza occupante: Lo scacchiere balcanico,* edited by Brunello Mantelli, 103–115. Trieste: Qualestoria, June 2002.

————. *Dittatore per caso.* Turin: L'ancora, 2001.

Gorla, Giuseppe. *L'Italia nella seconda guerra mondiale: Diario di un milanese ministro del Re nel Governo Mussolini.* Milan: Baldini and Castoldi, 1959.

Halder, Franz. *War Diary, 1939–1942.* 2 vols. Novato, CA: Presidio Press, 1988.

Hehn, Paul. *The Struggle Against Yugoslav Guerrillas in World War II.* Boulder, CO: Eastern European Monographs, 1980.

Hoptner, J. B. *Yugoslavia in Crisis 1934–1941.* New York and London: Columbia University Press, 1962.

Judah, Tim. *The Serbs: History, Myth and Destruction of Yugoslavia.* 2d. ed. New Haven and London: Yale University Press, 2000.

Jukic, Iliya. *The Fall of Yugoslavia.* New York: Jovanovich, 1974.

Karchmar, Lucien. "Draža Mihailović and the Rise of the Četnik Movement, 1941–1942." 2 vols. Ph.D. diss., Stanford University, 1973.

Knox, MacGregor. *Common Destiny: Dictatorship, Foreign Policy, and War in Fascist Italy and Nazi Germany.* Cambridge: Cambridge University Press, 2000.

Lederer, Ivo J. *Yugoslavia at the Paris Peace Conference: A Study in Frontiermaking.* New Haven: Yale University Press, 1963.

Loi, Salvatore. *Le operazioni delle unità italiane in Jugoslavia 1941–1943*. Rome: SME-US, 1978.

MacDonald, David Bruce. *Balkan Holocausts? Serbian and Croatian Victim-Centered Propaganda and the War in Yugoslavia*. Manchester and New York: Manchester University Press, 2002.

Maiocchi, Roberto. *Scienza italiana e razzismo fascista*. Florence: La Nuova Italia, 1999.

Manoschek, Walter. "'Coming Along to Shoot Some Jews?' The Destruction of the Jews in Serbia." In *War of Extermination: The German Military in World War II, 1941–1944*, edited by Hannes Heer and Klaus Naumann, 39–54. New York and Oxford: Berghahn Books, 2000.

Marjanović, Jovan. *Collaboration of D. Mihailović's Četniks with the Enemy Forces of Occupation 1941–1944*. Belgrade: Arhivski Pregled, 1976.

Martin, David. *The Web of Disinformation: Churchill's Yugoslav Blunder*. London: Harcourt, 1990.

Milazzo, Matteo J. *The Chetnik Movement & The Yugoslav Resistance*. Baltimore and London: The Johns Hopkins University Press, 1975.

Minniti, Fortunato. "Profili dell'iniziativa strategica italiana dalla non belligeranza alla guerra parallela," *Storia contemporanea* XXIII, no. 6 (1987): 1113–1197.

Monzalli, Luciano. "La questione della Dalmazia e la politica estera italiana nella primavera del 1941." *La rivista dalmatica* LXVIX (1998): 31–44.

Nenezić, Dragan S. *Jugoslovenske Oblasti Pod Italijom 1941–1943*. Belgrade: Vojnoistorijski Institut Vojske Jugoslavije, 1999.

Novak, B.C. *Trieste 1941–1954: The Ethnic, Political and Ideological Struggle*. Chicago: Chicago University Press, 1970.

Ortona, Egidio. *Diplomazia di guerra: Diari 1937–1943*. Bologna: Mulino, 1993.

Pavlowitch, Stevan K. *Unconventional Perceptions of Yugoslavia 1940–1945*. New York: East European Monographs, 1985.

———. *Yugoslavia*. New York: Praeger, 1975.

Pelagalli, Sergio. "Il generale Pietro Gàzzera al ministero della guerra (1928–1933)." *Storia contemporanea* XX, no. 6 (December 1989): 1007–58.

Piccini, U. *Una pagina strappata*. Rome: Corso, 1983.

Piemontese, Giuseppe. *Twenty-Four Months of Italian Occupation of the Province of Ljubljana*. Ljubljana: S.C., 1946.

Pirjevec, Joze. *Il giorno di San Vito Jugoslavia 1918–1992: Storia di una tragedia*. Turin: Nuova Eri, 1998.

Poliakov, Léon, and Jacques Sabille. *Jews under the Italian Occupation.* Paris: Éditions du Centre, 1955.

Rallo, Michele. *L'epoca delle rivoluzioni nazionali in Europa (1919–1945).* 2 vols. Rome: Settimo Sigillo, 1989.

Rich, Norman. *Hitler's War Aims.* New York: Norton, 1973.

Roberts, Walter R. *Tito, Mihailović and the Allies, 1941–1945.* New Brunswick, NJ: Rutgers University Press, 1973.

Roatta, Mario. *Otto milioni di baionette: L'esercito italiano in guerra 1940–1944.* Milan: Mondadori, 1946.

Rodogno, Davide. *Il nuovo ordine mediterraneo.* Turin: Bollati Boringhieri, 2003.

———. "La repressione nei territori occupati dall'Italia fascista tra il 1940 ed il 1943." In *L'Italia fascista potenza occupante: Lo scacchiere balcanico,* edited by Bruno Mantelli, 45–83. Trieste: Qualestoria, 2002.

Sala, Teodoro. "Fascisti e nazisti nell'Europa sudorientale: Il caso croato (1941–1943)." in *Le potenze dell'Asse e la Jugoslavia: Saggi e documenti 1941–1943.* edited by Enzo Collotti and Teodoro Sala, 49–76. Milan: Feltrinelli, 1974.

———. "Guerriglia e controguerriglia in Jugoslavia nella propaganda per le truppe occupanti italiane (1941–1943)." *Il movimento di liberazione in Italia* XXIX, no. 108 (1972): 91–114.

———. "Occupazione militare e amministrazione civile nella 'provincia' di Lubiana (1941–1943). In *L'Italia nell'Europa danubiana durante la seconda guerra mondiale,* edited by E. Collotti, T. Sala, and G. Vaccario, 73–93. Milan: Feltrinelli, 1966.

Schmider, Klaus. *Partisanenkrieg in Jugoslawien 1941–1944.* Hamburg: Mittler, 2002.

———. "Auf Umwegen zum Vernichtungskrieg? Der Partisanenkrieg in Jugoslawien, 1941–1944." In *Die Wehrmacht: Mythos und Realität,* edited by Rolf-Dieter Müller and Hans-Erich Volkmann, 901–922. Munich: Oldenbourg, Verlag, 1999.

Schreiber, Gerhard. "Due popoli, una vittoria? Gli italiani nei Balcani nel giudizio dell'alleato germanico." In *L'Italia in guerra 1940–1943,* edited by P. P. Poggio and B. Micheletti, 95–124. Brescia: Fondazione "Luigi Micheletti," 1992.

Scotti, Giacomo. *Buono Taliano: Gli Italiani in Yugoslavia 1941–1943.* Milan: La Pietra, 1977.

Scotti, Giacomo and Luciano Viazzi, *L'inutile vittoria: La tragica esperienza delle truppe italiane in Montenegro.* Milan: Mursia, 1989.

———. *Occupazione e guerra italiana in Montenegro: Le aquile delle Montagne Nere.* Milan: Mursia, 1987.

Sepić, Dragovan. "La politique italienne d'occupation en Dalmatie 1941–1943." In *Les systèmes d'occupation en Yougoslavie 1941–1945*, 377–424. Belgrade: L'institute pour l'étude du mouvement ouvrier, 1963.

Shelah, Menachem. *Un debito di gratitudine: Storia dei rapporti tra l'esercito italiano e gli ebrei in Dalmazia (1941–1943).* Rome: SME-US, 1991.

———."Italian Rescue of Yugoslav Jews." In *The Italian Refuge: Rescue of Jews During the Holocaust*, edited by Ivo Herzer, 205–217. Washington, D.C.: The Catholic University Press, 1989.

Shorrock, William I. *From Ally to Enemy: The Enigma of Fascist Italy in French Diplomacy.* Kent OH and London: The Kent State University Press, 1988.

Simoni, L. *Berlino ambasciata d'Italia 1939–1943* (Rome: Migliaresi, 1946).

Spazzali, Roberto. "Il campo di concentramento dell'isola di Melato (Molat) (1941–1943) *Rivista dalmatica* 3 (July-September 1996): 169–87.

Stavrianos, L. S. *The Balkans Since 1943.* New York: Holt, Rinehart, and Winston, 1958.

Steinberg, Jonathan. "Types of Genocide? Croatians, Serbs, and Jews, 1941–1945." In *The Final Solution: Origins and Implementation*, edited by David Cesarani, 175-193. London and New York: Routledge, 1996.

———. "The Roman Catholic Church and Genocide in Croatia, 1941–1945." *Studies in Church History* 29 (1993): 463–479.

———. *The Axis and the Holocaust 1941–1943.* London and New York: Routledge, 1991.

Talpo, Oddone. *Dalmazia: Una cronaca per la storia (1941).* Rome: SME-US, 1995.

———. *Dalmazia: Una cronaca per la storia (1942).* 2d ed. Rome: SME-US, 2000.

———. *Dalmazia: Una cronaca per la storia (1943–1944).* Rome: SME-US, 1994.

———. "Porto Ploče: Tentativo tedesco di affaciarsi in Adriatico (1942)" *Rivista Dalmatica* 70 (1999): 145–51.

———. "Diario di Franceso Giunta Governatore della Dalmazia." *La rivista dalmatica* LXV (1994): 1–16.

Tanner, Marcus. *A Nation Forced in War.* 2d ed. New Haven and London: Yale University Press, 2001.

Tomasevich, Jozo. *War and Revolution in Yugoslavia, 1941–1945: Occupation and Collaboration.* Stanford, CA: Stanford University Press, 2001.

———. *War and Revolution in Yugoslavia, 1941–1945: The Chetniks.* Stanford: Stanford University Press, 1975.

Trevor-Roper, H. R. *Hitler's Secret Conversations 1941–1944*. New York: Signet Books, 1953.

Trifkovic, Srdja. *Ustaša: Croatian Separatism and European Politics, 1929–1945*. London and Aiken, SC: The Lord Byron Foundation for Balkan Studies, 1988.

———. "Rivalry Between Germany and Italy in Croatia, 1942–1943." *The Historical Journal* 36, no. 4 (1993): 879–904.

Verna, Frank Philip. "Notes on Italian Rule in Dalmatia under Bastianini, 1941–1943." *International History Review* XII, no. 3 (August 1990): 528–547.

———. "Yugoslavia Under Italian Rule 1941–1943: Civil and Military Aspects of the Italian Occupation." Ph.D. diss., University of California, 1985.

Voigt, Klaus. *Il refugio precario: Gli esuli in Italia dal 1933 al 1945*. Florence: La Nuova Italia, 1996.

West, Richard. *Tito and the Rise and Fall of Yugoslavia*. New York: Carroll and Graf, 1996.

Wheeler, Mark. "Pariahs to Partisans in Power: The Communist Party of Yugoslavia." In *Politics of Retribution in Europe: World War II and its Aftermath*, edited by Tony Judt, 110–51. Princeton, NJ: Princeton University Press, 2000.

———. *Britain and the War For Yugoslavia, 1940–1943*. Boulder, CO: East European Monographs, 1980.

Zanussi, Giacomo. *Guerra e catastrofe d'Italia*. 2 vols. Rome: Corso, 1945.

Živojinovic, Dragoljub R. "Yugoslavia." In Neville Wylie, *European Neutrals and Non-Belligerents During the Second World War*, 217–37. Cambridge: Cambridge University Press, 2000.

# Notes

1. Cited in Ivo J Lederer, *Yugoslavia at the Paris Peace Conference: A Study in Frontiermaking* (New Haven: Yale University Press, 1963), pp. 73–75.

2. A recent study on Italy and the Paris Peace Conference is H. James Burgwyn's *The Legend of the Mutilated Victory: Italy, the Great War, and the Paris Peace Conference, 1915–1919* (Westport CT and London: Greenwood Press, 1993).

3. DDI, VII, VII, Mussolini to Badoglio, 2 October 1926; MacGregor Knox, *Common Destiny: Dictatorship, Foreign Policy, and War in Fascist Italy and Nazi Germany* (Cambridge: Cambridge University Press, 2000), p. 123.

4. Still the best study on Mussolini's diplomacy during the 1920s is by Alan Cassels, *Mussolini's Early Diplomacy* (Princeton, NJ: Princeton University Press, 1970).

5. An important study on Italy and the Croatian separatists is by James J. Sadkovich, *Italian Support for Croatian Separatism* (New York: Garland, 1987). For particulars on Italian subsidy of terrorism in Eastern Europe, see H. James Burgwyn's *Il revisionismo fascista* (Milan: Feltrinelli, 1979).

6. Cited in Renzo De Felice, *Mussolini il duce: Gli anni del consenso* (Turin: Einaudi, 1974), p. 381, n. 1.

7. GD, r. 10, 14.90.11, 27 December 1929.

8. GD, r. 10, 14.90.11, 27 December 1929; DDI, VII, VIII, 360, Guariglia to Galli, 12 February 1930; 423, Guariglia to Grandi, 13 March 1930.

9. DDI, VII, IX, 370, Grandi to Mussolini, 12 November 1930.

10. GD, r. 22, 25.90.40, July 1932.

11. Sergio Pelagalli, "Il generale Pietro Gàzzera al ministero della guerra (1928–1933)," *Storia contemporanea* XX, no. 6 (December 1989): 1045.

12. William I. Shorrock, *From Ally to Enemy: The Enigma of Fascist Italy in French Diplomacy* (Kent, OH and London: The Kent State University Press, 1988), p. 49.

13. Eric Gobetti, *Dittatore per caso* (Turin: L'ancora del Mediterraneo, 2001), p. 70.

14. Gobetti, *Dittatore per caso*, p. 77.

15. Gobetti, *Dittatore per caso*, p. 93.

16. Count Galeazzo Ciano, *Ciano's Diplomatic Papers*, Hugh Gibson, ed. (London: Oldham's Press, 1948), pp. 98–105.

17. Count Galeazzo Ciano, *The Ciano Diaries 1939–1943* (Garden City, NY: Doubleday, 1946), 7 February 1939.

18. Dragoljub R. Živojinović, "Yugoslavia," in *European Neutrals and Non-Belligerents During the Second World War*, ed. Neville Wylie (Cambridge: Cambridge University Press, 2000), p. 221.

19. A good study, if a little dated, is by J. B. Hoptner, *Yugoslavia in Crisis 1934–1941* (New York and London: Columbia University Press, 1962).

20. DDI, IX, III, 194, Conversation between Ciano and Pavelić, 23 January 1940.

21. *The Ciano Diaries*, 9 April and 10 May 1940.

22. DDI, IX, IV, 848, Croatian National Committee to Ciano, 10 June 1940.

23. Martin Creveld, *Hitler's Strategy, 1940–1941: The Balkan Clue* (Cambridge: Cambridge University Press, 1973), p. 11.

24. *The Ciano Diaries*, 7 March 1940, 11 November 1940.

25. DGFP, D, IX, 360, Mackensen to Foreign Ministry, 1 June 1940; 373, Mussolini to Hitler, 2 June 1940.

26. DGFP, D, X, 73, Foreign Ministry Memorandum, 1 July 1940; DDI, IX, V, 161, Alfieri to Ciano, 1 July 1940.

27. DGFP, D, X, 129, Conversation between Hitler and Ciano, 8 July 1940; *Ciano's Diplomatic Papers*, Conversation between Ciano and Hitler, 7 July 1940.

28. Franz Halder, *War Diary, 1939–1942*, 2 vols. (Novato, CA: Presidio Press, 1988), I: 549 (14 August 1940).

29. DGFP, D, X, 343, The Foreign Intelligence Department of the Wehrmacht to the Chief of the OKW (Rintelen Report), 9 August 1940.

30. ACS, Graziani Papers, 58, f. 47, sf. 9, 18 and 22 August 1941.

31. DDI, IX, V, 427, Alfieri to Ciano, 16 August 1940; DGFP, D, X, 353, Conversation between Ribbentrop and Alfieri, 17 August 1940.

32. Mario Roatta, *Otto milioni di baionette: L'esercito italiano in guerra dal 1940 al 1944* (Milan: Mondadori, 1946), p. 120.

33. *The Ciano Diaries*, 11 November 1940.

34. *Ciano's Diplomatic Papers*, pp. 408–11.

35. DGFP, D, XI, 383, Mussolini to Hitler, 22 November 1940.

36. DDI, IX, VI, 236, Pavelić to Anfuso, n. 1, 260, Anfuso to Ciano, 8 December 1940, and 392, Anfuso to Ciano, 2 January 1941.

37. DGFP, D, XI, 549, Ribbentrop to legation in Jugoslavia, 21 December 1940, and 551, Heeren to Foreign Ministry, 23 December 1940.

38. L. Simoni, *Berlino ambasciata d'Italia 1939–43* (Rome: Migliaresi, 1946), p. 209.

39. DDI, IX, VI, 553, Ciano to Mussolini, 8 February 1941, Annex V.

40. DGFP, D, XII, 76, Mussolini to Hitler, 22 February 1941.

41. DGFP, D, XII, 45, Weizäckers memorandum, 12 February 1941.

42. DDI, IX, VI, 671, Anfuso to Mussolini, 2 March 1941, and 672, Anfuso to Mameli, 3 March 1941; DGFP, D, XII, 117, Conversation between Mussolini and Hitler, 2 March 1941, and 182, Mackensen memorandum, 19 March 1941; Simoni, *Berlino ambasciata d'Italia*, p. 212.

43. Collotti believes that Cetković threw himself in the arms of the Third Reich blinded by the expansionist ambition of seizing Salonika. Enzo Collotti, "Penetrazione economica e disgregazione statale: Premese e conseguenze dell'aggressione nazista alla Jugoslavia," in Enzo Collotti and Teodoro Sala, *Le potenze dell'Asse e la Jugoslavia: Saggi e documenti 1941/1943* (Milan: Feltrinelli, 1974), pp. 21–22.

44. Breccia is particularly critical of the British for irresponsibly by urging the Yugoslavs to resist with only vague and unfounded promises of military support. Alfredo Breccia, *Jugoslavia 1939–1941: Diplomazia della neutralità* (Milan: Giuffrè, 1978), chapter seven.

45. Cited in Srdja Trifkovic, *Ustaša: Croatian Separatism and European Politics, 1929–1945* (London and Aiken, SC: The Lord Byron Foundation for Balkan Studies, 1998), p. 99.

46. Creveld, *Hitler's Strategy, 1940–1941*, p. 143.

47. A phrase turned by Trifkovic, *Ustaša*. p. 100.

48. Simoni, *Berlino ambasciata d'Italia*, p. 216.

49. DGFP, D, XII, 226, Mackensen to Berlin, 28 March 1941.

50. NAW, T-821, 128, 320–21, Guzzoni note for von Rintelen, 30 March 1941.

51. NAW, T-821, 127, 798–99, Mussolini to Cavallero, 29 March 1941; 128, 553–54, Roatta to Ambrosio, 2 April 1941; DGFP, 289, D, XII, Mussolini to Hitler, 6 April 1941.

52. NAW, T-821, 127, 798, Mussolini to Cavallero, 29 March 1941.

53. NAW, T-821, 128, 251–54, CS report, 29 March 1941, 128, 456–59, CS report, 29 March 1941.

54. Fortunato Minniti, "Profili dell'iniziativa strategica italiana dalla non belligeranza a la guerra parallela," *Storia contemporanea* XVIII, no. 6 (December 1987): 1113–95.

55. NAW, T-821, 128, 320–21, Guzzoni to von Rintelen, 30 March 1941.

56. NAW, T-821, 128, 553–54, Roatta to Ambrosio, 2 April 1941.

57. DDI, IX, VI, 837, Mameli to Ciano, 3 April 1941.

58. Breccia, *Diplomazia della neutralità*, p. 449.

59. DDI, IX, VI, 838, Ciano to Mameli, 3 April 1941.

60. DGFP, D, XII, 281, Hitler to Mussolini, 5 April 1941.

61. Fortunato Fattuta, *La campagna di Jugoslavia, aprile 1941–settembre 1943* (Campobasso, 1996), p. 35.

62. Details of Italy's short war against Yugoslavia are found in Salvatore Loi's *Le operazioni delle unità italiane in Jugoslavia (1941–1943)*, (Rome: SME-US, 1978), pp. 60, 133–38.

63. DDI, IX, VI, 792, Hitler to Mussolini, 27 March 1941; DGFP, D, XII, 224, Hitler to Mussolini, 28 March 1941.

64. Jozo Tomasevich, *War and Revolution in Yugoslavia, 1941–1945: Occupation and Collaboration* (Stanford, CA: Stanford University Press, 2001), p. 48.

65. DDI, IX, VI, 795, Mussolini to Hitler, 28 March 1941; DGFP, D, XII, 226, Mackensen to Berlin, 29 March 1941.

66. Filippo Anfuso, *Da Palazzo Venezia al Lago di Garda (1936–1945)*, (Bologna: Cappelli, 1957), pp. 157–64.

67. Norman Rich, *Hitler's War Aims* (New York: Norton, 1973), p. 198.

68. Peter Broucek, *General in Zwielicht: Die Lebenserinnerungen Edmund Glaises von Horstenau*, 3 vols. (Vienna: Boehlhaus, 1980, 1983, 1988), II: 82.

69. Trifkovic, *Ustaša*, p. 108.

70. This is the view of L. S. Stavrianos, *The Balkans Since 1453* (New York: Holt, Rinehart, and Winston, 1959, p. 172.

71. Eric Gobetti writes that Pavelić on his journey to Zagreb was accompanied by 240 followers. "Da Marsiglia a Zagabria: Ante Pavelić e il movimento ustaša in Italia (1929–1941)," in *L'Italia fascista potenza occupante: lo scacchiere balcanico*, ed. Brunello Martelli (Trieste: Qualestoria, XXX 1 (June 2002):114.

72. Broucek, *Glaise von Horstenau*, p. 98.

73. Oddone Talpo, *Dalmazia: Una cronaca per la storia (1941)* (Rome: SME-US, 1995), pp. 309–10.

74. PP, Diary, 24 April 1941. Pietromarchi worked out his plan for Dalmatia with the help of Oscar Randi, a native of Zara and irredentist, who held a high office in the Ministry of Public Culture.

75. PP, Diary, 24 April 1941.

76. Renzo De Felice, *Mussolini l'alleato: L'Italia in guerra* (Turin: Einaudi, 1990), I: 383, n. 2.

77. PP, Luca Pietromarchi, "Il problema della Dalmazia nei rapporti politici ed economici tra l'Italia e la Croazia Marzo 1942," *Storia e politica internazionale*, pp. 3–24.

78. DDI, IX, VI, 914, Salata to Anfuso, 15 April 1941.

79. ASMAE, GABAP, 46, Report of 11 April 1941.

80. *The Ciano Diaries*, 30 April 1941.

81. *The Ciano Diaries*, 29 April 1941.

82. Giovanni Ansaldo, *Il giornalista di Ciano: diari 1932–1943* (Bologna: il Mulino, 2000), pp. 296–97.

83. DDI, IX, VI, 923, Mussolini to Ciano, 17 April 1941.

84. NAW, T-821, 128, 145–46, The German military attaché to the CS, 13 April 1941.

85. DGFP, D, XIII, 363, Ribbentrop to Rome, 17 April 1941.

86. Ciano, *Ciano's Diplomatic Papers*, p. 436.

87. DGFP, D, XII, 328, Ribbentrop to Kasche, 12 April 1941.

88. PP, Diary, 24 April 1943.

89. DGFP, D, XII, 385, Conversation between Ciano and Hitler, 22 April 1941.

90. PP, Diary, 24 April 1943.

91. DGFP, D, XII, 394, Unsigned memorandum, 24 April 1941.

92. DGFP, D, XII, 398, Schmidt memorandum, 24 April 1941.

93. Trifkovic, *Ustaša*, p. 125.

94. Trifkovic, *Ustaša*, p. 125; DGFP, D, XII, 605–06, Weizsäcker memorandum, 8 June 1941.

95. *The Ciano Diaries*, 25 April 1941.

96. PP, Diary, 8 May 1941.

97. *The Ciano Diaries*, 26 April 1941.

98. PP, Diary, 8 May 1941.

99. Luciano Monzali, "La questione della Dalmazia e la politica estera italiana nella primavera del 1941," *La rivista dalmatica* LXVIX (1998): 43.

100. PP, Diary, 8 May 1941.

101. Broucek, *Glaise von Horstenau*, p. 113.

102. PP, Pietromarchi, "Il problema della Dalmazia," pp. 20–21.
103. See, for example, the report of the General Director of the IRI, Donato Menichella, to Mussolini, in DDI, IX, VII, 131, 17 May 1941.
104. Stevan K. Pavlowitch, *Unconventional Perceptions of Yugoslavia 1940–1945* (New York: East European Monographs, 1985), p. 108.
105. Fatutta, *La campagna di Jugoslavia*, p. 35.
106. According to the German Ministry of Foreign Affairs: Of a population of 6,300,000, Croats, 3,385,000; Serbs, 3,300,000; Muslims, 1,925,000; Germans, 700,000; Hungarians, 150,000; Slovaks, 65,000; Jews, 40,000; Slovenes, 30,000; Italians, 5,000. Frank Philip Verna, "Yugoslavia Under Italian Rule 1941–1943: Civil and Military Aspects of the Italian Occupation" (Ph.D. diss., University of California, 1985), p. 77.
107. DDI, IX, VII, 117, Casertano to Ciano, 16 May 1941; Talpo, *Dalmazia: Una cronaca per la storia, (1941)*, pp. 323–24.
108. DGFP, D, XI, 385, Conversation Ciano and Ribbentrop, 22 April 1941.
109. Talpo, *Dalmazia: Una cronaca per la storia (1941)*, p. 202.
110. DDI, IX, VII, 923, Mussolini to Ciano, 17 April 1941.
111. DGFP, D, 378, Conversation between Ribbentrop and Ciano, 21 April 1941.
112. DGFP, D, XI, 385, Conversation Ciano and Ribbentrop, 22 April 1941; PP, Diary, 21 April 1941.
113. *The Ciano Diaries*, 21 May 1941.
114. *The Ciano Diaries*, 26 May 1941.
115. ASMAE, GABAP, b. 50, Report by Captain Dr. Ugo Villani to MAE.
116. PP, Diary, 8 July 1941.
117. PP, Diary, 8 July 1941.
118. PP, Diary, 8 May and 8 July 1941.
119. PP, Diary, 8 July 1941.
120. Perić referred to Muslim petitions begging annexation of their Sandžak homelands to Croatia. Pietromarchi retorted: "Democratic regimes avail themselves of this stuff [plebiscites and petitions]; but not in this Fascist century. Today responsibility for decisions lies with leaders." Afterward, Ciano "jokingly" remarked: "Do you believe that the Sandžak is your feudal state? We must give something to the Croats." But he too was getting impatient: "It is a question

of six million people, born less than two months ago, who wish to conduct imperialism at our expense." PP, Diary, 25 June 1941.

121. PP, Diary, 8 July 1941.

122. Giacomo Scotti & Luciano Viazzi, *Occupazione e guerra italiana in Montenegro: Le aquile delle montagne nere* (Milan: Mursia, 1987), p. 64.

123. DGFP, D, XII, 363, Ribbentrop to Mackensen, 17 April 1941.

124. *The Ciano Diaries*, 29 April 1941.

125. Ansaldo, *Il giornalista di Ciano*, p. 299.

126. The title of a fine recent study by Davide Rodogno, *Il nuovo ordine mediterraneo* (Turin: Bollati Boringhieri, 2003).

127. Matteo J. Milazzo, *The Chetnik Movement & The Yugoslav Resistance* (Baltimore and London: The Johns Hopkins University Press, 1975), p. 6.

128. Broucek, *Glaise von Horstenau*, II: 17.

129. Milazzo, *The Chetnik Movement*, p. 10.

130. Loi, *Le operazioni delle unità italiane in Jugoslavia*, p. 142; Carlo Falconi, *The Silence of Pius XII* (Boston: Little Brown, 1970), p. 274. Smilja Avramov, *Genocide in Yugoslavia* (Belgrade: BIGZ, 1995), 235, citing Italian estimates, gives the following figures: Croats: 4,800,000; Serbs, 1,850,000; Germans, 146,000; Magyars, 70,000; Slovenes, 37,000; Czechs, 45,000; Others, 35,000.

131. Aleksa Djilas, *The Contested Country: Yugoslav Unity and Communist Revolution 1919–1953* (Cambridge MA and London: Harvard University Press, 1991), pp. 110–14.

132. Jonathan Steinberg, "The Roman Catholic Church and Genocide in Croatia, 1941–1945," *Studies in Church History* 29 (1993): 469.

133. Jonathan Steinberg, "Types of Genocide? Croatians, Serbs, and Jews, 1941–1945," in *The Final Solution: Origins and Implementation*, ed. David Cesarani (London and New York: Routledge, 1996), p. 179.

134. Cited in Trifkovic, *Ustaša*, p. 141.

135. These figures are taken from Jonathan Steinberg, "Croatians, Serbs, and Jews," p. 175, and David Bruce MacDonald, *Balkan Holocausts? Serbian and Croatian Victim-Centered Propaganda and the War in Yugoslavia* (Manchester and New York: Manchester University Press, 2002), p. 162.

136. Broucek, *Glaise von Horstenau*, p. 98.

137. Tomasevich, *Occupation and Collaboration*, p. 400.

138. NAW, T-821, 248, 440–45, Report from Croatia, 19 May 1943.

139. S. Bianchini and F. Privitera, *6 aprile 1941: L'attaco italiano alla Jugoslavia* (Milan: Marzorati, 1993), p. 67.

140. A careful historian notes that "the Croatian militia were often egged on by local priests." Steinberg, "The Roman Catholic Church and Genocide in Croatia," p. 470.

141. Tomasevich, *Occupation and Collaboration*, p. 370.

142. Trifković, in his *Ustaša*, provides a comprehensive description of Ustaša atrocities.

143. Tomasevich, *Occupation and Collaboration*, pp. 533–34.

144. Marcus Tanner, *Croatia: A Nation Forced in War*, 2d ed. (New Haven and London: Yale University Press, 2001), pp. 148–49.

145. Tomasevich, *War and Revolution in Yugoslavia: Occupation and Collaboration*, p. 489.

146. ACS, Carte Morgagni, b. 68, Viaggio Zagreb, 16–20 maggio XIX. Report to Mussolini. I would like to thank Malte Koenig for bringing this file to my attention.

147. NAW, T-821, 127, 1025, Mussolini to Ambrosio, 23 April 1941.

148. Mario Dassovich, *Fronte Jugoslavo 1941–'42* (Udine: Del Bianco, 1999), pp. 15–16.

149. NAW, T-821, 128, 389-94, Ambrosio to the War Ministry, 23 April 1941, 226-29, Ambrosio to the War Ministry, 16 May 1941.

150. Talpo, *Dalmazia: Una cronaca per la storia (1941)*, p. 406.

151. Loi, *Le operazioni delle unità italiane in Jugoslavia*, p. 144.

152. Falcone, *The Silence of Pius XII*, p. 299.

153. Djilas, *The Contested Country*, p. 121.

154. NAW, T-821, 232, 05–06, Dalmazzo to the 2nd Army, 10 May 1941.

155. Talpo, *Dalmazia: Una cronaca per la storia (1941)*, D. 5, Monticelli to Dalmazzo, 16 June 1941, pp. 472–73.

156. Talpo, *Dalmazia: Una cronaca per la storia (1941)*, D. 6, Ambrosio to Casertano, 21 June 1941, pp. 474–76.

157. Talpo, *Dalmazia: Una cronaca per la storia (1941)*, D. 7, Bastianini to MAE, 24 June 1941, pp. 477–49.

158. The report of General Gian Carlo Re of 5 April 1941, cited in Dassovich, *Fronte Jugoslavo 1941–'42*, p. 44, n. 47. While the "official" Italian military historians Talpo and Loi can be criticized for rendering apologias for the conduct and accomplishments of the Italian armies in Yugoslavia, they present ample evidence to prove that the commanders and soldiers of the 2nd Army afforded help and shelter to persecuted Jews and Orthodox Serbs.

159. NAW, T-821, 53, 697–702, Dalmazzo to the 2nd Army, 17 January 1942.

160. Tim Judah, *The Serbs: History, Myth and the Destruction of Yugoslavia*, 2d ed. (New Haven and London: Yale University Press, 2000), p. 118.

161. Steven K. Pavlovitch, *Yugoslavia* (New York: Praeger, 1975), p. 144.

162. Nora Beloff, *Tito's Flawed Legacy: Yugoslavia & the West since 1939* (Boulder, Colorado: Westview Press, 1984), p. 68.

163. NAW T-821, 232, 20, VI Army Corps report, 15 May 1941.

164. *The Ciano Diaries*, 10 June 1941.

165. Cited in Talpo, *Dalmazia: Una cronaca per la storia (1941)*, p. 202.

166. ASMAE, GABAP, b. 28, Coselschi report, 4 June 1941, and 50, Coselschi report, 19 June 1941. In a German report, Coselschi, in a rousing speech delivered to an Ustaša audience, made no mention of the Serbs. NAW, T-501, 266, 363–364, Glaise report, 11 August 1941.

167. Gian Nicola Amoretti, *La vicenda italo-croata nei documenti di Aimone di Savoia (1941-1943)*, (Rapallo: Ypotesis, 1979), p. 93.

168. ASMAE, GABAP, b. 34, MI report, 22 July 1941.

169. To ease Bastianini's burden, Casertano suggested that Jews in Dalmatia be sent to camps in Italy. ASMAE, GABAP, Casertano to Pietromarchi, 1 August 1941.

170. DDI, IX, VII, 443, Casertano to Ciano, 1 August 1941.

171. Cited in Pawlovitch, *Unconventional Perceptions of Yugoslavia*, p. 117.

172. Cited in Tomasevich, *Occupation and Collaboration*, p. 241.

173. DDI, IX, VII, 247, Alfieri to Ciano, 12 June 1942.

174. DDI, IX, VII, 446, Host Venturi to Mussolini, 1 August 1941.

175. DDI, IX, VII, 446, Host Venturi to Mussolini, 1 August 1941

176. Antonello Biagini and Fernando Frattolillo, eds., DS (SME-US), DS, V, IV, Tomo II, Allegati, D. 71, Allegato 1, Ambrosio to SC, 8 August 1941.

177. DS, V, IV, Tomo II, Allegati. D. 71, Allegato1, Ambrosio to CS, 8 August 1941.

178. USSME, N I-II, b, 724, Ambrosio to SMRE, 11 June 1941.

179. AVII, b. 309, contains many Croatian memoranda containing complaints of Italian partiality toward Orthodox Serbs. See also Loi, *Le operazioni delle unità italiane in Jugoslavia*, p. 167.

180. DS, V, IV, Tomo II, D. 93, Ambrosio to SMRE, 12 August 1941.

181. NAW, T-821, 232, 332, VI Army Corps to 2nd Army, 20 July 1941, and 417-19, "Contacts with rebel elements," 4 August 1941.

182. A view expressed by a Slav historian, T. Covacev, cited in Dassovich, *Fronte Jugoslavo 1941–'42*, p. 25, n. 5.
183. Talpo, *Dalmazia: Una cronaca per la storia (1941)*, pp. 543–47.
184. Talpo, *Dalmazia: Una cronaca per la storia (1941)*, D. 8, Ciano to Casertano, 10 August 1941, p. 591.
185. Ortona, *Diplomazia di guerra*, p. 157.
186. Talpo, *Dalmazia: Una cronaca per la storia (1941)*, p. 518.
187. NAW, T-821, 474, 535, 2nd Army note on the occupation of the demilitarized zone, 30 August 1941; 398, 1013, 2nd Army report, 9 October 1941.
188. PP, Commissione Centrale di Epurazione, b 2.3, no.1.
189. DDI, IX, VII, 474, Casertano to Ciano, 13 August 1941.
190. DDI, IX, VII, 486, Casertano to Ciano, 16 August 1941.
191. Talpo, *Dalmazia: Una cronaca per la storia (1941)*, p. 518.
192. NAW, T-501, 267, The German general in Agram to OKW, 18 August 1941.
193. DGFP, D, XIII, 217, Ribbentrop to Kasche, 20 August 1941, n. 4.
194. DGFP, D, XIII, 219, Ribbentrop to Kasche, 21 August 1941.
195. ASMAE, GABAP, b. 32, Bastianini to Pietromarchi, 2 September 1941.
196. ASMAE, GABAP, b. 40, Ambrosio report, 15 August 1941, italics in the original.
197. Trifkovic, *Ustaša*, p. 152.
198. This becomes clear in a note he sent to General Dalmazzo. USSME, M-3, b. 59, Ambrosio to Dalmazzo, 26 December 1941.
199. AVII, b. 309, f. 4, NDH promemoria, 20 August 1941 and f. 5, NDH promemoria, 20 October 1941.
200. AVII, b. 309, f. 18, General Zupano memorandum, undated.
201. Zbornik, XIII,, bk. I, D. 328, Oxila report, 23 August 1941.
202. Talpo, *Dalmazia: Una cronaca per la storia (1941)*, p. 537.
203. The 2nd Army felt otherwise. Its Office of Political Affairs held that the occupation and transfer of Italian power took place without undue difficulties. "90% of the Orthodox population . . . had returned to their homes, invoking Italian protection and, in many instances, requesting annexation of the area to Italy." This document is cited in Verna, "Yugoslavia Under Italian Rule," pp. 395–98.
204. DS, V, IV, Tomo II, D. 20, Ambrosio to Army Chief of Staff, 7 October 1941.

205. USSME, N I-II, DS, b. 568, Report of Colonel Umberto Salvatores, the commander of the Italian garrison at Gračac, 6 September 1941.

206. ASMAE, GABAP, b. 41, Conversation between Pietromarchi and Pavelić in Zagreb, 25-27 October 1941.

207. Talpo, *Dalmazia: Una cronaca per la storia (1941)*, p. 888.

208. ASMAE, GABAP, b. 32, Unsigned note for the foreign minister, 30 September 1941; Zbornik, XIII, bk. I, D.154, Ambrosio to his commanders, 5 October 1941; Talpo, *Dalmazia: Una cronaca per la storia (1941)*, p. 890.

209. ASMAE, GABAP, b. 31, Note for the Foreign Minister, 7 October 1941; b. 33, Pietromarchi to Casertano, 8 October 1941.

210. Talpo, *Dalmazia: Una cronaca per la storia (1941)*, p. 892.

211. ASMAE, GABAP, b. 34, Pietromarchi to Bastianini, 10 October 1941.

212. ASMAE, GABAP, b. 34, Pietromarchi to Horst Venturi, 12 February 1942.

213. ASMAE, GABAP, b. 34, Pietromarchi to Alberto Calisse, 8 November 1941.

214. ASMAE, GABAP, b. 30, MFA unsigned memorandum, 30 September 1941 and AP, b. 31, Memorandum for the Foreign Minister, 7 October 1941.

215. Beloff, *Tito's Flawed Legacy*, p. 72.

216. Walter R. Roberts, *Tito, Mihailović and the Allies, 1941–1945* (New Brunswick, NJ: Rutgers University Press, 1973), pp. 33–34.

217. Cited in Judah, *The Serbs*, p. 119.

218. Interestingly, the Germans were not confident that Nedić was serving them as a loyal "Quisling." A high-level German report describes the situation: "The Nedić government organizes resistance openly within the framework of its administration but practices it covertly, while Mihailović organizes resistance clandestinely and practices it openly. Not to be trusted; neither his police forces. Quite wrong to place any reliance on the Nedić government." The 1942 Meyszner Report on Serbia. SS-Gruppenführer and Generalleutnant of Police, 29 August report, cited in *South Slav Journal* 5 (Autumn 1982): 43–46.

219. For a succinct study, see Christopher S. Browning, "The Wehrmacht in Serbia Revisited," in *Crimes of War: Guilt and Denial in the Twentieth Century*, eds. Omer Bartov, Atina Grossmann, and Mary Nolan (New York: The New Press, 2002), pp. 31–40.

220. Mark Wheeler, "Pariahs to Partisans to Power: The Communist Party of Yugoslavia," in *Politics of Retribution in Europe: World War II and its Aftermath*, ed. Tony Judt (Princeton, NJ: Princeton University Press, 2000), pp. 137–38.

221. Jovan Marjanović, *Collaboration of D. Mihailović's Chetniks with the Enemy Forces of Occupation 1941–1944* (Belgrade: Arhivski Pregled, 1976), D. 5, Minutes of talks between Mihailović and Ger. High Command in Serbia, 11 November 1941, pp. 20–28; Milazzo, *The Chetnik Movement*, pp. 37–38.

222. ASMAE, GABAP, 34, Bastianini to Pietromarchi, 7 Novembere 1941.

223. Talpo, *Dalmazia: Una cronaca per la storia (1941)*, pp. 895–97.

224. For a discussion of Partisan atrocities during the battle of Pljevlja, see Dassovich, *Fronte jugoslavo 1941–'42*, pp. 92–97.

225. Lucien Karchmar, "Draza Mihailović and the Rise of the Četnik Movement, 1941–1942" (Ph.D. diss., Stanford University, 1973), I: 480–81.

226. DDI, IX, VII, 746, Casertano to Ciano, 13 November 1941.

227. ASMAE, GABAP, b. 28, Inspector General Ciro Verdiani to MI, 14 November 1941.

228. ASMAE, GABAP, b. 32, Mussolini to Ambrosio, 2 November 1941.

229. Talpo, *Dalmazia: Una cronaca per la storia (1941)*, p. 913.

230. DDI, IX, VII, 699, Pietromarchi to Ciano, 30 October 1941.

231. ASMAE, GABAP, b. 32, Conversation between Pietromarchi and General De Blasio, 15 November 1941.

232. PP, L.2, Italo-Croatian Permanent Economic Commission Report.

233. ASMAE, GABAP, b. 32, Pietromarchi to Bastianini, 29 November 1941.

234. ASMAE, GABAP, b. 33, Conversation between Pietromarchi and Ambrosio, 12 December 1941.

235. NAW, T-821, 356, 540–44, Ambrosio to SME, 2 January 1942.

236. DDI, IX, VIII, 26, Conversation between Ciano and Pavelić, 15 December 1941, Annex: Meeting between the Italian and Croatian delegates.

237. Emphasis mine.

238. *The Ciano Diaries*, 15 December 1941.

239. *The Ciano Diaries*, 15 December 1941.

240. Amoretti, *La vicenda italo-croata*, pp. 45–46.

241. NAW, T-821, 53, 697–702, Dalmazzo to 2nd Army, 17 January 1942; 64, 1305–08, Dalmazzo to Ambrosio, 22 December 1941, 64, 1123, Ambrosio to the Army General Staff, 22 December 1941.

242. USSME, M-3, b. 59, Mussolini's meeting with Ciano, Roatta, Ambrosio, Casertano, and General Magli, 18 December 1941.

243. DDI, IX, VIII, 40, Ambrosio to Cavallero, 18 December 1941.

244. *The Ciano Diaries*, 17 December 1941.

245. PP, Diary, 3 January 1942.

246. *The Ciano Diaries*, 29 December 1941.

247. PP, Diary, 5 January 1942.

248. DDI, IX, VIII, 81, Pietromarchi to Casertano, 29 December 1941.

249. NAW, T-821, 64, 993–1002, Meeting of Italian generals, 30 December 1941.

250. NAW, T-501, 264, 515–17, Glaise to OKW, 26 January 1942.

251. DDI, IX, VIII, 195, Ambrosio to Cavallero, 23 January 1942.

252. DS, V. VI, Tomo II, D. 12, Ambrosio to Mussolini 21 February 1942.

253. ASMAE, GAPAB, b. 51, Mazzolini to MAE, 5 May 1941.

254. ASMAE, GABAP, b. 53, MAE to Paolo Thaon di Revel of the Finance Ministry, 1 July 1941.

255. ASMAE, GABAP, b. 54, Ciano to Minister of Finances and War, 26 June 1941.

256. Milovan Djilas, *Memoir of a Revolutionary* (New York: Harcourt, Brace, and Jovanovich, 1973), p. 385.

257. DDI, IX, VII, 375, Mazzolini to Pietromarchi, 11 July 1941.

258. Verna, "Yugoslavia Under Italian Rule," p. 198.

259. Zbornik, III, bk 4, D. 149, Pirzio Biroli memorandum, 15 July 1941.

260. Cavallero, *Diario*, 17 July 1941.

261. The Ciano Diaries, 17 July 1941.

262. Scotti and Viazzi, *Occupazione e guerra italiana in Montenegro*, p. 131.

263. Zbornik, III, bk. 4, D. 152, Pedrazzali to his troops, 21 July 1941.

264. NAW, T-821, 356, 717–21, Pirzio Biroli to CS, 15 July 1941.

265. USSME, N I-II, b. 374, Mentasti directives of 5 and 14 August 1941.

266. Zbornik, III, bk. 4, D. 166, Pirzio Biroli memorandum on reprisals, 8 August 1941; Verna, "Yugoslavia Under Italian Rule," p. 212; Scotti and Viazzi, *Occupazione e guerra italiana in Montenegro*, pp. 236–37.

267. Pavlowitch, *Yugoslavia*, p. 122.

268. Milovan Djilas, *Wartime* (New York: Harcourt, Brace, and Jovanovich, 1973), pp. 8, 23–24, 37, 81; Richard West, *Tito and the Rise and Fall of Yugoslavia* (New York: Carroll and Graf, 1996), pp. 108–09.

269. Beloff, *Tito's Flawed Legacy*, p. 68.

270. Dassovich, *Fronte Yugoslavo 1941–'42*, pp. 32–33. Djilas denies that he stood to the left of Tito and that he was primarily responsible for the ferocious Partisan reprisals. It was, in his view, a rumor started by Četniks and perpetrated by Edvard Kardelj. See his *Wartime*, p. 83.

271. NAW, T-821, 356, 652–62, Pirzio Biroli to CS, 2 August 1941, Annotation: "Seen by the Duce."

272. NAW, T-821, 356, 652–62, Pirzio Biroli to CS, 2 August 1942. Annotation: "Seen by the Duce."

273. NAW, T-821, 356, 652–62, Pirzio Biroli to CS, 2 August 1942. Annotation: "Seen by the Duce."

274. Admitted by Mazzolini. See his report of 22 July in ASMAE, GABAP, b. 54, 22 July 1941.

275. ASMAE, GABAP, b. 52, Pietromarchi to War Ministry, 29 July 1941.

276. Carlo Spartaco Capogreco, "Una storia rimossa dell'Italia fascista: L'internamento dei civili jugoslavi (1941–1943)," *Studi storici* (January-March 2001): 227; Scotti and Viazzi, *Occupazione e guerra italiana in Montenegro*, pp. 215.

277. Stephen Clissold, *Whirlwind: An Account of Marshal Tito's Rise to Power* (London: Cresset Press, 1949), p. 80.

278. Gino Bambara, *Jugoslavia settebandiere: Guerra senza retrovie nella Jugoslavia occupata (1941-1943)*, (Brescia: Vannini, 1988), p. 102. Fatutta states that Italy suffered a total of 4,000 casualties, a third of the occupying force, in dead, wounded, and dispersed. Fattuta, *La campagna di Yugoslavia*, p. 61.

279. NAW, T-821, 356, 664–78, Pirzio Biroli report, 12 August 1942, 750–53, Pirzio Biroli report, 1 December 1941; DDI, IX, VIII, 796, Pirzio Biroli to Ciano, 1 December 1941.

280. NAW, T-821, 356, 664–78, Pirzio Biroli report, 12 August 1942.

281. NAW, T-821, 356, 664–78, Pirzio Biroli report, 12 August 1942.

282. DS, V, Tomo II, D. 19, Pirzio Biroli to SME, 18 October 1941.

283. ASMAE, GABAP, b. 49, Report by the Commissioner of Civil Affairs Rulli to MAE, 18 October 1941.

284. The proclamation of 31 October is reproduced in NAW, T-821, 356, 829.

285. USSME, N 1-11, DS, b. 463, Pirzio Biroli to Office of Civilian Affairs, 6 November 1941.

286. Verna, "Yugoslavia Under Italian Rule," p. 220.

287. USSME, N I-II, DS, b. 463, Pirzio Biroli memorandum, 13 October 1941.

288. Davide Rodogno, "La repressione nei territori occupati dall'Italia fascista tra il 1940 ed il 1943," in *L'Italia fascista potenza occupante*, p. 51.

289. NAW, T-821, 356, 814–19, Rulli to Ciano, 10 December 1941.

290. Scotti and Viazzi, *Occupazione e guerra italiana in Montenegro*, p. 328.

291. Cited in Scotti and Viazzi, *Occupazione e guerra italiana in Montenegro*, p. 328.

292. Cited in Scotti and Viazzi, *Occupazione e guerra italiana in Montenegro*, p. 348.

293. NAW, T-821, 356, 756, Unsigned memorandum for the Duce, from Zara, 28 November 1941. One can deduce that the author was Bastianini, since the memo was written on a typewriter he commonly used, was sent from his headquarters in Zara, and was posted directly to the Duce, with whom he was on intimate terms.

294. For Pirzio Biroli's reports, see the following: NAW, T-821, 356, 820–28, 837–39, 2 December 1941.

295. DDI, IX, VIII, 805, Ciano to Pirzio Biroli, 2 December 1941; NAW, T-821, 356, 754, Cavallero to Pirzio Biroli, 3 December 1941.

296. NAW, T-821, 356, 754, Cavallero to Pirzio Biroli, 3 December 1941.

297. Scotti and Viazzi, *Occupazione e guerra italiana in Montenegro*, p. 183.

298. Zbornik, III, bk. 4, D. 205, Pirzio Biroli proclamation, April 1942. The first part of the proclamation carrying the April date is reproduced in its original Italian. Giacomo Scotti and Luciano Viazzi, *L'inutile vittoria: La tragica esperienza delle truppe italiane in Montenegro* (Milan: Mursia, 1989), pp. 153–54, cite this proclamation but date it January 1942.

299. Capogreco, "Una storia rimossa dell'Italia fascista," p. 229; Scotti and Viazzi, *L'inutile vittoria*, p. 114. This ratio was later reduced to 1:1 and 1:2. Talpo, *Dalmazia: Una cronaca per la storia (1942)*, p. 1187.

300. PP, Diary, 6 January 1942.

301. The sobriquet earned by Pirzio Biroli during his command in Ethiopia.

302. These figures are drawn from Tone Ferenc, *La provincia 'italiana' di Lubiana: Documenti 1941–1942* (Udine: Istituto friulano per la storia del movimento di liberazione, 1994), pp. 71–85.

303. He wrote: "It was an error on Italy's part to have "annexed" the regions of Yugoslavia assigned to it and yet worse to have introduced immediately Italian civil administration and fascist institutions." Roatta, *Otto milioni di baionette*, pp. 166–67.

304. NAW, T-821, 128, 343–48, Ambrosio report, 25 April 1941.

305. Tone Ferenc has published minutes of the fourteen member council under Grazioli's chairmanship in his *"Gospod Visoki Komisar Pravi..." Sosvet za Ljubljansko Pokrajino [Consulta per la Provincia di Lubiana] Documenti* (Ljubljana: CIP, 2001).

306. Karchmar, "Draža Mihailović and the Rise of the Četnik Movement," I: 46–47.

307. Mario Cuzzi, *L'occupazione italiana della Slovenia (1941–1943), (*Rome: SME-US, 1998), pp. 63–74. Cuzzi carefully analyzes the ideological origins and political and social nature of the Slovene collaborators.

308. Cuzzi, *L'occupazione italiana della Slovenia*, pp. 73–86.

309. Michele Rallo, in his *L'epoca delle rivoluzioni nazionali in Europa*, 2 vols. *(1919–1945)* (Rome: Settimo Sigillo, 1989), II: 65, makes a distinction between Grazioli's Italianization program and the harsher German denationalization efforts.

310. Carlo Spartaco Capogreco, *Renicci. Un campo di concentramento in riva al Tevere (1942–43)* (Cosenza: Fondazione Ferramonti, 1998), pp. 19–20.

311. These figures are drawn from Rodogno, *Il nuovo ordine mediterraneo*, p. 157.

312. Ferenc, *La provincia 'italiana' di Lubiana*, D. 30, Grazioli to SP and XI Army Corps, 28 October 1941, pp. 195–198.

313. DS, V, Tomo II, D. 30, Ambrosio to SME, 15 October 1941.

314. Cuzzi, *L'occupazione italiana della Slovenia*, pp. 44–45.

315. Cuzzi, *L'occupazione italiana della Slovenia*, pp. 49–50.

316. Tone Ferenc, "Le système d'occupation des nazis en Slovénie," in *Les systèmes d'occupation en Yougoslavie 1941–1945* (Belgrade: Karlovy Vary, 1963).

317. Ferenc, *La provincia 'italiana' di Lubiana*, D. 36, Memorandum drafted by General Taddeo Orlando and edited by Robotti forwarded to 2nd Army, End of November 1941, pp. 227–41.

318. Ferenc, *La provincia 'italiana' di Lubiana*, D. 25, Robotti to field commanders, 5 October 1941, pp. 185–87; NAW, T-821, 271, 624–34, Robotti notes for a meeting with the High Commissioner, 7 November 1941.

319. This attitude was typical of the XI Army Corps. For example: "Every-one must be considered our enemy." NAW, T-821, 271, 443–50, Subjects to be dealt with by army command, 30 January 1942.

320. Tomasevich, *Occupation and Collaboration*, p. 103.

321. USSME, N I-II, DS, b. 1374, Ambrosio to SMRE, 7 January 1942.

322. ACS, PCM, p.1.1.13, f. 36146, Mussolini's proclamation 19 January 1942; NAW, T-821, 505, 271, Mussolini to 2nd Army, 21 January 1942; Tone Ferenc, *"Si ammazza troppo poco": Condannati a morte—ostaggi—passati per le armi nella provincia di Lubiana 1941–1943* (Ljubljana: Istituto per la storia moderna, 1999), p. 16. At the end of December 1941, Mussolini had already become frustrated by Grazioli's refusal to accept the military's broad definition of "the guilty ones." NAW, T-821, 64, 993–1002, Meeting of the Italian generals, 30 December 1941.

323. Apparently, however, Mussolini's edicts got entangled in red tape or were subverted by Grazioli's clever evasions, for the Minister of Interior Guido Buffarini-Guidi in May 1942 saw fit to remind Grazioli to make the public security forces available to Robotti's command. Dassovich, *Fronte Jugoslavo 1941–'42*, pp. 165–66.

324. Ferenc, *"Si ammazza troppo poco,"* p. 15, which contains a printed copy of Roatta's communication to Robotti of 3 February 1942.

325. Text of the proclamations can be found in Ferenc, *"Si ammazza troppo poco,"* D. 18, pp. 110–11, and D. 29, p. 117. See also Cuzzi, *L'occupazione italiana della Slovenia*, pp. 198–99, and Bambara, *Jugoslavia settebandiere*, pp. 52–54.

326. Ferenc, *Rab–Arbe–Arbissima: Konfinacije, Racije in Internacije v Lubljanski Pokrajini 1941–1943* (Ljubljana, CIP, 2000), D. 62, Robotti report, undated, pp. 83–88. Ferenc claims that 18,708 men were taken in for questioning and 878 sent to concentration camps during this roundup. Ferenc, *La provincia "italiana' di Lubiana*, p. 339, n. 3.

327. Ferenc, *Rab–Arbe–Arbissima*, D. 92, Grazioli to SPD and MI, 25 March 1942, p. 110.

328. Ferenc, *Rab–Arbe–Arbissima*, D. 55, Roatta to XI Army Corps, 14 March 1942, pp. 78-80, D. 59, Roatta to XI Army Corps, 15 March 1942, p. 82.

329. NAW, T-821, 271, 304–07, Conversation between Grazioli and Robotti, 30 April 1942.

330. *The Ciano Diaries*, 18 May 1942.

331. NAW, T.821, 271, 111–16, Conversation between Grazioli and Robotti, 17 September 1942.

332. NAW, T-821, 271, 701–04, Robotti to Ambrosio and Grazioli, 31 October 1941; Capogreco, "Una storia rimossa dell'Italia fascista," p. 214.

333. NAW, T-821, 271, 183–89, Conversation between Robotti and Grazioli, 14 June 1942; Ferenc, *Rab–Arbe–Arbissima*, D. 136, Robotti to field commanders, 27 May 1942, D. 175, Orlando to XI Army Corps, 25 June 1942, p. 173; Cuzzi, *L'occupazione italiana della Slovenia*, pp. 210–11.

334. Ferenc, *Rab–Arbe–Arbissima*, D. 139, Commissario Rosin to Grazioli, 28 May 1942, p. 139.

335. Capogreco, "Una storia rimossa dell'Italia fascista," p. 216.

336. Giuseppe Piemontese, *Twenty-Four Months of Italian Occupation of the Province of Ljubljana* (Ljubljana: S.C., 1946), p. 54.

337. Ferenc, *Rab–Arbe–Arbissima*, D. 192, Orlando report of the *rastrellamento* of Ljubljana (27 June–1 July), 4 July 1942, pp. 184–86.

338. Ferenc, *Rab–Arbe–Arbissima*, D. 265, Prefect Marcello Tullarigo, inspector for war services, to MI, 12 August 1942, pp. 233–35.

339. Cuzzi, *L'occupazione italiana della Slovenia*, pp. 198–99.

340. Ferenc, *Rab–Arbe–Arbissima*, D.177, Grazioli to SPD and MI, 25 June 1942, p. 175; D. 216, Grazioli to SPD and MI, 16 July 1942, p. 175.

341. These reports are scattered throughout Ferenc's book *Rab–Arbe–Arbissima*.

342. This practice was graphically described by the Carabinieri officer G. De Filippis in his report to his superior attached to the XI Army Corps Command. Ferenc, *Rab–Arbe–Arbissima*, D. 181, De Filippis to the CC.RR of XI Army Corps, 26 June 1942, p. 177, D. 226, De Filippis to the CC.RR of XI Army Corps, 20 June 1942, pp. 206–27.

343. Ferenc, *"Si ammazza troppo poco,"* D. 22, Commissario Rosin to Gazioli, 30 July 1942, pp. 153–57.

344. Ferenc, *La provincia 'italiana' di Lubiana*, D. 73, Robotti to Supersloda, 12 May 1942, pp 397–400.

345. Wheeler, "The Communist Party of Yugoslavia," p. 139.

346. Joze Pirjevec, *Il giorno di San Vito: Jugoslavia 1918–1992 Storia di una tragedia* (Turin: Nuova Eri, 1998), pp. 162, 169.

347. NAW, T-821, 61, 787–92, Robotti to Roatta, 12 June 1942.

348. NAW, T-821, 271, 491–99, Notes taken by XI Corps Commander, 8 January 1942.

349. Cuzzi, *L'occupazione italiana della Slovenia*, p. 240.

350. B.C. Novak, *Trieste 1941–1954: The Ethnic, Political and Ideological Struggle* (Chicago: Chicago University Press, 1970), *passim*.

351. Ferenc, *La provincia 'italiana' di Lubiana*, D. 91, Meeting of Mussolini, Cavallero, Ambrosio, Robotti, Coturri, Piccini, and De Blasio, 31 July 1942, pp. 478–83.

352. NAW, T-821, 62, 708–10, Robotti-chaired meeting, 12 July 1942.

353. Cuzzi, *L'occupazione italiana della Slovenia*, pp. 78–86.

354. Cuzzi, *L'occupazione italiana della Slovenia*, p. 83.

355. Cuzzi, *L'occupazione italiana della Slovenia*, pp. 87–91.

356. NAW, T-821, 271, 304–07, Conversation between Grazioli and Robotti, 30 April 1942.

357. NAW, T-821, 61, 787–92, Robotti to Roatta, 12 June 1942.

358. Ferenc, *La provincia 'italiana' di Lubiana*, D. 100, Conversation between Grazioli and Robotti, 20 September 1942, p. 512, n. 4.

359. Rodogno, *Il nuovo ordine mediterraneo*, p. 370.

360. NAW, T-821, 252, 306–07, Roatta to CS, 12 September 1942, 315–17, Rožman memorandum to Robotti, and Robotti's comments, 12 September 1942.

361. Cuzzi, "I Balcani, problemi di un'occupazione difficile," p. 349.

362. NAW, T-821, 271, 257–59, copy of an oral communication made by the 2nd Army in a meeting at Fiume, 23 May 1942.

363. Ferenc, *Rab–Arbe–Arbissima*, D. 133, Extract of a communication made by Roatta in a meeting at Fiume, 23 May 1942, p. 134.

364. Cuzzi, *L'occupazione italiana della Slovenia*, p. 201.

365. Cited in Tone Ferenc, "Gli italiani in Slovenia 1941–1943," in *L'Italia in guerra 1940–1943*, eds. Bruna Micheletti and Pier Paolo Poggio (Brescia: Annali della Fondazione "Luigi Micheletti," (1990–91), p. 162; T-821, 62, 353–65, Roatta memorandum, 8 June 1942.

366. PP, Diary, 12 July 1942.

367. NAW, T-821, 60, 1083-86, Robotti to Roatta, 25 May 1942.

368. NAW, T-821, 271, 322–27, Subjects for the attention of General Robotti, 12 April 1942.

369. NAW, T-821, 271, 798–99, Robotti to field commanders, 23 July 1942.

370. NAW, T-821, 218, 1001, Robotti memorandum, 18 July 1942.

371. NAW, T-821, 62, 557, Grazioli and Robotti proclamation to the Slovene people, 15 July 1942.

372. NAW, T-821, 218, 662, Roatta memorandum, 13 August 1942.
373. NAW, T-821, 498, 1038, Grazioli and Robotti Proclamation, 17 September 1942.
374. PP, Diary, 24 July 1942.
375. Ugo Cavallero, *Diario 1940–1943* (Ciarrapico, 1984), 31 July 1942; Ferenc, *La provincia 'italiana' di Lubiana*, D. 91, Meeting between Mussolini and his generals at Gorizia, 31 July 1942, pp. 478–83.
376. "Be careful of the Slovenian throng of Catholics and 'white guards' who don't amount to anything. Their contribution must be considered as a concession that we make to them, not a concession that they make to us." Cited in Ferenc, *La provincia 'italiana' di Lubiana*, D. 92, IX Army Corps report of meeting at Kočevje, 2 August 1942, pp. 484–87.
377. Cavallero, *Diario*, 31 July 1942.
378. Ferenc, *La provincia 'italiana' di Lubiana*, D. 91, Meeting between Mussolini and his generals at Gorizia, 31 July 1942, p. 483, n.11.
379. Ferenc, *La provincia 'italiana' di Lubiana*, D. 92, Record of the meeting held by the commander of the XI Army Corps at Kočevje, 2 August 1942, pp. 484–87
380. Francesco Fatutta, "Cronache di guerriglia in Iugoslavia," Part 3: in *Studi storico-militari 1994* (Rome: SME, 1996), p. 754; Fatutta, *La campagna Jugoslava*, p. 110.
381. Ferenc, *La provincia 'italiana' di Lubiana*, D. 94, Grazioli to SPD and MI, 16 August 1942, pp. 491–93.
382. Cuzzi, *L'occupazione italiana della Slovenia*, pp. 228–29.
383. Ferenc, "Gli italiani in Slovenia," p. 163; Ferenc, "La provincia 'Italiana' di Lubiana, p. 117.
384. Cited in Sala, "1939–1943. Jugoslavia 'neutrale' e Jugoslavia occupata," p. 100. Ferenc uses the phrase as the title of his book, *Si ammazza troppo poco*.
385. Ferenc, *"Si ammazza troppo poco,"* D. 35, Robotti to Grazioli, 25 May 1942, p. 122, and D. 36, Robotti to Grazioli, 25 May 1942, p. 123.
386. Robotti revealed these fears in a private letter to General De Blasio. NAW, T-821, 271, 724–26, 20 December 1941.
387. Ferenc, *La provincia 'italiana' di Lubiana*, D. 105, Robotti to Grazioli, 3 December 1942, pp. 530–32.
388. Talpo, *Dalmazia: Una cronaca per la storia (1941)*, D. 11, Giorgio Suppiej to the secretary of the Fascist party, 1 May 1941, p. 276.

389. Cited in Frank P. Verna, "Notes on Italian Rule in Dalmatia under Bastianini, 1941–1943," *International History Review* XII, no. 3 (August 1990): 532.

390. Dragovan Sepić, "La politique italienne d'occupation en Dalmatie 1941–1943, in *Les systèmes d'occupation en Yougoslavie 1941–1945* (Belgrade: L'institute pour l'étude du mouvement ouvrier, 1963), p. 388.

391. Cited in Verna, "Yugoslavia Under Italian Rule," p. 353.

392. NAW, T-821, 128, 355, Giustiniani to MAE, 3 May 1941.

393. ACS, PCM, p.1.1.13, f.16452, sf. 40, Bastianini to PCM, 17 November 1941.

394. Sepić, "La politique italienne d'occupation en Dalmatie 1941–1943," pp. 405-06; Capogreco, "Una storia rimossa dell'Italia fascista," p. 222.

395. ACS, PCM, p. 1.1.13, f. 16452, sf. 45, Bastianini to Russo, 5 September 1941.

396. ACS, PCM, p. 1.1.13, f. 16452, sf. 45, Ministry of Education to Bastianini, 7 October 1941.

397. Verna, "Yugoslavia Under Italian Rule," pp. 340–42.

398. Talpo, *Dalmazia: Una cronaca per la storia (1941)*, p. 506; ASMAE, GABAP, 28, Pietromarchi to Bastianini, 31 July 1941.

399. Cited in Jonathan Steinberg, *All or Nothing: The Axis and the Holocaust 1941-1943* (London and New York: Routledge, 1991), p. 31.

400. ACS, PCM, p.1.1.13, f.16452, sf. 31, Bastianini to Mussolini, 26 July 1941.

401. Talpo, *Dalmazia: Una cronaca per la storia (1941)*, D. 8, Ciano to Casertano, p. 591.

402. Egidio Ortona, *Diplomazia di guerra: Diari 1937–1943* (Bologna: Mulino, 1993), p. 157.

403. Verna, "Notes on Italian Rule in Dalmatia," p. 535.

404. ASMAE, GABAP, b. 50, Bastianini report, 30 November 1941.

405. ACS, PCM, p. 1.1.13, f. 16452, sf. 74, Bastianini to Mussolini, 16 November 1941.

406. Talpo, *Dalmazia: Una cronaca per la storia (1941)*, D. 2, Bastianini to PCM and MI, 28 October 1941, pp. 845–47.

407. Verna, "Notes on Italian Rule in Dalmatia," p. 538.

408. ACS, PCM, p. 1.1.13, f. 16452, sf. 72, Bastianini to PCM, 17 November 1941.

409. ACS, PCM, p. 1.1.13, f. 16452, sf. 72, Bastianini to PCM, 28 October 1941.

410. ACS, PCM, p.1.1.13, f. 36146, 19 January 1942.
411. Talpo, *Dalmazia: Una cronaca per la storia (1942)*, 2nd ed. (Rome: SME-US, 2000), pp. 223–27. Mussolini's purpose, however, was not to rob Bastianini of power or downgrade Dalmatia's civil status but to solve a thorny problem. Families of soldiers killed in the annexed regions received a normal pension—death by reason of service—whereas those families of soldiers fallen in the occupied areas obtained the much higher war pension. By declaring both occupied and annexed areas "zones of operation," the families of all fallen soldiers would qualify for war pensions. But Mussolini's efforts to do military justice caused no end of jurisdictional confusion in the annexed province of Dalmatia. Cuzzi, "I Balcani, problemi di un'occupazione difficile," p. 352.
412. PP, Diary, 23 January 1942.
413. ACS, PCM, p.1.1.13, f. 57412, 24 January 1942.
414. NAW, T-821, 55, 966–68, Armellini to Roatta, 29 March 1942.
415. ACS, PCM, p. 1.1.13, f. 16452, sf. 74, Bastianini to Mussolini, 9 July 1942.
416. NAW, T-821, 51, 251-53, Armellini to De Blasio, 9 March 1942; 232–33, Armellini to Roatta, 3 May 1942; 224–25, Armellini to Roatta, 8 May 1942.
417. NAW, T-821, 410, 31–32, Bastianini to Roatta, 31 March 1942.
418. Talpo, *Dalmazia: Una cronaca per la storia (1942)*, p. 237.
419. ACS, PCM, p. 1.1.13, f. 16452, sf. 74, Bastianini memorandum for Mussolini, 31 May 1942; NAW, T-821, 51, 1034, Note for the Duce, unsigned, 31 May 1942.
420. NAW, T-821, 51, 218–23, Bastianini to Roatta, 19 April 1942.
421. Talpo, *Dalmazia: Una cronaca per la storia (1942)*, p. 237.
422. NAW, T-821, 64, 367–69, Memorandum on the annexed territories, 31 July 1942.
423. Dassovich, *Fronte jugoslavo 1941–'42*, p. 171.
424. ACS, PCM, p. 1.1.13, f. 16452, sf. 74, Bastianini memorandum for Mussolini, 1 June 1942.
425. ACS, PCM, p. 1.1.13, f. 16452, sf. 74, Bastianini to Mussolini, 21 June 1942; Talpo, *Dalmazia: Una cronaca per la storia (1942)*, p. 247.
426. Cuzzi, "I Balcani, problemi di un'occupazione difficile," p. 353.
427. ACS, PCM, p. 1.1.13, f. 16452, sf. 74, Bastianini to Mussolini, 29 June 1942.

428. ACS, PCM, p. 1.1.13, f. 16452, sf. 74, Bastianini to Mussolini, 9 July 1942.

429. NAW, T-821, 64, 416, Military promemoria, 13 July 1942.

430. NAW, T-821, 64, 423–30, Bastianini to the public security forces, 12 July 1942.

431. NAW, T-821, 64, 942–43, Armellini to Roatta, 6 July 1942.

432. NAW, T-821, 64, 330, Armellini to Roatta, 14 June 1942.

433. NAW, T-821, 63, 972–73, Armellini to Supersloda, 30 June 1942.

434. NAW, T-821, 63, 975, Armellini to Roatta, 14 June 1942.

435. NAW, T-821, 64, 325–31, Armellini to Supersloda, 17 June 1942, 953–56, Armellini to Roatta, 2 July 1942.

436. NAW, T-821, 64, 306–12, Bastianini to prefects and police units, 23 June 1942.

437. NAW, T-821, 64, 477–79, Armellini to Bastianini, 19 July 1942.

438. NAW, T-821, 64, 300, Armellini to Supersloda, 22 June 1942.

439. NAW, T-821, 64, 907–08, Armellini to Supersloda, 21 June 1942; Talpo, *Dalmazia: Una cronaca per la storia (1942)*, pp. 253–56.

440. Talpo, *Dalmazia: Una cronaca per la storia (1942)*, D. 6, Armellini to Roatta, 29 May 1942, pp. 332–36.

441. NAW, T-821, 64, 395–98, Armellini to Supersloda, 18 July 1942.

442. NAW, T-821, 64, 77–79, Armellini to Bastianini, 19 July 1942, 953–56, Armellini to Roatta, 2 July 1942.

443. Talpo, *Dalmazia: Una cronaca per la storia (1942)*, D. 6, Armellini to Roatta, 29 May 1942, pp. 332–36.

444. Talpo, *Dalmazia: Una cronaca per la storia (1942)*, D. 13, Bastianini to Mussolini, 10 July 1942, pp. 351–54.

445. ACS, PCM, p.1.1.13, f.16452, sf.120, Bastianini to Armellini, 15 July 1942; Talpo, *Dalmazia: Una cronaca per la storia (1942)*, pp. 270–71.

446. NAW, T-821, 64, 405, Bastianini to Roatta, 15 July 1942.

447. Ortona, *Diplomazia di guerra*, pp. 170–71.

448. ACS, PCM, p.1.1.13, f.16452, sf. 120, Bastianini to Russo, 16 July 1942.

449. NAW, T-821, 64, 967, Questione Eccellenza Bastianini, 25 June 1942.

450. Giacomo Zanussi, *Guerra e catastrofe d'Italia: Giugno 1940–giugno 1943*, 2 vols. (Rome: Corso, 1945), I: 287.

451. NAW, T-821 64, 305, CS to Roatta, 25 July 1942.

452. NAW, T-821, 64, 385, General Magli to the CS for General Robotti, 25 July 1942.

453. Zanussi, *Guerra e catastrofe d'Italia*, I: 248.

454. Talpo, *Dalmazia: Una cronaca per la storia (1942)*, p. 278.

455. Zbornik, XIII, bk. 2, D. 80, Roatta memorandum on the situation in Dalmatia, 23 July 1942.

456. Cavallero, *Diario*, 1 August 1942.

457. Rodogno, *Il nuovo ordine mediterraneo*, p. 327.

458. NAW, T-821, 64, 579-82, Bastianini to SPD and MI, 11 October 1942; Talpo, *Dalmazia: Una cronaca per la storia (1942)*, pp. 635–38. The Inspector General of Public Safety, Ciro Verdiani, submitted a long report to the Minister of Interior describing the deteriorating economy and lack of respect for Italian authority on the part of the native Croats produced by Communist agitation and violence. Verna, "Yugoslavia Under Italian Occupation," pp. 411–14.

459. NAW, T-821, 64, 583–86, Roatta's annotation of a letter of the governor of Dalmatia dated 11 October 1942.

460. NAW, T-821, 498, 1091, Roatta to Bastianini, 21 August 1942.

461. Ortona, *Diplomazia di guerra*, 10 October 1942.

462. Talpo, *Dalmazia: Una cronaca per la storia (1942)*, p. 997. Talpo obtained this report of Bastianini from the British archives.

463. Rodogno holds that Mussolini intended to utilize Bastianini's "totalitarian" denationalization program as a model to graft onto Italy at the end of a victorious war.

464. Zbornik, XIII, bk. 2, D. 80, Roatta memorandum, 23 July 1942.

465. Paul Hehn, *The Struggle Against Yugoslav Guerrillas in World War II* (Boulder, CO: Eastern European Monographs, 1980), p. 101.

466. *The Ciano Diaries*, 6 January 1942.

467. For a discussion on this point from the inside, see Zanussi, *Guerra e catastrofe d'Italia*, I: 241–43.

468. USSME, M-3, b. 75, Ambrosio to corps commanders, 6 January 1942.

469. Giacomo Scotti, in his *Buono Taliano: Gli Italiani in Yugoslavia 1941– 1943* (Milan: La Pietra, 1977), cites many examples of the effectiveness of Communist propaganda in weakening the will of the Italian soldier which, according to him, in many instances caused desertions.

470. In general, I hesitate to cite figures from either Italian or Yugoslav sources on Italians, Partisans, or Yugoslav citizens killed, wounded, or "dispersed" under Italy's occupation thanks to bias and the inherent difficulty in tabulating accurate figures of war casualties and desertions in guerrilla campaigns.

471. A copy of the 3C Memorandum, a small booklet, can be found in AVII, b. 93, f. 1. It is reproduced in Massimo Legnani, "Il 'ginger' del generale Roatta: Le direttive della 2nd armata sulla repressione antipartigiana in Slovenia e Croazia in *Italia contemporana*," 209–10 (December 1997–March1998): 159–74.

472. Bianchini and Privitera, *6 aprile 1941*, p. 72.

473. NAW, T-821, 395, 71, Ambrosio to the XI Army command, 26 September 1941.

474. T. Sala, "Guerriglia e controguerriglia in Jugoslavia nella propaganda per le truppe occupanti italiane (1941–1943), *Il Movimento di liberazione in Italia* XXIX, no. 108 (1972): 91–114, and Enzo Collotti, *L'Europa nazista: Il progetto di un nuovo ordine europeo (1939-1945)* (Florence: Giunti, 2002), p. 266.

475. Ferenc, *"Si ammazza troppo poco,"* D. 2, Ambrosio to V Army Corps, 23 October 1941, p. 139.

476. AVII, b. 93, f. 1, Roatta's 3C Circular, 1 March 1942.

477. USSME, N I-II, b. 724, Roatta to the Governor of Dalmatia, the High Commissioner of Ljubljana and the Prefect of Carnaro, 5 March 1942.

478. NAW, T-821, 218, 152–57; 410, 1040–47, Roatta memorandum and appendix "A" to 3C circular, 7 April 1942.

479. Ferenc, *"Si ammazza troppo poco,"* p. 21.

480. AVII, b. 93, f. 2, Roatta's Circular 3CL, 1 December 1942.

481. Roatta's orders 800 of 12 January 1943 and 568 6 January 1943 to V and XVIII Army Corps, cited in frame 1216, United Nations War Crimes Commission.

482. For a concise review of German occupation policies in Serbia, see Browning, "The Wehrmacht in Serbia Revisited," pp. 31–40.

483. Zanussi, *Guerra e catastrofe d'Italia*, I: 218.

484. ASMAE, GABAP, b. 35, Pietromarchi's memorandum for Ciano, 28 January 1942.

485. NAW T-821, 53, 1173–79, 2nd Army to SME, 2 February 1942; Talpo, *Dalmazia: Una cronaca per la storia (1942)*, D. 13, Ambrosio to Roatta, 13 February 1942, pp. 170–71; USSME, DS, b. 1222, Roatta to field commanders, 15 February 1942.

486. Talpo, *Dalmazia: Una cronaca per la storia (1941)*, D. 12, "Sassari" division to VI Army Corps, 12 November 1941, p. 1006.

487. West, *Tito and the Rise and Fall of Yugoslavia*, p. 99.

488. Talpo, *Dalmazia: Una cronaca per la storia (1942)*, pp. 432–33.

489. Milazzo, *The Chetnik Movement*, p. 76.
490. DDI, XI, VIII, 345, Roatta to Ambrosio, 6 March 1942.
491. Jozo Tomasevich, *Revolution in Yugoslavia, 1941–1945: The Chetniks* (Stanford: Stanford University Press, 1975), p. 214.
492. NAW, T-821, 65, 299–301, Roatta memorandum on talks held in Zagreb, 13 April 1942.
493. Talpo, *Dalmazia: Una cronaca per la storia (1941)*, pp. 913–14.
494. Hehn, *The Struggle Against Yugoslav Guerrillas in World War II*, pp. 61–62.
495. NAW, T-821, 53, 697–702, Dalmazzo to the 2nd Army, 17 January 1942.
496. Clissold, *Whirlwind*, p. 117.
497. David Martin *The Web of Disinformation: Churchill's Yugoslav Blunder* (London: Harcourt, 1990), p. 80.
498. Cited in Jonathan Steinberg, *All or Nothing.* pp. 43–44.
499. DDI, XI, VIII, 345, Roatta to Ambrosio, 6 March 1942.
500. USSME, M-3, b. 89, Roatta minute, undated.
501. Talpo, *Dalmazia; Una cronaca per la storia (1942)*, pp. 21-22.
502. AVII, b. 309, f. 20, Mihailović to Djordjić and Djurišić, 20 December 1941; Talpo, *Dalmazia: Una cronaca per la storia (1942)*, D. 7, Mihailović to Četnik commanders, pp. 150–55.
503. For a discussion of Mihailović's politics, see Karchmar, *Draža Mihailović and the Rise of the Četnik Movement, passim.*
504. USSME, M-3, b. 59, Conversation between Ambrosio and Mussolini, 28 December 1941.
505. DDI, IX, VIII, 139, Casertano to Ciano, 13 January 1942.
506. General Gian Carlo Re, the Italian military attaché in Zagreb, wrote very pessimistic reports on the ability of the Axis to prevent Partisan insurgency in eastern Bosnia from spilling over to the Italian-occupied zones. USSME, DS, b. 1371, General Gian Carlo Re to Superesercito and the Air Ministry, 16 and 30 January 1942, and 11 February 1942.
507. NAW, T-501, 264, 515–19, Glaise to OKW, 26 January 1942.
508. USSME, M-3, b. 89, Roatta report, February 1942.
509. USSME, M-3, b. 89, Roatta to CS, 5 February 1942.
510. DDI, IX, VIII, 274, Pietromarchi to Ciano, 16 February 1942.
511. PP, Diary, 4 March 1942.
512. DDI, IX, VIII, 274, Pietromarchi to Ciano, 16 February 1942.

513. These quotes are cited in Hehn, *The Struggle Against Yugoslav Guerrillas*, pp. 79, 82, 88.

514. Francesco Fatutta, "Croniche di guerriglia in Jugoslavia: Parte 2: Gennaio-giugno 1942," in *Studi storico-militari-1993* (Rome: SME-US, 1996), p. 246.

515. Hehn, *The Struggle Against Yugoslav Guerrillas*, p. 110.

516. Talpo, *Dalmazia: Una cronaca per la storia (1942)*, D. 14, Meeting of German, Italian, and Croatian army generals, 3 March 1942, pp. 172–75. Article 10 of the Abbazia agreement reads: "The signatories of the treaty pledge themselves not to negotiate either with the Četniks or with the Communists." Cited in Hehn, *The Struggle Against Yugoslav Guerrillas*, p. 113.

517. Klaus Schmider, *Partisanenkrieg in Jugoslawien 1941–1944* (Hamburg: Mittler, 2002), p. 120.

518. Hehn, *The Struggle Against Yugoslav Guerillas*, pp. 109–11. For General Kvaternik's views, see Talpo, *Dalmazia: Una cronaca per la storia (1942)*, D. 17, 8 March 1942, pp. 185–88. In latter March the Germans were apprised that Roatta intended to billet air and land forces in Sarajevo. Schmider, *Partisanenkrieg in Jugoslawien*, p. 137.

519. Broucek, *Glaise von Horstenau*, pp. 142, 434; Talpo, *Dalmazia: Una cronaca per la storia (1942)*, D. 13, Ambrosio to the 2nd Army, 13 February 1942, pp. 170–71. Ambrosio wrote: *"Avoid all negotiations with the Četniks."*

520. NAW, T-821, 70, 429–32, Minutes of a meeting between Italian, German, and Croatian generals, 28 March 1942.

521. Talpo, *Dalmazia: Una cronaca per la storia (1942)*, p. 75.

522. NAW, T-821, 70, 85–88, Roatta to Bader, 31 March 1942.

523. NAW, T-821, 98–100, Kvaternik to Roatta, 31 March 1942; NAW, T-821, 70, 328–32, De Blasio to Pietromarchi, 25 April 1942. The German record reports the opposite: that General Laxa "admitted that the Croatian government was still negotiating with the insurgents in Herzegovina." Hehn, *The Struggle Against Yugoslav Guerrillas*, pp. 119-20. Vrančić met with Jevdjević in the presence of an Italian representative on 23 March 1942. NAW, T-821, 70, 470–72, Operation "B," 28–29 March 1942.

524. Trifkovic, *Ustaša*, p. 168.

525. Talpo, *Dalmazia: Una cronaca per la storia (1942)*, pp. 76–77.

526. Schmider, *Partisanenkrieg in Jugoslawien*, p. 123.

527. USSME, M-3, 58, General Roatta to General Bader, 31 March 1942.

528. NAW, T-821, 271, 340-52, Meetings between Roatta, Bader, and Laxa, 28–29 March 1942; Talpo, *Dalmazia: Una cronaca per la storia (1942)*, pp. 76–77.

529. NAW, T-821, 53, 1173–79, Roatta to SME, 30 January 1942.

530. PP, Diary, 22 March 1942.

531. Karchmar, *Draža Mihailović and the Rise of the Četnik Movement*, I: 499.

532. Talpo, *Dalmazia: Una cronaca per la storia (1942)*, D. 19, De Blasio, Chief of Staff of the 2nd Army, to Pietromarchi, 25 April 1942, pp. 193–98.

533. NAW, T-821, 70, 440–41, Meeting of Italian, German, and Croatian generals, 29 March 1942. General Bader later gave the order that the population must be "treated with comprehension and justice": the villages in which arms and munitions were found or that had favored rebels were to be burned; bourgeois elements suspected of having supported the rebels were to be interned. NAW, T-821, 70, 174, Bader directive for operations in Bosnia, 10 April 1942.

534. Schmider, *Partisanenkrieg in Jugoslawien*, p. 122.

535. NAW, T-821, 271, 340–52, Meetings between Roatta, Bader, and Laxa, 28–29 March 1942.

536. USSME, M-3, b. 58, General Roatta to General Bader, 31 March 1942.

537. DDI, IX, VIII, 454, Castellani to Ciano, 15 April 1942.

538. Schmider, *Partisanenkrieg in Jugoslawien*, p. 130.

539. Schmider, *Partisanenkrieg in Jugoslawien*, p. 134.

540. Talpo, *Dalmazia: Una cronaca per la storia (1942)*, pp. 77–78.

541. Talpo, *Dalmazia: Una cronaca per la storia (1942)*, p. 79; Schmider, *Partisanenkrieg in Jugoslawien*, p. 123.

542. DDI, IX, VIII, 454, Castellani to Ciano, 15 April 1942.

543. Roatta, in his Circular 4C, NAW, T-821, 248, 1 April 1942, described that the Italian troops, after heroically holding out against the Partisans in snow and biting cold, broke the siege and administered heavy losses on the enemy in men and provisions once the weather had cleared.

544. NAW, T-501, 268, 445–46, Glaise report, 13 April 1942; DDI, IX, VIII, 454, Castellani to Ciano, 15 April 1942, Annex, Roatta to Ambrosio, 13 April 1942; USSME, M-3, b. 58, General Roatta to General Bader, 31 March 1942; Talpo, *Dalmazia: Una cronaca per la storia (1942)*, p. 78.

545. NAW, T-821, 65, 299–301, Roatta memorandum on talks with Pavelić in Zagreb, 13 April 1942.

546. DDI, IX, VIII, 454, Castellani to Ciano, 15 April 1942, and Annex: Roatta to Ambrosio, 13 April 1942.
547. PP, Diary, 10 and 25 April 1943.
548. Talpo, *Dalmazia: Una cronaca per la storia (1942)*, D. 19, De Blasio to
Pietromarchi, 25 April 1942, pp. 193–98.
549. Hehn, *The Struggle Against Yugoslav Guerrillas*, p. 127.
550. DDI, IX, VIII, 468, Castellani to Pietromarchi, 21 April 1942.
551. NAW, T-821, 70, 878–84, Unsigned note from the Italian military
attaché in Belgrade, 20 May 1942.
552. NAW, T-821, 70, 328–32, De Blasio to Pietromarchi, 25 April 1942;
USSME, M-3, b. 64, Roatta to Superesercito, 21 April 1942, and
Roatta to the 2nd Army Office of Operations, 22 April 1942.
553. NAW, T-821, 70, 328–32, De Blasio to Pietromarchi, 25 April 1942.
554. NAW, T-501, 268, 449–51, Glaise report, 6 April 1942, 318–20,
Glaise report, 8 June 1942, 326–28, Glaise report, 11 June 1942;
Hehn, *The Struggle Against Yugoslav Guerrillas*, p. 125.
555. Talpo, *Dalmazia: Una cronaca per la storia (1942)*, p. 82.
556. NAW, T-821, 65, 368, Roatta to SME, 30 April 1942.
557. NAW, T-821, 70, 878–89, General Umberto Fabbri to 2nd Army,
20 May 1942.
558. Scotti and Viazzi, in *L'inutile vittoria*, p. 331, however, believe that
the peremptory German order to break off Operation *Trio* in mid
May was premature and allowed the Partisans to get away.
559. NAW, T-821, 398, 604, Roatta's 4C circular, 1 April 1942.
560. These figures are taken from Talpo, *Dalmazia: Una cronaca per la storia
(1942)*, p. 86.
561. Talpo, *Dalmatia: Una cronaca per la storia (1942)*, p. 82.
562. General Dalmazzo, for one, was quite critical over the Italian withdrawal from both the 1st and 2nd zones for opening up these areas to the nefarious influence of both the Ustaša and the Partisans.
Talpo, *Dalmazia: Una cronaca per la storia (1942)*, D. 9, Dalmazzo to
2nd Army, 9 June 1942, pp. 515–17.
563. NAW, T-501, 268, 304–06, Glaise report, 18 June 1942.
564. ASMAE, GABAP, b. 32, Pietromarchi memorandum, 29 April 1942.
565. PP, Diary, 6 and 19 January, 1942.
566. Karchmar, *Draža Mihailović and the Rise of the Četnik Movement*, I: 401.
567. PP, Diary, 30 June 1942.
568. PP, Diary, 30 June 1942.
569. PP, Diary, 15 September 1942.

570. PP, Diary, 30 June 1942.

571. Scotti and Viazzi, *L'inutile vittoria*, p. 148.

572. Tomasevich, *The Chetniks*, p. 212.

573. PP, Diary, 31 July 1942.

574. PP, Diary, 27 August 1942.

575. Pavlowitch, *Yugoslavia*, p. 127; Marjanović, *Collaboration*, D. 16, Agreement Between Montenegrin Četnik, and Nationalist Leaders with Italian Governor of Montenegro, 21 July 1942, pp. 46–49.

576. PP, Diary, 27 August 1942.

577. PP, Diary, 22 June 1942.

578. Pavlowitch, *Yugoslavia*, p. 128.

579. Karchmar, and the books by Scotti and Viazzi.

580. Capogreco, "Una storia rimossa dell'Italia fascista," p. 229.

581. NAW, T-501, 268, 449, Glaise report, 6 April 1942.

582. General Dalmazzo wrote Roatta that Vrančić engaged the Četniks for the sole purpose of lining them up in the common endeavor "to chase Italy out of Dalmatia." USSME, M-3, b. 66, Dalmazzo to Roatta, 23 April 1942.

583. NAW, T-501, 268, 122-23, Glaise report, 13 October 1942.

584. ASMAE, GABAP, b. 31, Pietromarchi memorandum, 10 May 1942; DDI, IX, VIII, 550, Ciano to Cavallero, 19 May 1942.

585. An excellent introduction to the subject of Italian economic imperialism in Croatia can be found in Teodoro Sala, "Fascisti e nazisti nell'Europa sudorientale. Il caso croato (1941–1943)," in *Le potenze dell'Asse e la Jugoslavia*, ed. E. Collotti and T. Sala (Milan: Feltrinelli, 1974), pp. 49–76.

586. Cited in Sala, "Il caso croato," p. 72.

587. Trifković, *Ustaša*, pp. 178–79.

588. AVII, b. 309, f. 12, Nota Verbale, 1 June 1942. The Italians evacuated Bosanski Petrovac on 25 May, Drvar five days later, Prozor and Glamo on 1 June. Talpo, *Dalmazia: Una cronaca per la storia (1942)*, pp. 508–10.

589. PP, Diary, 18 May 1942.

590. Talpo, *Dalmazia: Una cronaca per la storia (1942)*, pp. 440–42.

591. AVII, p. 309, f. 12, Nota Verbale, 1 June 1942.

592. Whereby the Italian army undertook to garrison and politically control the second zone and to occupy the third zone, which met the objective of protecting the Orthodox from the Ustaša. The text of the 19 June agreement can be found in NAW, T-821, 410, 160–72.

593. AVII, b. 309, f. 12, Nota Verbale, 1 June 1942.
594. NAW, T-821, 65, 299, Roatta's report on the conference in Zagreb, 13 April 1942.
595. NAW, T-821, 52, 237–45, Clarifications of the 19 June Agreement, Roatta to Supersloda, 28 June 1942.
596. PP, Diary, 12 September 1942.
597. ASMAE, GABAP, b. 35, Pietromarchi memorandum for Ciano, 22 June 1942.
598. NAW, T-821, 60, 418–19, Ambrosio to SME, 4 February 1942.
599. NAW, T-821, 410, 420–26, Roatta memorandum, 10 May 1942. "Evidently the Zagreb government, for internal political reasons, regretted the concessions it made . . . the Croatian authority, whenever confronted by difficulties regarding the life of the population, foists the blame on our military authority. To those who complain: "what do you want us to do?" They say: "Here the Italians dominate. Turn to them." This is supposed to be the odious side (quite exaggerated) of [Italy's] exercise of "civil power" with respect to the population, to which the Poglavnik has alluded verbally. *In substance*, given the mentality of the central and outlying Croatian authority, given the armed struggle in the troubled regions in question, and given the diverse zones interspersed between garrisons which escape our authority . . . the "civil powers" have not been exercised anywhere on a large scale, and in a *positive* manner, but on a reduced scale, and in a sense prevalently of *a veto*. In other words we have rarely been able to say: "Do this" (because it would have been a dead letter), but we have said, "Don't do this." As a result, despite the obstructionism, we have succeeded, having on hand the necessary force. The "don't do this" consists essentially in the measures there appertaining to the operations in impeding provisions or manifestations susceptible to upsetting the public order or pacification, and in having to remove—after difficulties—the most hostile [Croatian] functionaries. Actually, the ambiance of Zagreb, in full euphoria for progress accomplished in a year, imagining . . . itself capable of putting the whole country promptly in order, is on the whole intolerant of [our] "civilian power." For this makes them appear, in the eyes of the population, in a state of tutelage because still "underage." . . . Moreover, in the case of the ex-Austrians (General Laxa at the head) there exists a hostility toward everything Italian. If we renounce "civil power" in the 2nd zone,

the hostile wing of the extremist Zagreb government will give a free hand to its own agents, and we will have a second edition, albeit reduced, of the summer 1941 persecutions. I am therefore of the opinion that we should not abandon the "civil power" in the occupied territories.

600. Talpo, *Dalmazia: Una cronaca per la storia (1942)*, D. 13, Roatta to CS, 12 June 1942, pp. 524–32. General Dalmazzo was no less critical of the NDH. USSME, M-3, b. 89, Dalmazzo to the 2nd Army, 24 May 1942.

601. *The Ciano Diaries*, 18 May and 10 June 1942.

602. PP, Diary, 6 July 1942.

603. DDI, XI, VIII, 536, Giustiniani to Ciano, 12 May 1941.

604. PP, Diary, 12 July 1942.

605. PP, Diary, 15 May 1942.

606. Talpo, *Dalmazia: Una cronaca per la storia (1942)*, D. 16, Pietromarchi memorandum for Ciano, 2 July 1942, p. 545.

607. Milazzo, *The Chetnik Movement*, p. 99.

608. Talpo, *Dalmazia: Una cronaca per la storia (1942)*, p. 611.

609. Cuzzo, "Il terzo anno," p. 358.

610. ACS, Minculprop, b. 3132, General Pièche to Polverelli, 7 October 1942.

611. ASMAE, GABAP, b. 37, Pietromarchi memorandum, 15 September 1942.

612. Hitler had this to say about the Croats: "If the Croats were part of the Reich, we'd have them serving as faithful auxiliaries of the German Führer, to police our marches. Whatever happens, one shouldn't treat them, as Italy is doing at present. The Croats are a proud people. They should be bound directly to the Führer by an act of loyalty." H. R. Trevor-Roper, *Hitler's Secret Conversations 1941–1944* (New York: Signet Books, 1953), p. 115.

613. Enzo Collotti, "Penetrazione economica e disgregazione statale: premesse e conseguenze dell'aggressione nazista alla Jugoslavia," in *The Third Reich and Yugoslavia, 1933–1945* (Belgrade: Institute for Contemporary History, 1977), p. 301.

614. NAW, T-501, 264, 1193, Glaise report, 10 July 1941; DGFP, D, 13, 113–15, Kasche to the Foreign Ministry, 10 July 1941.

615. Broucek, *Glaise von Horstenau*, p. 162.

616. NAW, T-821, 53, 661-64, unsigned report, 21 May 1942.

617. NAW, T-821, 55, 556–57, Dalmazzo to Roatta, 9 June 1942.

618. NAW, T-821, 410, 10–13, Robotti memorandum, undated.

619. Oddone Talpo, "Porto Ploče: Tentativo tedesco di affaciarsi in Adriatico (1942) *Rivista Dalmatica*, 70 (1999): 145–51. Pietromarchi claims that he also reserved for Italy the right to build the connecting railroads. PP, Diary, 1 June 1942.

620. Giuseppe Gorla, *L'Italia nella seconda guerra mondiale: Diario di un milanese, ministro del Re nel Governo Mussolini* (Milan: Baldini and Castoldi, 1959), 10 August 1942, pp. 337–38.

621. Amoretti, *La vicenda italo-croata*, p. 89.

622. PP, Diary, 23 June 1942.

623. DDI, IX, VIII, 646, Pietromarchi to Ciano, 23 June 1942; ASMAE, GABAP, b. 36, Bastianini to Pietromarchi, 9 July 1942.

624. Cuzzi, "I Balcani, problemi di un'occupazione difficile," p. 357.

625. Collotti and Sala, *Le potenze dell'Asse e la Jugoslava*, pp. 125-31.

626. NAW, T-821, 63, 843, Armellini to Supersloda, 2 August 1942.

627. Talpo, *Dalmazia: Una cronaca per la storia (1942)*, pp. 572–73.

628. PP, Diary, 1 June 1942.

629. Milazzo, *The Chetnik Movement*, p. 76.

630. Talpo, *Dalmazia: Una cronaca per la storia (1942)*, pp. 448-50; NAW, T-821, 347, 820–23, Statement by Draža Mihailović, 16 July 1942. A brief Italian report of the Četnik meeting can be found in USSME, M-3, b. 51, A portion of a report of the VI Army Corps, 7 August 1942; Milazzo, *The Chetnik Movement*, pp. 94-95.

631. Pavlovich, *Yugoslavia*, p. 148. In the trial of Mihailović published by the Yugoslav government, the meeting convened by Mihailović is described as taking place on 13 July 1942 in the village of Avtovac in Herzegovina. This official report emphasizes Mihailović's domination of the proceedings and conveys a tighter chain of command in Četnik ranks than one gleans from the Italian sources.

632. Mario Dassovich, *Fronte jugoslavo 1943* (Udine: Del Blanco, 2000), p. 10.

633. For this interpretation of Tito and the Partisans in this section, I have drawn mainly on Stevan Pavlowitch, *Yugoslavia*, pp. 134–37. Throughout his works on wartime Yugoslavia, Pavlowitch makes arresting and eminently fair judgments on people, movements, and events.

634. AVII, b. 93, General Esposito report, undated.

635. PP, Diary, 25 June 1942.

636. ASMAE, GABAP, b. 32, Castellani to FM, 13 October 1942.

637. NAW, T-821, 63, 690–93, Roatta meeting with Trifunović, 10 September 1942.

638. Milazzo, *The Chetnik Movement*, pp. 97–98.

639. USSME, M-3, b. 89, Roatta meeting with Trifunović and Jevdjević, 21 September 1942.

640. USSME, M-3, b. 51, Portion of a VI Army Corps report, 7 August 1942; NAW, T-821, 252, 299, Castellani to MFA [in German translation], 23 August 1942.

641. NAW, T-821, 31, 351-53, Roatta meeting with Trifunović, and Jevdjević, 21 September 1942; ASMAE, GABAP, b. 26, Supersloda memorandum, 4 July 1942.

642. USSME, M-3, b. 89, Roatta's report on his talks with Četnik leaders, 23 September 1942.

643. USSME, M-3, b. 89, Roatta's report on the Četnik militia, 26 September 1942.

644. USSME, M-3, b. 89, Roatta's report on his talks with Četnik leaders, 23 September 1942.

645. Milazzo, *The Chetnik Movement*, p. 107.

646. USSME, M-3, b. 54, Roatta to V Army Corps, 18 September 1942.

647. USSME, M-3, b. 89, Colonel Carà's report on his conversations with Trifunović and Jevdjević, and the journalist Grdjić, 22 September 1942.

648. Talpo, *Dalmazia: Una cronaca per la storia (1942)*, D. 8, Roatta to CS, 5 December 1942, pp. 1250–52.

649. Talpo, *Dalmazia: Una cronaca per la storia (1942)*, D. 9, Pièche to MAE, no date, pp. 1253–59, D. 10, G. A. Spechel, for the Governor, to MAE, 11 February 1943, pp. 1255–56, and D. 11, Head of the Dalmatian cabinet to MAE, Statute: Promulgated by General Draža Mihajlović on 1 December 1942 in Šahović, Monenegro, undated, pp. 1257–60.

650. Talpo, *Dalmazia: Una cronaca per la storia (1942)*, D. 6, Cavallero to Supersloda, 17 September 1942, p. 832.

651. The Italians broke down the numbers as follows: Trifunović had a force of 18,320 that were dependent on the 2nd Army and 6,000 of his own; Jevdjević had around 10,000 men at his disposal. USSME, M-3, b. 89, Annex to Roatta's report on the Četnik militia, 26 September 1942.

652. Oddone Talpo, *Dalmazia: Una cronaca per la storia (1943–1944)* (Rome: SME-US, 1994), D. 13, General Rosi memorandum, 3 May 1943, p. 698; NAW, T-821, 288, 256, Robotti to VI Army Corps, 8 May 1943; 404, 729-30, Robotti note, 8 May 1943.

653. ASMAE, GABAP, b. 38, Roberto Ducci memorandum, 15 April 1943.

654. ASMAE, GABAP, b. 38, Robotti to CS, 8 May 1943.

655. NAW, T-821, 52, 305–12, 329–37, 376, on the Zagreb meeting, 19 September 1942.

656. NAW, T-821, 54, 05, 24 August 1942; 53, 744, 23 September 1942.

657. ASMAE, GABAP, b. 30, Giardini to MAE, 25 September 1942.

658. NAW, T-821, 448, 417, 2nd Army report, 15 November 1942, 383, 2nd Army report, 15 January 1943.

659. Četnik atrocities against the Muslims are detailed in Tomasevich, *The Četniks*, pp. 256–61.

660. NAW, T-821, 410, 1001–03, Muslim petition to 2nd Army, 11 September 1942.

661. NAW, T-821, 59, 659–60, Spigo to Roatta, and Roatta marginal comments, 12 August 1942.

662. Amoretti, *La vicenda italo-croata*, p. 122.

663. USSME, M-3, b. 993, Dalmazzo report, 2 September 1942; Talpo, *Dalmazia: Una cronaca per la storia (1942)*, p. 597; PP, Diary, 16 September 1942.

664. USSME, N I-II, b. 993, Report of a meeting on 12 October 1942 in Spalato, Generals Roatta, Santovito, Spigo, and Primieri, 14 October 1942; Talpo, *Dalmazia: Una cronaca per la storia (1942)*, p. 749.

665. USSME, N I-II, b. 993, Report of a meeting on 12 October 1942 in Spalato, Generals Roatta, Santovito, Spigo, and Primieri, 14 October 1942.

666. Talpo, *Dalmazia: Una cronaca per la storia (1942)*, D. 22, Solari Bozzi report, 30 October 1942, pp. 897–905; D. 23, Pièche to MAE, 7 October 1942, pp. 906-13.

667. Tomasevich, *Occupation and Collaboration*, pp. 439–40.

668. PP, Diary, 15 February 1942.

669. Broucek, *Glaise von Horstenau*, pp. 165–66. In January 1943 Glaise noted that the elder Kvaternik now harbored less animosity toward Serbs, but not so son "Dido," who, he told Glaise, was no longer his offspring but that of Pavelić for carrying on the Ustaša's murder-

ous ways. The elder Kvaternik asked Glaise: "Tell me dear friend, do you believe a word he [Pavelić] says? Glaise wrote that unfortunately he could not answer with an unqualified "Ja," for that would make him appear "as a stupid chap." NAW, T-501, 264, 564–70, Glaise to Schuchardt, 10 January 1943. See Schmider, *Partisanenkrieg in Jugolsawien*, pp. 161–62, for Glaise's earlier recommendations for a regime change in Zagreb.

670. ASMAE, GABAP, b. 35, Pietromarchi note for Ciano, 22 June 1942; Talpo, *Dalmazia: Una cronaca per la storia (1942)*, p. 452; ASMAE, GABAP, b. 26, Castellani to MFA, 4 July 1942.

671. Dassovich, *Fronte jugoslavo 1941–'42*, p. 220.

672. Talpo, *Dalmazia: Una cronaca per la storia (1942)*, p. 613.

673. Talpo, *Dalmazia: Una cronaca per la storia (1942)*, D. 13, Baldoni memorandum, 14 October 1942, pp. 857–58.

674. USSME, M-3, b. 89, Roatta to corps commanders, 18 October 1942; NAW, T-821, 410, 1256–60, Note by the 2nd Army on incidences and excesses attributed to the Četniks; 503, 43–45, Roatta to Lorković, 31 October 1942, 53-55, SIM to 2nd Army, 11 October 1942.

675. Talpo, *Dalmazia: Una cronaca per la storia (1942)*, D. 2, Baldoni to MAE, 17 September 1942, pp. 821–22.

676. NAW, T-821, 503, 50–52, Spigo to 2nd Army, 24 October 1942.

677. NAW, T-821, 503, 18, Roatta to V Army Corps, 18 September 1942.

678. USSME, M-3, b. 89, Roatta to corps commanders, 18 October 1942; NAW, T-821, 31, 338–41, Roatta to corps commanders, 18 October 1942; USSME, N I-II, b. 1222, Roatta report on agreements reached with Pavelić on use of Četnik MVAC units, 18 October 1942; NAW, T-821, 503, 43–45, Roatta to Lorković, 31 October 1942.

679. Talpo, *Dalmazia: Una cronaca per la storia (1942)*, p. 769.

680. Zanussi, *Guerra e catastrofe d'Italia*, I: 268.

681. Tomasevich argues that Roatta, by freely moving Četnik units around and arming additional troops, broke many promises to Croatian officials to keep them confined to Herzegovina and to foreswear any additional recruitment. *Occupation and Collaboration*, pp. 258–61.

682. Talpo, *Dalmazia: Una cronaca per la storia (1942)*, D. 15, A report on the views of Roatta to MAE, 14 October 1942, pp. 863–64.

683. AVII, b. 93, f. 24, Roatta to CS, 11 October 1942.

684. Tomasevich, *Occupation and Collaboration*, pp. 260-62.

685. PP, 3, 1, Ivo Herzer, "How Italians Rescued Jews," in *Midstream*, June–July 1983.

686. Klaus Voigt states that there were 38,000 Jews, including refugees, under Ustaša domination. *Il refugio precario: Gli esuli in Italia dal 1933 al 1945* (Florence: La Nuova Italia, 1996), p. 243.

687. AVII, b. 309, f. 30, untitled, 24 November 1941.

688. Voigt, *Il refugio precario*, p. 245.

689. PP, Diary, 26 March 1942.

690. Rodogno, *Il nuovo ordine mediterraneo*, pp. 444–45.

691. Danial Carpi, "The Rescue of Jews in the Italian Zone of Occupied Croatia," in *Rescue Attempts During the Holocaust: Proceedings of the Second Yad Vashem International Historical Conference, April 1974*, eds. Yisrael Gutman and Efraim Zuroff (Jerusalem: 1977), pp. 508–09.

692. Rodogno, *Il nuovo ordine mediterraneo*, p. 445.

693. NAW, T-821, 405, 716–17, Bastianini to Roatta, 7 July 1942.

694. PP, Diary, 12 July 1942.

695. Cited in Steinberg, *All or Nothing*, p. 53.

696. Menachem Shelah, "The Italian Rescue of Yugoslav Jews," in *The Italian Refuge: Rescue of Jews During during the Holocaust*, ed. Ivo Herzer (Washington, D.C.: The Catholic University Press, 1989), p. 209.

697. ASMAE, GABAP, b. 42, for the two drafts of the memorandum, unsigned, 18 August 1942.

698. ASMAE, GABAP, b. 42, Appunto for the Duce, unsigned, 21 August 1942, which bears Mussolini's *"nulla osta"* in the upper right hand corner.

699. PP, Diary, 24 August 1942.

700. PP, Diary, 28 August 1942.

701. PP, Diary, 13 September 1942.

702. Castellani to Pietromarchi, 11 September 1942, cited in Carpi, "The Italian Rescue of Yugoslav Jews," p. 513.

703. USSME, N I–II, b. 993, Roatta to CS on a meeting at Ragusa with Croatian officials, 31 August 1942.

704. NAW, T-821, 405, 682, Roatta to the Croatian commissioner general and VI Army Corps, 10 September 1942.

705. NAW, T-821, 405, 680, Roatta to the Croatian commissioner general and VI Army Corps, 24 September 1942.

706. NAW, T-821, 405, 749, Roatta to CS, 22 September 1942.

707. ASMAE, GABAP, b. 42, Castellani to Pietromarchi, 24 September 1942.

708. PP, Diary, 14 October 1942.

709. PP, Diary, 18 October 1942.

710. Broucek, *Glaise von Horstenau*, p. 148.

711. NAW, T-501, 268, 116-18, Glaise to OKW, 17 October 1942.

712. ASMAE, GABAP, b. 42, Unsigned memorandum, 23 October 1942, and Unsigned memorandum; Cavallero to Supersloda, 28 October 1942.

713. Zanussi, *Guerra e catastrophe d'Italia*, I: 265-66; Menachem Shelah, *Un debito di gratitudine: Storia dei rapporti tra l'Esercito Italiano e gli ebrei in Dalmazia (1941–1943)* (Rome: SME-US, 1991), pp. 112–13.

714. NAW, T-821, 405, 833–35, Amodio, to V Army Corps, 8 November 1942.

715. ASMAE, GABAP, b. 42, Amodio, to V Army Corps, 8 November 1942.

716. NAW, T-821, 405, Pièche to MAE, 4 November 1942.

717. ASMAE, GABAP, b. 42, Castellani to MAE, 3 December 1942; NAW, T-821, 405, 856, Extracts from a memorandum of the commander, unsigned, 12 November 1942.

718. Voigt, *Il refugio precario*, p. 286.

719. PP, Diary, 31 March 1943.

720. PP, Diary, 31 March 1943.

721. Léon Poliakov and Jacques Sabille, *Jews under the Italian Occupation* (Paris, Éditions du Centre, 1955), pp. 147–48.

722. PP, Diary, 11 March 1943.

723. ASMAE, GABAP, b. 42, Bastianini to Castellani, 31 March 1943.

724. ASMAE, GABAP, b. 42, Castellani to MAE, 20 March 1943.

725. Ferenc, *Rab–Arbe–Arbissima*, D. 468, 2nd Army report, 10 July 1943, pp. 414–15.

726. Shelah, "The Italian Rescue of Yugoslav Jews," p. 216.

727. Voigt, *Il refugio precario*, p. 250.

728. Rodogno, *Il nuovo ordine mediterraneo*, p. 482.

729. Shelah, *Un debito di gratitudine*, p. 101.

730. Talpo, *Dalmazia: Una cronaca per la storia (1942)*, p. 786.

731. Talpo, *Dalmazia: Una cronaca per la storia (1942)*, D. 25, Roatta memorandum on military meeting at Sušak, 22 November 1942, p. 927.

732. Schmider, *Partisanenkrieg in Jugoslawien*, pp. 180–81.
733. Talpo, *Dalmazia: Una cronaca per la storia (1942)*, p. 1176.
734. Karchmar, *Draža Mihailović and the Rise of the Četnik Movement*, II: 556.
735. PP, Diary, 18 December 1942.
736. Steinberg, *All or Nothing*, pp. 83-84.
737. Cited in Steinberg, *All or Nothing*, p. 61.
738. NAW, T-821, 21, 962–87, Conversation between Ciano and Hitler, 18 December 1942.
739. Quote is Ambrosio's. NAW, T-821, 125, 816–17, Conversation between Pirzio Biroli and Robotti, 3 March 1943.
740. NAW, T-821, 21, 962–87, Conversation between Ciano and Hitler, 18 December 1942, during which Hitler stated: "Germany has no interest of a political character [in Croatia]."
741. PP, Diary, 31 December 1942.
742. PP, Diary, 18 October 1942.
743. Talpo, *Dalmazia: Una cronaca per la storia (1943–1944)*, p. 383.
744. DDI, IX, IX, 422, Cavallero to Mussolini, 18–19 December 1942; Cavallero, *Diario*, 24 January 1943. At the Italo-German conference in Salzburg on 7-10 April 1943, the Germans complied with the Italian insistence on a joint command. Talpo, *Dalmazia: Una cronaca per la storia (1943–1944)*, D. 12, Meeting at Salzburg, 12 April 1943, p. 521.
745. USSME, N I-II, b. 1222, Cavallero to Roatta, 10 January 1943.
746. PP, Diary, 3 January 1943.
747. PP, Diary, 8 January 1943.
748. PP, Diary, 8 January 1943.
749. PP, Diary, 6 January 1943.
750. Cavallero, *Diario*, 3 January 1943, pp. 646–47; Talpo, *Dalmazia: Una cronaca per la storia (1943–1944)*, p. 24.
751. Talpo, *Dalmazia: Una cronaca per la storia (1943–1944)*, p. 26; Ciano, *Diary*, 2 January 1943.
752. Talpo, *Dalmazia: Una cronaca per la storia (1943–44)*, D. 4, Castellani to MAE and the Italian legation in Zagreb, undated, pp. 200–04.
753. Schmider, *Partisanenkrieg in Jugoslawien*, pp. 186–87.
754. Talpo, *Dalmazia: Una cronaca per la storia (1943–44)*, p. 27.
755. PP, Diary, 27 January 1943; Schmider, *Partisanenkrieg in Jugoslawien*, pp. 207–08.
756. Schmider, *Partisanenkrieg in Jugoslawien*, pp. 207–08.

757. NAW, T-501, 264, 564–70, Glaise to Schuchardt, around 10 January 1943; DDI, IX, IX, 422, Cavallero to Mussolini, 18–19 December 1942.

758. Zanussi, *Guerra e catastrofe d'Italia*, I: 283-84.

759. Ciano, Diary, 6 January 1943.

760. AVII, b. 368, f. 5, Roatta to XVIII Army Corps, 29 January 1943.

761. Talpo, *Dalmazia: Una cronaca per la storia (1943–1944)*, p. 385.

762. PP, Diary, 9 February 1943.

763. Zbornik, IV, bk 9, D. 211, Roatta to CS, 12 January 1943.

764. *The Ciano Diaries*, 2 January 1943.

765. DDI, IX, IX, 510, Castellani to Ciano, 18 January 1943.

766. Talpo, *Dalmazia: Una cronaca per la storia (1943–1944)*, D. 4, Castellani to MAE, 10 January 1943, pp. 200–04.

767. AVII, b. 364, f. 1, Roatta to field commanders, January 1943.

768. *The Ciano Diaries*, 6 January 1943.

769. Trifkovic, *Ustaša*, p. 186.

770. Loi, *Le operazioni delle unità italiane in Jugoslavia*, p. 212; *The Ciano Diaries*, 6 January 1943.

771. PP, Diary, 6 January 1943.

772. Zbornik, 1V, bk. 9, D. 217, Supersloda to CS, 12 January 1943.

773. PP, Diary, 27 January 1943.

774. PP, Diary, 27 January 1943.

775. PP, Diary, 11 October 1942.

776. PP, Diary, 27 January 1943.

777. PP, Diary, 18 January 1943.

778. PP, Diary, 8 February 1943.

779. NAW, T-821, 126, 011-347, Conversations between Ambrosio and Warlimont, 5, 6, 12, and 27 February 1943.

780. AVII, b. 368, f. 1, Robotti to CS, 4 February 1943.

781. NAW, T-821, 125, 810 and 815, Conversation between Roatta and Robotti, 4 and 8 February 1943; Talpo, *Dalmazia: Una cronaca per a storia (1943–1944)*, D. 8, Conversation between Robotti and the German generals Löhr and Lüters, 8 February 1943, pp. 210–15.

782. AVII, b. 368, f. 1, Robotti to CS, 4 February 1943.

783. Talpo, *Dalmazia: Una cronaca per la storia (1943–1944)*, D. 9, Conversation between Casertano and Kasche, 9 February 1943, pp. 216–20.

784. NAW, T-821, 298, 11–12, Robotti to field commanders, 27 February 1943.

785. USSME, N I-II, b. 1222, General Re report on German operations, 18 February 1943.

786. Fatutta, *La campagna di Iugoslava*, p. 127.

787. Yugoslav historians soft-pedal Partisan atrocities while Italian defenders of their military righteously endeavor to even the record. Through choice quotations, Dassovich, in *Fronte jugoslavo 1943*, pp. 51–52, succinctly summarizes the radically differing viewpoints on the question of Partisan treatment of Italian war prisoners that was brought to a head in the Battle of Neretva. Evidence of the massacre of Italian prisoners is given by an Italian medical doctor, which can be found in Talpo, *Dalmazia: Una cronaca per la storia (1943–1944)*, D. 13, pp. 229–35. Djilas, in his *Wartime*, p. 220, owns up to the Partisan massacre of the entire third battalion of the 259th regiment.

788. USSME, N I-II, b. 1222, Robotti to Piazzoni, 5 March 1942.

789. Milazzo, *The Chetnik Movement*, p. 122.

790. Cited in F.W. Deakin, *The Brutal Friendship: Mussolini, Hitler and The Fall of Italian Fascism*, 2 vols. (Garden City, NY: Doubleday Anchor Books, 1966), I: 183–84. The full text of Hitler's letter can be found in DDI, IX, X, 31, Hitler to Mussolini, 16 February 1943.

791. Cited in Deakin, *The Brutal Friendship*, I: 62.

792. Cited in Talpo, *Dalmazia; Una cronaca per la storia (1943–1944)*, p. 36.

793. Cited in Deakin, *The Brutal Friendship*, I: 163.

794. Cited in Deakin, *The Brutal Friendship*, I: 187. For the Italian minutes of the meeting, see NAW, T-821, 125, 531–34, Meeting at the Palazzo Venezia, 26 February 1943.

795. Cited in Deakin, *The Brutal Friendship*, I: 193, 195.

796. Schmider, *Partisanenkrieg in Jugoslawien 1941–1944*, p. 223.

797. PP, Diary, 1 March 1943.

798. NAW, T-821, 126, 340–47, Meeting between Ambrosio and Warlimont, 27 February 1943.

799. For these military talks, see NAW, T-821, 125, 531, CS report, 24 February 1943, 340, CS report on the meeting at the Palazzo Venezia, 25 February 1943, 26 February 1943; PP, Diary, 1 March 1943.

800. PP, Diary, 1 March 1943.

801. Talpo, *Dalmazia: Una cronaca per la storia (1943–1944)*, D. 17, Summary of German-Italian meetings of 26, 27, 28 February 1943, 2 March 1943, pp. 248–50; Schmider, *Partisanenkrieg in Jugoslawien*, p. 225.

802. Cited in Deakin, *The Brutal Friendship*, I: 188.

803. Deakin, *The Brutal Friendship*, I: 197.

804. NAW, T-501, 264, 518–29, Glaise to Schuchardt, 26 May 1943.

805. Vladimir Dedjer, *Tito* (New York: Simon & Schuster, 1953), pp. 191–94.

806. Milazzo, *The Chetnik Movement*, p. 129; Srdjan Trifkovic, "Rivalry Between Germany and Italy in Croatia, 1942–1943," *The Historical Journal* 36, no. 4 (1993): 902. Loi, in *Le operazioni delle unità italiane in Jugoslavia*, p. 218, claims that the Četniks beat the Partisans in Montenegro. See also Tomasevich, *Occupation and Collaboration*, p. 144.

807. Fattuta, *La campagna di Jugoslavia*, p. 130.

808. USSME, N I-II, b. 1222, Robotti to the German command, 6 March 1942.

809. Talpo, *Dalmazia: Una cronaca per la storia (1943–1944)*, pp. 106–08.

810. NAW, T-821, 250, 17-29, Pirzio Biroli report, undated.

811. Tomasevich, *The Chetniks*, pp. 244–47; Schmider, *Partisanenkrieg in Yugoslawien*, p. 251.

812. Beloff, *Tito's Flawed Legacy*, p. 81. Beloff cites Yugoslav sources to support her contention that Tito, in his moment of distress, was prepared to align with Germany to destroy the Četniks. See also the accounts in Pavlowitch, *Yugoslavia*, p. 141, and Roberts, *Tito, Mihailović and the Allies*, p.108, which support Beloff.

813. Trifkovic, *Ustaša*, p. 217; Tomasevich, *The Chetniks*, p. 247.

814. PP, Diary, 20 January 1943.

815. PP, Diary, 26 February 1943.

816. PP, Diary, 6 January 1943.

817. PP, Diary 3 January 1943. The last part of this quote is in the original Latin: "Nec cennis nec sine iis."

818. DDI, IX, X, 23, Casertano to Bastianini (Conversation between Casertano and Mussolini), 15 February 1943.

819. DDI, IX, X, 24, Casertano to Bastianini, 15 February 1943,

820. DDI, IX, X, 61, Conversation between Mussolini and Ribbentrop, 26 February 1943.

821. DDI, IX, X, 24, Casertano to Bastianini, 15 February 1943.

822. DDI, IX, X, 62, Casertano to Mussolini, 27 February 1943.

823. ASMAE, GABAP, b. 37, 5 January 1943.

824. DDI, IX, X, 186, Casertano to Mussolini, 3 April 1943.

825. DDI, IX, X, 142, Casertano to Mussolini, 22 March 1943.

826. DDI, IX, X, 142, Casertano to Mussolini, 22 March 1943.

827. PP, Diary, 30 March 1943.

828. PP, Diary, 29 April 1943.

829. PP, Diary, 3 May 1943.

830. DDI, IX, VIII, 461, Lanza d'Ajeta to Romano, 17 April 1942.

831. ASMAE, GABAP, b. 32, Casertano to FM, 17 March 1943.

832. PP, Diary, 13 February 1943.

833. Talpo, *Dalmazia: Una cronaca per la storia (1943–1944)*, p. 604.

834. Trifkovic, *Ustaša*, p. 219.

835. Broucek, *Glaise von Horstenau*, pp. 170–73.

836. NAW, T-501, 264, 556-60, Glaise to Warlimont, 15 February 1943.

837. NAW, T-501, 264, 556–60, Glaise to Warlimont, 15 February 1943; Trifkovic, *Ustaša*, p. 219.

838. Schmider, *Partisanenkrieg in Jugoslawien*, pp. 240–41.

839. Schmider, *Partisanenkrieg in Jugoslawien*, p. 287.

840. ASMAE, GABAP, b. 37, Unsigned memorandum for the Duce, 22 February 1943.

841. PP, Diary, 13 February 1943.

842. PP, Diary, 13 February 1943.

843. Schmider, quoting German sources, gives a figure of 10,000 Muslims massacred. *Partisanenkrieg in Jugoslawien*, p. 196.

844. Talpo, *Dalmazia: Una cronaca per la storia (1943–1944)*, D. 25, Pierantoni to MAE, 7 March 1943, pp. 266-68.

845. NAW, T-821, 31, 370–79, notes on Mihailović and his relations with Četnik leaders.

846. NAW, T-821, 247, 746, Memorandum for the SME on the attitude of the Četniks, 20 March 1942.

847. Verna, "Yugoslavia Under Italian Rule," p. 467.

848. Trifkovic, *Ustaša*, p. 186.

849. AVII, b. 368, f. 5, Robotti memorandum on his meeting with Ambrosio and Mussolini, 5 March 1943.

850. NAW, T-821, 125, 816–23, Conversation between Pirzio Biroli and Robotti, 3 March 1943.

851. NAW, T-821, 31, 335–36, Robotti to CS, 8 March 1943; 125, 817–19, Conversation between Pirzio Biroli and Robotti, 3 March 1943. Pirzio Biroli, as Pietromarchi remarked, was by far and away the greatest champion of the Četniks. PP, Diary, 4 March 1943.

852. AVII, b. 368, f. 5, Robotti memorandum on his meetings with Ambrosio and Mussolini, 5 March 1943.

853. AVII, b. 368, f. 5, Robotti memorandum on his meetings with Ambrosio and Mussolini, 5 March 1943.

854. NAW, T-821 247, 746–48, SME report on the Četniks, 20 March 1943.

855. NAW, T-821, 128, 1007–14, Unsigned memorandum, 11 March 1943.

856. Cited in Deakin, *The Brutal Friendship*, I: 202.

857. DDI, IX, X, Mussolini to Hitler, 9 March 1943.

858. Talpo, *Dalmazia: Una cronaca per la storia (1943–1944)*, p. 68.

859. Cited in Tomasevich, *The Chetniks*, p. 247.

860. Talpo, *Dalmazia: Una cronaca per la storia (1943–1944)*, D. 26, Political situation, 4 April 1943, pp. 269–75.

861. Tomasevich, *The Chetniks*, p. 241.

862. Tomasevich, *The Chetniks*, p. 230.

863. NAW, T-821, 247, 762-65, Dattilo Gustavo to SME, 13 February 1943, 722–723, a report on German use of the Četniks in Bosnia for the SC, 16 March 1943.

864. AVII, b. 249, f. 1, Conversation between Robotti and General Lüters, 10 March 1943.

865. Dassovich, *Fronte jugoslavo 1943*, pp. 64–65.

866. Loy, *Yugoslavia*, pp. 250–51.

867. Milazzo, *The Chetniks*, p. 135.

868. Deakin, *The Brutal Friendship*, I: 182.

869. F.W.D. Deakin, *The Embattled Mountain* (New York & London: Oxford University Press, 1971), pp. 181–82.

870. The Italians picked up reports in late January and February of talks between Partisan and Četnik agents. Talpo, *Dalmazia: Una cronaca per la storia (1943)*, p. 79.

871. Karchmar, *Draža Mihailović and the Rise of the Četnik Movement*, II: 598–99.

872. Talpo, *Dalmazia: Una cronaca per la storia (1943–1944)*, D. 29, pp. 280–82, which contains an undated copy of a report allegedly composed by Mihailović to his Četnik commanders in Montenegro, submitted to the 2nd Army on 8 April 1943.

873. NAW, T-821, 31, 370, 2nd Army memorandum for talks with Četnik commanders, 24 February 1943.

874. Quoted in Talpo, *Dalmazia: Una cronaca per la storia (1942)*, p. 1158.

875. Talpo, *Dalmazia: Una cronaca per la storia (1943–1944)*, D. 29, A copy of a report that Mihailović was said to have delivered to Četnik Nationalists of Montenegro, 8 April 1943, pp. 280–82.

876. Talpo, *Dalmazia: Una cronaca per la storia (1943–1944)*, pp. 127–28.
877. For a telling discussion of this point, see Enzo Collotti, *L'Europa nazista*, pp. 233–34.
878. DDI, IX, X, 220, Ambrosio to Mussolini, 12 April 1943; Talpo, *Dalmazia: Una cronaca per la storia (1943–1944)*, p. 390.
879. PP, Diary, 10 March 1943.
880. Talpo, *Dalmazia: Una cronaca per la storia (1943–1944)*, D. 15, Conversation between Rosi and Robotti, 12 April 1943, pp. 534–35, and D. 15, Ambrosio to Robotti, 12 April 1943, pp. 536–37.
881. Talpo, *Dalmazia: Una cronaca per la storia (1943–1944)*, pp. 391–92, and D.15, Ambrosio to SME, 12 April 1943, pp. 536–37.
882. NAW, T-501, 264, 538–40, Glaise to OKW, 6 May 1943.
883. ADAP, E, V, 347, Hitler conversation with Pavelić, 27 April 1943.
884. Collotti, *L'Europa nazista*, p. 242.
885. DDI, IX, X, 348, Bastianini to Mussolini, 21 May 1943.
886. Cited in Deakin, *The Brutal Friendship*, I: 353.
887. PP, Diary, 3 May 1943.
888. PP, Diary, 18 May 1943.
889. PP, Diary, 18 May 1943.
890. Tomasevich, *The Chetniks*, p. 253.
891. PP, Diary, 23 April 1943.
892. Talpo, *Dalmazia: Una cronaca per la storia (1943–1944)*, D.1, Robotti to SME, 8 May 1943, pp. 661–62.
893. Trifkovic, *Ustaša*, p. 190.
894. PP, Diary, 3 May 1943.
895. PP, Diary, 18 May 1943.
896. DDI, IX, X, 328, Pierantoni to Mussolini, 15 May 1943; Talpo, *Dalmazia: Una cronaca per la storia (1943–1944)*, p. 564, and D. 6, Piazzoni report, 30 May 1943, pp. 671–75.
897. Milazzo, *The Chetnik Movement*, p. 144; Tomasevich, *Occupation and Collaboration*, p. 145.
898. Talpo, *Dalmazia: Una cronaca per la storia (1943–1944)*, D. 2, Castellani to MAE, 6 May 1943, pp. 663–64.
899. NAW, T-821, 126, 398–402, Conversation between Ambrosio and Rintelen, 19 May 1943.
900. Cited in Talpo, *Dalmazia: Una cronaca per la storia (1943–1944)*, p. 577.
901. Pavlowitch, *Yugoslavia*, p. 142.
902. Loi, *Le operazioni delle unità italiane in Jugoslavia*, p. 254. An Italian military report from Montenegro broke down Italian losses as fol-

lows: 290 dead, 541 wounded, and 1502 dispersed. 12,000 enemy dead were reported, 3,000 at the hands of the Italians, who, the report gloated, executed most of the prisoners that had been taken. NAW, T-821, 250, 06–10, Report on military operations in 1943 against Partisan forces in Montenegro, 22 July 1943.

903. Tomasevich, *The Chetniks*, p. 254.

904. Cited in Verna, "Yugoslavia Under Italian Rule," p. 263.

905. Talpo, *Dalmazia: Una cronaca per la storia (1943–1944)*, D. 18, Pierantoni to MAE, 30 April 1943, pp. 543-45.

906. Talpo, *Dalmazia: Una cronaca per la storia (1943–1944)*, D. 16, Report by the VI Army commander, 1 July 1943, pp. 704–07.

907. ASMAE, GABAP, b. 38, Ducci report, 15 April 1943.

908. NAW, T-821, 294, 592, 2nd Army to VI Army Corps, 2 April 1943.

909. Talpo, *Dalmazia: Una cronaca per la storia (1943–1944)*, p. 594.

910. Talpo, *Dalmazia: Una cronaca per la storia (1943–1944)*, p. 565.

911. Milazzo, *The Chetnik Movement*, p. 130.

912. Talpo, *Dalmazia: Una cronaca per la storia (1943–1944)*, D. 9, The address by the German commandant to the citizens of Mostar, 4 June 1943, pp. 684–85.

913. Dassovich, *Fronte Yugoslavo 1943*, p. 106.

914. Talpo, *Dalmazia: Una cronaca per la storia (1943–1944)*, pp. 804–05.

915. NAW, T-821, 31, 332, SME to 2nd Army, 31 May 1943; Dassovich, *Fronte Jugoslavo 1943*, pp. 105–06.

916. DDI, IX, X, 380, Pierantoni to Mussolini, 1 June 1943.

917. Talpo, *Dalmazia: Una cronaca per la storia (1943–1944)*, D.10, Piazzoni Proclamation, 1 June 1943, p. 686.

918. Tomasevich, *The Chetniks*, p. 256.

919. PP, Diary, 21 May and 8 June 1943.

920. Talpo, *Dalmazia; Una cronaca per la storia (1943–1944)*, D. 6, Mussolini to Giunta, 21 April 1943, p. 500. Robotti, however, still told his commanders that they should not "abandon" Četnik formations but to make use of them as much as possible. AVII, b. 368, Robotti meeting with his commanders, 21 April 1943.

921. DDI, IX, X, 391, Pierantoni to Mussolini, 4 June 1943; NAW, T-821, 31, 327–30, Report of the Salonica meeting, 2 June 1943.

922. PP, Diary, 8 June 1943.

923. DDI, IX, X, 426, Pietromarchi to Bastianini, 16 June 1943; ASMAE, GABAP, b. 32, Pietromarchi to Bastianini, 16 June 1943. For Pirzio

Biroli's own explanations for calling on the Germans for military support, see NAW, T-821, 347, 578–602, Pirzio Biroli's report to the Duce, July 1941–June 1943, 26 June 1943.

924. NAW, T-821, 31, 332, SME to 2nd Army, 29 May 1943.

925. Tomasevich, *Occupation and Collaboration*, pp. 145, 262.

926. Milazzo, *The Četnik Movement*, p. 148.

927. Talpo, *Dalmazia: Una cronaca per la storia (1943–1944)*, D. 8, Castellani to MAE, 28 March 1943, pp. 503–04.

928. Talpo, *Dalmazia: Una cronaca per la storia (1943–1944)*, p. 805.

929. Talpo, *Dalmazia: Una cronaca per la storia (1943–1944)*, p. 612.

930. Cited in Talpo, *Dalmazia: Una cronaca per la storia (1943–1944)*, p. 835.

931. Talpo, *Dalmazia: Una cronaca per la storia (1943–1944)*, D. 22, CS memorandum, 23 July 1943, pp. 731–33.

932. Talpo, *Dalmazia: Una cronaca per la storia (1943-1944)*, p. 585.

933. NAW, T-821, 347, 831, VI Army Corps to 2nd Army, 1 July 1943.

934. NAW, T-821, 31, 245, 2nd Army to VI Army Corps, 24 May 1943; 286, 03, 2nd Army to VI Army Corps/SIM, 4 July 1943. In January 1944, isolated and abandoned by everybody outside his movement, Mihailović backed away from a "Greater" or "homogeneous" Serbia by declaring at a Congress held in the village of Ba that the future Yugoslavia would adopt a monarchical trialist federation.

935. NAW, T-821, 289, 537, 2nd Army to VI Army Corps, 14 July 1943; 286, 10, 2nd Army to CS/SIM, 14 July 1943; 289, 608, 2nd Army to VI Army Corps, 20 July 1943.

936. DDI, IX, X, 497, Pierantoni to Mussolini, 11 July 1943.

937. DDI, IX, X, 501, Ambrosio to MAE, 12 July 1943.

938. DDI, IX, X, 507, Pierantoni to Mussolini, 14 July 1943.

939. AVII, b. 364, f. 5, Conversation between Jevdjević and Croatian Colonel Sarnbek, 29 January and 16 March 1943.

940. The ultimate fate of Italy's most stalwart Četnik allies is described by Martin, *The Web of Disinformation*, pp. 81–88. Djilas reports in *Wartime*, pp. 252–53, that the Germans, after capturing and interning Djurišić, brought him back to Montenegro to fight by their side against the Partisans.

941. Cuzzi, *L'occupazione italiana della Slovenia*, p. 242.

942. Cuzzi, in "I Balcani," p. 351.

943. Roatta reported Mussolini as saying: "The Duce has said that he [Grazioli] does not count for anything and don't take him into ac-

count . . . In case he should bother you again write a letter once more, and I will write him directly telling him plainly that, save the administration of the province, don't get into anything." NAW, T-821, 271, 33–39, Roatta memorandum, 22 November 1942.

944. Ferenc, *Rab–Arbe–Arbissima*, D. 370, CC.RR Commander Tommasini to Command 210 of the CC.RR, 2 January 1943, p. 335.

945. Ferenc, *Rab–Arbe–Arbissima*, D. 382, Giovanni Domenis to the Fascist Federal Secretary, 12 January 1943, pp. 342–43.

946. NAW, T-821, 61, 620–26, Robotti to Roatta, 26 October 1942.

947. NAW, T-821, 60, 906–10, Roatta to Robotti, 8 December 1942.

948. Ferenc, *Provincia 'italiana' di Lubiana*, D. 97, Grazioli to SPD and MI, 24 August 1942, pp. 498–502.

949. NAW, T-821, 61, 731–33, Roatta to Robotti, 6 December 1942.

950. U. Piccini, *Una pagina strappata* (Rome: Corso, 1983), pp. 21–22.

951. Cuzzi, *L'occupazione italiana della Slovenia*, p. 254.

952. Ferenc, *Rab–Arbe–Arbissima*, D, 292, Robotti note, 11 September 1942, p. 253.

953. NAW, T-821, 61, 627, Robotti to field commanders, 18 October 1942.

954. NAW, T-821, 405, 1299–1300, Robotti to field commanders, 20 April 1943.

955. NAW, T-821, 405, 1299–1300, Robotti to field commanders, 20 April 1943.

956. Piemontese, *Twenty-Four Months of Italian Occupation*, Allegato 1, Orlando memorandum, 20 March 1942.

957. Piccini, *Una pagina strappata*, p. 31.

958. Dassovich, *Fronte jugoslavo 1943*, p. 96.

959. Dassovich, *Fronte jugoslavo 1943*, p. 95.

960. Ferenc, *Rab–Arbe–Arbissima*, D. 355, Gambara note, 17 December 1943, p. 326.

961. Ferenc, *Rab–Arbe–Arbissima*, D. 356, Gambara note, 17 December 1943, p. 326.

962. Ferenc, *Rab–Arbe–Arbissima*, D. 361, Gambara to Supersloda, 18 December 1942, p. 329. At this penultimate hour of Italian rule in Slovenia, Italian bureaucrats from the Interior Ministry to the XI Army Corps, snarled in red tape, unclear directives, and inter-service rivalries, still had not carefully sorted out collaborators taken in for protection against Partisan reprisals and suspected Partisan sympathizers. On 30 April the Interior Ministry assumed sole au-

thority for releasing internees. Ferenc, *Rab–Arbe–Arbissima*, D. 434, MI, Gabinetto of the ministry, 30 April 1943, p. 388.

963. Ferenc, *Rab–Arbe–Arbissima*, D. 365, Gambara to XI Army Corps, 23 December 1943, p. 332.

964. For example the report of the Carabinieri captain Di Furia, sent to the Carabinieri command at the XI Army corps on 17 December 1942, in Ferenc, *Rab–Arbe–Arbissima*, D. 357, p. 327. In NAW, T-821, 448, 682–94, Political and military notice, 15 May 1943, the fear is expressed that the release of internees that had recently taken place in Slovenia would be regarded as an act of weakness by the Balkan peoples.

965. Ferenc, *Rab–Arbe–Arbissima*, D. 444, Sacripanti to the Carabinieri command of the XI Army Corps, 18 May 1943, p. 396.

966. Ferenc, *"Si ammazza troppo pocco,"* D. 39, Ermanno Rossi to the "Isonzo" division, 3 March 1943, p. 170.

967. Ferenc, *Rab–Arbe–Arbissima*, D. 463, Robotti to the 2nd Army, 4 July 1942, pp. 410–11.

968. For example, see Cuzzi's argument, *L'occupazione italiana della Slovenia*, p. 255.

969. NAW, T-821, 448, 641–52, Political and military news, 15 February 1943.

970. NAW, T-821, 448, 654–69, Political and military news, 15 March 1943, 670-81, 15 April 1943, and 727, 15 August 1943.

971. Dassovich, *Fronte jugoslavo 1943*, p. 93.

972. Cuzzi, *L'occupazione italiana della Slovenia*, pp. 258, 260–61.

973. USSME, N I-II, b. 1114, Colonel Brucchietti report, 27 March 1943.

974. Piemontese, *Twenty-Four Months of Italian Occupation*, Allegato XXVIII, Gambara note on reprisals, 4 May 1943.

975. NAW, T-821, 288, 866–68, General Pietro Scipione to Gambara, 29 June 1943.

976. NAW, T-821, 288, 864–65, Gambara to Robotti, 1 July 1943.

977. NAW, T-821, 288, 861–62, Robotti to Gambara, 2 July 1943.

978. NAW, T-821, 125, 824–25, Conversation Gambara with "il capo," 5 March 1943.

979. Ferenc, *Rab–Arbe–Arbissima*, D. 397, Gambara to XI Army Corps, 2 February 1943, pp. 363–64, and Robotti's order that the power over the camps be kept in Gambara's hands, in D. 409, Robotti to XI Army Corps, 17 February 1943, p. 371.

980. Cited in Ferenc, "Gli italiani in Slovenia," p. 164.

981. Ferenc, "La provincia did Lubiana," p. 117.

982. Cuzzi, *L'occupazione italiana della Slovenia*, p. 275, n. 17.

983. Ferenc, *La provincia 'italiana' di Lubiana*, D. 96, Grazioli to SPD and MI, 16 August 1942, pp. 495–98.

984. Capogreco, "Una storia rimossa dell'Italia fascista," p. 220.

985. Ferenc, *"Gli italiani in Slovenia,"* pp. 165–68.

986. Capogreco, *Renicci*, p. 27.

987. Capogreco, "Una storia rimossa dell'Italia fascista," p. 215. According to an Italian website, on 25 February there were 5,343 internees, of which 1,643 were children. www.romacivica.net/inpiroma/deportazione/deportazionecampi1.htm. The concentration camp of Gonars was located in the province of Udine.

988. Ferenc, *"Si ammazza troppo poco,"* p. 18. An Italian website yields the following figures: Civilian hostages who were shot, 1,500; shot on the spot, 2,500; death by torture, 84; tortured and burnt alive, 103; men, women, and children who died in concentration camps, 7,000. Total, 13,087. www.storiaXXIsecolo.it/deportazione. For more information, see also www.romacivica.net/inpiroma/deportazione/deportazionecampi1.htm.

989. NAW, T-821, 405, 1310-13, Robotti minutes of a meeting with Giunta, 17 March 1943.

990. Talpo, *Dalmazia: Una cronaca per la storia (1943–1944)*, p. 330.

991. Talpo, *Dalmazia: Una cronaca per la storia (1943–1944)*, D. 4, Giunta to Rossi, 2 April 1943, pp. 488–90.

992. Oddone Talpo, "Diario di Francesco Giunta Governatore della Dalmazia," *La rivista dalmatica* LXV (1994): 1–16.

993. NAW, T-821, 405, 804–05, Unsigned, but must be Giunta to Zerbino, 20 April 1943.

994. NAW, T-821, 405, 804–05, Unsigned, but must be Giunta to Zerbino, 20 April 1943.

995. ACS, PCM, p. 1.1.13, f.16452, sf. 161, Giunta to Mussolini, 16 April 1943.

996. NAW, T-821, 286, 186–91, Robotti to Roatta, 13 July 1943. See also Robotti's brief summary of his meeting with Giunta on 21 June in 286, 209-11, Robotti to Giunta, 11 July 1943.

997. Talpo, *Dalmazia: Una cronaca per la storia (1943–1944)*, pp. 317–18.

998. NAW, T-821, 286, 192–94, Spigo to Robotti, 30 March 1943.

999. Talpo, *Dalmazia: Una cronaca per la storia (1943–1944)*, p. 331.

1000. NAW, T-821, 286, 195–97, Robotti to SME, 23 April 1943.

1001. Talpo, *Dalmazia: Una cronaca per la storia (1943-1944)*, D. 2, Giunta to Rossi, 27 March 1943, pp. 482–83.

1002. NAW, T-821, 286, 198–99, Spigo to Robotti, 13 July 1943.

1003. NAW, T-821, 286, 224–25, Robotti to Giunta, 20 July 1943.

1004. Talpo, *Dalmazia: Una cronaca per la storia (1943–1944)*, p. 791.

1005. NAW, T-821, 286, 213–18, Robotti memorandum on conversations with Giunta, 13 July 1943.

1006. NAW, T-821, 286, 186–91, Robotti to Roatta, 13 July 1943; 285, 535–38, Robotti to Roatta, 24 July 1943.

1007. Talpo, *Dalmazia: Una cronaca per la storia (1943–1944)*, p. 799.

1008. Talpo, *Dalmazia: Una cronaca per la storia (1943–1944)*, p. 812.

1009. PP, Diary, 26 April 1943.

1010. Capogreco, "Una storia rimossa dell'Italia fascista," p. 225.

1011. Talpo, *Dalmazia: Una cronaca per la storia (1942)*, D. 2, Dr. Girolamo Mileta to Bastianini, pp. 1228–31.

1012. See his reply in Talpo, *Dalmazia: Una cronaca per la storia (1942)*, D. 3, Bastianini to Dr. Girolamo Mileta, pp. 1233–37.

1013. Roberto Spazzali, "Il campo di concentramento dell'isola di Melato (Molat) (1941–1943)," *Rivista Dalmatica* 3 (July-September) 1996: 169–87.

1014. Talpo, *Dalmazia: Una cronaca per la storia (1943–1944)*, p. 609, and D. 20, Unsigned memorandum, 17 June 1943, and unsigned Annex, pp. 718–25.

1015. PP, Diary, 31 December 1942.

1016. Talpo, *Dalmazia: Una cronaca per la storia (1943–1944)*, p. 576.

1017. ASMAE, GABAP, b. 31, Pierantoni to MAE, 11 June 1943. A reproduction can be found in Talpo, *Dalmazia: Una cronaca per la storia (1943–1944)*, D. 15, 11 June 1943, pp. 700–03.

1018. ASMAE, GABAP, b. 31, Pierantoni to MAE, 11 June 1943.

1019. ASMAE, GABAP, b. 31, Pietromarchi to Francesco Scammacca, the foreign ministry representative at the CS, 19 June 1943.

1020. ASMAE, GABAP, b. 31, Pierantoni to MAE, 11 June 1943.

1021. Talpo, *Dalmazia: Una cronaca per la storia (1943–1944)*, p. 603.

1022. NAW, T-821, 247, 722–23, Memorandum on German employment of the Četniks, signature illegible, 16 March 1943.

1023. Talpo, *Dalmazia: Una cronaca per la storia (1943–1944)*, D. 16, Situation at the end of June 1943, 1 July 1943, pp. 704–07.
1024. This point was made by Pieter Lagrou, "Irregular Warfare and the Norms of Legitimate Violence in Twentieth Century Europe," delivered at the Bologna conference, *Guerra ai civili*, 19 June 2002.
1025. These figures are taken from Schmider, *Partisanenkrieg in Jugoslawien*, p. 588, and Tomasevich, *The Chetniks*, p. 255.
1026. NAW T-821, 252, 64–85, SC report, 1 August 1943.
1027. Talpo, *Dalmazia: Una cronaca per la storia (1943–1944)*, p. 1097.
1028. Scotti and Viazzi, *Occupazione e guerra italiana in Montenegro*, p. 14. Germany's losses in Yugoslavia between May 1941 and August 1944 were as follows: 10,300 dead and 3,800 missing. Schmider, *Partisanenkrieg in Yugoslawien*, p. 586.
1029. Cited in Beloff, *Tito's Flawed Legacy*, pp. 75–76.
1030. Cited in Beloff, *Tito's Flawed Legacy*, p. 76.
1031. PP, Diary, 12 March 1942.
1032. Zbornik, XIII, bk 2, D. 80, Roatta memorandum, 23 July 1942, and D. 83, Roatta memorandum, 28 July 1942.
1033. NAW, T-821, 64, 953–56, Armellini to Roatta, 2 July 1942.
1034. Quoted in Avramov, *Genocide in Yugoslavia*, p. 380.
1035. NAW, T-821, 271, 456–60, Meeting at Verconico, 28 January 1942.
1036. NAW, T-821, 410, 1025–31, Roatta report, 28 February 1942.
1037. Iliya Jukic, a former Yugoslav diplomat, in his *The Fall of Yugoslavia* (New York: Jovanovich, 1974), pp.129, reports without documentation that Roatta in 1942 showed interest in establishing contacts with the British through some of Mihailović's commanders. "'If the Central Powers win,' he told them, 'Italy will be able to help establish a strong Serbian state in the center of the Balkans as a counterbalance to German omnipotence. If the Western Powers win, the Serbs will testify at the peace conference to the humane conduct of the Italians during the occupation.' Did Roatta through Mihailović make a desperate attempt to reach an agreement with Britain and the United States?"
1038. PP, Diary, 13 May 1943.
1039. Rodogno, in *Il nuovo ordine mediterraneo*, pp. 186–87, argues that Roatta wilfully overestimated the Partisan forces arrayed against the 2nd Army, which enabled him to delineate a drastic, and specifically "Fascist," counterinsurgency strategy in keeping with his proclivity of "working toward the Duce."

1040. His letter can be found in NAW, T-821, 410, 314–15, Nunzio Francesco Borgongini to the 2nd Army, 12 July 1943.

1041. NAW, T-821, 410, 565–69, Robotti to 2nd Army, September 1943.

1042. NAW, T-821, 404, 504–07, and 729–30, Robotti notes of 12 April and 8 May 1943.

1043. PP, Diary, 18 January 1943.

1044. NAW, T-821, 404, 732–33, Robotti to V Army Corps, 8 May 1943.

1045. NAW, T-821, 404, 1375–76, Robotti to V Army Corps, 19 May 1943, 1377–78, Robotti to SME, 19 May 1943, 1412–13, Robotti to SME, 8 July 1943.

1046. NAW, T-821, 410, 580–83, Robotti memorandum, 4 September 1943.

1047. PP, Diary, 16 March 1943.

1048. PP, Diary, 31 January 1943.

1049. DDI, IX, X, 501, Ambrosio to MAE, 12 July 1943.

1050. PP, Diary, 18 August 1943.

1051. NAW, T-501, 266, 206, Glaise report, 14 December 1941.

1052. Talpo, *Dalmazia: Una cronaca per la storia (1943–1944)*, pp. 312-13.

1053. A discussion on the Italian laws of war can be found in Dassovich, *Fronte Jugoslavo 1941-'42*, pp. 202–03, and Talpo, *Dalmazia: Una cronaca per la storia (1942)*, pp. 569–70, and pp. 647–48, n. 41.

1054. Ferenc, *La provincia "italiana" di Lubiana*, p. 193, n. 3.

1055. NAW, T-821, 271, 501–12, Notes of a 2nd Army command meeting, 30 December 1941.

1056. NAW, T-821, 55, 622–24, Roatta to Robotti, 4 April 1942.

1057. USSME, N I–II, b.724, A note on "rebel bands" by Francesco Delfino, Colonel of the Royal Carabinieri attached to the 2nd Army, 20 November 1941.

1058. NAW, T-821, 398, 581, Robotti memorandum, 10 June 1942.

1059. NAW, T-821, 62, 353–65, Roatta to field commanders, 8 June 1942.

1060. ARS, b.1788, Roatta to the governor of Dalmatia, the High Commissioner of Italian Slovenia, and the prefect of Carnaro, 5 March 1942.

1061. NAW, T-821, 60, 885–86, Roatta to 2nd Army, 20 March 1942.

1062. NAW, T-821, 63, 843, Armellini to Supersloda, 2 August 1942.

1063. Talpo, *Dalmazia: Una cronaca per la storia (1942)*, pp. 569–70.

1064. PP, Diary, 18 August 1943.

1065. There is a tendency by Scotti and Viazzi of describing the Italian officers as sowers of mindless death and destruction and as "Fascist" evildoers as opposed to the common Italian soldier—an essentially humane individual. This distinction rings true. But their use of "Fascist" perhaps covers too many soldiers in the Italian military. No question about the Squads, but many Italian generals in Yugoslavia were at best lukewarm Fascists while others had no hesitation in criticizing *squadristi* excesses.

1066. In AVII, b. 572, one finds Italian reports on Carabinieri *rastrellamenti* and atrocities. One such document asserts that 144 men and two women were shot on 21 March 1943. Many hostages were killed in retaliation for Partisan murder of Slovenes collaborating with Italy. It is obvious that the prefects of Spalato and Zara, Paolo Zerbino and Gaspero Barbéra, were most assiduous in carrying out cruel policies against the local population.

1067. PP, Diary, 8 June 1943.

1068. ARS, 1788, XII, f. 2, Roatta note on internments, 8 September 1942. Rodogno, when summarizing Roatta's internment categories, based on a document he consulted in the Interior Ministry carrying the same date, 8 September 1943, cites the term "repressive" in place of "precautionary," the term utilized by Roatta in his own note. Rodogno, *Il nuovo ordine mediterraneo*, p. 418. As Capogreco points out, the distinctions between "precautionary," "repressive," and "protective" became hopelessly blurred in both Italian internment policy and application. *Una storia rimossa*, pp. 213–14.

1069. Capogreco, *Una storia rimossa*, pp. 213–14.

1070. Ferenc, *Rab–Arbe–Arbissima*, D. 300, Benedettini Carlo for the War Ministry to the 2nd Army Command, 2 October 1942, p. 258.

1071. Ferenc, *Rab–Arbe–Arbissima*, D. 324, Mussolini's proclamation number 143, 19 November 1942, p. 276.

1072. Mussolini, OO, XXX, p. 97; "Il Piccolo di Trieste," 11 June 1941, cited in Ferenc, *La provincia 'italiana' di Lubiana*, p. 286, n. 13.

1073. NAW, T-821, 61, 776, Roatta note, 2 June 1942.

1074. He would "transfer a large part of the population, settle them in the Kingdom, and put Italians in their place." ARS, 1788, XII, f. 2, Roatta note on internments, 8 September 1942. Also see Capogreco, *Renicci*, p. 15, n. 7.

1075. ARS, II, XI C.A., b. 662/III, Robotti note, 1 November 1942; Ferenc, *La provincia 'italiana' di Lubiana*, D. 78, p. 411, n. 3.

1076. NAW, T-821, 60, 1047, Bindi, for the MI to Grazioli, 11 June 1942.

1077. NAW, T-821, 60, 1048, Bindi, for the MI to Grazioli, 13 June 1942.

1078. ARS-II, A.C., b. 16/I, Roatta to Robotti and Grazioli, 9 September 1942.

1079. ARS-II, XI C.A., b. 661 a/IX, Roatta memorandum on Slovenes interned, 16 December 1942.

1080. Ferenc, *Rab–Arbe–Arbissima*, D. 353, Roatta report on concentration camps, 16 December 1942, pp. 322–24.

1081. Ferenc, *Rab–Arbe–Arbissima*, D. 328, Medical Captain Carlo Alberto Lang report on the Arbe camp, 14–19 November 1942, pp. 281–82.

1082. Ferenc, *Rab–Arbe–Arbissima*, D. 337, Medical Colonel Perpetti report on the sanitary conditions in Arbe, 30 November 1942, pp. 291–94.

1083. NAW, T-821, 398, 34–50, Report on the Arbe concentration camp, 11 December 1942.

1084. Ferenc, *Rab–Arbe–Arbissima*, D. 371, De Filippio to the Carabinieri command of the XI Army Corps, 3 January 1943, pp. 335–36.

1085. NAW, T-821, 398, 03–21, Giuseppe Gianni to Supersloda, 3 December 1942.

1086. Carlo Spartico Capogreco, *I Campi del duce: L'internamento civile nell'Italia fascista (1940–1943)*, (Turin: Eiuaudi, 2004), pp. 77–78. The latest Yugoslav study arrives at the following figures. Under Italian occupation, 149,639 persons were interned at one time or another and 92,902 people imprisoned. Dragan S. Nenezić, *Jugoslovenske Oblasti Pod Italijom 1941–1943* (Belgrade: Vojnoistorijski Institut Vojske Jugoslavije, 1999), p. 159.

1087. Roy Carroll, *Manchester Guardian Weekly*, 11 July 2001.

1088. Capogreco, *Renicci*, p. 31.

1089. NAW, T-821, 498, 977, Roatta to Grazioli, April 1942. References to this commission, which was located in the Office of Civil Affairs, in the documents consulted in this book are very rare. On this occasion, the commission was asked to review proposals to intern the families of rebel leaders, to reduce the ration cards of such families, and to forbid them safe-conduct passes.

1090. NAW, T-821, 410, 1040–47, Roatta to field commanders, and Appendix "A" and Appendix "B" to the 3C circular, 7 April 1942.

1091. NAW, T-821, 410, 1040–47, Roatta to field commanders, and Appendix "A" and Appendix "B" to the 3C circular, 7 April 1942.

1092. NAW, T-821, 62, 353–65, Roatta to field commanders, 8 June 1942.

1093. NAW, T-821, 498, 965–66, Roatta to field commanders, 13 August 1942, 961–62, Roatta to field commanders, 10 September 1942.

1094. NAW, T-821, 498, 965–66, Roatta to field commanders, 13 August 1942, 961–62, Roatta to field commanders, 10 September 1942.

1095. In late June, the Italian troops in Montenegro shot 180 interned "Communists" as reprisal for the Partisans' execution of war prisoners, nine officers and "some troops." NAW, T-821, 133, 1485, General Roncaglia to CS, 25 June 1943.

1096. Gerhard Schreiber, "'Due popoli, una vittoria'? Gli italiani nei Balcani nel giudizio dell'alleato germanico," in *L'Italia in guerra 1940–1943*, eds. P. P. Poggio and B. Micheletti (Brescia: Fondazione "Luigi Micheletti," 1992), p. 111.

1097. Cited in Philip J. Cohen, *Serbia's Secret War* (College Park, TX: Texas A&M University Press, 1996), p. 99, who draws this information from the Zbornik collection, v.14, bk. 1, D. 180, p. 672.

1098. John Cornwell, *Hitler's Pope. The Secret History of Pius XII* (New York: Penguin, 1999), p. 254.

1099. Roberto Maiocchi has recently written an important book on the subject of Italian racism: *Scienza italiana e razzismo fascista* (Florence: La Nuova Italia Editrice, 1999).

1100. Aaron Gillette, *Racial Theories in Fascist Italy* (London and New York: Routledge, 2002), pp. 130–80.

1101. Steinberg, *All or Nothing*, p. 35.

1102. Browning, "The Wehrmacht Revisited in Serbia," p. 38.

1103. For this discussion on German repression I have drawn heavily on Schmider's book, *Partisanenkrieg in Jugoslawien*, and, particularly, his informative article, "Auf Umwegen zum Vernichtungskrieg? Der Partisanenkrieg in Jugoslawien, 1941–1944," in *Die Wehrmacht: Mythos und Realität*, eds. Rolf-Dieter Müller and Hans-Erich Volkmann (Munich: Oldenbourg Verlag, 1999), pp. 901–22.

1104. Steinberg, *All or Nothing*, p. 37.

1105. This is a conclusion shared by Collotti, Ferenc, and Sala. For citations and further discussion, see Collotti, *L'Europea nazista*, p. 282.

1106. Walter Manoschek, "'Coming Along to Shoot Some Jews?'" The Destruction of the Jews in Serbia," in *War of Extermination: The German Military in World War II, 1941–1944*, eds. Hannes Heer and Klaus Naumann (New York and Oxford: Berghahn Books, 2000), pp. 39–51.

1107. See the following interesting articles by Filippo Focardi on this theme, "L'Italia fascista come potenza occupante nel giudizio dell'opinione pubblica italiana: La questione dei criminali di guerra (1943–1948)," in *L'Italia fascista potenza occupante: Lo scacchiere balcanico,* ed. Brunello Mantelli (Trieste: Qualestoria, June 2002), pp. 157–83, and "'Bravo italiano' e 'cattivo tedesco': Riflessioni sulla genesi di due immagini incrociate," *Storia e Memoria* (Genoa: Istituto Storico della Resistenza in Liguria, 1996), pp. 55–83.

1108. Most notably by Filippo Focardi, in his article, "'Bravo italiano' e 'cattivo tedesco,'" pp. 55–83.

1109. Tomasevich, *Occupation and Collaboration*, pp. 737–38, cites two authoritative historians who estimate real wartime population losses of between 900,000 and 1,150,000.

1110. There seems to be a rough agreement among the Italians, Germans, and the Nuremberg Court that the Ustaša represented approximately five percent of the Croat population. Of course this does not include surmises on the number of sympathizers who were glad to see the elimination of Orthodox Serbs, Jews, and gypsies from territories they claimed to be part of a "Greater Croatia."

1111. ASMAE, GABAP, b. 38, Ducci memorandum, 15 April 1943.

1112. ASMAE, GABAP, b. 38, Ducci memorandum, 15 April 1943.

1113. NAW, T-821, 347, 729–46, Pièche to MAE, 774-79, Pièche to MAE, 9 September 1942; 248, 440-45, Pièche to MAE, 18 January 1943; PP, 2, 3, Pièche report, 17 March 1943.

1114. NAW, T-821, 410, 898-909, Zuccolin memorandum, 19 December 1941.

1115. PP, Diary, 27 February 1942.

1116. PP, Diary, 8 June 1943.

1117. PP, Diary, 8 June 1943.

1118. PP, Diary, 8 June 1943. Pietromarchi wrote on 10 December 1942: "Whatever is the outcome of the war, the germs delivered by Fascism in this old Europe will not die. The truths that it has diffused will be reaffirmed and the European people will have to inform their styles and systems by absorbing these truths." PP, Diary, 10 December 1942.

1119. ASMAE, GABAP, b. 32, Pietromarchi memorandum, 5 June 1943.

1120. ASMAE, GABAP, b. 32, Pietromarchi to Bastiniani, 16 June 1943.

1121. PP, Diary, 26 July 1942.

1122. PP, Diary, 26 July 1942.
1123. PP, Diary, 18 June 1943.
1124. PP, Diary, 24 July 1943.
1125. DDI, IX, X, 429, Pietromarchi to Alfieri, 17 June 1943.
1126. In the weeks following Mussolini's fall, the Palazzo Chigi did not change its Balkan policy. The newly appointed Italian minister plenipotentiary to Zagreb, Luigi Petrucci, held that the creation of a great Croatia, with German support, was the least damaging solution in the Balkans from the point of view of Italian interests. Italy must therefore be friendly with the Croats and cease coddling the Četniks. NAW, T-821, 31, 267–72, Conversation between Roatta and Petrucci, 11 August 1943.

# Index